D1566393

The guiding theme of this volume is that contemporary political science owes much of its present character to its past. In the twelve essays, the contributors – all practicing political scientists – explore the emergence and transformation of political traditions and research programs that have helped make political science what it is today. Included are histories of political themes and ideals (democracy, race, political education), conceptual and philosophical frameworks (the state and pluralism, behavioralism, policy analysis, public opinion, biology and politics), and theoretical projects and programs (realism in international relations, spatial theory of elections, rational choice, and historical approaches to institutional analysis). Each essay provides special insight and a distinct approach to particular episodes, moments, trends, and aspects of the history of academic political science. The volume as a whole provides a general overview of the history of the discipline and the variety of ways disciplinary history can illuminate the present.

Political Science in History

Political Science in History

Research Programs and Political Traditions

Edited by

James Farr
University of Minnesota

John S. Dryzek
University of Melbourne

Stephen T. Leonard
University of North Carolina

CAMBRIDGE
UNIVERSITY PRESS

Published by the Press Syndicate of the University of Cambridge
The Pitt Building, Trumpington Street, Cambridge CB2. 1 RP
40 West 20th Street, New York, NY 10011-4211, USA
10 Stamford Road, Oakleigh, Melbourne 3166, Australia

First published 1995

Printed in the United States of America

Library of Congress Cataloging-in-Publication Data

Political science in history : research programs and political
  traditions / edited by James Farr, John S. Dryzek, Stephen T.
  Leonard.
  p. cm.
  Includes bibliographical references (p.) and index.
  ISBN 0-521-47422-1 (hardcover). – ISBN 0-521-47955-X (paperback)
  1. Political science – United States – History. 2. Political
science – Research – United States – History. I. Farr, James (James F.).
II. Dryzek, John S., 1953– . III. Leonard, Stephen T., 1954– .
JA84.U5P6117 1995
320'.072073 – dc20   94-25321
                   CIP

A catalog record for this book is available from the British Library.

ISBN 0-521-47422-1 hardback
ISBN 0-521-47955-X paperback

Contents

vi   *Contents*

Preface

With this collection of essays we invite reflection on the history of American political science. We asked our contributors to take a historical approach to their topics in the belief that to understand the present and possible futures of political science, one has to understand its history. We hope that their efforts might encourage readers to come to the same conviction and perhaps even engage in their own reflection on the history of political science. Our justification for this project rests ultimately on the arguments it starts, not on whether readers agree with everything that is contained here.

While we do not want the historiographical orientation or thematic structure of the volume to become too much of a distraction, a few words on these matters may be in order. First, this is a volume on American political science, but we have not constrained our contributors by setting down rigid intellectual or geographical boundaries on what constitutes the discipline. We did set a chronological boundary with the establishment of professional political science in the late nineteenth century, though occasionally a glance further back is appropriate. Some of our contributors have generous understandings of the intellectual boundaries of American political science. Others are more narrow. Sometimes American political science appears imperial in its influence across national boundaries and in defining whole realms of inquiry outside the United States. In other instances, American political science appears closed and withdrawn, preoccupied with peculiarly American concerns while ignoring or radically altering discourses appropriated from elsewhere. Sometimes these foreign discourses are taken more seriously. And sometimes the discipline is best understood by what it fails to do as much as by what it actually does. The boundaries of the discipline are a function of the questions practitioners ask and the ways they ask them. We impose no narrower definition of these boundaries.

This openness is reflected in the range of topics and themes that we have included. Our goal is not to catalogue the discipline's subfields and their histories. Instead, the various essays cover an expansive set of research programs, political traditions, methodological agendas, and intellectual debates. The discipline is truly the work of many hands, and when viewed from a variety of perspectives it acquires shapes and meanings that cannot be discerned from any single point of view.

While we did aspire to a degree of comprehensiveness in our coverage, we cannot pretend that this volume embodies all possible topics, themes, or perspectives that might be considered important. Indeed, we are missing a number of essays that we felt would further round out its content. We pursued – and even thought we had secured – essays on systems theory, structural functionalism, political development, and gender. Each of these topics fell through for various reasons. Yet even if we had been able to include these essays, many readers would no doubt find gaps in the coverage. We could of course appeal to constraints of space, or time, or personal limitations to excuse our oversights, but these are obvious enough to require no elaboration. Instead, we invite readers who see limits in the thematic structure of the volume to engage the history of the discipline through the themes they believe important. This would fulfill the intention with which we began: to invite reflection on the history of American political science.

To our essayists – Terence Ball, Jack Donnelly, John Ferejohn, J. A. W. Gunn, John G. Gunnell, Joseph P. McCormick II, Cheryl M. Miller, Karen Orren, David Schlosberg, Kenneth A. Shepsle, Stephen Skowronek, Douglas Torgerson, and Hanes Walton Jr. – go special thanks for their willingness and their work. Our editor, Alex Holzman, was consistently encouraging and judicious in his advice. The reviewers for Cambridge University Press offered insightful comments and helpful suggestions from which all the authors benefitted. Finally, since this is a coedited volume, the editors would like to thank each other for the pleasures of shared work.

Contributors

Terence Ball received his Ph.D. from the University of California at Berkeley and is presently Professor of Political Science at the University of Minnesota. His interests include political theory, environmental ethics, and the history and philosophy of the social sciences. He is the author of *Transforming Political Discourse* (1988) and, most recently, *Reappraising Political Theory* (1994).

Jack Donnelly is Andrew W. Mellon Professor of Political Science at the Graduate School of International Studies, University of Denver. He is the author of many books and articles on the topic of human rights, including *The Concept of Human Rights* (1985), *Universal Human Rights in Theory and Practice* (1991), and *International Human Rights* (1993). He teaches in the areas of political theory and international relations.

John S. Dryzek is Professor of Political Science at the University of Melbourne. His books include *Rational Ecology: Environment and Political Economy* (1987) and *Discursive Democracy: Politics, Policy, and Political Science* (1990). His writings are mostly in the areas of democratic theory, disciplinary history, environmental politics, public policy analysis, philosophy of social science, critical theory, and public opinion.

James Farr is Professor of Political Science at the University of Minnesota. He is the author of several essays in the history and philosophy of the social sciences, as well as coeditor of *Political Innovation and Conceptual Change* (1989) and *Discipline and History: Political Science in the United States* (1993). He is currently investigating theories of the state and the practice of citizen education in the United States.

John Ferejohn is Catherine S. G. Munro Chair in Political Science and Senior Fellow of the Hoover Institution at Stanford University. He has written extensively in the areas of formal political theory and American politics. He is author of *Pork Barrel Politics* (1974), coauthor of *The Personal Vote: Constituency Service and Electoral Independence* (1987), and coeditor of *Information and Democratic Processes* (1990).

J. A. W. Gunn has been a professor in the Department of Political Studies, Queen's University, Kingston, Ontario, since 1970. His books include *Politics and the Public Interest* (1969), *Factions No More* (1972), *Benjamin Disraeli: Letters* (1982); and *Beyond Liberty and Property* (1983). His latest work, provisionally entitled *Queen of the World: Opinion in the Public Life of France*, is due to appear in 1995.

John G. Gunnell is Professor of Political Science at the State University of New York in Albany. He is the author of many works on political theory, philosophy of the social sciences, and the history of political science. His recent books include *Between Philosophy and Politics: The Alienation of Political Theory* (1986) and *The Descent of Political Theory: The Genealogy of an American Vocation* (1993).

Stephen T. Leonard is Associate Professor of Political Science at the University of North Carolina at Chapel Hill. He is the author of *Critical Theory in Political Practice* (1990) and an editor of *Intellectuals and Political Life* (forthcoming). His work has appeared in several edited volumes, the *American Political Science Review*, and *Political Theory*. He is currently working on a study of political radicalism in seventeenth-century England.

Joseph P. McCormick II is Associate Professor and Director of the Master of Arts in Public Administration program at Howard University in Washington, DC. His teaching and research interests are in the areas of African-American electoral politics, the political behavior of interest groups in the environmental justice movement, and the interaction of science, technology, and public policy.

Cheryl M. Miller is Associate Professor of Policy Sciences and Political Science at the University of Maryland, Baltimore County. She has published articles on bureaucratic accountability and legislative oversight in such journals as *Public Administration Review*, *Policy Studies Review*, and *Congress and the Presidency*. Her current research focuses on the emergence and role of state black legislative caucuses.

Karen Orren is Professor of Political Science at UCLA. Her most recent book is *Belated Feudalism: Labor, Law, and Liberal Development in the United States* (1991). With Stephen Skowronek, she is founder and managing editor of *Studies in American Political Development*.

David Schlosberg is a Ph.D. candidate in the Department of Political Science at the University of Oregon. He is currently working on a dissertation examining the development of the theory of pluralism, with a focus on new political practices in the environmental movement in the United States.

Kenneth A. Shepsle is Professor of Government at Harvard University. He has published extensively in the field of formal political theory and has applied this approach to the study of the U.S. Congress and other institutions. He is the coeditor of *Perspectives on Positive Political Economy* (1990) and author of *Models of Multiparty Electoral Competition* (1991). Currently he is completing research on the comparative study of government formation in parliamentary democracies.

Stephen Skowronek teaches American politics at Yale University. He is the author of *Building a New American State: The Expansion of National Administrative Capacities, 1877–1920* (1982) and *The Politics Presidents Make: Leadership from John Adams to George Bush* (1993). With Karen Orren he is founder and managing editor of *Studies in American Political Development*.

Douglas Torgerson teaches political theory and organization theory at Trent University, where he is Director of Administrative Studies. He is the author of *Industrialization and Assessment: Social Impact Assessment as a Social Phenomenon* (1980) and coeditor of *Managing Leviathan: Environmental Politics and the Administrative State* (1990). He is also editor of the journal *Policy Sciences*.

Hanes Walton Jr. is Professor of Political Science at the University of Michigan. His latest work is *The Native Son Presidential Candidate: The Carter Vote in Georgia* (1992). He is presently preparing a research reader on African-American politics.

Introduction

James Farr, John S. Dryzek, and Stephen T. Leonard

I

The present condition of political science in the United States is not easily diagnosed. But whatever else may be said, the present condition is both temporally and temperamentally a *post*behavioral one. The present condition of American political science, that is, takes its measure in time and attitude from the behavioral era that galvanized the identity of the discipline at midcentury. Although behavioralism never achieved the status of a unified paradigm or a universally accepted research program, its emphasis on creating a predictive science of politics, its language of behavior and process, and its liberal pluralism certainly provided a sharpened focus for the discipline in the 1950s and 1960s, whether as an umbrella for empirical research or as a target for disciplinary critics. Whatever its merits or shortcomings, behavioralism focussed the discipline in a singular and dramatic way, and its success in doing so has kept its memory alive in numerous arguments over the "state of the discipline" ever since.

Memory notwithstanding, behavioralism no longer focusses the discipline in the 1990s. Neither, it would appear, does much of anything else. What we are calling "the postbehavioral condition" certainly does not represent any revolutionary achievement or any ideological consensus about the discipline as a whole. There has not been a "postbehavioral revolution" or any consensus about a policy-relevant "postbehavioralism" of the sort that David Easton hoped to inaugurate in 1969 when he addressed the American Political Science Association (APSA) as its president. In his recent 1991 presidential address to the APSA, Theodore Lowi argued that the past few decades of political science in the United States have been shaped not by one, but by three hegemonic projects: public opinion, public policy, and public choice. Each has secured a stable niche in the discipline. But none has achieved anything remotely like universal acceptance; and many other altogether different projects proceed quite independently of them. Instead, there now exist not only multiple approaches to empirical research, but also multiple agendas for the discipline as a whole, including those relating to its teaching and service missions.

There are at present three responses to the proliferation of approaches and agendas that now characterizes the postbehavioral condition of American political science. These three in turn invite a fourth response.

The first expresses dismay and bemoans the loss of disciplinary focus provided by behavioralism. On this account, political science is fractured into countless smaller communities that have little to say or to do with one another. Many of those articulating this response are themselves erstwhile behavioralists who helped to revolutionize the discipline in the 1950s and 1960s. In a much-discussed essay (1988a), for example, Gabriel Almond laments the "separate tables" that now constitute the discipline. In his metaphor, diners at each table represent a school of thought that converse with one another but largely ignore conversations taking place at the other tables. His "broad cafeteria of the center" has dissipated along with behavioralism. Heinz Eulau (1977) and Seymour Martin Lipset (quoted in Finifter 1983) have expressed similar anxieties about the discipline's "drift" and "decline" since the passing of behavioralism. Even David Easton – whose presidential address (1969) symbolically marked the decline of behavioralism's prominence, just as his *Political System: An Inquiry into the State of Political Science* (1953) symbolically marked its confident emergence – finds little coherence in the contemporary scene. In recent reflections, he has acknowledged not only that the disciplinary focus provided by behavioralism has passed, but that no single coherent alternative – even postbehavioralism – has emerged to replace it. Indeed, he avers that "there are now so many approaches to political research that political science seems to have lost its purpose" (1990, 143).

The expression of dismay associated with this first response, it bears noting, is not limited to those who once avowed behavioralism or hoped for a policy-relevant postbehavioralism. Recent disciplinary historians who have been roundly critical of behavioralism as a misguided attempt to scientize the study of politics – like David Ricci (1984), as well as Raymond Seidelman and Edward Harpham (1985) – have argued that the discipline at least once had *an* agenda to focus its collective energies. In their view, however, this agenda was not principally to scientize politics, but to provide a realistic assessment and actual encouragement of democracy and progressive change in the United States. In Ricci's terms, the agenda all along involved a "tragic" pursuit of incompatible scientific and democratic goals, but at least it was an agenda. Tragic or not, Seidelman and Harpham conclude that political science as a tradition of realistic, politically engaged inquiry has plainly ended.

A second response argues that the multiplicity of approaches and agendas is deceiving inasmuch as most of them are not genuine candidates for a political *science* worthy of the name. In effect, this response raises a scientific battle cry for one particular research agenda as the scientific successor of a failed behavioralism. Other research agendas are thereby shunted aside without much serious engagement. A particularly striking example of this response is articulated by William Riker, who identifies his version of rational choice theory with the very discipline of political science (1982a). By singling out one research program – in this case one of the three hegemonic projects identified by Lowi – Riker lays claim to having discerned and cultivated the design for scientific progress most deserving of the discipline's postbehavioral loyalties.

A third response eschews both despair and scientific hegemony, embracing and even celebrating disciplinary diversity. J. Donald Moon, for one, has recently argued (1991) that fragmentation is inevitable so long as there exist competing definitions of the very nature of politics and of science. This inevitability is further guaranteed by the very capacity of social scientific knowledge to influence the objects of its study. Turning what is a vice for some into a virtue for the discipline as a whole, Moon casts diversity as desirable insofar as it vitiates the effects of institutional, theoretical, and methodological ossification. Dogan and Pahre (1990) develop a more extended argument for expecting creativity and innovation at the conflict-producing intersection of various research agendas. For them, conflict issues in cross-fertilization and disciplinary hybrids that are better able to adapt to an ever-changing agenda of problems confronting practitioners (see also Moon, 1975; Ball, 1976; and Dryzek, 1986). In short, the contemporary fragmentation of political science should not be the cause of dismay or the occasion to advocate one partisan research agenda. Much less should it be diagnosed as suffering from a multiple personality disorder, even if some of its symptoms – notably a lack of communication across adherents of different research programs or orientations – may require treatment.

These three responses are at odds with one another in their diagnoses of the present condition of postbehavioral political science. Yet they share one thing in common, if only implicitly. Each *takes for granted the importance of the discipline's past* – and especially behavioralism – for understanding its present. More particularly, each presupposes (and in varying degrees realizes) a historical sensibility about the development of the discipline since the behavioral era. The first implies and tentatively develops a historical narrative about the decline and fragmentation of the discipline as a whole, the second a narrative about the successful march of a single research program in pursuit of science, and the third a narrative about the creativity and interdisciplinary communication made possible by the inevitable diversity of research agendas that has developed in recent years. Doubtless, more could be done by way of filling in and further specifying the historical details that would lend weight and substance to these competing narratives (or, rather, these narrative-sketches). But our point is only to suggest that such historical narratives (or narrative-sketches) are logically presupposed in these – or in any other – diagnoses of the postbehavioral condition of political science.

Yet another response to the postbehavioral condition – the one that informs our intentions in bringing this volume together – is possible. It seizes explicitly on the historical sensibilities implied but not developed by the first three. It summons attempts to fill in the historical details and to fill out the historical narratives implied in current reflections on the state of the discipline. Sometimes this involves fortifying the divide that behavioralism marks in the history of the discipline. Sometimes, however, it entails throwing intellectual life lines back across the historical divide created by behavioralism, locating antecedents and possible models of disciplinary identity that go beyond the constraints of behavioralism. At any rate, whatever the diagnostic particulars of this self-conscious historical turn, it provides a larger canvas on which to portray how the discipline metamorphosed into its present shape, as well as to sketch various avenues leading to possible futures. This fourth response, in short, encourages a form of reflection on the contemporary condition of the discipline whose own empirical work consists in recounting the episodes, moments, trends, and developments in the history of political science.

This historically oriented response to the present condition of the discipline can itself be situated in terms of an important development in postbehavioral political science. This development has not been fully noticed or appreciated. Despite the much-espied fragmentation in its research, political science has become much more hospitable to history and to historical investigation than behavioralism ever was. Perhaps this development is precisely due to the ahistorical orientation of much of behavioralism, a point made long ago by Robert Dahl in his famous "epitaph" for the behavioral protest movement (1961b). Now, it would be an exaggeration to say that the discipline as a whole has taken a historical turn. But the range of research programs, approaches, and agendas now self-consciously articulated in historical terms is quite striking.

Consider, for example, the state-centered and policy-oriented investigations of American political development found in the work of Skocpol, Skowronek, Orren, Bensel, and others (see, e.g., references in Orren and Skowronek, Chapter 12, this volume). Many shorter historical works of this sort now appear in the pages of *Studies in American Political Development*. Moreover, political scientists associated with rational choice theory have turned the tools of game theory to episodes in the past, including conflicts in the classical world, voting patterns during England's Long Parliament, debates over federalism in the late eighteenth century, party realignments in mid-nineteenth-century United States, the rise of bureaucratic influence on agricultural policy in the early twentieth century, and much else besides (see, e.g., references in Ferejohn, Chapter 10, and in Shepsle, Chapter 11, this volume). Many other important studies with striking historical dimensions or subjects have appeared in the pages of *Social Science History* (first published in 1976), a journal that has sustained a cross-disciplinary interest in applying various quantitative and qualitative methods of the social sciences *to* history. More recently, *Social Science History* has acknowledged that "in fact the intellectual interchange goes both ways" and that its recent essays "help us see how historical research and thinking have been at play in disciplinary research ordinarily considered nonhistorical" (Monkkonen 1991, 199). The subfield of political theory has of course always been interested in the history of political thought. But even there, commitment to history and sustained reflection on historical methods of textual interpretation has redoubled as a result of the flourishing of "the new history of political thought" associated with the work of Quentin Skinner, J. G. A. Pocock, and John Dunn, and more recently, in the wake of poststructuralist and postmodernist "genealogies of knowledge/power" of the sort associated with the work of Michel Foucault. Many other examples are readily found in other areas of research and in various subfields of the discipline that corroborate the point:

There is a growing body of postbehavioral literature that makes history, both as subject and method, central to political science inquiry.

The contributions to this volume represent examples of this fourth response to the postbehavioral condition. Together, they offer ways of understanding the past and present, as well as the past *in* the present state of academic political science. Working in a genre that includes the historically oriented substantive works just mentioned, they are engaged in an exploration of political science that parallels or merges with broader historical studies of the discipline and of the social sciences more generally, as found in the recent work of Novick (1988), Morawski (1988), Almond (1990), Turner and Turner (1990), Ross (1991), Gordon (1991), Baer, Jewell, and Sigelman (1991), Easton, Gunnell, and Graziano (1991), Gunnell (1993), and Farr and Seidelman (1993). Like these works, the essays herein certainly display a range of judgments about the past and the present, from the partisan to the sympathetic to the critical.

With respect to subjects, we have aspired to a degree of comprehensiveness in our coverage while fully cognizant of the fact that the vast scope of the discipline precludes any exhaustive or noncontroversial choice of themes and topics. The essays here encompass not only the three hegemonic projects identified by Lowi – public opinion, public policy, and public choice – but also the still more inclusive project of behavioralism and, from an earlier era, the focus on the state, which for several decades veritably constituted political science. The essays also cover some of the discipline's most long-lived and/or influential traditions of research: realism in international relations, Darwinian biology, and rational choice theory (as applied to the spatial theory of elections). Two essays present competing versions of the "new institutionalism" against the background of the old. Another essay remembers civic education and pedagogical commitment as a central disciplinary concern; yet another traces the discipline's ambivalent relationship to the prospects of democratic self-government among the citizenry. What the discipline has historically missed – or dealt with in only limited or questionable fashion – is also instructive, as the essay on race demonstrates.

This considerable diversity of subjects ranges over the *intellectual products* of political science. Each essay thereby narrates a story of change – sometimes development and sometimes decline – in the various concepts, theories, methods, research programs, or philosophical foundations that have historically identified the work of political scientists. The personalities and professional events of the discipline are cer-

tainly intimated in each essay, but the narrative emphasis squarely falls
on what political scientists have thought, said, or written about politics
in the broader intellectual context of the discipline's various approaches
and agendas. The changes of these intellectual products over time are
explained in the volume both internally and externally. They are explained, that is, both by endogenous processes of theoretical refinement
or empirical testing, and by exogenous processes brought on by crises
or conflicts in the political world. Indeed, the essays in this volume collectively suggest – as some of them also individually do – that the defining characteristic of intellectual change in political science is the mutual
determination of internal scientific developments and external political
events.

If the essays in this volume help to overcome the alleged dichotomy
between internal and external history, they also help to call into question yet other dichotomies. For example, Dryzek and Leonard (1988) in
an earlier article divided recent historians of political science into two
camps: Whigs and skeptics. Whigs understood the past as a prologue to
a happy present or imminent future, whereas skeptics understood it as
the record of unremitting error down to our time. But however much this
bifurcated schemata captured what *had* passed for the discipline's history writing – and even that is debatable (see Farr et al. 1990) – the essays in this volume do not fall so neatly into this or any other dichotomy.
They suggest instead that the historiographical landscape now appears
both more complex and more defensible.

Another example of this defensible complexity in historiographical
orientation and of the overcoming of alleged dichotomies becomes evident in how our essayists orient their histories vis-à-vis current debates
and disputes. At first glance, some are more evidently "presentist": The
subjects that they address, as well as their terms for addressing them, are
dictated by present concerns. They begin their narratives in the nearer
past or run the past rather quickly up to the present without too much
delay over distant figures, theories, or debates. The narrative is then
quite plainly "related to" the present condition and explicitly made to be
diagnostic of it. Our two final essays – each presenting its own version
of the "new institutionalism" – are particularly provocative examples of
this more evidently presentist style. And they even make their historical
narratives directly serve research agendas that presently compete for the
hearts and minds of political scientists as they look to the future.

Other essays, by contrast, are more evidently "historicist" in orientation: Their subjects and terms of reference closely follow the past de-

bates in which they originally figured. They begin their narratives in a more-distant past or stop it at a considerable temporal remove from the present after a much more fine-grained investigation of the figures, theories, and debates in question. The connection to the present is therefore not nearly so evident, in part because of the extent of empirical research about the past that is on display.

But the differences between presentist and historicist approaches blur on closer scrutiny. Our initially identified presentists *are* indeed aware that there is a past with which they must genuinely contend, and in its own terms. And our historicists, however much they may bracket or belay present concerns, *do* speak to their contemporaries. Consider, for example, the first essay in the volume by John G. Gunnell. Although initially historicist in its treatment of the decline of the discourse of "the state" – a discourse that virtually constituted academic political science between the mid-nineteenth and the early twentieth centuries – Gunnell also shows how apparently long-abandoned themes may have presentist implications. As he argues, the eclipse of statist discourse, beginning with the rise of pluralist theory in the 1920s and all but completed by the 1950s, left a "discursive residue" that "still permeates both political science and political theory." Shunted to the margins of the discipline and then all but extinguished as pluralism rose up to replace it, discourse about "the state" remained an implicit presupposition of pluralism itself, for it was in large part *against* notions of "the state" that pluralism established its disciplinary ascendency in the first place. Moreover, at a time when we hear more than one voice for "bringing the state back in" (Evans, Rueschemeyer, and Skocpol 1985; Almond 1990), returning to those debates should help us think more clearly about how we might interpret the present discourse of the state in relation to the "discursive residue" left by pluralism itself.

Thus, current debates may have more historical depth than may at first sight be apparent, and even features of debates in the past that appear without immediate contemporary relevance may prove quite important in making sense of our present dilemmas. As Quentin Skinner has suggested in connection with returning to the debates of the 1540s (much less the 1920s) for some purchase on the present-day debate over negative and positive liberty (a debate, one might note, not unrelated to debates over pluralism and the state):

It may be precisely those aspects of the past which appear at first glance to be without contemporary relevance that may prove upon closer acquaintance to be of the most immediate philosophical significance. For their relevance may lie in the fact that, instead of supplying us with our usual and carefully contrived pleasures of recognition, they enable us to stand back from our own beliefs and the concepts we use to express them, perhaps forcing us to reconsider, to recast or even . . . to abandon some of our current beliefs in the light of these wider perspectives. (1984, 202)

It is in this spirit that as certain of the essays intimate, one might reconsider how early treatments of race shape the present contours of inquiry into the politics of race, or even peruse once again Aristotle's account of practical judgment when attempting to think more adequately about the future of policy studies.

All of this attests to both the effects of the postbehavioral condition and what we believe is the potential of a historically oriented response to that condition. That our contributors are not all of one mind in that response is of course signally important. But it is equally important that they show how *any* adequate response must find at least part of its grounding in a historically informed reconstruction of the postbehavioral condition.

II

Speaking in different ways to our postbehavioral condition, then, the essays in this volume provide historical narratives of some of the most important and influential approaches and agendas in the intellectual history of American political science. The chronological development of the discipline has helped to situate the essays in the order that they appear. Thus, discussion of the state precedes that of rational choice theory, pedagogical concerns precede those of behavioralism, public opinion precedes the new institutionalism, and so on, because the former have generally been the subject of more long-standing disciplinary debates than have the latter in each case. The former usually helped to galvanize the discipline at an earlier point in time, and so their principal figures are generally more distant. But even these are relative judgments, since there are very many obvious overlaps in the essays.

In "The Declination of the State," John G. Gunnell begins with the late 1800s when political science was understood to be "the science of the state." His narrative turns quickly to the debate between statists and pluralists that emerged in the 1920s when "the science of the state" first

came under serious attack. Pluralists – essentially following the lead of
Harold Laski – criticized statists in the discipline for having a monistic
theory of authority and for raising the state to metaphysical heights over
the give-and-take of groups in society. They also saw in the study of
groups a more methodologically progressive way of proceeding than the
alleged legalism and formalism of the past. Yet not all political scientists signed on to the scientific and political agenda of pluralism, as the
writings of W. Y. Elliott make clear. Fearing the "sublimation" of politics to society and a scientistic self-understanding of the discipline,
Elliott also strove to retain an idealistic tradition of liberalism that associated the state with a "community of purpose" that had authority over
and gave meaning to the politics of groups and interests. At stake in this
debate, as Gunnell makes clear, was not only the identity of the discipline as a science of politics, but the nature of American liberalism itself. Committed to telling an essentially internalist story about this
development (or in this case an aspect of the decline) of the discipline,
Gunnell closely follows the terms and texts of those earlier debates.
However, he clearly shows how the debates of the 1920s not only fore-
shadowed but were virtually replayed in the controversy between later
pluralists and their critics in the 1950s and 1960s. Their "discursive
residue" remains with us, even now.

   Clearly related to the debate over liberalism in American political science was the debate over democracy itself. In a narrative that begins
with Woodrow Wilson and runs down to Daniel Bell and Seymour Martin Lipset, Terence Ball presents an account of the "ambivalent alliance"
that political science has struck with American democracy. Echoing the
even earlier tensions over American democracy in the Jeffersonian and
Jacksonian eras, political scientists in the United States have generally
been democratic in self-conception, but nonetheless skeptical about the
qualities necessary for self-government that are to be found in ordinary
citizens, much less the mass public. One might even say that political
scientists, in different ways and at different times, have been intent on
saving American democracy from itself. Thus were Wilson's and A.
Lawrence Lowell's hopes for reform of the civil service at the expense
of congressional government and popular opinion, Walter Lippmann's
trust in experts over a "phantom public" of "omnicompetent citizens,"
and the later various hopes for an end of ideology or at least for an apathetic public to unfetter the representative and bureaucratic institutions
of America's brand of democratic government. Ball traces these
changes not mainly to an internal dialogue between scientists and intel-

lectuals, but to the contingent constellations of political forces at particular times. Moreover, he suggests that political scientists have not been and could not have been normatively neutral in offering their different accounts of American democracy. Believing it to be at a crossroads today, he encourages the discipline in this postbehavioral era to take heed of its pedagogical responsibilties in order to be as concerned with the education of ordinary citizens as with the training of specialists.

It is the history of political science *as* pedagogical practice that Stephen Leonard expressly sets out to narrate. This narrative is a timely one inasmuch as many political scientists these days have called for "citizen education" and "service-learning" as essential components of the discipline's self-understanding. Leonard gives historical grounding to these sentiments by looking back to the writings of thinkers like Francis Lieber, Woodrow Wilson, Charles Merriam, and the "revolutionaries" of the behavioral era. But he does so in such a way as not to romanticize what has previously passed as the pedagogical purposes of political science. Although always committed to an effective pedagogical project, political scientists often cast the terms of this project in a variety of not always compatible ideals, some of which were at a competitive disadvantage in relation to others because of the discipline's theoretical, institutional, and ideological preoccupations. Opening, then closing off or marginalizing the ideals of educating citizens, statesmen, and civil servants, political science eventually made its own disciplinary self-reproduction – the pedagogy of future political scientists – its main educative concern. With the advent of postbehavioralism, this trajectory of development is more or less exhausted, and the pedagogical identity of the discipline opens up. And as Leonard suggests, those committed to a renewal or, better, a restructuring of the educative mission of the discipline today might be well advised to consider the reasons why the pedagogical purposes of political science took the shape they did.

Among these pedagogical possibilities, the education of the public itself was predicated on the idea that public opinion mattered most in democratic government. Although the very idea of public opinion goes back to the formation of modern states in the seventeenth and eighteenth centuries, it gained particular salience with the rise of democratic states in the nineteenth century. In that context, it came under the scrutiny of political scientists who formed and then sustained the discipline in the United States and elsewhere. This is the point of departure for J. A. W. Gunn's historical accounting of the concept and its theoretical uses. In a narrative that covers the views of Lippmann, Tonnies, Sait, Blumer,

Rogers, Berelson, Key, Converse, Noelle-Neumann, and many others, Gunn traces changes in the meaning and use of the concept, as well as in the methodologies that have attended its disciplinary deployment. It was survey research in particular that revolutionized public opinion, making it virtually synonymous with what the polls measured. Displacing older holistic notions about the public mind, survey research introduced an understanding that was based on the aggregation of individual and even private opinions. More recently, however, there has been a return to certain holistic notions, in particular that we cannot understand the concept or study the phenomenon without reference to collective behavior, manipulative psychology, or unintended "spirals of silence." The history of these wide shifts in the study of "public opinion" provides ample evidence for why political scientists should not expect the emergence of one syncretic definition of the term or one agreed-upon research strategy for studying the phenomena it names. But lest that seem a methodological failure, Gunn's essay reminds us that the concept remains, for better or worse, at the center of democratic politics. Moreover – and more historically – public opinion remains under the influence of the past if only because the political theory that attributes normative significance to the content of the public mind cannot be replaced by mere data. The issues that give significance to the phenomenon and the analysis that explored the meaning of the concept are with us still.

Methodological uncertainties and political portent also attend the history of biological thinking in political science, especially after the Darwinian revolution in the late nineteenth century. In their narrative, John S. Dryzek and David Schlosberg examine one of the more persistent (if discontinuous) research programs that spans over a century of political science in the work of Davies, Masters, and many others. During this century of work, Darwinian thinking was implicated not only in the debates about a genuine science of politics and society, but also in debates that were more demonstrably political and ideological. This is evident in early works like William Graham Sumner's *What the Social Classes Owe to Each Other* and Henry Jones Ford's *The Natural History of the State*, as well as in later invocations of eugenics and more recent ones of sociobiology. After a period of eclipse, roughly equivalent with the rise of behavioralism, the postbehavioral contribution to this research program has emerged within the subfield of biopolitics. This latest version of the program now accepts an essentially interactionist perspective that connects nature with human choice and political culture. While the scientific and ideological vagaries that are evident in the history of the Darwinian research program as a whole have yet to be eliminated, this interactionist outlook nonetheless indicates how practitioners might counteract ideological misuses of biological thinking in politics. Dryzek and Schlosberg's narrative has the consequence of encouraging certain trends in biopolitics, especially those that are self-consciously nondeterministic and that renounce the idea that nature has any single truth to tell us about politics and society. Their conclusion is consistent with the third, welcoming, response to postbehavioral fragmentation that we noted earlier.

Biological thinking was at its ideological and scientific worst when used in the study of race, especially at the turn of the century. This is the historical point of departure for the study by Hanes Walton, Cheryl M. Miller, and Joseph P. McCormick. Noting the essentially racist conclusions reached by the likes of John W. Burgess at the discipline's founding in the 1880s, they narrate the transformations in the discipline's rather fitful treatment of race. Indeed, they discover two very different traditions of research – one they call "race relations politics," the other "African-American politics" – using as their historical evidence the content of articles in the discipline's oldest and most prominent journals, *Political Science Quarterly* and *American Political Science Review*. The former tradition has generally dominated the pages of these key journals of the discipline, when the subject of race has been taken up at all. One of the consequences of this dominance, the authors argue, has been to implicate the discipline in the accommodation of "race relations" to the institutional status quo and its implicit inequalities. Walton, Miller, and McCormick clearly favor the second, African-American politics tradition, one in which empowerment has been the key concept and clear-cut goal. Its future is quite clearly tied to the course of present and future events, as well as the discipline's overall response to those events.

As noted in connection with pluralism, the concept of the "state" has been of signal importance in the history of political science. With glances back at the tradition of modern political thought that cast politics principally in terms of "reasons of state" and realpolitik, Jack Donnelly narrates another tradition of state-centered analysis – realism in international relations. Tracing the academic history of realist conceptualizations of international politics, Donnelly intimates both the ambiguity and limitations of realist thinking. Premised on assumptions of individual egoism, interstate anarchy, and the importance of national power and international security – the meanings and implications of which realists were never fully agreed upon – realism was roundly attacked from a variety of perspectives for its theoretical deficiencies, methodological naiveté, and political inadequacies. And although a rescue effort has been recently mounted by "neo-realists," even this has been ineffective in stemming the loss of vitality that followed from that most injurious of conclusions that critics inflicted on the body of the realist paradigm, namely, that realism was, quite simply, *unrealistic* because of its essentially static theoretical and philosophical constructs.

It was frustration not so much with realism as with the very language of the state that was dramatically vented by the "behavioral revolutionaries" of the 1950s and 1960s. While a few earlier figures like Arthur Bentley and Charles Merriam received praising reminiscences, the behavioralists generally sought a wholesale transformation of the discipline. Instead of "the state" and legal-formal methods, they preferred and developed research strategies to study "behavior" and "process," "system" and "groups." At stake, in their view, was the fate of a genuinely predictive science of politics against the tradition of normative and historical inquiry, as well as the hopes of a scientific explanation of the liberal pluralist processes allegedly at work in American politics. Emphasizing the writings of Easton, Truman, Dahl, and Eulau, James Farr engages in a remembrance of the revolution, tracing the course of the debates over science and politics that attended the dramatic rise and equally dramatic demise of behavioralism as a movement in the discipline. Calling his a "forensic history," he stays close to the terms of the debates that consumed behavioralists and their critics, whether those debates pointed "in" toward the discipline's scientific aspirations or "out" toward the political events bounded by the end of World War II and the beginnings of the end of the Viet Nam War. Indeed, so important were these debates to the identity of the discipline at midcentury that they are still being reminisced about, particularly at a time when no equally galvanizing movement is to be found. Political scientists of different generations are sorting out what it means to be in a *post*behavioral era, and they cannot but remember the behavioral revolution and its impact on the present in doing so.

The postbehavioral era was symbolically ushered in by David Easton in 1969 during the height of the protests against the Viet Nam War and struggles over civil rights for African-Americans, conflicts that found their way into the halls of academic political science. It was Easton's plea that the discipline become more evidently relevant to the political world outside its academic enclave. The most convenient way to characterize this in the discipline's language was to encourage a turn to policy and policy studies. It is with "the policy turn" during this postbehavioral period that Douglas Torgerson begins his narrative of the discipline's concern with the analysis of public policy. Yet he proceeds to situate the policy turn in terms of a broader history that in the middle distance is populated by the likes of Harold Lasswell and John Dewey and in the far distance by none other than Aristotle. Critical of the positivist and technocratic tendencies in much of applied policy analysis, Torgerson reconsiders the purchase on the topic provided by Aristotle's conception of prudence, or practical judgment. The reflective, interpretive, critical, and action-orienting perspectives embodied in what Aristotle called *phronēsis* warrants its particular praise in our context, especially when appropriated by hermeneutic and critical theorists. At stake in this historical reconstruction is not only an academic practice, but "an open-ended form of public life" to which political science can yet contribute.

Whether political science contributes to public life in this precise way remains to be seen, of course. But we may be fully confident that, given its history, political science will continue to study electoral behavior – the most distinctive feature of public life in representative democracies – with every theoretical and methodological means available. One of the most important transformations in the study of electoral behavior resulted as a consequence of the introduction of rational choice theory and spatial modeling. Thanks in particular to the work of Anthony Downs in the late 1950s, a "spatial theory of elections" emerged to consume the attentions of a whole new generation of political scientists associated with game theory. The philosophical and methodological orientations of this new generation of game theorists increasingly distanced them from the older traditions of inquiry associated with public opinion research or with institutional analyses of electoral politics. John Ferejohn attends closely to the developments in the spatial theory of elections in the thirty-five years that have passed since the publication of Downs's classic, *An Economic Theory of Democracy*. Ferejohn is interested in the "internal" history of this theory rather apart from developments in American electoral politics as such. Even then, he is less interested in assessing the history of its empirical adequacy so much as the development of new techniques and perspectives in game theory. With this historiographical framework in place, he turns to assess an issue central to the coherence of the spatial model of elections as a rational choice theory, namely, whether campaign platforms rationally can have predictive or informational value for the voter. The ensuing historical narrative works over the various affirmations and denials of the rationality at stake here. Ferejohn concludes his narrative by endorsing the view that in certain situations defined by a single-dimensional ideology, campaign platforms have informational content and voters decide rationally when using them. With the present state of the discipline fully in mind, Ferejohn ends by calling not only for further theoretical development, but for further clarification of the philosophical foundations of spatial modeling and rational choice theory as such. The coherence of these calls is made possible by the history he has narrated.

The final two essays are intended to justify two very different research programs in political science that ironically go under the same name – "the new institutionalism." While both are critical of an "old" institutionalism in the past, each seizes upon different failures of the past and each advocates very different futures for the discipline. Kenneth A. Shepsle makes out a case for a new institutionalism that is informed by game theory and public choice. In this way, his essay clearly overlaps the research program discussed by Ferejohn. The old institutionalism was, in Shepsle's assessment, too preoccupied with the state and with describing the minutiae of its formal-legal institutions. Behavioralism was a scientific advance on the old institutionalism, but it otherwise "expressed a profound disinterest in institutions at all." In favoring sociology and psychology, behavioralism turned institutions into veritable epiphenomena, mere shells to be filled by atomized individuals and their roles, values, and statuses. It was the subsequent revolution – the rational choice revolution of the 1970s – that favored economics and made possible a new institutionalism, one that conceptualized institutions as game forms that provide the rules and settings for rational agents who seek to optimize their behavior. Like rational choice theory, the new institutionalism is, in Shepsle's version, an equilibrium theory; and his history of it is an analysis of the various ways that equilibrium has been conceptualized – including his own conception of "structure-induced equilibrium." The narrative concludes with a series of research paths that the new institutionalism needs to follow, as well as with a more general proclamation about the present and future of the discipline:

In the end, rational choice theory promises to drive a wedge between political thought and political theory, making the latter both a synthesis of its earlier roots and a genuinely scientific enterprise. More importantly, political science need no longer concede the study of institutions to the economists.

If Karen Orren and Stephen Skowronek are right, there is no reason to concede the study of institutions to rational choice theorists either. Their version of the new institutionalism emphasizes the historical study of institutions, especially those associated with the dynamics of state development. This work is new, they aver, not because it is concerned with history "writ large":

Rather it is historical, because it brings questions of timing and temporality in politics to the center of the analysis of how institutions matter. It is new because, in so doing, it breaks down the conception of order in time that has been the centerpiece of the study of American institutions in all of its incarnations past and present.

Their narrative subsequently commences to criticize the conceptions of order that have been at work in the old institutionalism, whether of the formal or the behavioral kind. Indeed, they even find the conception of an equilibrium that is necessary to rational choice theory and to Shepsle's brand of institutionalism to be just another episode in the history of order. Having brought us up to the present, Orren and Skowronek proceed to lay out the elements of their own new institutionalism, including claims that institutions have disparate and nonsimultaneous origins, that they control persons or other institutions, that they are purposive or intentional, and that they are typically created in relation to other institutions. The elements they delineate make clear that their effort is really one to rethink the philosophical foundations of the study of institutions, especially those dealing with temporality, change, and the meaning of history itself. In this way – and in a fitting end to the volume as a whole – they show how a history of political science can be made to help in the postbehavioral effort to make political science itself more historical.

The essays in this volume are healthy signs, in our view, of a renewed historical sensibility in political science, of a curiosity about and critical engagement with the discipline's past, and of the turn to the history of the discipline to address our present and future prospects. There are many ways to make this turn, as the essays make clear, and their very diversity allows us to sympathize with the spirit if not quite the letter of a recent observation by Gabriel Almond. Consciously echoing George

Orwell, Almond contends that "whoever controls the interpretation of the past in our professional history writing has gone a long way toward controlling the future" (1988a, 835). A less Orwellian and more palatable version might well read, "Those who contribute to the interpretation of the past in our professional history writing help establish the grounds for the development of the discipline's future." In our postbehavioral context, this is not only what we should expect. It may even constitute the basis for some hope that political science in the present and the future can deepen what it learns from its past.

1

The Declination of the "State" and the Origins of American Pluralism

John G. Gunnell

> Let us set briefly the problem with which all modern political the-
> ory is faced: the sphere in which autonomy may be and should be
> permitted to what English political theory has termed *voluntary
> associations*.   W. Y. Elliott

This essay is devoted principally to exploring the transformation in the
concept of the state and, in all senses of the word, its declination in the
field of political science subsequent to World War I. The principal focus is on the controversy about pluralism that emerged during the 1920s.
This represented an important juncture in the discursive evolution of the
discipline and in the structure of the profession, and its residue still permeates both political science and political theory. My intention is to reconstruct in detail this transfigurative conversation, with all its thrusts
and parries, and my purpose is to indicate the ways in which it changed
the content and form of the internal history of political science.[1] I also
want to suggest that, in an important sense, this controversy was about
the nature of political reality, about the meaning of liberal democracy,
and about the professional identity of political science and its relationship to politics.

By the mid-1950s, what liberalism meant in political science, and political theory, was pluralism. Pluralism had become both the standard
explanatory and descriptive account of politics and a normative theory
of liberal democracy. David Truman's application of what he took to be
Arthur Bentley's group theory of politics to an analysis of the "governmental process" had provided an influential image of the workings
of representative government (Bentley 1908; Truman 1951a; Latham
1952; Gross 1955). Although Truman briefly mentioned the early pluralist school, he did not explicitly employ the concept of pluralism. The

reconstitution of the concept was largely a product of the 1960s and a consequence of the work of Robert Dahl and his theoretical defense of "polyarchal democracy" as well as a number of allied arguments. Pluralism, Dahl (1956) suggested, was actually also a description of how the American political system worked, against what he described as Madisonian and populist images. And few would suggest that Dahl's (1961) famous study of New Haven politics was less than an implicit endorsement of pluralism as a normative theory of democracy.

During the late 1950s and early 1960s, the pluralist account of politics was progressively sedimented in the discourse of political science and closely associated with behavioralism, which had become the dominant methodological persuasion in the field as well as the basis of disciplinary identity. By the end of the 1960s, however, it had also become a consistent object of criticism – both as a description of politics and as an adequate theory of democracy and form of democratic practice (McCoy and Playford 1967; Connolly 1969).

There was a variety of immediate factors, both contextual and internal, that are relevant and commonly invoked in explaining what precipitated this second debate about pluralism and determined its particular character. Not the least of these was the infusion of German emigré ideas that were hostile to liberalism and pluralism (Gunnell 1988). Equally important was the internal critique of political science as implicitly conservative and as detached from political issues (Green and Levinson 1970; Surkin and Wolfe 1970). Yet the fundamental issue, as well as the terms of the discussion, had been long immanent in the discipline. Far more than the participants were conscious of it, the debate was the perpetuation of an indigenous form that was more determinative than either the somewhat accidental contextual circumstances that may have shaped the particular character of the discussion or the ideologies that attached themselves to it.

At the beginning of the 1960s, Sheldon Wolin (1960), for example, attacked the pluralist account of liberalism and charged it with undermining "the political." Henry Kariel (1961) suggested that it was a threat to constitutionalism. In the middle of the decade, Grant McConnell (1966) criticized the ascendancy of private power over democratic public interest. At the end of the 1960s, Theodore Lowi (1969) attributed the pathology of contemporary American politics to "interest-group liberalism." They, like many other representative critics of the period, were responding both to their image of the contemporary political situation and to the dominant descriptive, explanatory, and prescriptive model of politics in mainstream behavioral political science. But however unique their arguments, concerns, and intellectual background may have been in some respects, they, as well as those they criticized, were participating in a discursive structure that was deeply embedded in the discipline and that had crystallized in the 1920s. Recent debates about returning to the concept of the state in political and social science have a similar pedigree (Easton 1981; Evans, Rueschemeyer, and Skocpol 1985; Almond 1988b).

Although it might be reasonable to suggest, at some level of abstraction, that pluralism, from the time of Madison and the *Federalist*, has been the dominant vision of American politics, it has not always been a positive image or the focus of political studies. Nineteenth-century political science made the state its subject matter (Gunnell 1990). This was most immediately and concretely a reflection of what constituted political studies in Germany. Francis Lieber had brought the subject matter of the "state" to the United States and adapted it to the traditional university curriculum and to an analysis of American politics. And the work of individuals such as Theodore Woolsey, at Yale, and John W. Burgess and Herbert Baxter Adams, at Columbia and The Johns Hopkins University, respectively, continued to adopt and adapt *Staatslehre* and transform it into an American science of politics.

The concept of the state performed a number of functions, both intentional and latent. It gave emerging political science a distinctive identity and domain that promised autonomy from other fields in a universe of differentiating social science, but it also involved something less obvious but persistently relevant to the theory and practice of American politics. Although the discussion of the state was often cloaked in the legalism of Austinian analysis and the arcane language of organic images grounded in German philosophy, the search for the state was the search for the meaning and locus of the American political community – a community that was neither practically visible nor theoretically easy to specify in a world of pluralistic politics and institutions. What is so strikingly clear in the nineteenth-century literature is the insistence that the state is not government. While the former was supreme, indivisible, divine, and omnipotent, the latter was a limited institutional agent. Although this distinction served such purposes as allowing a simultaneous defense of national unity and noninterventionist government, the search for the state, as in Germany, was nothing less than the search for what often seemed counterfactual, the search for the *Volk*, the community – a real organic entity. It was a search for the "people" – the entity that loomed so large in eighteenth-century republican thought but that at the same time seemed to dissolve, in the *Federalist*, into rapacious individuals and divisive groups whose centrifugal tendencies were inhibited only by vigorous and creative leadership and by the institutional mechanics of constitutional artifice.

By the turn of the century, the state remained the subject matter of political science, but despite the retention of a metaphysical aura and assumptions about its Teutonic patrimony, it was on the road toward being demystified and transformed into the institution of government in the work of individuals such as Woodrow Wilson (1889) and W. W. Willoughby (1896). This, however, did not diminish its status. While many continued to find conservative solace in the idea of the state, Progressivists, like a previous generation of more radical social scientists, saw the state, now as government, as an instrument of social reform and as a vehicle for a constituent democratic majority that might be awakened by the results of realist social inquiry. For political scientists as a whole, then, the state, for a variety of reasons, remained deeply implicated in their identity. Yet as an account of political reality, the nineteenth-century organic vision was atrophying in the face of images of society and government that were beginning to appear intractably pluralistic. The traditional paradigm was even more dramatically disrupted by the advent of World War I and the overt American rejection of German philosophy, and its vision of the state, as the culpable source of authoritarian and imperialistic politics.

By the end of the first decade of the twentieth century, there were few, if any, who clung to the views that characterized the apotheosis of the idea of the state in the final decades of the nineteenth century. There was, however, very little direct confrontation with the arguments of Burgess or other propagators of the German organic theory. And the principal textbooks of the day still maintained that the state was the subject of political science. Even though the commitment to the state was not always based on the same theoretical grounds and ideology, it was pervasive. The loss of the idea of the state as a rationale for limited government and as a surrogate for the "people" did not diminish its acceptance by the succeeding generation of political scientists who struggled with the problem of American diversity.

There is a persistent myth in the scholarship on the history of political science that the demise of the nineteenth-century image of the state was part of a transition from historicism to scientism and involved a rejection of the ideas of Burgess, Willoughby, and others (see, e.g., Ross 1991).

While the generation that followed Burgess at Columbia, and even some of his contemporaries and close colleagues such as William A. Dunning, drifted away from his particular conception of the state, and particularly the racist elements, and diverged even more sharply ideologically, this was *not* what precipitated the debate about the state that erupted in the 1920s. Charles Merriam certainly welcomed and propagated the new trends in empirical social science, but this was more a change in the content of the idea of science than a shift in the basic commitment to science. Merriam never took it upon himself to challenge his teacher Burgess, or to challenge the paradigm of the state. Although there may be several dimensions to the explanation of this fact, one factor was certainly the continuity in areas of fundamental agreement (Gunnell 1992). Merriam, like many others, came to accept the notion that society was fragmented, but this was not, anymore than for someone such as Charles Beard or Bentley, a cause to depreciate the state. The state remained the solution to the problem. In the work of Merriam, what might be called pluralism was increasingly accepted as an account of social reality, but it was hardly a normative thesis. The state remained the locus of liberal democracy and the vehicle for the solution of social problems.

From the beginnings of the discipline, pluralism, or political and social diversity, had been construed as a pathology, and the circumstances of the late nineteenth and early twentieth centuries did little to ameliorate this concern that cut across ideological lines. For Wilson, the problem was fragmentation in both government and society, and Jesse Macy (1917), as well as many others, continued to see political science, through government, as an answer to the problem of controlling proliferating and conflicting interests. There is a long-standing myth that the nineteenth-century study of the state did not pay attention to the particulars of politics and the various interests in society. Individuals such as Lieber and Woolsey cataloged and discussed a plethora of political diversity while at the same time seeking unity in the idea of the state. But after the turn of century, in the work of both political scientists and sociologists, the focus on interest groups, as political reality, increased.

Although Bentley's work was neither well understood nor immediately very influential, his emphasis on groups was neither unrepresentative nor unnoticed. And Beard's (1913) account of the creation of the American constitution and the economic basis of politics challenged the idea of collective unity that had sustained the traditional theory of the state. A pluralist account of social reality was, by 1920, gaining strength, and, at least implicitly it was a challenge to the concept of the state as an organic community underlying government. But as a normative thesis challenging the idea of state authority, pluralism was hardly congenial to individuals such as Merriam and others who pursued a vision of national democratic consolidation and social control. Merriam was disillusioned with the Progressivist image of a democratic public that, awakened by the factual revelations of a realist social science, would rise up and take control from corrupt politicians and economic elites.

What was required was a social science that spoke to and through elites and that through civic education and the manipulation of public opinion, would foster the creation of a democratic public that would be represented by the state. For Merriam, as for Lasswell after him (1927), propaganda could be used for good as well as evil. What was emerging in the 1920s was an image of an irrational splintered society, propelled by self-interest and acting through the vagaries of public opinion, in which there was no definable public. This was exemplified in the work of Graham Wallas (1908), A. Lawrence Lowell (1913a), Walter Lippmann (1914), and Frank Kent (1924). Merriam (1922; Merriam and Gosnell 1924) himself found that American society was fractured by parties and that individuals did not participate.

It fell to Harold Laski to redeem "pluralism" and explicitly introduce the concept into the discourse of political science. It was principally in response to his claims, and to the ideas of those he implicated in his arguments, that the debate about the state was generated and that pluralism as a theory of liberal democracy was invented. By the mid-1920s, the concept of pluralism and the idiom of pluralistic theory had become common currency, while a decade earlier the concepts had been virtually absent from the literature. Pluralism was viewed as a "critical political theory" directed against the "conservative political theory" of "state monism" (Gettell 1924; Hsiao 1927).

In England, by the beginning of the war, there was already hostility toward the traditional theory of the state. Sir Ernest Barker not only condemned German philosophy and the "worship of power" in the work of writers such as Nietzsche and Treitschke, but criticized John Austin's theory of sovereignty as never having fitted English "polyarchism" (Barker 1914, 1915, 1918). This theme of the "discredited state" was pursued by Laski. He argued against both the idea of an omnipotent state as the source of law and the notions of philosophical absolutism with which it was allied (Laski 1917, 1919; Duguit 1919). But at the same time, he systematically turned to pluralism not only as an account of social reality but as a theory of democratic society. His early work represented a constant attack on idealism, the monistic theory of the state, the idea of state sovereignty, and on the Austinian inspired emphasis on formal legal aspects of the state as the subject of social science. Most of this work, largely in the form of collected essays, was published while he was at Harvard (from 1916 to 1920), and much of his philosophical inspiration and justification came from his reading of John Dewey and William James. Laski left Harvard and returned to England after negative student and administrative reaction to his public discussion and support of the Boston police strike. The university had offered its services to the city, and Lowell, now president, admonished Laski that it was not the place of a professor to speak out on political issues (see Deane 1955). What he initiated and left behind was a debate about the state that would precipitate a new theory of liberal society and contribute to a transformation in the identity of political science.

Laski ridiculed the "exaltation of unity" that had evolved in political theory from Dante to Hegel and that had been more recently represented by Bismarck and Treitschke. He excoriated the "mysticism" attending attempts at "monistic reduction," which presented the state as a holistic "personality" and obscured and subordinated the social elements that comprised it. Each church, town, university, and labor union had its own distinct reality and "group-life" and "will." The image of the state in "political theory," and the concept of sovereignty as its "instrument," was simply the counterpart and consequence of philosophical idealism's notion of a metaphysical "absolute" as the basis of human judgment. Laski opposed this Jamesian image of the pluralistic universe, which, he suggested, led to the political idea of a federated republic and to an "individualistic" and "pluralistic theory of the state."

Laski argued that, as a philosophical principle, the whole is not known before its parts and has no moral superiority. The parts are in themselves distinct, not part of a seamless web in which their reality derives from their relationship to something greater. Consequently, he claimed, the "State is but one of the variety of associations and groups to which the individual belongs" and to which allegiance is paid. The source of law was, in fact, not a command of a sovereign, as Austin had insisted, but something sociologically generated from the "opinion" of individuals and instances of their consent or "fused good-will." The only reason that the state was supreme on occasion was that it managed to "obtain general acceptance" of the "constituent wills from which the group will is made" and "prove itself" (as Dewey suggested) on an "experimentalist" basis. Any real disagreement on the part of its elements rendered it impotent and the assumption of sovereignty meaningless.

Laski sought support for his arguments in Aristotle's idea of mixed government and suggested that this conception of the polity offered "a pragmatist theory of the state" in which progress came not from uniformity but from variation and conflict. Yet he rejected what might also be understood as Aristotle's claim that the state was more important because its concerns were more comprehensive or that it had a larger moral purpose. He argued that, in fact, it usually represented only a portion of society, and its purposes were, in principle, no more superior than those of a church or trade union. Even though Parliament, for example, might be the formal seat of authority, its dictates were in the end the result of a "vast complex of forces," and public acceptance of those dictates was a "pragmatic" affair (Laski 1917, 1–25).

These ideas were explicitly inspired and formulated in the context of Laski's associations with Roscoe Pound, Felix Frankfurter, and Herbert Croly, as well as the jurisprudence of Oliver Wendell Holmes, but he more explicitly drew on the work of Maitland, Figgis, and Gierke and their research on pluralism in medieval society. He identified himself as a "frank medievalist." He also attempted, through his studies of the Reformation and other instances of religious dissent, as well as more modern examples such as syndicalism in France and the guild socialism of G. D. H. Cole, to give historical and rhetorical depth to his claims about pluralism and his animadversions against the worship of the state and the dogma of its moral superiority. While the modern state had sought its independence from religion, it attempted, he claimed, to appropriate for itself that same kind of universality.

Laski's primary concern was actually England and the conservatism of Parliament and common law, and he found in the United States what he believed was in many respects an exemplification of his theoretical claims about the "moral insufficiency" of the idea of the unitary state. He argued that the very fact of the American Revolution, as well as the nature of the government of the United States manifest in the principles of federalism and the separation of powers, demonstrated the "absurdity" and the practical abolition of Austin's theory of sovereignty and Dicey's image of a unitarian and omnipotent state. He argued that the American founders had taken the states as a "foundation to be built upon" and did not attempt "to create a complete system of government" at the national level. And this, he argued, was still sociologically apparent in the "fundamental diversity of circumstance" in the country, "in the variety of its group life, and in the wide distribution of sovereign power" that promised the "guarantee of its perennial youth" and the preservation of liberty." The eminent, imminent, and immanent danger, however, was, as in all modern countries, that of "centralization" and the loss of local autonomy (Laski 1917, 268–82).

Although one might be tempted, including Laski himself, to say that he developed a pluralistic theory of the state, he actually did not so much offer an alternative theory of the state as attempt to destroy every attribute of the state as conventionally conceived and, through concrete case studies, to demonstrate the absence of any historical essence. In successive essays, he moved more and more toward the notion that "what we term state-action is, in actual fact, action by government" (1919, 30), which in turn amounted to little more than what was functionally accepted by groups in society and made operative. And since there was never any ultimate assurance that government would be obeyed, as history seemed to so clearly demonstrate, the idea of sovereignty was a myth.

Mary Parker Follett's work was an interesting and intellectually challenging move in this conversation, but even though it must be counted as contributing to the transformation of pluralism into a normative theory of democracy, it did not become a major factor in the evolution of the discussion. She focused on the group as the essence of political life, but her concern was less to depreciate the idea of state than to reconstitute it in terms of a theory of group democracy. Follett's image of the group was hardly that of parties and interests, which, she believed, tended to constitute the reality of contemporary government – masked by the fiction of democracy. Neither representative government nor attempts at direct government were working, and when collective unity was achieved, it often meant the assimilation of the individual, which she considered the basic "unit of politics," in the "crowd." She argued that the "twentieth century must find a new principle of association" and that this should be "group organization," which would entail a "new method in politics" (Follett 1918, 3, 75). Democracy could work and achieve a common good only if political life was revitalized by, and defined in terms of, "the organization of non-partisan groups" such as those represented by neighborhoods and occupations. Follett argued that although "pluralism was the most vital trend in political thought," it had not developed an adequately positive political theory that answered the questions of what was to be done with diversity and how to move to "a true Federal State" and eventually a "World State." In her view, "the organization of men in small local groups" provided the basis for a "continuous political activity which ceaselessly creates the state" as a wider collective democratic community (1918, 7, 11, 13).

Laski (1935) was moving in the Marxist direction of claiming that government, or the state, really was and had always been controlled by a particular segment of society and a dominant economic interest. But he argued that it had also been subject to all sorts of limitations including the conscience of the individual, institutional checks, group diversity, and popular resistance and revolution. The real question was that of political obligation or why people obey authority. His answer was basically that government was forced to gain support, and this "leads to a pluralistic theory of society" and to a definite distinction between state and society. Since the "State is only one among many forms of association" and no more in harmony with the goals of society or morally and legally superior than a union or lodge, it had no special claim to authority. "The state is based upon will; but the wills from which its will is eventually formed struggle amongst each other for survival." This description, he claimed, was "realism," while the notion that the state can be identified with some general community was idealism. The state was simply mortals governing, and that is why it must be limited by democratic institutional means such as the separation of powers and representation (Laski 1919, 65–9).

Just as government was, or should be, rendered into parts, so was society "basically federal in nature." The great danger, for Laski, continued to be modern centralization, which tended to depreciate the principle and reality of consent and to obscure the fact that the state, like a "Darwinian species," only, at least properly, "summarizes a general social experience" and has no separate validation (1919, 74, 109). He continued to hold up the United States as a paradigm but at the same time suggested a sense of crisis based on the fact that this "political democracy confronts the most powerful economic autocracy the world has ever seen," while the separation of powers gives way to the decline of Congress and administrative centralization. Yet despite "its corrupt politics," the "withdrawal of much of its ability from governmental life, its exuberant optimism, and a traditional faith in its orthodox political mechanisms that may well prove disastrous," there was hope. This rested on its revolutionary and democratic heritage, the growth of organized labor, social protest and progressive experimentation, the rebirth of natural rights ideas, and legal decisions such as those of Holmes and Brandeis, which held the state subject to law (1919, 116).

Laski pursued the same themes in a third volume, yet by this point the monistic state and the pluralistic state were no longer simply different theoretical accounts. He went beyond the claim that the *theory* of sovereignty had "fallen from its high estate." The monistic state was presented as the characteristic structure of contemporary political power. Pluralism was offered as an alternative normative program in opposition to the "unified sovereignty of the present social organization" and devoted to the substitution of "coordination" for "hierarchical structure." Laski's goal was the "partition" of sovereignty and the creation of social "federalism." He continued to stress the manner in which government was controlled by dominant economic power and how liberty was incompatible with power in the hands of "a small group of property owners" (Laski 1921, v, 209). He still sought his exemplars in the Conciliar movement of the Middle Ages, Edmund Burke, and early American federalism.

With the decline of the state as a conception of political reality, Merriam and others, like later generations of political scientists, sought the identity and authority of political science more in its method rather than its subject matter, but this notion of methodological identity was not without its problems. The ideas of science and the state had been intimately entwined in the nineteenth century in that the state was conceived as the object of science, and science was understood as the basis of the authority of knowledge. The decline of the state signified the loss of a distinct and substantive object, and this, in turn, required the reconstitution of the identity of political science – a task to which Merriam devoted much of his life. It also required rethinking the issue of the relationship between political science and politics. It is in these terms that it is possible to explain in part the manner in which the controversy about the state and pluralism developed. Those who argued against pluralism as both a descriptive and normative thesis may, in some instances, have been, in the narrow sense, ideologically motivated, but more immediately and generally, what was at stake was the professional identity and authority of political science and the very meaning of liberalism.

First of all, pluralism provided little basis for distinguishing political science from sociology, psychology, and economics – and in fact, seemed to indicate its subservience to these fields. The domain of political science and the nature of political theory, whose boundaries had been carefully and assiduously circumscribed prior to World War I by Willoughby and others, were called into question. Second, if political science did not have access to the deeper scientific subject matter of the state, its claim to knowledge and its long sought social authority were in jeopardy. Finally, pluralism threatened the notion that there was, after all, a "people," which in turn called into question the very idea of liberal democracy as it had been heretofore conceived. It was not the empiricism of the new science of politics, advocated by individuals such as Merriam, that bothered the critics as much as its interdisciplinary character and the rejection of the conception of political reality represented by the idea of the state.

Many, including, for example, Dunning (1917), praised Laski's repudiation of unitary sovereignty, but the problem that Laski bequeathed to American political science was that of how, as Walter Shepard (1919) asked, conflicts between groups could be resolved without the supreme will of the state. Ellen Deborah Ellis (Smith College), however, was the first to articulate, and to attempt to give a schematic account of, the controversy that had taken shape. She emphasized that what had emerged was an increasingly distinct theory of "pluralism," which could be juxtaposed to "monism" – the "long accepted state theory of political science" (Ellis 1920, 394). The latter represented the state as the distinct, unitary, and absolute political association and sovereign organ of society and as something standing behind government and as the creator of liberty and rights. Ellis noted, accurately, that the pluralist challenge to these assumptions sprung less from a factual disagreement than from the belief that the state should be limited. She suggested that pluralist theory leavened some of the more dubious elements of traditional statism, such as the excessive emphasis on authority exemplified in German philosophy, and it called "attention to the present bewildering development of groups within the body politic, and to the fact that these groups are persistently demanding greater recognition in the governmental system." The difficulty, however, in her view, was that pluralism offered no solution to this problem and tended to "lay the way open to a very disorganized and casual political organization," which would be a threat to both order and liberty and which disguised the inescapable fact that, in the end, any real and true state must be a "unitary state" in which there is "one supreme loyalty and political sovereign" (Ellis 1920, 405–7). Ellis also pressed the failure of pluralism, and particularly notions of guild socialism, to distinguish adequately, both historically and analytically, between state and government and thereby to "overthrow the very citadel of the state itself" (Ellis 1923, 211).

Francis W. Coker (Yale), who had been an assistant to Dunning at Columbia, perceptively questioned whether pluralists such as Duguit and

Laski really advanced the same kind of ideas as Gierke, Maitland, and Figgis. He also suggested that the new pluralists had created a straw man and that, apart from syndicalism, none of the more recent ideas required "any abandonment of the essential features of the conventional theory of state sovereignty" (Coker 1921, 211). Coker accurately sensed that the emerging dichotomy between monism and pluralism was somewhat artificial, but he was not able to articulate the underlying concerns that propelled the debate. He continued to worry about the emphasis on pluralism and interest groups and about the manner in which theorists such as George Sabine, who, he believed, tended to concur with Gierke, Figgis, Laski, Krabbe, and Duguit, contributed to disparaging the idea of the state and the role of state authority in preserving "liberal values" (Coker 1924). And this was really what was principally at stake here – *whether liberal democracy was grounded in the state or in society.*

In 1922, Sabine participated in the translation and introduction of Krabbe's work *The Modern Theory of the State.* He still associated political theory with the philosophy of the state, but he applauded Krabbe for offering a new conception of state sovereignty as embodied in law and free from organic images of authority. Sabine's pluralist sympathies were evident, but he tried to mediate some of the controversies of the day. With respect to the debate between "monism" and "pluralism," he suggested that these were less competing theories than different "points of view" – one looking at legal structure and the other looking at process or development (Sabine 1923). But this abstract conciliatory approach obscured the increasingly deep-seated intellectual division.

William Yandell Elliott, an assistant professor at the University of California, began systematically to attack those who he believed were undermining the idea of state authority and the sovereignty of law (Elliott 1924, 1925). He believed that he had found a theme in the "varied currents of contemporary political theory which seems to have set against the conception of unitary sovereignty as the basis of the structure of the state." The claims of pragmatists, realists, and pluralists were, in his view, inviting social chaos and were out of place "in so closely knit a unity as is formed in the modern state" (1924, 251). For Elliott, pluralism was closely allied to syndicalism and such dangerous doctrines as those of Sorel. Laski was Elliott's principal target at the time, and he saw him, not surprisingly, given Laski's rhetoric, not only as following Barker's attack on the idea of the state, but as a "disciple" of James and as an advocate of Dewey's experimentalism (Elliot 1924, 275).

By the mid-1920s, the debate had definitely taken on a life of its own, and Laski was little more than a symbol. His arguments had never actually been very carefully analyzed in the literature, and by the time he wrote *The Grammar of Politics*, his own focus had shifted away from the critique of monism to the problem of the challenge to "the liberal theory of the state" presented by Marx's analysis. While he still affirmed much of the pluralist critique, he believed that pluralism had not sufficiently taken account of "the nature of the state as an expression of class-relations" both in "democratic" societies and in emerging authoritarian regimes (Laski 1925, iii, xi). Only in a classless society could there be a fundamental transformation in the state. The changing image of the state, however, was apparent in a work such as that of R. M. MacIver, who, while seeking something of a middle way in the controversy, implicitly undermined many of the assumptions that were crucial to earlier state theory.

MacIver argued that the "theory of the state has too long been dominated by the legislative conception of sovereignty" and that political thought today recognizes the "limited and relative character of sovereignty." It was necessary, he argued, to look at the state as a product of "social evolution" with no "perfected form" and to understand that it is only "*one* of the organs of the community" and that "the great associations are as native to the soil of society as the state itself" (MacIver 1926, 468, 475). The claim to legal absolutism was no different than the manner in which ecclesiastical law was dominant in its particular sphere. The state was essentially one of many social "corporations" and less the source of law than the guardian. Behind the state, MacIver claimed, was society or the "community," which constituted the unity or "solidarity of men" and of which the state was only a limited agent. But even if it were in no special way the "home of man," it was more than the product of clashing associations, and it represented, especially in its democratic manifestation, the most extensive and fundamental type of membership and provided a "form of unity to the whole system of social relationships" (1926, 479–86).

This somewhat ambivalent formulation was still not at all congenial to Elliott, since it gave the state no ultimate authority over social groups (Elliott 1927). Ellis suggested that after attempting to extricate itself from "a supernatural or metaphysical theory" and from the field of law and a formal juristic analysis of the state, political science was now besieged by disciplines such as sociology, economics, and ethics. Political science was at a "crossroads" where it was necessary to ask whether it was any longer possible to "attempt to reestablish it as a distinctive discipline?" (Ellis 1927, 773). The pluralist and sociological accounts of Krabbe, Duguit, Cole, and Laski, as well as the work of individuals such as Merriam, may have attempted to reach the "realities" behind the idea of the state, but, Ellis argued, they also tended to eliminate any distinctive political reality or meaning of sovereignty. In her view, even Willoughby did not adequately articulate what she called "the political" and distinguish a perspective on the "purely political character of the state" (Ellis 1927, 784).

Willoughby, who despite his criticisms of Burgess and German philosophy still clung to a version of the more traditional juristic view of the state, was also among those who criticized the position of Krabbe, Duguit, and Sabine. He challenged the critique of sovereignty that threatened the domain of political science, but he also attacked the critics for failing to distinguish between legal and ethical validity – between fact and value or political science and politics (Willoughby 1926). Sabine (1928) continued to defend Krabbe and argued that juristic formalism was too simple an approach to deal with modern political developments. By the mid-1920s, however, the two most articulate representatives in the discussion were Elliott and G. E. G. Catlin, and there is something ironic in this fact. Elliott, the leading critic of scientism and pluralism, and one of the few to view these "isms" in tandem during this period, was an American who did his undergraduate work at Vanderbilt and his doctorate at Oxford (1923). G. E. G. Catlin, who conjoined and defended scientism and pluralism, was an Oxford undergraduate who took his doctorate at Cornell (1924).

Catlin declared that "politics is concerned with a field of human behavior characterized by the recurrences of specific behavior patterns," particularly group processes, which can be defined psychologically and measured by various quantitative and statistical means (Catlin 1927a, 255). He applauded the pluralist position and its attack on the "absolute state," as well as its embrace of factual realism, but like Willoughby, he complained that it was still an "ethical philosophy," which treated politics from a "liberal" perspective, rather than a "dispassionate study of actual human behavior." Although he wished to transform pluralism into an empirical account of political reality and to retreat from a normative theory, he left no doubt that the purpose of social science was social control just as the purpose of natural science was control over nature, and he insisted on the inherent complementarity of science and democracy. He argued, however, that it was first necessary, as in the relationship between biology and medicine, to find some "basal principles of political method" and establish "a behaviorist science of politics" that would allow sound diagnosis of political problems and administrative and legislative treatment (Catlin 1927b, x–xi, 284, 295).

Elliott, now, in 1928, an assistant professor at Harvard, where he would rise to prominence and direct over a hundred dissertations, brought together his strictures against pluralism and scientism, which together, he believed, constituted "the pragmatic revolt in politics" – and in political science. Part of this work had been written as a doctoral thesis at Oxford just after World War I, but it incorporated articles and reviews published during the 1920s that focused on Laski, Duguit, Sorel, Mussolini, and others he counted as pragmatists and enemies of the liberal state. Although Elliott's principal teacher, A. D. Lindsay, was one of those who proclaimed that the "theory of the sovereign state has broken down" and who stressed the variety of corporate personalities and communities of interest in society (Lindsay 1914, 136), it was to him that the book was dedicated and to whom Elliott, in part through exposure to Kant, attributed the greatest intellectual influence. For Elliott, there were two traditions of pluralism, and he found inspiration in what he conceived as the older organic one that he believed Lindsay still represented. His "greatest stimulant," however, was, despite the wide disagreement, Laski, who he continued to perceive as the principal formulator of modern pluralist theory.

Elliott set out to rescue the concept of the state, and the book bears an uncanny resemblance to works written a generation later attacking scientism and pluralist liberalism – albeit often from a different ideological perspective. What is evident in Elliott's opus was a distinct concern about the manner in which pluralism threatened the identity of political theory, and political inquiry in general, as well as the very idea of a distinct and autonomous political domain and democratic community.

Elliott argued that there was, "in practice as well as theory," a "revolt against political rationalism" that was manifest in the contemporary attacks on "the constitutional and democratic state" in Europe both by "Capitalistic Fascism" and by the syndicalist and communist left wing of the Marxist movement. The philosophy behind these incursions, which "gives them their ideology and their values," was, he claimed, pragmatism, but this was, ironically, basically an American intellectual product despite its explicit appearance in the work of individuals such as Sorel and Mussolini. Although such events as the war and its aftermath and the "development of modern capitalistic industrialism" had undoubtedly created strains, a concerted attack on the foundations of liberal democracy had been mounted. Part of what made pragmatism so dangerous in Elliott's view, more so than even the dogmas of Bolshevism, was the fact that it was so totally "skeptical of absolutes" and thereby threatened to undercut both political philosophy and political practice, as well as their conjunction (Elliott 1928, viii). He emphasized his critical agenda, but his purpose was ultimately to reconstruct the associational identity of the constitutional state and, consequently, the study of politics.

The attack on state authority was, he argued, a pervasive one that was in evidence everywhere – from labor unions, dictatorships of the Left and Right, and those seeking a world state. While pluralism sought to discredit the state, fascism, in reaction, aimed at creating an excessively and repressively organic one. Through force and violence, both pluralism and fascism subverted law, public discussion, the franchise, and other characteristics of liberal constitutional society. Contemporary political science, however, had failed to discern what was happening. It was itself infused with pragmatism and focused on scientific descriptive studies to such a degree that "there is not a single contemporary political theorist in America who is to be counted among those of the first order." While pragmatism had the virtue of looking at political phenomena in context, rather than dealing with abstractions, it had made political science increasingly politically irrelevant and had failed to deal with man as a moral being and as a "purposive animal" endowed with the speculative reason that gives meaning to facts in both science and politics (Elliott 1928, 4–5).

Elliott directly attributed these trends, that had now reached "alarming proportions," to the philosophies of James and Dewey. As a consequence of their influence, "mainstream American political science" had become "behavioristic in terms of psychology and positivistic in terms of philosophy." Values had been neglected, and there were simply "too few political theorists and too many technicians, engineers, scientists or artists in America." The result was that philosophy and political practice had become disassociated as scientists joined politicians in an attitude of "pragmatic skepticism." Pragmatism, in the narrow sense, had gained a strong hold on academic life, but it also represented a more general world historical antiintellectual trend. It was reflected in the "revolt against the sovereignty of the personalized state and against parliamentarianism" that was manifest in syndicalism and the ideas of Sorel, the "more chastened pluralism" of Laski, Duguit's theory of *droit objectif*, and the "Fascist 'efficiency' gospel of Mussolini." The ideas of James had informed the work of individuals such as Laski and Sorel, who repudiated the state as "a moral agent and legal overlord," as well as the fascist attack on rational theories of the state (Elliott 1928, 7–10).

According to Elliott, there had been a long intellectual decline from Kant and the Age of Reason to Dewey and James, whose ideas had both infiltrated political practice and informed the "group theory of the state." Since "thought and act form a unity in history," it was possible to see past ideas in such present facts as the "general strike," which set class above the state, and the fascist justification of dictatorship. The idea of the "reality of group selves, including the state, forms the rock upon which Idealism and pragmatism have alike gone aground with their ships of state" (Elliott 1928, 31–2). While the former went to extremes with the notion of group "unity," the latter denied unity altogether. Pragmatism treated all groups except the state as moral persons, and this led to an instrumentalist and functional attitude that eventually "reenthroned" the state as a necessity and produced fascism. Thus, despite their different practical manifestations, pluralism and fascism rested on the same intellectual foundation.

Elliott claimed that practical manifestations of the pragmatic philosophy were visible in various aspects of what was called "modernism" – whether in education or politics. The traditional theory of the state had been dismissed as vicious and as not fitting the facts – and the facts were *groups*. "The life of certain groups within the state, notably trade unions and professional associations, has become a more real thing in men's experience than the common political life represented by the state." According to Elliott, philosophical rationalism and the idea of state sovereignty were mutually entailed in that both emphasized the priority of an organizing reason over diverse parts, while pragmatism stressed instinct, will, and plurality. "If Hegel was the apologist of Prussianism, Duguit is not less that of Fascism" (Elliott 1928, 40, 43).

Although Elliott conceded that pragmatism made a reasonable point when it challenged Hegelian philosophical absolutism and idealism, it went too far. Its "anti-intellectualistic pluralism begins with individualism, goes through groups, and culminates in force as an abstract power in the organically absolute state of Fascist theory" (1928, 64). When this philosophy is put into practice, it becomes "the mother of a brood of revolutionary theories of the state." Elliott argued that "constitutional government," on the other hand, represented the "same effort at political synthesis that conceptual logic does for thought synthesis. It must shun alike pluralism and absolutism" while providing an ideal and an "accepted rule fixing political responsibility" (1928, 75). Such a political system provides a kind of unity that inhibits both the centrifugal forces of pluralism and the centripetal forces of dictatorship while at the same time creating a kind of moral whole and a community of purpose in which sovereignty becomes a "reality."

Elliott was not advocating a return to the legalistic Austinian view of sovereignty, but the concept, even if something of a fiction, was, he believed, a necessary part of the idea of constitutional government. Those such as Laski who had discredited the idea of the state had moved in the direction of positing sovereign groups that raised the threat of corporatism and elevated, for example, freedom of religious sects above community interest. But the most important point that Elliott wished to make, echoing earlier American theorists of the state, was that the federal government possessed only a limited or delegated sovereignty. The institution of government was the "creature of the political community" and the representative of "the federal state created by the Constitution" (Elliott 1928, 106–7).

Elliott had been influenced by his new European colleague at Harvard, Carl Friedrich, and he fell into the naive belief that while other countries were abandoning liberalism and representative institutions, "the new Germany seems steadfast in its practice of parliamentary government under the benign moderation of Hindenburg" (Elliott 1928, 315). Although he could not accept Carl Schmitt's critique of parliamentary decision making, he sympathized with Schmitt's savage attack on pluralist liberalism and saw much of what Schmitt called modern political romanticism in pluralist thought and practice. Elliott reprised his earlier criticisms of Laski as another "disciple" of James and the foremost opponent of the idea of unitary sovereignty. Even though he found *The Grammar of Politics* more constructive and maybe "the most important contribution that has been made to recent political theory" (Elliott 1928, 167), he stressed Laski's affiliation with the labor party and his tendency to sacrifice the very individual he was concerned about through the destruction of the state and the unleashing of group interest. Elliott, however, was hardly simply an ideologue of conservative interests and an advocate of noninterventionist government. His concern was the loss of state authority, which was of equal concern to many with a quite different political philosophy.

What Elliott found in all these varieties of pluralism – whether what he termed the romanticist versions, represented by Sorel and Laski, or

the functional instrumental types, characteristic of Cole's guild socialism, as well as various internationalist movements – was the "sublimation" of the political realm in subpolitical groups and the loss of any
distinct idea of a political community. The alternative that he envisioned
was a return to the tradition of liberalism represented by T. H. Green and
by more recent works such as Norman Wilde's *The Ethical Basis of the
State* (1924), which called for a "community of purpose" that stood
above particular associations. This image of political authority, of the
state as "a community of purpose," might, he admitted, be to some degree a "mythos," but it was a barrier to fascism. Individuals such as
Dewey, with his attack on Austin, and Duguit, with his dismissal of anything approximating a general will and a political community in favor
of force and habit, surrendered any such ground. They instead raised up
groups as political reality and thereby in effect constituted "an apology
for the Fascist ideal of a 'disciplined' national organism" (Elliott 1928,
247, 250). While they saw the state as government and government as
merely a social instrument, Elliott insisted that the "constitutional
state . . . is the political community" whose purpose and will was expressed in law (1928, 298).

The practical immediate outcome of these intellectual trends was, Elliott claimed, as he had already argued in an earlier article, Mussolini,
the "prophet of the pragmatic era in politics." Even if not always named
as such, the method of fascism was pragmatism, and Elliott noted that
"Mussolini attributes his own intellectual shaping to William James, on
equal terms with three great pragmatists in politics: Machiavelli, Nietzsche, and the syndicalist, Georges Sorel" (Elliott 1928, 316). After the
failure of Wilson and the League of Nations, pragmatism became, Elliott argued, the *Zeitgeist* of our time and the essence of both political
action and political thought.

His answer was to make political authority paramount without at the
same time creating a "super-organism." He developed what he called a
"co-organic," as opposed to an organic, theory of groups. This recognized that a group consisted of an organic, largely economic, instrumental consensus but was also properly identified in terms of a defining
moral purposive consensus of individuals that, in the case of the political association or the state as a group, was the subject of political science. He claimed that the co-organic type of political association was
historically manifest in the Anglo-American constitutional state and that
pluralism and fascism were aberrations. Coolidge's action in the han-
dling of the Boston police strike seemed to him an appropriate example

of the co-organic constitutional state in action – hardly a sentiment that Laski would have shared.

Despite the intellectual distance between them, Catlin presented a long and surprisingly temperate, if somewhat wry, review of Elliott's polemic. He claimed that it was "indubitably the book of the year in political theory" and an important exposition of the "new liberalism" – which would actually be welcomed by those wishing a defense of the old liberalism with its emphasis on idealism and statism. Catlin suggested that Elliott stood to Laski like T. H. Green to Mill (Catlin 1929, 259). Harold Lasswell, while obviously in disagreement in many respects, also reviewed the book cautiously and suggested that because it broadened the perspectives of students of government, it should be "welcomed with enthusiasm" (Lasswell 1929–30, 134–5). But Lasswell, himself, was far from believing that group conflict was the key to a democratic society.

Catlin did, however, take serious issue with the notion that Mussolini could be best understood as a pragmatist, since, according to Catlin, he appeared closer to a Platonist. He argued that it was in fact the kind of philosophy espoused by Elliott that threatened individual rights by its insistence that the "state is the good, the beautiful, and the true." Nationalism, Catlin claimed, was "one of the most dangerous social poisons of our age" and a danger to the rule of law and constitutional morality and that in this respect Elliott was "on the side of Mussolini." For Catlin, internationalism and respect for local rights offered a better hope (Catlin 1929, 261–3). Although he agreed with Elliott that "facts" do not yield norms, he maintained that knowledge of facts explains norms and illuminates what is possible for human purpose (Catlin 1929, 260, 265).

By the end of the decade, the controversy had lost its coherency, but what had taken place was a debate, surely, about political reality. It was also the beginning of a very distinct disagreement about liberalism and about the basis of the identity of political science and political theory. It was not altogether an accident that the dialogue about pluralism was attached to the issue of scientism, and it was not simply because groups constituted a more obvious empirical subject matter than the state. Scientism was the basis on which one dimension of the discipline attempted to predicate the identity of the field in the wake of the decline of the state – a basis that was inadequate on several grounds from the perspective of individuals such as Elliott. "Methodism" in political science would continue to be blamed for forgetting both the idea and practice of politics (Wolin 1969).

40   *John G. Gunnell*

During the last half of the decade, pluralism, in the work of individuals such as Peter Odegard (1925) and Pendelton Herring (1929), was clearly gaining ground as an empirical descriptive account of American politics, but there were also signs of a return to the *Federalist* image of pluralism as an account of popular government and to the idea that the "people" and the "public interest" could be conceived in these terms (Dickinson 1929). There would continue to be ambivalence about the virtue of groups and pluralist theory during the 1930s (Coker 1934), but pluralism was progressively transformed into a normative account of American politics and liberal democracy (Garson 1978). Part of this development was the growing sense that American politics was the outpost of democracy in a political universe where totalitarian centralism and statism were becoming increasingly prominent. Consequently, as it would be so frequently and explicitly argued in later years, the theory of liberal democracy must be found in the practice of American political life.

Note

1. For a discussion of the methodological premises governing this essay and the emphasis on "internal" history, see Gunnell (1991). With respect to some of the broader substantive themes related to this discussion, see Gunnell (1993).

2

An Ambivalent Alliance: Political Science and American Democracy

Terence Ball

I

The "American Science of Politics," as Bernard Crick (1959) once referred to the academic discipline of political science, has long had an uneasy and ofttimes ambivalent relation to its subject matter. This subject matter is two sided. On the one side is the general realm of politics, or (in some quarters) "the political." The other and more specific side is American politics, or more specifically still (and with a nod toward Tocqueville), democracy in America. My aim here is to advance several conjectures about that ambivalent relationship. The first is that political science, insofar as it is (or claims to be) scientific, is bound to be suspicious of and skeptical toward the un- or ill-informed opinions and prejudices of ordinary citizens. My second claim is that political science in a setting that is not only academic but also American and therefore putatively democratic cannot take, and has not taken, a normatively neutral view of the civic or political education of Americans (particularly young and/or recently arrived ones). My third contention is that there has been something of a seesawing back and forth between a hopeful and a despairing view of the rationality and educability of the citizenry. My fourth and final claim is that the direction of the swing has been historically variable. That is, hope and despair have been more or less rational responses to contingent constellations of political forces, fears, and possibilities at particular times or moments.

   Since these claims constitute too tall an order to fill in a single essay, I propose to illustrate their plausibility by examining several episodes in the history of American political science. I therefore make no claim to completeness. My aim is simply to suggest that the history of American political science is in important respects part of the history of American politics. Claims about its "scientific" status, its "value neutrality" and policy relevance, its immunity to "ideology" and assorted foreign influences – these and other facets and features of American political science become intelligible (and, indeed, interesting) only when they are located within the larger intellectual and political context in which this discipline sought its niche and legitimacy within the American polity.

I propose to proceed as follows. I begin by sketching, very briefly and with the fewest possible strokes, a picture of two alternative visions of political science as a vocation. The first holds that that science's primary (though not exclusive) task lies in the enlightenment and education of the citizenry; the second, that political science should serve the state as an instrument of social control. I then attempt to show how the tension between these two visions gets played out in three periods or moments in the history of American political science. These are, respectively, the Wilsonian moment, the Progressive period, and the era of the behavioral revolution. Despite their diversity and obvious theoretical and methodological differences, all are in one way or another illustrative of political science's concern – or perhaps preoccupation – with the (in)capacity of American citizens to govern themselves. In the first period, the 1880s, political scientists showed an increasing distrust of democracy generally, and civic education more especially. In Woodrow Wilson's hands political science became fixated on the themes of "leadership" and a "science of administration" in the service of the state. By the turn of the century, American political science had severed all connections with the moral sciences. Aspiring to be a descriptive and explanatory science, its new sources of inspiration and insight included theories of evolution via natural selection as well as new work in psychology. The second or Progressive period saw the discovery of the unconscious and sometimes irrational impulses that figure in the thought processes of ordinary citizens. These discoveries provided grist for the mill not only for skeptical Progressives but also for a discipline that remained deeply suspicious of its own subject matter. I then try to show how this "discovery" influenced and affected conceptions of "public opinion" as a fleeting, fickle, malleable, and indeed, manufactured thing incapable of discovering, much less addressing, questions of the public interest (the idea of a public interest being predicated upon intelligent and informed public opinion). I then go on to argue that this thin view of democracy is thinned still further, in the third period, by the fear, fueled by the rise of totalitarian regimes in Russia and Europe, of the authoritarian and even totalitarian possibilities of popular government. I contend that some American political scientists' analysis of American politics during the early phase of the "behavioral revolution" represented an attempt to show that America was not Weimar – that uniquely American conditions precluded the possibility that democracy in America might be its own worst enemy.

II

I begin by sketching a distinction so crude that it amounts, almost, to a caricature. And yet, like any caricature, this one contains a good deal of truth. One vision of what political science should (aspire to) be stresses its educative mission or, more specifically still, its responsibility for the political education of the citizenry. Versions of this view, which has its origins in eighteenth-century "moral science," can be found in Thomas Jefferson, James Witherspoon, Samuel Stanhope Smith, Francis Lieber, and later, John Dewey and the young Charles Merriam. The second vision downplays the "political" and emphasizes the "science" in political science. More specifically, it sees political science as, in a quite literal sense (and with a nod toward Foucault) a "discipline" – a social science of civic control that serves the state by, among other things, training specialists in public administration and allied fields.[1] This view was advanced by, among others, Woodrow Wilson.

In the latter half of the nineteenth century, political science was tugged between the Scylla of disinterested science and the Charybdis of committed pedagogy. Fascinating yet frightening phenomena – sectionalism, civil war, immigration, urbanization – seemed to cry out not only for study but for correction and reform. Big-city politics, in particular, presented a veritable panorama of political problems too large to ignore. To some, the rise of political "machines" headed by bosses and run by ward heelers seemed to be the newer and more menacing version of the "machine that would go of itself" (Kammen 1987). Wave after wave of immigrants came from Ireland, Italy, Scandinavia, Russia, Eastern Europe, and elsewhere. New and not knowing "the ropes," they relied on and gave rise to Tammany and other big-city machines (Erie 1989). Muckraking journalists like Lincoln Steffens and Upton Sinclair might expose the corruption; but how might it be corrected? The solutions most commonly proposed were "honest government" and "social control." But if honesty made for the best policy, how might citizens be made honest as well as wise to the ways of the ward heeler? And how might the masses be controlled, both for their own good and that of the society at large?

One answer to both questions was that citizens – especially but not exclusively newly arrived ones – must be educated in the ways of democracy and the civic life. It was an answer that Jefferson would have recognized and appreciated. But for the most part political scientists at the turn of the century lacked Jefferson's faith in education. The older Enlightenment view – expressed succinctly in Helvetius's dictum *l'éducation peut tout* – was no longer an article of faith even, or perhaps especially, among educated Americans. Too much was beginning to be known about the unconscious and irrational impulses that cloud clear thinking even as they motivate most people's actions.

If the social sciences generally, and political science in particular, were unable to enlighten and emancipate the citizenry, they might at least aspire to control them and thereby chasten and dampen enthusiasm for the various crackpot plans and schemes then being peddled by populists, socialists, and other political snake-oil salesmen (Ross 1991, ch. 4). And they might also press for political reforms that would make machines and bosses less powerful and therefore less appealing to the poor and newly arrived. There was nothing necessarily "democratic" in these schemes for political reform and social control. They were instead intended to save American democracy from itself. The end being (ostensibly) democratic, and democratic means being ofttimes untrustworthy, it remained only to find the most efficient means to achieving that end. It is in this context that the works of several influential political scientists of the period can be read.

Among the most famous, and arguably the most influential, of these works is Woodrow Wilson's *Congressional Government* (1885). Wilson's title describes what he detests: government by the Congress. That body of busybodies can achieve nothing of lasting value; it can only bicker, barter, and trade. The solution to bad and corrupt government at the federal level lay in a strong executive, in the form of a president freed of old and outworn constitutional shackles. The balance of power between the legislative and executive branches needs to be tilted toward the latter. Wilson was, as Garry Wills observes, the first proponent (save perhaps Hamilton a century earlier) of "the imperial presidency" (Wills, 1992).

What then happens to the older republican and newer democratic idea of government of the people, by the people, and for the people? Wilson's answer is that the president, not a motley collection of congressmen, best embodies and represents "the popular will." From his youth Wilson had been an avid reader and ardent admirer of Thomas Carlyle's *Heroes and*

Hero Worship (1841) and, later, of Walter Bagehot's *The English Constitution* (1867). From the former he gained an admiration for strong men of genius and will who make, and do not merely live in, the world. And from the latter he acquired an abiding respect for the English parliamentary system, with a strong prime minister at the head of a unified government. Wilson's politics – and his conception of the place and role of political science – reflects these early influences and represents a break with the older discourse of democratic-republican politics.

"I am," Wilson declared somewhat disingenuously, "pointing out facts, – diagnosing, not prescribing remedies" (1885, 315). Yet the "facts" as Wilson framed them seemed quite clearly to call for correction of a certain kind. Echoing Bagehot, Wilson held that the main drawback of the U.S. Constitution was that the framers, fearing the emergence of an American counterpart of George III, had constitutionally precluded the kind of strong executive needed to check the legislature (Wilson 1885, 309-10). "The English Constitution," Wilson continued, "is now superior [to ours] because its growth has not been hindered or destroyed by the too tight ligaments of a written fundamental law." The U.S. Constitution fetters the executive even as it exacerbates "the natural, the inevitable tendency of every system of self-government like ours . . . to exalt the representative body, the people's parliament, to a position of absolute supremacy" (1885, 311).

The best, and perhaps indeed the only, antidote and counterweight to a diverse and ofttimes divided plurality is to be found in a singular and strong-willed president who will not follow popular opinion so much as to mold and then represent the "popular will." The presidential will precedes and makes possible the popular will. A professor, a political scientist who became a president of the fledgling American Political Science Association – and a future president of the United States – Wilson saw citizens much as a teacher sees his unkempt charges. A little learning and a lot of discipline can go a long way toward chastening high-spirited democrats, damping down their enthusiasm, and banking the fires of radicalism. It is in this very thin and restricted sense – that the aim of a science of politics is to contain and restrain "enthusiasm" – that the Wilsonian (and later Progressive) science of (reformist) politics had some connection with its eighteenth century ancestor. But if that earlier science had been deployed to contain religious enthusiasm, its successor aimed to curb democratic energy and excess (Farr, 1988a). The entropy feared by Jefferson might perhaps be put to more positive political use. A bit of ennui among the electorate might not be a bad thing, especially if it had the effect of discrediting Congress and elevating the executive branch beyond its eighteenth-century confines. "Leadership" *peut tout*.

Neither the Congress nor the executive can execute; they legislate, he leads, leaving it to others to execute; hence, the importance, in Wilson's view, of "administration," and of political science in the training of administrators. Wilson saw his as the Age of Administration, a "fourth stage" in the history of the nation. The first, "the period of federal construction," he notes, "is long passed." The second, "the season of constitutional development," is also gone, and "questions of constitutional interpretation are no longer regarded as of pressing urgency." The third era, that of the Civil War, "has been fought, even the embers of its issues being now almost extinguished." And so, says Wilson, "We are left to that unexciting but none the less capitally important business of every-day peaceful [read: piecemeal and nonradical] development and judicious administration to whose execution every nation in its middle age has to address itself." Yet America has so far failed to meet the challenge of middle age. "It cannot be said that these new duties have as yet raised up any men eminently fit for their fulfillment. We have had no great administrators since the opening of this newest stage, and there is as yet no visible sign that any such will soon arise." Perhaps, he mused, administration deals with "matters of a too quiet, business-like sort to enlist feeling or arouse enthusiasm" (Wilson 1885, pp. 202–3).

If in the eighteenth century the science of politics strove to dampen religious enthusiasm, its twentieth-century successor should aim to arouse enthusiasm for "administration" and the training of a cadre of professional administrators and civil servants who, like Hegel's disinterested "universal class," would be above politics and partisanship. One of the primary tasks of political science, as Wilson maintained more or less consistently, was to train these selfless servants of the modern administrative state. "Administration" *fait tout*.

There is, of course, a danger of attributing too much influence or importance to what was, after all, an academic book. *Congressional Government* was hardly a block-busting best seller (although it had, by 1895, gone through eighteen reprintings). But it – along with *The State* (1898) and Wilson's classic article "The Study of Administration" (1887a) – was read with considerable interest and attention by would-be reformers who wished to find some way of reconciling their progressivism with their commitment to democracy. Nor did Wilson confine his writing to academic books and journals. He was an indefatigable contributor to the popular press and middle-brow magazines. His message in all three venues remained much the same: science in the service of reform; the dangers of democratic excess; the need, in consequence, for a Congress checked and chastened by a strong executive; and the heretofore overlooked importance of administration.

Wilson's writings, both academic and popular, were also part of a larger literary genre about the limits of democracy and the intellectual and civic limitations of democratic citizens and their representatives. One of these – Henry Adams's best-selling and oft-pirated novel *Democracy* – had appeared only five years earlier, in 1880. Deeply pessimistic and certainly no Progressive, Adams nevertheless articulated the darker fears of many Progressives: Simply put, the masses are not up to the task of governing themselves; their representatives are corrupt, incompetent, and exhibit an unfortunate but understandable tendency to pander or at least pay lip service to what they perceive to be the popular will or to shape it by chicanery and demagoguery; and, as a result, American democracy is its own worst enemy. The conclusion was quick in coming: American democracy must be saved from itself, and by almost any means.

These claims and this conclusion were couched in a variety of idioms, both practical and theoretical. Among the former was the idiom of the muckrakers who focused on "corruption," albeit not of the old classical republican variety. And among the latter were two theoretical idioms in which intentionality and rationality – surely two prerequisites of the older republican and newer democratic politics – did not figure prominently: the Darwinian theory of evolution via natural selection and theories of individual and group psychology that emphasized the unconscious and irrational aspects of individual and collective behavior. All three idioms were incorporated into reformist (and particularly Progressive) thinking about democracy and became central features of a political *science* that could lay claim to being more than warmed-over common sense.

III

At the turn of the century muckraking journalists like Lincoln Steffens (1904) showed how city governments were ridden with graft and corruption. The term "corruption" had, in Steffens's and other muckrakers' hands, only a distant and tenuous connection with the classical republican understanding of the term. For Steffens and his fellow reform-minded journalists, elected and appointed officials were corrupt, citizens merely misinformed or ignorant. That there might be some sort of symbiotic relation between corrupt officials and ignorant citizens merely proved the Progressives' point that the relation must be broken once and for all and citizens saved from themselves by whatever means.

Various schemes to take the profit out of politics – by, for example, appointing salaried "city managers" in place of elected mayors and urban bureaucrats in place of city councilmen – were all the rage among Progressives. Not since Hegel had praised the Prussian bureaucracy as the selfless and purely public-spirited "universal class" (a title that Marx was later to confer on the proletariat) had such scorn been heaped upon mean-spirited and merely partisan politics, and such kudos accorded the gray and faceless servants of the public interest who were, in reality, tax collectors and the stampers of passports and other documents devised and demanded by the modern state.

To invoke the name of Hegel and the noun "state" in the same (long and Germanic) sentence should occasion no surprise. For they form a natural pair that ought not be taken lightly for our present purpose. The most important and influential late-nineteenth- and early-twentieth-century political scientists – Burgess perhaps foremost among them – did their graduate work in Germany and returned with renewed respect for the reforms that the state might accomplish. They thereby reaffirmed the direction taken earlier by Frances Lieber, the German emigré who perhaps more than any other self-described "political scientist" set the tone, if not the agenda, for state-sponsored schemes for political reform (Farr 1990). The German term for this academic-cum-political enterprise – *Staatslehre* – suggests more strongly than "political science" something of the increasingly intimate connection between an academic discipline and its political aims and aspirations within the setting supplied by the modern state. In American political science, "political" phenomena were increasingly couched in the idiom of the state. Part of this preference is, of course, practical: The state was more than a theoretical entity, and a force to be reckoned with. But this practical preference was powerfully reinforced by theoretical thinking that viewed the state in "scientific" terms, as an entity selected for success, so to speak, by forces or factors beyond any mortal's ken or control.

Hegel had, of course, supplied his own evolutionary account of the prehistory that had set the stage for the emergence of the modern state as the preeminent actor in modern politics (Avineri 1972). But it was not until the latter part of the nineteenth century that Germanic and Hegelian proclivities were joined, as it were, with English and Darwinian thinking that the state as a theoretical and scientifically sanctioned species really reached the take-off stage. Although intended by Darwin to account for a restricted range of natural phenomena, his theory of progress and evolution via "natural selection" was quickly picked up and adapted to partisan political purposes. Herbert Spencer in England and William Graham Sumner in the United States propounded a set of views that came to be called (colorfully if somewhat misleadingly) "social Darwinism." Meanwhile, on the Left, European and American socialists were also claiming Darwin's mantle. At Marx's graveside in 1883, Friedrich Engels claimed that Marx and Darwin were fellow scientists-in-arms, and a host of "scientific socialists" soon joined the chorus (Ball 1979).

In the United States, non-Marxian socialists like Edward Bellamy appropriated an "evolutionary" view of political progress predicated on the idea that the best and (in hindsight) most rational changes come about not by conscious deliberation but by a process of adaptation and natural selection. In effect, Bellamy joined Emersonian optimism with Darwinian science. "We design it thus and thus," Emerson had written half a century before; "It turns out otherwise, and far better" (quoted in Drukman 1971, 136). Bellamy's best-selling utopian novel, *Looking Backward* (1888), envisioned a state-socialist United States having come into being by a process having nothing to do with politics and everything to do with "evolution." "The [institutional] solution," says his hero's host Dr. Leete, "came as the result of a process of industrial evolution that could not have terminated otherwise. All that society had to do was to recognize and cooperate with that evolution, when its tendency had become unmistakable" (Bellamy 1960, 49). Nor did the new socialist society require much in the way of political deliberation and action: Scientific planning and managerial know-how had realized the old Saint Simonian dream of substituting the administration of things for the governing of men. "We have no parties or politicians," Dr. Leete declares, and therefore no "demagoguery and corruption" (Bellamy 1960, 56).

However much they might misunderstand or distort Darwin, such "Darwinian" notions had a powerful appeal in the American academy, and nowhere more than in departments of political science.[2] The important point for my purposes here is that a "science of politics" had been and was being powerfully transformed, from one that focused on conscious civic deliberation to one that viewed aims and intentions as irrelevant and part of some larger and more pervasive pattern of historical development that might, in hindsight, be recognizably progressive.

The state, according to Henry Jones Ford in *The Natural History of the State* (1915), had evolved by stages from a primitive to a more complex and sophisticated form. One of the primary purposes of political science was to understand these evolutionary processes, the better to appreciate how human tinkering and interference tend to make things worse (Ford 1903, 1906). The most egregious interference came from those who meant well and had high hopes for humanity's self-improvement. But human beings generally, and *Homo democraticus* more especially, were imperfect creatures with a misplaced pride in their own capacity for self-government. The skepticism of Ford and other would-be Darwinians was also powerfully reinforced by the introduction of yet another theoretical idiom, that of psychology.

The science of psychology was hardly new, of course. But in its earlier sense "psychology" was that part of the moral sciences that inquired into such matters as how humans learn language, acquire ideas, store and recall memories, and such. Psychology's greater grandfather was the Locke of the *Essay Concerning Human Understanding*. But the science of psychology underwent a sea change at the turn of the century. In Europe, and later in the United States, Freud was a key figure. Closer to home, William James's *Principles of Psychology* (1890) and, as it were, its companion volume and case study, *The Varieties of Religious Experience* (1902), painted a picture of the human psyche that Locke and his progeny could scarcely have recognized. The human mind was not a *tabula rasa* but an evolving organ and an instrument of adaptation that takes an active part in processing the data of cognition. But the mental furnishings that make cognition possible were not confined to Kant's well-ordered categories of time, space, and causality; on the contrary, we understand the world via a motley collection of preconceptions, prejudices, emotions and well- or ill-founded beliefs whose function is to bring some semblance of order to what would otherwise be a "blooming, buzzing confusion."

James had very little to say about the political implications of his ideas, nor did he develop these in any systematic way. But two of his Harvard colleagues were soon to do so. One was the visiting English Fabian, Graham Wallas; the other, the patrician political scientist A. Lawrence Lowell. In *Human Nature in Politics* (1908) Wallas complained that political science continued to cling to an outmoded view of human nature generally, and theories of perception, cognition, and motivation in particular. And as a result, its "intellectualist" theories of politics generally, and of democratic politics in particular, are out of date.

Most people, most of the time, are motivated by irrational impulses, drives, fears, and phobias of which they are wholly unaware. And when such creatures act collectively or in concert, as citizens, they are incapable of the kind of calm, cool, rational deliberation required by classical republican or democratic theory.

To the degree that democracy depends on the ordinary citizen's capacity for clear thought and rational deliberation, this disturbing discovery not only undermined democracy; it also cast considerable doubt on the efficacy of education, especially civic or political education, to enlighten the citizenry and to put them on their guard against demagogues, party bosses, and ideologues of every conceivable coloration. The calls to arms being issued by radicals of the Right and Left appealed to fears, resentments, and deep-seated anxieties that had no necessary connection with "reality" but that were powerful nonetheless. The discoveries that had revolutionized the science of psychology, Wallas claimed, ought to be revolutionizing political science as well.

Much influenced by his Harvard colleague William James, A. Lawrence Lowell in effect answered Wallas's challenge. In *Public Opinion and Popular Government* (1913a) Lowell applied James's psychological insights to political behavior. The mind of the citizen is a human mind; and the human mind, far from being the model of rational cognition described by Locke and his progeny or the proponents of "moral sense" theory, is little better than a bundle of prejudices and preconceptions through which one makes some sense (however slight or skewed) of an otherwise puzzling and confusing external world. Add to this the fact that the political world of policy and legislation is even more "external" or foreign to most people, and it becomes plain that the ideally rational, informed, and deliberative democratic citizen is a romantic Jeffersonian fiction to which few, if any, actual citizens can compare. And what is worse, the chasm between civic capacity and systemic need grows wider by the week. As American society becomes more complex and the administrative apparatus of the state more technical, government must be guided less by ordinary citizens and more by experts whose knowledge, advice, and credentials citizens are not competent to judge. Nor are most citizens likely, or even able, to acquire the necessary knowledge. And so, said Lowell,

the amount of knowledge needed for the administration of public affairs is increasing more rapidly than the diffusion of such knowledge, and . . . this is lessening the capacity of the ordinary citizen to form an opinion of his own on the

52   Terence Ball

various matters that arise in conducting the government. If so, the range of questions about which the public cannot form a real opinion tends to enlarge. . . . This is particularly true where the special knowledge of experts is involved, because it is not easy for the community at large to weigh expert opinion. Few things are, in fact, more difficult, or require greater experience; and yet the number of questions on which the advice of experts is indispensable grows with every advance in technical knowledge and mechanical invention. (1913a, 49–50)

The upshot is twofold. So far as American political science is concerned, the traditional task of educating citizens is less important than is the training of experts in public administration and allied fields. And so far as American democracy is concerned, the role of the citizen is considerably diminished. He (women still did not have the vote) lacks not only knowledge of complex political and administrative matters, but what is worse, also the time, energy, interest, and intelligence to acquire and apply such knowledge.

Lowell's analysis predated by a decade the thesis made famous by Walter Lippmann. As a student at Harvard (in the illustrious class of 1910 that included John Reed and T. S. Eliot), Lippmann had studied not only with William James, but with Graham Wallas and Lowell (with whom he, as a socialist, disagreed deeply and openly). But like Lowell, Lippmann became ever more skeptical of the ordinary citizen's capacity to understand, much less control, political phenomena. And as World War I had shown, most citizens were receptive to patriotic propaganda, big lies, and half-truths. His *Public Opinion* (1922), followed three years later by *The Phantom Public* (1925), amounted to a scathing attack on the very idea – and indeed the ideal – of the "omnicompetent citizen." Like Wallas and Lowell, Lippmann argued that most people's perceptions of political phenomena are filtered through preconceptions and prejudices, or what he termed "phantoms," that shape – or more often misshape – their views. "Public opinion" refers, then, not to the opinings of an informed public, but to the chaotic collection of phantasms and fantasies that constitute most people's mental furniture. Nothing so shifting and fickle could form the foundation for coherent legislation or rational public policy.

Lippmann's attack prompted a passionate but characteristically low-keyed critique from John Dewey. Reviewing *Public Opinion* in the *New Republic*, Dewey called Lippmann's book "perhaps the most effective indictment of democracy as currently conceived ever penned" (Dewey [1922] 1983, 286). And later, in *The Public and Its Problems* (1927), Dewey again acknowledged the power of Lippmann's analysis – an analysis that, if correct, undermined if it did not destroy the very idea of democratic citizenship (Dewey [1922] 1983, 288; [1927] 1984a, 116-17n). For if most individuals are incapable of rational self-rule, it follows that they are, collectively, incapable of self-government. And from this follows the corollary that "the many" must, for their own good, be ruled by the wise "one" or "the few." Dewey agreed with Lippmann's puncturing of the "illusion" of an informed and omnicompetent public whose opinions are the result of rational deliberation. But instead of blaming citizens, Dewey pointed an accusing finger at inadequate social science, and at psychology in particular. "Had it not been for the misleading influence of a false psychology," Dewey wrote, "the illusion might have been detected in advance" ([1927] 1984a, 158). A true psychology – and a pedagogy predicated upon it – pointed the way out of this political impasse.

For my purposes here, three points about the Lippmann–Dewey debate and its aftermath are of particular significance. The first is that Lippmann was answered systematically and at some length not by a political scientist, but by a philosopher. As an academic discipline, political science had to a very considerable extent ceased to be a critical and prescriptive enterprise; that task was left to philosophers like Dewey and – later still – to "traditional" or "normative" political theorists. To see how professional political science viewed the Lippmann–Dewey debate is, to say the least, instructive.

Lippmann's *Public Opinion* was reviewed in the *American Political Science Review* by Arthur N. Holcombe of Harvard, who praised it as "a true masterpiece [that] will give aid and comfort to all teachers of political science" and invaluable instruction to their students (Holcombe 1922, 501). But four years later, when Lippmann's *The Phantom Public* was reviewed by Wisconsin's Arnold Bennett Hall, the tone was markedly different. Civic education and "political theory" were downplayed, and "science" extolled. "Most writing that appears under the name of political theory," wrote Hall,

might better be called political literature. Certainly it is not a theory in any scientific sense, for a true political theory is a generalization that accurately explains the facts of political behavior. Unfortunately, most so-called political theory . . . seems to derive its influence from the lure of the literary form in which it is expressed [and the] emotional ideals [it calls forth].

Having thus excoriated political theory, Hall paid Lippmann a left-handed compliment. *The Phantom Public*, he concluded, "is excellent literature [that] does not contain scientific generalizations based on objective evidence" (Hall 1926, 199–200).

The *American Political Science Review* dealt differently with Dewey's *The Public and Its Problems*. Dewey's book, being presumably a work of "philosophy," was not reviewed at all. This omission, in itself, might seem insignificant. But the publication of *The Public and Its Problems* coincided almost exactly with William Bennett Munro's 1927 APSA Presidential Address. "Political science, if it is to become science," said Munro, "should first of all obtain a decree of divorce from the philosophers" (Munro 1928, 8). The divorce of political science from political philosophy was also tantamount to a divorce between political science and political pedagogy. "All around us," Munro observed,

gigantic campaigns of civic education are being carried on, by organizations of every kind, . . . inspired by the hope of improving the attitude of the citizen toward his government, and especially his sense of civic duty. . . . To a considerable extent, the money that is being spent upon these so-called campaigns of civic education represents pure futility and waste.

These campaigns, he concluded, "rest upon formulas concerning civic duty that are not merely unscientific but ridiculous" (Munro 1928, 7).

One should not, of course, make too much of book reviews and APSA presidential addresses. Such evidence is circumstantial at best. But it does suggest that, by coincidence or design, American political science was by degrees disavowing its older educative mission, embracing "science," and eschewing "philosophy." Each embrace and disavowal carried with it implications for democracy and democratic citizenship.

This in turn suggests a second feature of American political science during this period. Dewey, like Witherspoon, Stanhope Smith, and other late-eighteenth- and early-nineteenth-century moral scientists – and quite unlike most mainstream political scientists – set great store by education generally, and civic education in particular (Dewey 1916). While paying lip service to the idea and the importance of civic education, various committees of the APSA had little to recommend, save to suggest periodically that political science was an important field of study and had something to contribute to the education of citizens. Increasingly, however, its importance lay less in the education of citizens than in the training of specialists. Civic education was best left to professional educators.[3]

A third feature also appears during this period. Rather than criticize or defend democracy, political science merely reconfigured its conception of citizenship and public opinion. If public opinion was, as Lowell and Lippmann argued, an ill-informed jumble of prejudices and passions, then so be it; that was merely another topic to be described in some detail and to be explained with the aid of theories of socialization, psychoanalysis, and other tools of this increasingly specialized trade. The study of "public opinion" quickly became a mainstay of political science.[4] And, not least, "public opinion" came increasingly to be viewed as malleable and manipulable – something that could be "molded" or "shaped" by better-informed, less fickle, and more rational elites. If democracy rested on the consent of the governed, it remains for the rational "few" to – in Lippmann's chillingly Orwellian phrase – "manufacture consent" (Lippmann 1922, 248).[5]

The next two decades – the era of the Great Depression and World War II – mark a pivotal point in the history of American political science, paving the way for the "behavioral revolution" of the postwar period. As I have attempted to argue elsewhere (Ball 1993), the Depression and World War II opened opportunities previously undreamed of by American social scientists, and political scientists in particular. Money, prestige and power were the rewards awaiting those disciplines that could exhibit their scientific bona fides and political utility. One way of telling the story of the behavioral revolution would emphasize the temptation too great to be resisted; another, which I shall now attempt, would stress what might be called the normative basis of behavioralism.

IV

Much that has been written about the behavioral revolution, both in defense and criticism, has focused on its supposedly scientific (or, some said, scientistic) pretensions, its putative political coloration (variously described as conservative, liberal, pluralist, or apolitical), its antipathy toward "traditional" or "normative" political theory, and so on. Behavioralism was variously condemned by critics – from conservative Straussians to radical New Leftists – for supposedly celebrating "stability" for its own sake, for its too-ready accommodation to the status quo, for its theoretical defense of undemocratic practices, and for partaking of the political lassitude of the Eisenhower era and, subsequently, the Cold War crusades of the Kennedy and Johnson years.[6] Some of the harshest and most heartfelt criticisms came from refugee scholars who saw in behavioralism an ostrich-like attempt to avoid politics altogether.[7]

My aim here is not to assess the accuracy or the fairness of these and other criticisms. I want instead to conclude by proposing a different "take" on that still-controversial era in the history of American political science. Because space is short, I shall state my claim briefly and baldly. American political science, as an academic discipline, was never much enamored of participatory democracy; indeed, it tended to be skeptical and wary of widespread and enthusiastic participation at the grass roots. This traditional antipathy was deepened further by the various horrors of the second quarter of the twentieth century. The Great Depression, the rise of fascism in Italy, Germany, and Spain, World War II and the Holocaust, and the phenomenon of Stalinism in the Soviet Union formed the backdrop against which at least some aspects of the behavioral revolution can be better understood. More specifically, the hope of avoiding any repetition of, and learning lessons from, these horrors colored the conception of democracy that can be discerned in the thinking of several key figures and the theories or analytical frameworks they proposed. But as the memory of these terrors began to fade in the face of new threats, and as a new generation was schooled in the new behavioralist orthodoxy, the normative basis of the revolution receded into the background. And there it lay, unrecognized both by younger behavioralists and by emigré and New Left critics alike.

Three episodes, each drawn from different research programs, seem to me to exemplify these developments. The first is the "functionalist" defense of apathy by Bernard Berelson (1952); the second is the "economic" theory of democracy developed by Anthony Downs (1957); and the third is the "end of ideology" thesis advanced by Edward Shils, Seymour Martin Lipset, and Daniel Bell in the late 1950s. Each in its own way exhibits the truth of Farr's contention that American political science has been something of a "scavenger discipline," taking its cues and borrowing its methods and theories from other social scientific disciplines (Farr 1982). But each of these three episodes also points, I think, to the normative basis of behavioralism. And each suggests something about behavioralism's emphasis – or, as critics charged, its overemphasis – on the conditions conducive to political stability.

Bernard Berelson, Paul Lazarsfeld, and William McPhee's *Voting* (1954) was in many ways a pioneering study. Subtitled *A Study of Opinion Formation in a Presidential Campaign*, it looked at length and in minute detail at data collected in Elmira, New York, during the 1948 presidential campaign. But perhaps the most controversial aspect of that work was a brief concluding chapter that had nothing to do with data or the methods of analyzing it: "Democratic Practice and Democratic Theory," written mainly by Bernard Berelson, advanced the controversial contention that widespread apathy could, on balance, be beneficial or "functional" for a democratic system. Nonparticipation promoted "stability" and precluded the kind of intense conflicts that had disrupted and eventually destroyed other democracies. A deeply divided but highly mobilized populace was, as Weimar showed, dangerous to democracy. Too much democracy – in the form of intense ideological division and high rates of participation – could destroy a democracy. "How," Berelson asked, "could a mass democracy work if all the people were deeply involved in politics?" And he answered that

lack of interest by some people is not without its benefits, too. . . . Extreme interest goes with extreme partisanship and might culminate in rigid fanaticism that could destroy democratic processes if generalized throughout the community. Low affect . . . – not caring much – underlies the resolution of many political problems. . . . Low interest [in politics] provides maneuvering room for political shifts necessary for a complex society in a period of rapid change. Compromise might be based upon sophisticated awareness of costs and returns – perhaps impossible to demand of a mass society – but it is more often induced by indifference. Some people are and should be highly interested in politics, but not everyone is or needs to be. Only the doctrinaire would deprecate the moderate indifference that facilitates compromise. (Berelson 1954, 314–15)

What from the perspective of classical republican (and latterly democratic) theory appears to be "an individual 'inadequacy' provides a positive service for the society" (1954, 316). With its focus on "functions" performed by and for the "system," Berelson's analysis bore at least a superficial similarity to the structural-functional systems approach then being advocated by Talcott Parsons in sociology and David Easton in political science.

But Berelson's borrowings were more catholic still, extending even to the patron saint of political economy. Implicitly invoking Adam Smith, Berelson defended the division of labor between an active and an apathetic citizenry.

We have learned slowly in economic life that it is useful not to have everyone [be] a butcher or a baker, any more than it is useful to have no one skilled in such activities. The same kind of division of labor – as repugnant as it may be – is serving us well today in mass politics. There is a division of political labor within the electorate. (Berelson 1954, 321)

While certainly not advocating "apathy without limit," Berelson does allow that some degree of indifference is necessary if democracy is not to destroy itself (1954, 322).

Later, during the backlash against behavioralism in the 1960s, critics, particularly those from the New Left, charged Berelson and his fellow behavioralists with advocating an "elite" conception of democracy in which an active "few" ruled the apathetic "many." The antidote they advocated was more participation (Duncan and Lukes 1963; Davis 1964). In reply, Robert Dahl made explicit what one might call the Weimar worry that animated Berelson and other behavioralists who wished to revise democratic theory so as to emphasize conditions conducive to consensus and systemic stability. "The rapid rise in electoral participation in the late years of the Weimar Republic," wrote Dahl, "did not make it a 'better' democracy, nor did it enable that Republic to solve its problems. Instead, it was associated with factors that transformed that experiment in democracy into a monstrous system, with very high rates of 'participation' of a kind, and where apathy was encouraged only in the concentration camps" (Dahl 1966, 301). The charge that Berelson (and Dahl, among others) had overemphasized systemic "stability" had, Dahl admitted, some merit. But, he added,

while we may have recently emphasized the conditions of democratic "stability" too much, and the conditions of democratic change too little, I doubt whether anyone who remembers the failure of "stable" democracies to emerge in the USSR, Italy, Germany and Spain will ever find it in himself to scoff at writers who focus on the conditions of democratic stability. What such writers are likely to have in mind when they think of democratic "instability" is not cabinet changes nor even piddling differences in regime but the possibility of democratic failures eventuating in brutal dictatorships in comparison with which even the worst polyarchy will seem like the promised land. (1966, 301n)

Dahl, like Lippmann and Harold D. Lasswell, allowed that Freud, whatever the inadequacy of his theory, had at least "made us all acutely aware of man's capacity for irrational, nonrational, impulsive, neurotic, and psychotic action in politics, unfortunately, as much as elsewhere" (Dahl 1956, 13). The Nazi and Soviet dictatorships served to underscore Freud's insights, which political scientists – and democratic theorists – ignore at their and everyone else's peril.

American political science, some suggested, might perform a public service by offering an alternative to intensely ideological, divisive, participatory democratic politics. To the irrationality of Weimar it might counterpose its own, certifiably American conception of democratic politics, in which rationality triumphs over irrationality and interest trumps ideology. That, at any rate, was Anthony Downs's aim in *An*

Economic Theory of Democracy (1957). Claims to the contrary by Barry (1970) and others notwithstanding, the "sociological" approach of Berelson and the "economic" model favored by Downs, did, despite obvious methodological differences, lead to remarkably similar or at least congruent conclusions.

Despite some rather overblown claims about its originality, Downs's book has a long line of ancestors stretching back to Mandeville and Adam Smith, David Ricardo and James Mill, not to mention Jeremy Bentham and Joseph Schumpeter.[8] Ever since Adam Smith and other eighteenth-century thinkers attempted to dampen religious "enthusiasm" and personal and political "passions" by dangling the carrot of "interests," political economists, political scientists, and assorted rational choice theorists have touted the primacy of interests over ideology (Hirchmann 1977). Human beings are calculating creatures, and *Homo politicus* is no exception to the rule that most people, most of the time, are – unless inexplicably blinded by ideology or some irrational passion – motivated mainly if not exclusively by considerations of self-interest. And what is true of individual voters and candidates for public office is perforce true of collectivities, including interest groups, political parties, governments, and even entire nations.

People who pay attention to their own interests and welfare are – so the "economic" argument runs – less likely to try to remake society along utopian lines. Politics becomes a more or less predictable enterprise. If a politics of self-interest and group interest is a chastened politics, immune to the infection of ideology and the excesses of enthusiasm, then American politics is probably its purest exemplar. The spirit of commerce, competition, and self-interest that both amazed and appalled Tocqueville, Mrs. Trollope, Charles Dickens, and other nineteenth-century observers, is not a national vice but a virtue of individual Americans that becomes evident only when projected onto a larger political screen and contrasted with the horrors produced by twentieth-century totalitarian regimes that subordinated individual interests to the greater interest of such supraindividual entities as *Volk* or nation or class.

In the American democracy, Downs claimed, candidates and political parties seek simply to win elections and to hold public office. And this they do not by proposing grandiose ideological schemes but by appealing to the interests of individuals and groups. Those who have the widest and most inclusive appeal, will win – this time, anyway. Periodic elections afford the losers another opportunity to change their platform and "mix" of proposed programs so as to appeal to more voters next

time. As for individual voters themselves, they – being rational actors – will "invest" only as much time and energy as their interests warrant. Reading, listening to, and learning about the candidates' views
takes time; and time, as the old adage says, is money. A rational citizen
will "spend" no more time/money than is necessary to acquire such information. Some will conclude that the cost is too high in relation to the
expected return and will neither incur the cost nor cast a vote. The phenomenon that Berelson had characterized as "apathy" is thereby recast
and redescribed in Downs's economic idiom as "rational abstention"
(Downs 1957, ch. 14). The relatively low rates of voter turnout are less
a condemnation of American democracy than a vindication of voter rationality. Abstention may be every bit as rational – indeed perhaps even
more so – as casting a vote.

Downs did acknowledge, however, that a polity's claim to be democratic could not be sustained in the face of universal or near-universal
apathy or abstention (Berelson's "apathy without limit"). Obviously a
sizeable part of the electorate has to vote. But why? After all, each rational voter will reason that his or her vote will make a miniscule or
nonexistent difference in the outcome of any particular election; and
since there are "costs" incurred by acquiring information, taking the
time to go to the polls, and so on, the costs clearly outweigh the benefits or "expected utilities"; and so the rational citizen ought not bother
to vote. The problem then becomes one of explaining why anyone in his
or her right (or rational) mind would vote. And Downs rose to the challenge by introducing an ad hoc – and distinctly non-"economic" – consideration into the calculus of voting. A rational individual would,
Downs suggested, be willing to pay the costs incurred in becoming informed and voting, even if he gained nothing save the satisfaction derived from "do[ing] his share in providing long-run benefits" by helping
to maintain the democratic system. But of course, this adjustment, as
critics were quick to point out, not only is incongruent with, but actually
contradicts, the most fundamental tenets of the "economic" or "rational
choice" program (see, e.g., Barry 1970, 20).

I have elsewhere made my own criticisms of Downs and other defenders of an "economic" approach to, and defense of, American
democracy (Ball 1988, ch. 6). And Downs himself has had second and
more self-critical thoughts about his project (Downs 1991). But its logical and theoretical shortcomings aside, we would do well to remember
the political backdrop against which Downs and other contemporaries
theorized. The memory of Weimar and other failed democracies still

loomed large, and high rates of "participation" were still seen as suspect and a mixed blessing at best. And American democracy, for all its flaws, seemed by comparison to be a workable and viable, if not always ideal, model.

But was this "model" generalizable and exportable? Or was it unique and, by implication, not amenable to being exported abroad? These questions are not of purely historical interest and import. Indeed they have, in the age of Reagan and, latterly, the "New World Order" announced by former President Bush, a renewed salience and urgency. Former President Bush's New World Order seemed, to me at least, to skip over and ignore a number of episodes in American political history. It was Wilsonian to the core, in that it sought – rhetorically, at any rate – to make the world safe for (American-style) democracy; and it ignored (or was more likely ignorant of) important objections raised against this ideal in the 1950s by historians and social scientists of the so-called consensus school.

Not the least of these objections was raised by Daniel Boorstin in his 1952 Walgreen Lectures, published in the following year as *The Genius of American Politics*. America's "genius" is that it is wholly without ideology or political philosophy; no "theory" animates its politics; in this political culture of prudence and compromise, the proverbial half-loaf proves much more attractive than the pie in the sky. Like Tocqueville, Boorstin noted that Americans are an atheoretical people, little given to philosophical abstraction or systematic speculation about politics and the good life. "The marvelous success and vitality of our institutions is equaled by the amazing poverty and inarticulateness of our theorizing about politics. No nation has ever . . . been less interested in political philosophy or produced less in the way of theory" (Boorstin 1953, 8). And this, Boorstin believed, is all to the good. The alternative would be a politics of ideology and, indeed, "idolatry":

The tendency to abstract the principles of political life may sharpen issues for the political philosopher. It becomes idolatry when it provides statesmen or a people with a blueprint for their society. The characteristic tyrannies of our age – naziism, fascism, and communism – have expressed precisely this idolatry. They justify their outrages because their "philosophies" require them. (1953, 3)

Often viewed in retrospect as a simple-minded celebration of American "exceptionalism" and of nonideological American "consensus" politics, Boorstin's book was in fact a warning against American adventurism abroad. It was, more specifically, a brief against Cold War era enthusiasts' aspirations of exporting American democracy to countries and cultures that do not share our history. Unlike its Soviet nemesis, the United States has "nothing in the line of a theory that can be exported to other peoples of the world." Indeed, "nothing could be more un-American than to urge other countries to imitate America. We should not ask them to adopt our 'philosophy' because we have no philosophy which can be exported" (1953, 1). If making the world safe for democracy meant re-making the world in America's image, then the world would not and could not ever be safe or democratic. This was, in the context of the early Cold War era – and is, even now, in the era of the New World Order – a startling and somewhat heretical claim.

But while Boorstin located America's genius in its antipathy to "theory," his fellow historian Louis Hartz argued that the American consensus was in fact deeply theoretical. In *The Liberal Tradition in America* (1955) Hartz claimed that Lockean liberal theory was so pervasive in our politics as to seem factual and commonsensical rather than theoretical. Lockean theoretical concepts and categories constituted practical political reality in America. American political culture was characterized by a widespread and unexamined belief in private property and the rights to life and liberty. Hartz's aim was less to celebrate than to describe this "Lockean consensus" and to trace out its implications. One of the more important of these implications was entirely congruent with Boorstin's, namely, that American political culture is unique and therefore unavailable for exportation abroad. This theme, implicit in *The Liberal Tradition*, became a central focus of Hartz's later *Founding of New Societies* (1964), where he argued that each nation's history opened some paths to political development even as it precluded others. A prudent American foreign policy would recognize this and refrain from trying to export – or impose by foreign aid or force of arms – an American-style economic or political system.

The first incarnation of the vaunted "end of ideology" – or what one might, at a stretch, call the Boorstin–Hartz thesis – was quickly picked up by political scientists eager to downplay the importance of "ideas" and "theories" of a normative or nonempirical kind. But this borrowing was partial and incomplete. Among political scientists, Boorstin's and Hartz's main message was, if not lost entirely, soon subordinated to the thesis that an American "consensus" prevailed, and precluded (or perhaps signaled the end of) "ideology" in politics (and, correspondingly, the demise or death of "traditional" or "normative" political theory in the academy). An American consensus at home meant that the emergence of millenarian or utopian political movements of a Marxist or any other kind was well-nigh impossible. The sectarian division and ideological conflict of Weimar was, in America, virtually impossible in principle. And what had always been true in America – that interest trumped ideology and a rational consensus prevailed – was about to become true in other parts of the world. Our consensual and nonideological City on a Hill showed the way to nations still benighted by ideology and sectarian conflict. The dictates of prudence will soon prevail and will necessarily preclude a politics of idealism or utopianism. Anyone in search of a workable ideal need look no further than our own doorstep. American-style democracy, declared Seymour Martin Lipset in *Political Man*, is "the good society itself in operation" (1960, 403). America was the good society, so to speak, by default and negation: It was neither Weimar riven by ideological division nor the Soviet Union or any other totalitarian society driven by devotion to a single, all-pervasive ideology. America was a pluralistic society characterized not by conflicting ideologies but by competing interests; a widespread consensus kept conflict manageable and within bounds; and the rest of the world would one day discover this and follow our lead.

While the first and second of these claims is made explicit by Dahl and others, the third remained largely implicit. I haven't the space here to document that claim. But let me conclude by pointing to one illustration. The idea that there exist certain specifiable "functional requisites" for a viable democracy was proposed by Lipset (1959, 1960) and other "empirical theorists" of democracy and was picked up by Almond and Verba (1963), among other comparativists. When one examines these "functional requisites" – low levels of class conflict, the existence and legitimacy of competing parties, widespread consensus regarding the "rules of the game," and so on – one discovers that they are met most fully in the United States. In the Almond–Verba version, a viable "civic culture" is one in which these requisites are met. And not surprisingly, the ideal-type of the civic culture is most fully exemplified in the political culture of the United States.

That the United States should serve as a model or template against which other nations and political cultures are compared and found wanting was, of course, antithetical to the analyses offered by Boorstin and Hartz. But it does provide some support for those enamored of the ideal of a New World Order in which an American consensus is to be exported to, or even imposed on, the rest of the world. The end of ideology – of alternative visions, ideas, and ideals – is not an unmixed blessing. Its supposed successor is said in some quarters to be the "end of history" (Fukuyama 1989). But both are wishful illusions, and the successor will doubtless go the way of its predecessor. If there is a larger lesson to be learned from this and earlier episodes, it is at once more important and more ambiguous.

V

It is perhaps trite but nonetheless true to say that American political science stands once again at a crossroads. On the one side it can celebrate "stability" even as it documents and distances itself from the civic inadequacies of the citizenry; or it can come down from its Olympian heights to take part in the education and enlightenment of the public. We face, as it were, a choice between two views and two vocations of political science. One view – call it the Wilsonian vision – holds that political science should be concerned with administration and the training of specialists at home, as well as the exportation of American-style democracy abroad. The other is the Jeffersonian (or, if you like, the Deweyan) vision that sees political science's role as preeminently educative. Political science should be concerned not only with the "training" of specialists but with the broader political education of citizens; for in political matters most citizens are apt to be only as interested, informed, and intelligent as their education allows and encourages them to be. That most citizens are ill-informed or uninformed and apathetic is less a condemnation of them than of the education they have received, in most instances, from the state. To the degree that the fate of democracy in the United States remains unsure and ambiguous, American political science bears, by design or inadvertence, some share of responsibility.

Notes

1. My nod toward Foucault is merely that, because, of course, he saw every enterprise – including education – as a form of "disciplinary power." He would not have recognized the distinction I draw here as a meaningful one.
2. See, generally, Degler (1991) and, with specific reference to political science, Dryzek and Schlosberg, "Disciplining Darwin," Chapter 5, this volume.
3. See, e.g., Woellner (1923).

4. See J. A. W. Gunn, Chapter 4, this volume.
5. Lippmann also spoke of "creating consent": "The creation of consent, is not a new art. It is a very old one which was supposed to have died out with the appearance of democracy. But it has not died out. It has, in fact, improved enormously in technic, because it is now based on analysis rather than rule of thumb. And so, as a result of psychological research, coupled with the modern means of communication, the practice of democracy has turned a corner. A revolution is taking place, infinitely more significant than any shifting of economic power. . . . None of us begins to understand the consequences, but it is no daring prophecy to say that the knowledge of how to create consent will alter every political calculation and modify every political premise" (Lippmann 1922, 248). Later, during the New Deal, some sympathetic political scientists spoke sanguinely of "engineering" the consent necessary for maintaining and legitimizing the new "democratic service state." Peter Odegard, for one, observed that "the engineering of consent for the changes necessary . . . calls for leadership of the highest order" (Odegard 1940, 164).
6. See, inter alia, McCoy and Playford (1967); Green and Levinson (1970); and Farr, Chapter 8, this volume.
7. For examples, see Strauss (1962), Voegelin (1952), Arendt (1958), and Christian Bay (1967). On the role of these and other refugee scholars as critics of "behavioralism" and champions of "political theory," see Gunnell (1993).
8. On Downs's other intellectual debts and affinities, see John Ferejohn, Chapter 10, this volume.

3

The Pedagogical Purposes of a
Political Science

Stephen T. Leonard

American political scientists have repeatedly claimed that an essential feature of their discipline is a commitment to the well-being of the body politic. A critical dimension of this commitment is a pedagogical ideal; it is through a pedagogy that academic political science, as a learned discipline, articulates how its relationship and commitment to the body politic is to be both understood and realized. As I shall try to show in this essay, the pedagogical purposes of American academic political science have changed over time, but what I also want to show is that the character of these changes is in large part a function of conceptual and practical transformations in light of which political scientists have modified their pedagogical self-understandings. A history of these changes does not of course tell us everything we need to know about academic political science (as the other essays in this collection attest), but it may well serve to clarify, or perhaps simply provoke us to reflect on, how the educative responsibilities of disciplinary practitioners ought to be understood.

It is difficult to see how these considerations can be avoided, if only because they have been part of the discipline's identity since its inception. Indeed, American political science took its beginnings as part of a mid- to late-nineteenth-century educational reform movement, and like most (if not all) educational reform movements, this one was in large part a response to perceived social and political problems. The challenge of defining the educative mission of the discipline was to craft a pedagogical program appropriate for addressing these problems. The founders of the discipline did so by drawing on and modifying pedagogical ideals inherited from their ("predisciplinary") predecessors as well as adding some of their own invention. And the legacy they bequeathed to subsequent generations of political scientists has required further development, modification, and transformation in the pedagogical purposes of political science.

In tracing these developments, I make no assumption that changes in the discipline's educative mission had to follow an inevitable path, driven by some constitutional contradiction at the heart of the disciplinary enterprise, whether expressed in terms of "tragedy" (Ricci 1984), "disenchantment" (Seidelman and Harpham 1985), a conflict between "advocacy and objectivity" (Furner 1975), or some other "essential tension." Rather, my narrative suggests that a constellation of forces – foremost among them the political self-understandings of political scientists, attitudes and arguments about the role of higher education, the institutional status and structure of the academy, and crucial changes in American society – together forged the pedagogical ideals of practicing political scientists. The results were seldom predictable, but one can see in them – at least in retrospect – elements of continuity and innovation that defined the constraints and opportunities of successive generations of practitioners.

All of this intimates the historiographical, historical, and practical themes of my essay. What remains is to flesh them out in more detail. As I argue, between the end of the Civil War and the turn of the century, the founders of the discipline advanced three distinct yet related pedagogical missions for the discipline: to educate citizens and political leaders for civic life, to reproduce scholars and researchers for the discipline itself, and to train bureaucrats for state administration. In the first two decades of the new century, political scientists moved to consolidate these missions, but changed circumstances forced many to begin developing a more narrowly defined account of the discipline's pedagogical purposes, and disciplinary reproduction displaced civic education and administrative training as the central purpose of political science pedagogy. After 1920, this constricted understanding was progressively refined and entrenched, and culminating with the "behavioral revolution" in the post–World War II years, it remained ascendant until the 1960s. Since that time, demands for educational reform, linked to widespread perception of social and political crisis, have opened up renewed concerns with the discipline's educative mission, and the challenge we face today is one of reconstituting the pedagogical purposes of academic political science – and in doing so perhaps reconstituting the discipline itself.

Readers are invited to draw their own lessons from this history. I will not assert that we neglect these issues at our own peril or make any other momentous claims for these concerns. But it seems to me that those who are by definition educators ought to occasionally reflect on their pedagogical self-understandings – or be willing to accept the conclusions of those who do it for them. That academic political science has an educative mission is given in its genesis, but the form and content of that mission is not necessarily given in – even if constrained by – the genesis of the discipline. Perhaps these are sufficient reasons for trying to come to grips with the pedagogical legacy we have inherited from our predecessors.

I. A Creation for Crisis: Academic Political Science as Political Pedagogy

By the end of the Civil War, the classical education provided in the "college way," what Frederick Rudolph (1990: 136) called "little more than a body of established doctrine, an ancient course of study, and a respectable combination of piety and discipline," was being eclipsed by a new vision of higher education suited to a dynamic and ever-changing society. The founding fathers of academic political science were among the most active proponents of this vision;[1] their conceptualizations of the educative mission of the discipline were expressions of that vision, and both the vision and its pedagogical implications were reflections of an intellectual and ideological commitment to republicanism as well as a changing analysis of the state.

Republicanism

The social background of many of those who were prominent in the creation of academic political science was that of "the cosmopolitan gentry," whose moral and political inclinations tended toward a defense of "Whig principles of property rights, limited majoritarianism, and elite governance" (Ross 1991: 94–5). Since most of those who attended college in the early to middle nineteenth century were white, English-speaking men who had sufficient property to provide them with the leisure to pursue a higher education (Lanham 1992: 34), these attitudes were both common and noncontroversial among the proponents of educational reform. Many of those who subscribed to these principles also understood them to embody the ideals of American republicanism stretching back to the eighteenth century, and the founders of academic political science were no different in this regard (see Ross 1991: 66–9).

Like most American republicans, the founders of academic political science also recognized that education was critical to the maintenance of republican commitment and virtue (see Cremin 1980: ch. 4). Thus did Francis Lieber, arguably *the* father of American academic political science, conceptualize the discipline (in 1858) as a contributing "branch of public instruction" in "that sacred cause of learning, inquiry, and of training to learn and inquire; of truth, culture, wisdom, of humanity" (Lieber 1880: 330, 329). Moreover, in the discourse of American republicanism, political science was the mode of knowledge that served to cultivate and reinforce the virtues of republican morality and politics (Crick 1959: ch. 1), a fact that made the educational mission of academic political science particularly central to the discipline's identity. Not just education in general, but *civic* education was the responsibility of political science. Civic education was important if only because for many republicans "the problem of good government" was a "problem of good men" (Crick 1959: 73), and this meant making both *good citizens* and *good leaders*.

This tradition of defining political science as the basis for a civic education in republican moral and political commitment was, then, an integral feature of early conceptions of political science as an academic discipline. Lieber certainly recognized as much when he cast political science as "the very science for nascent citizens of a republic" (1880: 343), and Andrew Dickson White recognized as much when, at the founding of the Department of History, Political, and Social Science at Cornell in 1868, he proclaimed political science as an essential component of the education of those who would "rise to positions of trust in public service" (quoted in Furner 1975: 280).

Now none of this may appear to present difficulties for defining the pedagogical mission of the new discipline; indeed, the idea that academic political science would commit itself to civic education appears to be little more than an extension of long-standing republican ideals. What is not readily apparent, however, is why these tasks required an *academic* discipline. And the answer the founders gave to this question marks the difference between them and their predecessors and contemporaries who were more or less content with the civic education provided in the old "college way."

Earlier – and many late-nineteenth-century – republicans had put great stock in the civic educative roles of popular schooling, a free press, voluntary associations, and the "old time colleges" (Cremin 1980: 104; Rudolph 1990: ch. 5). By contrast, the proponents of academic political science – and many others who were supporters of the university movement (Rudolph 1990: 111–12) – saw these institutions as both deficient and defective: deficient because they had done little to stem the rising tide of democratic excesses; defective because they were unable to meet the unprecedented needs of the republic as it moved toward the last century of the millennium.

In the wake of Jacksonian democracy, which dominated American political discourse from 1828 through the Civil War (Morison 1972: 161), academic political science had to be a science (as Lieber no doubt intentionally put it) of and for "*nascent* citizens" (my emphasis). How else could one educate people who had been given the privileges, but had yet to learn the constraints, of republican self-government? If American democracy was to succeed in fulfilling the destiny of the republic, democratic politics had to be tutored in republican civilities. Thus, it had become evident to the founders of the discipline that the "fundamental truths" of political science "ought to be ingrained in the minds of every one that helps to crowd your public schools" (Lieber 1880: 353). Yet the fact that in America "individual liberty is enjoyed in a degree in which it has never been enjoyed before" and that "political action is carried to a greater intensity than in any other land" meant that more needed to be done to preserve and dispense the teachings of American republicanism. Indeed, Lieber insisted, "Nowhere is the calming effect of an earnest and scientific treatment of politics more necessary" than in America (1880: 351). And as the venue of this "earnest and scientific treatment," the modern academy offered the means to remedy the defects of other educative institutions.

Two related implications that had crucial bearing on the future development of the discipline followed from this argument. The first was that the "truths of political science" might now become the more or less exclusive intellectual property of academic political scientists.[2] The second was that this intellectual property had to be differentiated from its precedent forms. One effect of these conceptual changes was to make the discipline responsible for guiding and shaping the content of civic education at every level of public instruction – a notion that may help explain why civic education remains a critical concern throughout the history of the discipline. But another effect was that the academy took on a political importance that it never had before.

This brings us to the defects of existing modes of education that prompted political scientists to cast their lot with the modern academy, and it is here that I must introduce the second important theme for understanding how the founders of the discipline defined its pedagogical mission.

The State

As other historians of the discipline have shown (see Haddow 1939: 240–53; Farr 1990; Gunnell 1991), the state was the object of early academic political science in two senses: It was that object which political science studied, and it was the object that political science knowledge would help steer. In their concerns with the state, academic political scientists were in one sense merely extending a theoretical theme that had been central to American republican discourse for some time (Farr 1991: 15), but their understanding of the state was such that both its study and steering entailed the need for new knowledge, new agents and institutions, and therefore new pedagogical endeavors for the discipline itself.[3]

The need for new knowledge arose in part from the perception that the state had become an increasingly complicated entity requiring well-ordered facts and generalizations that would be useful in its guidance (Farr 1991: 12). And in this, the discipline had to become more rigorous in its inquiries; the "body of established doctrine" and "ancient course of study" in the old college curriculum, and the simple truths that were the coin of popular education, were by definition inadequate to this need. To the extent that the modern academy could provide by its "earnest and scientific treatment" the remedy of this defect, and insofar as academic political science was central to the academy's (political) educative mission, the value of both the discipline and its institutional venue were considerable indeed.

The needs of intellectual rigor helped secure the institutional foundations of academic political science, but it was the content of those needs that further buttressed the case for an academicized discipline and an expanded pedagogical program. Whatever the importance of civic education in the discipline's educative identity, there was also a need for a class of experts who were capable of producing the necessary knowledge as well as those who were trained in the techniques for applying the findings of political science to the complex task of steering the modern state. In short, what were needed were scholars and bureaucrats. And the inability of existing modes of education to create scholars and bureaucrats was another part of their defect.

It was not until the early 1880s that these new pedagogical tasks became central to the discipline's identity, but their groundwork had been laid years earlier. For example, Lieber and Theodore Dwight Woolsey, perhaps the two most influential advocates of the new discipline, had participated in many discussions advocating reform of higher education, and the model they advanced was that of a specialized, professional academy much like the modernized German university system (Rudolph 1990: 128–9). Each in his own way contributed to the conceptual innovations that allowed scholarly and bureaucratic training to take their place in the discipline's pedagogical program. Lieber's influence lay primarily in his articulation of the intimate connection between higher education – especially the modern university – and the state, arguing that the modern university would be "the highest apparatus of modern civilization" in preserving the "greatest of institutions" – the state itself (Lieber 1880: 330, 357). In this scheme, the academic scholar was responsible for upholding republican ideals in a way that "no government, no censor, no suspicious partisan . . . no party . . . no connections" could influence and for acting in a way that would enable his example to become "an element of living statesmanship" (1880: 373, 374).

Woolsey's contribution to this changing pedagogical program came primarily in the form of focusing attention on the needs of bureaucratic effectiveness. In what would become his widely cited text, *Political Science, or the State Theoretically and Practically Considered*,[4] the great bulk of the work attended a variety of subjects more or less directly related to the administrative tasks of government (Haddow 1939: 242), thereby shifting the discourse of the state away from concerns of republican virtue toward considerations of efficiency and effectiveness. The reception that Woolsey's book received confirmed that significant changes in the self-understandings of political scientists were afoot, and these changes were further confirmed a short time later by the positive reception afforded Dorman Eaton's study, *The Civil Service in Great Britain* (Eaton 1880; see Waldo 1948: 28; Crick 1959: 32–3).

With discursive foundations for an expanded pedagogical program now established, it remained only to pursue their implications. What Lieber anticipated in linking the academy to the state was the importance of educating scholars. In 1872, Daniel Coit Gilman – himself an advocate and editor of Lieber's work[5] – appeared to take this demand to heart in his inaugural address as president of the University of California, where he defined the modern university as "a group of agencies organized to advance the arts and sciences of every sort, and train young men as scholars for all the intellectual callings of life" (in Rudolph 1990: 333). But the most influential example of what this implied for the discipline of political science was set by the work of John Burgess in the form of the Columbia School of Political Science.

In his role as the prime mover behind the Columbia experiment, initiated in 1880, Burgess hoped to establish a program that would supply scholars to the expanding universities. This project, as he put it, would serve to "do something for democracy, even in letters and science" (Burgess 1934: 199), and as John Gunnell (1991: 146) points out, it is difficult to quarrel with Burgess's assessment of Columbia's leadership in this task of disciplinary reproduction. To be sure, Burgess shared his contemporaries' ideals regarding other pedagogical tasks for the discipline. He had, after all, conceived the Columbia School of Political Science as an American version of France's Ecole Libre des Sciences Politiques (a training school for high-level civil servants and statesmen [Furner 1975: 280]), and the Columbia Board of Trustees' resolution establishing the program stated that it was "designed to prepare young men for the duties of public life" (quoted in Haddow 1939: 180n27).[6] Yet on reading his recollections on the development of the Columbia School (in Burgess 1934: 191–244), one cannot help being struck by Burgess's preoccupation with more narrowly conceived scholarly and academic concerns. His judgments of his colleagues and his students are shot through with claims about their scholarly standing and potential, and his plan for the school includes extended discussions of how American scholars would be educated, how a political science journal would be started, how an Academy of Political Science would be created, and how a series of published works in political science would be established.

As we shall see shortly, these were to prove the rudiments of a later dominant form of disciplinary identity and pedagogical emphasis, and Burgess's Columbia School is widely acknowledged as the model of what academic political science would soon become (see Crick 1959: 26–9; Somit and Tanenhaus 1967: 16–21; Gunnell 1991: 143–9), but that time – and the conceptual and practical changes that made it possible – were still in the future. In context, Burgess's concerns with developing a pedagogy for disciplinary reproduction were, as Bernard Crick (1959: 28) argues, more a matter of emphasis than difference with other political scientists. And as John Gunnell (1991: 28) suggests, it was certainly true that Burgess (and those of like mind) understood the development of scholarship to be a complementary feature of a broader pedagogical mission, including the tasks of civic education and the training of bureaucrats. But whatever these ideals, the fact of the matter is, while Burgess was advancing his pedagogical ideal, concerns about civic education and the education of scholars were being displaced by a growing preoccupation with the need to train effective civil servants.

It is difficult to pinpoint any particular reason political scientists embraced the cause of civil service reform with such enthusiasm; perhaps it is best to say that the change was over-determined. For the second generation of academic political scientists (from about the mid-1870s on), the movement for reforming higher education must have appeared a qualified success. New, modern universities were springing up yearly, even monthly, and many of those that had been around for a long time were undergoing radical restructuring (see Rudolph 1990: ch. 13). At the same time, the continued excesses of the "Gilded Age," rampant corruption in politics, and widespread demands for civil service reform outside the academy (Morison 1972: 34–5) must have had significant influence on political scientists. Taken together, these provided a ripe context for the emergence of calls for the discipline to dedicate itself to the education of civil servants.

Interestingly enough, these concerns – like those undergirding demands for educational reform and the discourse of the state in political science – were also understood as part of a continued commitment to republicanism (Waldo 1948: 28), but the fact that it was *bureaucrats* who might carry forth the torch of republican virtue certainly marked a significant revision of what those commitments entailed.[7] Whereas bureaucracy was for the founding fathers of the American republic a kind of necessary evil that might threaten liberty, it became for many political scientists in the last two decades of the nineteenth century a kind of necessary good for the preservation of republican progress.[8] And although many advocates of civil service reform believed that much of this mission could be accomplished by imparting a sense of republican moral and ethical integrity to bureaucrats, there were many others who were placing more and more emphasis on another part of that mission, namely, just teaching bureaucrats how to do their jobs effectively and efficiently.

Further changes in conceptions of the state, some of which had been intimated in Woolsey's work, exacerbated these differences. During the 1880s and 1890s, calls were heard for abandoning "idealistic" accounts of the state for more "realistic" ones, for ending "speculation" about the state and engaging in "empirical" examination of how it worked, and for getting away from complex "organic" notions of the state and discerning the relationships between the "parts" of the whole. As these themes were worked out, the focus of statist discourse became increasingly governmental – thus creating an enlarged disciplinary niche for a civil service pedagogy – and the realm of appropriate state concerns became increasingly administrative – thus pushing moral concerns to the margins and efficiency concerns to the center of civil service pedagogy. Moreover, these concerns not only pushed civic education and disciplinary reproduction to the margins of the discipline's pedagogical mission, but they also began to reshape the ways in which civic education and the reproduction of scholars was understood.

Some of these effects were previewed by Charles Kendall Adams at the founding of the School of Political Science at the University of Michigan in 1881. His discontent with the potential for civic education was obvious. Arguing that America had "no governing class," that "the son of the lowest has the same political pathway open before him as the son of the highest," and that the result had been an increasing "reliance . . . on the baser arts of political manipulation" (Adams 1881: 11–12), Adams called for the creation of an expert civil service that would serve to replace "the responsible aristocracy that America neither had nor wanted" (Crick 1959: 25).

Other effects were previewed by Woodrow Wilson. Although an advocate of civic education (see Wilson 1887a), Wilson was also critical of what he took to be an excessive preoccupation with moral and ethical niceties in conceptions of the state (see Wilson 1889) as well as being a strong advocate of efficiency and effectiveness in government (see Wilson 1887b; see also Haddow 1939; Crick 1959: 26; Seidelman and Harpham 1985: 49; and the essay by Terence Ball, Chapter 2, this volume).[9] I need not rehearse Wilson's influential role here, for it would be some years before that influence would be fully recognized.[10] But for the purposes of the moment, the important point about Wilson's contribution was that it signaled a reconceptualization of the meaning of good scholarship, and thus a change in the way that the training of scholars would proceed. Much like the content of civic education had to conform to the demands of civil service reform, the education of scholars was to be made over so that "The Study of Politics" (to use the title of one of Wilson's provocative essays) was coextensive with the study of the administrative state.[11] Still, the full effects of these innovations were yet to be realized.

By the last decade of the century, then, practitioners of academic political science had before them three distinct pedagogical tasks: civic education, reproduction of the discipline, and supplying bureaucrats for the state. As I have suggested, the demands of educational reform and perceptions of social and political crisis, modified by changing theoretical notions and institutional conditions, had not only given rise to these pedagogical tasks, but also opened up possibilities for altering the ways in which they were ordered and understood. At the turn of the century, academic political scientists began to consolidate the discipline's educative mission. Their efforts would show just how far – and at what costs – the changes of the 1880s and 1890s could be realized.

II. Pedagogical Consolidation and Professionalization: 1900–1920

Over the last two decades of the nineteenth century, American political scientists increasingly turned their attention to understanding the actual workings of the American republic and the state. "Practical politics, political corruption, the processes of administration, elections and primaries, public opinion, and in a tentative way political psychology were becoming the new fields for investigation" in academic political science (Haddow 1939: 248). The founding of the American Political Science Association (APSA) in 1903 can be taken as the moment when these concerns were given legitimacy in the definition of the discipline's intellectual identity. As the "Americanization" of the discipline proceeded apace – more of the professorate was being trained in the United States, more of the scholarship cited was American in origin, and more attention was being given to teaching American politics subjects (Somit and Tanenhaus 1967: 61) – the educative mission of academic political science became more tightly bound to reforming the American polity. This would prove to be a formula fraught with difficulties.

Although the stated aim of the APSA was to promote "the scientific study of politics, public law, administration and diplomacy" (Willoughby 1904: 109), this did not mean that the association was to be concerned only with promoting that study for its own sake, any more than it had meant this for the founding fathers of the discipline. Political science was certainly a science *of* politics, but at the same time it was still a science *for* politics.

This was readily apparent in the speed with which the founding members of the association moved to bolster the discipline's educative responsibilities.[12] Soon after the APSA was founded and Frank Goodnow was elected to its presidency, a Section on Instruction (hereafter,

APSA SOI) was appointed.[13] Posing the question (and the title of the section's first [1905] report) "What Do Students Know about American Government before Taking College Courses in Political Science?" the section members found that most public school and many college students were ignorant about the workings of government and most public officials were unfamiliar with the findings of the social sciences (APSA SOI 1906).[14]

There were many moments of continuity and change in these findings. First, consider the implications for the task of civic education. On the one hand, a critical premise of the report was that "popular" modes of civic education were still deficient, much as they had been for the early advocates of the new discipline. "It is impossible to believe," said W. A. Schaper, "that our political training by billboards, newspaper headlines and stump speeches" is adequate for creating an "enlightened" citizenry (APSA SOI 1906: 225). On the other hand, another critical premise of the report was that the moral and ethical basis of "enlightenment" was supplanted by knowledge of *government* as the primary deficiency of American politics. Indeed, the report recommended that throughout "the entire educational system, from the primary school to the University," there was a need for basic education in the workings of American government, and short of this, at least "every candidate for a college degree should be required to have attained a certain proficiency in American government" (1906: 227). Here, then, was one realization of the conceptual sea change that I intimated in the previous section; civic education would still be a responsibility of academic political science, but educating citizens and leaders in the operations of American government – not republican virtue – would now constitute the basis of that civic education.

Other moments of continuity and change were also present in the report. The importance of *academic* political science as the source of proper training for civil service was clearly acknowledged in the claim that the modernized universities could be commended for their part in "reforms undertaken in recent years," but the discipline had to remain committed to meeting "the demand for trained men" in "departments of the federal service" (APSA SOI 1906: 226). We have seen how this was anticipated in the developments of earlier decades, and in light of the report's emphasis on the need for government officials to be attentive to the findings of the social sciences, one can also see that the report's concern with efficiency and effectiveness had its precedent in the past.[15] However, the report went beyond the belief that academic political science must bear responsibility for training bureaucrats, for it also appeared to suggest that this task must become the *primary* pedagogical concern of the discipline. To be sure, all recipients of a college degree were to have a "proficiency in American government," and higher education was to be geared toward "fitting a young man systematically and thoroughly for a public career" whether as "attorneys, judges and administrative officers" (1906: 226), but it was the last of these that was singled out for emphasis. Thus, every level of education had to be attentive to teaching the rudiments of American government, but the highest level of education – the university – was to focus on the most immediate and important need for the republic, namely, producing well-trained bureaucrats.

The adjustment of civic education to match the changing discourses of republicanism and the state were readily apparent, as was the effect of these changes in raising the prominence of civil service training in the ordering of the discipline's pedagogical mission. And what of the education of scholars? The 1905 report did not address this concern, but it did intimate an accommodation for disciplinary reproduction: By suggesting that civil service training was the discipline's most urgent pedagogical task and that the *universities* were the exclusive venue for that training, the report implied that good scholarship was a presupposition of reform.

A report presented by the instruction committee of the APSA in 1907, now working under the cumbersome title of The Committee of Five of the American Political Science Association in Instruction in American Government in the Secondary Schools (hereafter, APSA COF), appeared to confirm this implication.[16] Like its predecessor, this committee assigned to the secondary schools and colleges the important responsibility of shaping "the judges, legislators, diplomats, politicians and office-seekers in the making," as well as educating "future citizens, too, in their most impressionable years" (APSA COF 1908: 221–2). But while the universities would also have some responsibility for educating citizens and statesmen, it was to the education of civil servants and scholars that they were called upon to turn their greatest efforts.[17]

These were bold assertions that reflected a goal more than a reality. The 1905 report by the Section on Instruction may have given the discipline high marks for its part in political reforms "undertaken in recent years," but there was plenty of evidence to suggest that many political scientists were convinced that there was still a long way to go in making good the discipline's pedagogical promise. One major obstacle to the realization of this promise was what prompted it in the first place; both the extent and pace of civil service reform was resisted by many politicians right through the end of the nineteenth century (White 1958: 303–27), and even when administrative reform became an established cause after the turn of the century, it was slow to be realized. Academic political scientists tried to adjust to these developments; for example, while they maintained the call for reform and a civil service pedagogy, many responded to slack demand for their pedagogical services by becoming personally involved in politics. This was a common pattern of activity throughout the late years of the nineteenth and right up through the second decade of the twentieth century, but it dropped off precipitously after 1920.[18]

The decline in personal participation can perhaps be explained as a response to the slow pace of reform – for some, however, a different explanation seemed to be in order. At the same time that some political scientists were suggesting that reform might be realized if only the discipline would turn its attention "more in the direction of governmental problems" (Willoughby 1907: 24), the study of "law-making activity and government," and "the tasks and problems of scientific administration" (Shaw 1907: 179), others were lamenting the fact that scholars and leaders, "both those classes to whom our political progress must be due" (Goodnow 1905: 46) were not yet communicating with each other adequately. How was this to be explained? One answer was that academic political science had not yet become scientific enough; if political leaders (let alone citizens) were not listening to political scientists, perhaps the reason was that political science was itself deficient.

This was a charge that would open whole new opportunities for academic political scientists once they had loosened the ties between administrative reform and the discipline's educative mission. It authorized a wholesale retreat back into the academy as well as a redoubled effort in producing "generations of scholars" who could "bring political science to a position of authority as regards practical politics" (Ford 1906: 206). But before that commitment became a widely perceived need or (as it would soon be) a reality that shaped the discipline's pedagogical identity, there were some conceptual innovations and institutional transformations that had to be completed.

The conceptual innovations were intimated by Henry Jones Ford as early as 1905. Ford's take on the discipline's failures focused on the need to develop *better knowledge* as a precondition of demands for political reform – not simply to demand that the knowledge that there was

80 *Stephen T. Leonard*

should be better utilized. Moreover, his account of what that knowledge entailed involved a recognition of the "transitory" character of "the national, popular state of Western civilization," the "instability of political forms," and the "processes of change" that affected politics. Furthermore, this required that the discipline work toward establishing theoretical foundations that were "objective" and not simply derived from "subjective . . . method" or "abstract terms [contingent] on the historical accidents of their origin" (Ford 1906: 199–203).

All of this suggested that there was a need to detach the discipline's intellectual identity from the American experience and to develop a science of politics that could account for all manner of political experiences regardless of their historical or geographical location. It also suggested the need to bring forth those "generations of scholars" who could create a form of knowledge that might "give rational determination to the destinies of nations" (Ford 1906: 206).

Now it would be a mistake to overstate the differences between Ford and many of his colleagues on these points, for his was not an idiosyncratic position. The APSA had, after all, dedicated itself to "the scientific study of politics"; it had created numerous committees and sections to focus scholarship on political practices that had both domestic and comparative import; *and* it had also dedicated itself to the task of purveying its findings to those outside the discipline by means of its educational mission. Similarly, Ford himself seemed to have a practical end in mind when he advocated a commitment to improving the discipline's knowledge claims. Nonetheless, Ford's demand for better knowledge, a more self-consciously comparative knowledge, and an *objective* knowledge, did offer an ideal in which the primary pedagogical purpose of academic political science might become nothing more than producing "generations of scholars."

Still, this ideal was only a possibility, a conceptual space that might be filled when civil service reform lagged behind its advocates' expectations or when political scientists retooled their political and theoretical self-understandings. What helped make the ideal a reality were two institutional transformations, both of which were effects of successful disciplinary organization. The first was what we might call "pedagogical Taylorism" – quite simply, the movement to divide and refine the different pedagogical tasks of the discipline.[19] In their attempts to define the institutional venue for civil service training efforts, many political scientists – like the members of those APSA committees that had written the 1905 and 1907 reports on instruction – had emphasized the peculiar place of the universities in the discipline's educative mission.[20] Yet time would show that the logic of pedagogical Taylorism outdistanced the capacity of the discipline to realize the goals that gave rise to it in the first place; when enthusiasm for civil service reform waned, all that was left of that peculiar place was the responsibility for undertaking "research work." Academic political science would certainly remain committed to civic education, even if only an education in American government, but the burden of that responsibility would be carried by those institutions for which – or those educators for whom – the demands of scholarship were not pressing. Academic political science would also remain committed to a pedagogy for bureaucrats, even if only a technocratic pedagogy, but it would do so by decentering the field of public administration, hiving off these interests in separate departments or within departments of political science, a process that was more or less complete by 1920.[21]

Perhaps none of this would have occurred if a second institutional transformation hadn't taken place in the interim. Simply put, academic political science had perhaps been *too successful* in realizing the goal of creating a mode of knowledge that "no government, no censor, no suspicious partisan . . . no party . . . no connections" could influence – a goal that Francis Lieber had sought a full half-century earlier. What had once been understood as *a cause for* creating an institution that could preserve republican teachings in a more systematic and scientific way now became *a cause of* increasing separation between good scholarship and an effective political education.

By World War I, the organization of modern higher education was more or less complete. Committees, departments, hierarchies, codes, standards – all of (what we now see as) the characteristic paraphernalia of the organizational structure of modern higher education were in place (Rudolph 1990: 440). Within the discipline itself, there was a parallel change as the number of political science departments increased, the number of doctoral degrees awarded grew, and the number of nonacademics associated with the profession declined (Somit and Tanenhaus 1967: 55–9). And when it came to accounting for the results of these developments in terms of the discipline's bearing on matters of practical politics, the balance sheet began to look somewhat lopsided.

The dangers of success had apparently become evident to practitioners by 1913. In that year, the APSA's Committee on Instruction in Government, or Committee of Seven (APSA COS), delivered a "Report on Instruction in Political Science in the Colleges and Universities" con-

taining a dire warning from Chester H. Rowell, who espied real difficulties in the fact that "university investigators write books which other
university men read, and meantime the practical work of government
blunders on, struggling as best it can on the knowledge and experience
which universities could collect" (APSA COS 1914: 263). The report
trucked out many now-familiar themes as well: a limited account of
civic education as education about government; the pedagogical division of labor between the universities on the one hand, and the colleges
and schools on the other; and the special role of the universities in training civil servants (see 1914: 264).[22] But the dire warning it contained
made these themes pale in comparison with the broader problem of making "research work" (1914: 264) a moment of political reform.

The Committee of Seven – like earlier APSA committees on instruction, like Henry Jones Ford, like nearly every political scientist who
wrote about such things since the creation of the discipline – clearly intended for "research work" to be understood as an integral part of reform efforts. Yet what happened between 1913 and 1920 – when
research work finally took center stage in the discipline's pedagogical
identity – can only be explained as a consequence of a growing recognition that while scholarship and reform were related, disciplinary practitioners were unable to convince others of the usefulness of their
findings.[23] Given this, and the limitations of civic education and civil
service reform, what better way to assert the discipline's value to the
body politic than to redouble the effort to produce a better form of
knowledge?

In the concatenation of failed endeavors, conceptual change, and institutional transformations, academic political science would seek first
and foremost to produce the kind of knowledge and those "generations
of scholars" that might bring political science to "a position of authority as regards practical politics," an effort that would require, as Charles
Merriam put it in 1923, "the willingness of many men and women to de-
vote long years of arduous and unremitting toil to the detailed study of
political problems" (Merriam 1923: 294). This model of pedagogical
identity would prove to be dominant for the next half-century of the discipline's history, but it was not without its own ambiguities. It elicited
bold claims from its partisans, but it was sustained only by the issuance
of promises that became increasingly difficult to realize. This would not
be the first time that political scientists would propose an ideal that
could not be met, but the result of this particular failure would be an opportunity to define the pedagogical identity of the discipline as akin only

to that in which the founders of academic political science had found themselves.

III. Pedagogical Constriction, Scholarship, and the Cause of Science, 1920–1960

It was in terms of the failed endeavors of administrative reform, the conceptual innovations that had effectively gutted the republican and statist assumptions of earlier political scientists, and the ambiguous institutional successes of academic political science that Charles Merriam called forth a commitment to the "unremitting toil" of inquiry, and it was in terms of these changes that he also called for a "new science of politics" that would entail a "reconstruction of the methods of political study and the attainment of larger results in the theoretical and practical fields" (Merriam 1921: 174). The enthusiasm with which many in the discipline agreed with Merriam was striking. As Somit and Tanenhaus note (1967: 110), Merriam's trumpet blast was followed by the appointment of an Association Committee on Political Research (1921), three National Conferences on the Science of Politics (1922, 1923, 1924), and eventually, an expansive role for political scientists in the creation of the Social Science Research Council.

Some may interpret these developments as a realization of an inherent tendency in the academization of political science, but (as I hope to have already intimated) there is good evidence to suggest that the increasingly vigorous turn toward the "science" in the discipline's identity was a response to contingencies neither anticipated nor desired. It was these contingencies that forced the constriction of the discipline's pedagogical mission. This said, it is nonetheless important to recognize (as I also hope I have shown) that there was much in the discipline's past that prepared the conceptual ground for this constriction. And it was this conceptual groundwork that enabled academic political scientists to turn (what might now be seen as) academic exile into a triumphant opportunity for the development of a full-blown science of politics.

Bold claims about potentials, problems, and appropriate processes of inquiry were advanced in the cause of science. The narrative line that these claims followed is familiar enough to any political scientist so as not to require my elaboration on its expressions: Good science could help us remedy our social and political ills, and while the road to science is long and steep, we could traverse it if we followed the examples of those who went before. This was, of course, a narrative line that had been taken by defenders of the discipline since its earliest days. But what made the expression of "scientism" in the 1920s particularly interesting for our purposes is that it was predicated on the promise that *method* was the key to the realization of true science (Gunnell 1983: 8–9).

One implication of this methodological preoccupation was that if good scholarship was good science and good science was defined by right method, then objectivity no longer required any particular political commitment. Indeed, where scientific objectivity was once understood as necessarily entailing political commitment – as it had for the founding fathers of the discipline – it now became a matter of political neutrality.

Why this conceptual change? Certainly one can locate a cause in the fact that the model of the natural sciences often informed the methodological self-understandings of political scientists (as Ross, 1991, and Ricci, 1984, seem to suggest). One could also locate a cause in the "declination of the state" in disciplinary discourse – which cut off the normative grounding of scientific objectivity – that the American state had provided for earlier practitioners. But it would be shortsighted to overlook the broader social and political context in which this methodological self-understanding became prevalent. In the 1920s there was a broad "counterrevolution" against the university movement. As Frederick Rudolph (1990: ch. 21) suggests, the German model, with its attendant emphases on specialization, professional detachment, elitism, and ivory-tower scholarship, was under attack for its failure to provide "a kind of finishing school for the people" and its failure to even adequately "shape all-around organization men" who were to be the descendants of republican gentlemen (1990: 448–9).[24] In addition, the Red Scares of the late teens had produced a series of vitriolic attacks on the professorate that continued well into the 1920s and 1930s (Morison 1972: 249). But determined to serve the public weal through professionalized, specialized intellectual inquiry, focusing attention on improving the quality of scholarship *and defining that quality in politically neutral ways* must have seemed both sensible and safe to many political scientists.

Whatever the cause, the equation of objectivity with neutrality was quickly met head on by critics of this new form of scientism. By the late 1920s, prominent political scientists, like William Yandel Elliott, Edward S. Corwin, and Charles Beard, began to question the equation.[25] Interestingly enough, many of their criticisms of scientism would later become the basis for telling critiques of the scientistic cause: that there was a large gap between the promise and the products of scientific inquiry (Elliott 1928: 89–90; Corwin 1929: 588) and that the abandonment of ethical considerations was wholly wrongheaded (Elliott 1928: 77; Corwin 1929: 591). These criticisms also had bearing on the substantive content of the discipline's pedagogical efforts (see, e.g., Elliott 1928: 77). But what they did not challenge was the belief that better scholarship was needed or that the reproduction of the discipline should be given highest priority (Somit and Tanenhaus 1967: 118, 119, 120).

The upshot was that challenges to scientism were deflected from becoming serious threats to the task of training "generations of scholars," and to the extent that these criticisms actually presupposed that pedagogical ideal, they were easily contained by allowing "normatively oriented" practitioners a place within the organizational structure of the discipline (Gunnell 1983: 9–10) and by following a strategy of journal article, textbook, and conference panel skirmishes that posed no fundamental threat to the discipline's educative identity. As we shall see, however, the capacity for containment eroded as the proponents of scientism grew bolder in their assertions.

In the meantime, those who were critical of the ordering of pedagogical priorities launched their own offensive. In 1926, the APSA once again attempted to take stock of the state of the discipline's educative mission, this time in the form of the Committee on Policy (APSA COP), and when the committee report was delivered in 1930, it appeared that the chair, Thomas H. Reed, meant to reconstitute the discipline's commitment to civic education and civil service training (APSA COP 1930: 18–24).[26]

Reed's reflections on the need for civil service training were pretty much what one would expect; expertise, efficiency, and effectiveness were his guiding themes. But the most interesting (and telling) proposals he advanced involved the creation of various sorts of outreach programs that might close the gap between a commitment to good scholarship and a commitment to civic education.[27] Although it has been suggested that this was nothing less than an effort to "recast the nature of American political science" that would have "drastically altered" the development of the discipline (Somit and Tanenhaus 1967: 87, 100), I think that a much more circumspect interpretation may be in order.

As Somit and Tanenhaus themselves point out (1967: 99), while many practitioners in the discipline might have been attracted by ideals of civic education, many others were not inclined to push too hard in reorienting the discipline. Moreover, many of the remedies sought – such as expanding the discipline's membership to include a larger public representation, creating numerous conferences that would bring together political scientists and politicians – failed, no doubt in large part *because* the discipline had *become* an academic guild first and foremost. But perhaps most importantly, it wasn't even clear that this "new" emphasis on civic education represented a true reorientation of the discipline; for the kinds of programs the Committee on Policy advocated entailed an emphasis on teaching the rudiments of American government through adult education programs, the public schools, and a national radio program. And in this, the new civic education movement represented nothing more than an implicit recognition of pedagogical Taylorism; it left untouched, or only lightly considered, the question of whether there might be a major problem involved in parceling out the discipline's pedagogical tasks to different educational institutions, and it certainly left open the conceptual space that an exclusive focus on the reproduction of scholars could – and did – fill. Finally, it should be noted that this new commitment to civic education, with its emphasis on the teaching of American government, was not really intended to make citizens critics of government or demanding of political change. Rather, civic education here meant giving citizens an understanding of existing institutions so that they might better appreciate the value of those institutions.

It is not my intention to besmirch this effort; it did, after all, suggest the kinds of projects that might revive the discipline's commitment to civic education, but in terms of the substantive content of those projects, and in terms of its explicit commitment to the same logic of pedagogical Taylorism that had informed its opponents' efforts, it scarcely threatened to reshape the discipline's pedagogical identity – at least not directly.

The indirect effect of this push for a renewal of disciplinary commitment to civic education proved profound indeed. So too did the effects of efforts to criticize scientism. The effect that they had, however, was not to change the hearts or minds of those who linked the advancement of scholarship and the advancement of science – it was to make them even more firmly committed to their ideals.

Bold claims in defense of the cause of science and scholarship were fortified by bold claims against any arguments critical of that cause. Many political scientists denigrated *any* attempts to cast the discipline's pedagogical responsibilities in terms of citizenship training – no matter how broadly or narrowly defined.[28] Some even went to far as to dismiss as "naive" those "gigantic campaigns of civic education" that were being carried out "by organizations of every kind" in the heady years before the Depression (Munro 1928: 7). At the same time, drawn into an ever more intense offensive by the intransigence of their critics, the advocates of scientism distanced themselves from those iconoclasts who would "politicize" political science, and calls for "leaving ethics to the philosophers" or criticisms of those who brought "the integrity of the guild into disrepute by prostitution of their talents for quick gain, notoriety, or unscientific reformism" (Leigh 1944: 534) became increasingly common up to and through the end of World War II.

This trajectory of discursive development in the discipline might have continued unabated, and the "behavioral revolution" that crystallized it might have occurred earlier, were it not for the momentary reflection that the war seemed to require of everyone, including academic political scientists. Following a now-established pattern, the members of the guild created yet another committee to take stock of their pedagogical identity. The committee for the Advancement of Teaching (APSA CAT) made a cursory nod to the principle of "periodic audits" of the discipline's educative responsibilities, but the fact that it recognized "the special factors that make the need especially acute right now" (APSA CAT 1951: 3) appeared to excuse the association's twenty-year lapse in auditing itself.

The contents of the report, however, suggested that there was more involved than a periodic or even a special audit, for they appeared to actually *endorse* the trajectory of disciplinary development that I have been discussing. The now-standard array of tasks in the discipline's pedagogical mission were all there: Citizenship education, education for the public service, and graduate instruction (the education of scholars) were all given extensive treatment in individual chapters. (There was even a chapter recognizing the effects of pedagogical Taylorism – "Better Teamwork between the High School and Colleges".)[29] To be sure, the report appeared to promise serious reflection on the pedagogical priorities of the discipline; civic education was given particular emphasis as a means of girding the polity for its "struggle" with "antithetical forces" (read: fascism and communism) (APSA CAT 1951: ix), many examples of civic educative efforts were cited, including some in which institutions of higher education were involved (1951: 29–41), and the committee recommended that "more could be done than is now being done to make citizenship a vivid, living reality for our students" (1951: 41). But the overall theme of the report was that things were fine just as they were. Little, it seemed, needed to be done to "improve the teaching of

political science" (1951: ix): There was already "far more 'practical' instruction in citizenship . . . than even most members of the profession
realize"; there were already many "unsung heroes . . . in colleges and
universities sprinkled from coast to coast" who were carrying out these
civic educative tasks; and even those courses that were not explicitly designed for civic education were helping since "a course does not have to
be 'practical' in its catalog description to be vital in fact," and there were
many professors who placed an "emphasis on citizenship in the beginning [usually American government] course" (1951: 36–7, 188–94).

Given this evidence (and I use the term loosely here), one might understand why the committee – and it was not alone – would claim that
"amongst political scientists in the United States, training for intelligent
citizenship is the predominant interest and emphasis."[30] This was certainly a misdescription of disciplinary attitudes (as Somit and Tanenhaus seem to suggest [1967: 196]), but a more provocative way of
reading the claim is to see it as rationalization of what the reality actually was; for if political scientists were already committed and engaged
in a pedagogy for citizenship, there was no need for them to change their
pedagogical emphases. And to the extent that the committee believed
that "if the political science profession is to improve its over-all effectiveness, the graduate school is obviously the starting point, for it is from
this source that future personnel must come and that changes in objectives and in methods must be introduced" (APSA CAT 1951: 246), it
actually endorsed the existing order of pedagogical priorities.

Put another way, it might be acknowledged that political scientists
were committed to civic education, but that their commitment was more
often than not cast in terms that already took for granted a disciplinary
identity that had become well fortified over the past thirty years. Indeed,
the great bulk of the report confirmed what had already become accepted disciplinary trends and pedagogical practices, and although it
was moderately critical of some of these, its central conclusions – that
the discipline was doing what it should be doing, and that it was in the
graduate programs that effective reform should begin – all but blunted
serious consideration of more radical educative reorientations.

It should come as no surprise, therefore, that the committee's report
drew little attention. Nor should it come as any surprise that other attempts by the association to become more actively involved in direct
forms of civic education (as in its relationship to the Citizenship Clear-
ing House–National Center for Education in Politics)[31] foundered after
a few short years (Somit and Tanenhaus 1967: 188, 197). Outside of

rather cursory remarks in APSA presidential addresses, a few scattered articles in disciplinary journals, or other marginal attempts to develop a programmatic plan for moving the discipline out of its academic enclave, there were no significant "movements" to reorient the discipline's educative identity over the next decade and a half. Thus, and finally, it should come as no surprise that the advocates of a scientistically grounded pedagogy for disciplinary reproduction were emboldened to declare that the discipline had finally reached its coming-of-age: The behavioral revolution was upon the discipline, and the pedagogical purpose of a political science was to continue to reproduce those "generations of scholars" for whom the scientific study of politics was their first and primary concern.

As James Farr (Chapter 8, this volume) notes, between the late 1940s and the late 1960s, especially during the 1950s, behavioralism galvanized the identity of the discipline in a way that had never happened before. It galvanized its partisans by providing them with a focus for attacking those who opposed scientism and the need to reproduce the discipline, and ironically enough it also galvanized the opponents of scientism and a narrow concern with disciplinary reproduction by providing them with a more clearly circumscribed target for their criticisms. These provocations, however, might never have amounted to more than a set of ongoing skirmishes – which they had already been for some time – if the system of higher education itself hadn't been challenged by the effects of broader social and political changes. And it was these, perhaps more than anything else, that turned the briefs for and against behavioralism into a fundamental opening of the educative mission of academic political science.

IV. Conclusion: The Challenge of a Postbehavioral Pedagogy

The groundwork of the behavioral revolution was laid by the forces that had turned the attempt to consolidate the educative pedagogical identity of political science into a cause for constricting that identity. Failed ideals of reform, conceptual innovation, and institutional transformations certainly played their part in opening opportunities for constriction, but these opportunities became actualized only under pressures in the 1920s that called the entire system of higher education to account for the contributions it was making to the public good. When political scientists responded to these pressures, many blamed the lack of disciplinary effectiveness in practical politics on the lack of disciplinary development in providing scientifically grounded and therefore authoritative knowledge. For decades this formula worked well enough, as the success of the behavioral revolution attested. But in the context of new pressures on the academy, old questions returned in a form that made the (now) time-worn platitudes of scientism and its concomitant commitment to disciplinary reproduction sound increasingly hollow, if not irresponsible.

Paradoxically, the new pressures on the academy were in part the result of processes presupposed by the ideal of disciplinary reproduction. Educating more and better scholars, after all, only made sense if the system of higher education was expanding, and expand it did. After the end of World War II, higher education in the United States grew by leaps and bounds as more and more students, many of whom would never have attended colleges or universities in earlier decades, sought out degrees (Rudolph 1990: 486). Not surprisingly, the expansion of the professorate kept pace (Somit and Tanenhaus 1967: 158–60). Disciplinary reproduction, it would seem, grew "under the twin spurs of an insatiable demand for faculty, and the concomitant insistence that professors hold doctorates" (1967: 158), and the pedagogical identity embodied in the behavioral revolution both advocated and benefited from these developments.

But if the needs of an expanding system and the insistence that professors be trained properly were complementary, the interests of the changing student body and the kind of training the professorate received were not. Many students questioned the value of the education that they received, and academics themselves began to doubt their educational ideals (see Oakley 1992: 269). Some students sought a more "practically useful" knowledge, and they demanded that professors supply it. For political science, this was a clear indictment of the highly abstract and jargon-laden discourse that had come to pass as high-quality scholarship. Other students demanded that the knowledge they were taught take account of their own life experiences, which were now far more diverse than in the past (Lanham 1992: 35). This had the effect of questioning not only the American politics emphasis of the discipline, but also the class and/or ethnic content of that scholarship. And still others – emboldened by the struggles for civil rights and against the war in Vietnam – insisted that higher education become an integral part of social and political revolution instead of an institution of reaction (see the essays in Weaver and Weaver 1969). This questioned the implicit political commitments obscured by claims of objectivity.

Thus, the emphasis on scholarship and disciplinary reproduction may have been facilitated by the *quantitative* needs of an expanding system of higher education, but the substantive content of scholarship and training for disciplinary reproduction was often at odds with the *qualitative* demands that the expanding system of higher education had opened.

As concerns of content superseded the needs of expansion, the effect within the discipline itself was to call into question its educative identity in both its substance and form. What was once expressed in two more or less distinct discourses – the critique of scientism and the critique of pedagogical priorities – became for many a single cause (see, e.g., the essays in Graham and Cary 1972). The behavioral revolution promised to finally make political science scientific, objective, value free; the revolution in higher education proved – or rather required disciplinary practitioners to recognize – that behavioral political science was political, partisan, and shot through with evaluative assumptions. By the late 1960s it was no longer possible for academic political scientists to ignore the fact that much of their work appeared as an apology for the status quo and that their preoccupation with disciplinary reproduction merely undermined their responsibilities to address broader public, political concerns. And as James Farr shows (Chapter 8, this volume), it was both critics and advocates of behavioralism who recognized this.

The collapse of the behavioral revolution thus gave way to the "postbehavioral" challenge of reconstituting the very foundations of the discipline, including its educative mission. If nothing else, the collapse of the behavioral revolution has had the meritorious effect of forcing political scientists to become more reflective, more often, and in more self-critical ways than they had been in the past. Indeed, since the 1960s and especially in the past decade, disciplinary self-reflection has become so common that it is difficult to keep pace with the literature.[32] No longer confined to the reports of APSA committees, association presidential addresses, and the occasional book or article, disciplinary self-reflection in the postbehavioral era might even be called a field of study in itself. Of course, some might interpret these developments as an expression of disciplinary disunity, something to be overcome; others may see it as a sign of healthy diversity and eclecticism (Crotty 1991: 3). However one interprets it, one thing is clear: The identity of academic political science is now open in a way that it may never have been – save those early years when the founding fathers of the discipline struggled to establish it.

Have we then come full circle since the days of the founding of the discipline? Perhaps not, for we are not now in the position of creating a discipline as much as we are in a position of trying to remake the creation we have inherited. But in another sense, perhaps we have; for the crisis of higher education we find ourselves in today, a crisis that the decline of the behavioral revolution and the current postbehavioral condition of political science are expressions of, requires us to respond to the challenge of remaking the discipline much as the founding fathers of the discipline had to respond to the challenge of creating it. In their time they had to justify the discipline as an answer to the same questions we face today: "Education for what? For whom? How and where?" (Thompson 1971: 25).

These questions are our legacy, the present crisis of higher education makes it imperative that we address them, and the open contours of the postbehavioral condition of the discipline is the ground from which we must proceed. If there is any merit in preserving academic political science, even in a radically altered form – and even this may be doubted – then the challenge of creating a postbehavioral pedagogy for political science may be nothing less than the challenge of recreating the discipline itself. American academic political science was born of a commitment to education; perhaps its rebirth will depend on our ability to define again what that commitment will be.

Notes

1. For example, Francis Lieber, John W. Burgess, Theodore Dwight Woolsey, Daniel Coit Gilman, Charles Kendall Adams, and Andrew Dickson White.
2. Lieber's vision of the kind of education the university would provide seemed very close to the "moral education" emphasized in the old-time colleges (see Ricci 1984: 59–60). Although this may make him more of a transitional figure in terms of the *content* of political education, his claims about the importance of the academy anticipated a different understanding of the *sources* of political knowledge.
3. John Gunnell (1990: 125) argues persuasively that it was through the state that the discipline defined its practical relationship to politics, and that the state and the university were integrally linked for political scientists (1990: 138–43). Gunnell is somewhat cautious in his explication of this link, but I

think a strong case can be made for an interpretation in which political scientists are seen as seeking, through the university, a vehicle for applying reformist plans to the state. What this means is that the growth of academic professionalism, ideals of reform, and the pursuit of "pure science" were *complementary* in character. It was only with later changes in the meaning of the state, of academic professionalism, and of scientific objectivity that this complementarity broke down.

4. Anna Haddow (1939: 240–1) notes that Woolsey's text, along with Wilson's and Burgess's work on the state, was one of the "most significant" in the political science literature during the "Gilded Age," and it was judged "the most scholarly and systematic presentation of the principles of political science which has appeared from the pen of an American" by one of Woolsey's contemporaries.

5. Gilman edited Lieber's collected papers (Lieber 1880) and characterized Lieber's work as having a major impact on "the most thoughtful students of politics" (quoted in Ross 1991: 67). As Ross also notes, Woolsey was a devout disciple of Lieber.

6. Nor should one underestimate Burgess's belief in the value of political science in preserving and expanding the "truths" of the American republican experience, his skepticism regarding the capacities of the popular classes, or his commitment to the principles of elite governance – as almost any of his "scholarly" work will attest.

7. As David Lowery (1993) argues, the status of the bureaucracy was always an important dimension of republican discourse. Most importantly for our purposes, however, is a change between earlier republican and later political scientific understandings of bureaucracy as a necessary institution. Indeed, Lowery's essay demonstrates how fears of the bureaucracy moved from its perceived threat to liberty to questions about its effectiveness as an agency of the governmental state.

8. Even the title of Leonard D. White's (1958) influential study of public administration (the practice, not the theory) during the postbellum period suggests the connection between republican sentiment and bureaucratic emphasis: *The Republican Era: A Study in Administrative History, 1869–1901.*

9. Waldo (1948: 26n12) suggests that Wilson's essay "The Study of Public Administration" (1887) attracted little attention for many years after its publication. Although this might be taken as an indication that concerns over governmental efficiency and bureaucratic reform weren't yet foremost in the minds of most political scientists, it should be noted – as Waldo does – that "the legal and descriptive studies upon which later offerings [in public administration] were to be based were [already] underway" in the last two decades of the nineteenth century. For our purposes, this is perhaps the central point of interest for the narrative at hand, for the studies that Waldo

mentions were integral aspects of the transformation of state discourse I
am addressing.

10. Leonard White argues that the period 1870–1900 were "years of stagna-
tion" in the development of administrative doctrine, although (interestingly) he notes the exception of those who were "reformers" and "students
of government" (White 1958: 396). Any decent social history of the period
will confirm White's intimation that there were many such people, but
more to the point is his claim that "only three" – Charles Francis Adams,
Woodrow Wilson, and Frank J. Goodnow – would be remembered by subsequent generations.

11. In his history of the "the political theory of american public administration," Dwight Waldo (1948: 28) argues that "between [G. L.] Prentiss'
[1877 *Our National] Bane* and Richard Henry Dana's *Merit Principle in
the Selection of the Higher Municipal Officers* of 1903 there is a great
gulf." That gulf as Waldo sees it, is characterized by the difference between
a belief in the need to reform public administration on moral grounds and
a belief in the need to reform public administration on grounds of increasing efficiency. For our narrative, the crossing of that gulf marks the ascendancy of efficient administration as one of the discipline's primary
pedagogical concerns. What it also marks, however, is the collapsing of
scholarship into inquiry for (technocratic) civil service reform.

12. The next few paragraphs are heavily indebted to the discussion in Somit
and Tanenhaus (1967: 81–3).

13. It is interesting to note that no committee on instruction was established
in 1903 when the APSA was formed. In 1904, the Executive Council of
the association replaced the 1903 "standing committees" with standing
"sections." Most of these involved reorganizing thematic emphases –
and it was here that the Section on Instruction was established. I have
been unable to figure out why instructional concerns were not considered in the formation of the APSA's organizational structure or why the
Executive Committee added a section on instruction a short time later.

Although much of the literature on the history of the discipline might
lead to the conclusion that this gap could be explained by tensions between
the pursuit of "scholarly" legitimation and "partisan" political concerns, I
am not convinced that this would be an appropriate framework of analysis
for this period. Given the fact that early political scientists drew such distinctions in ways different than we do (indeed, their definition of scholarly
identity did not equate scientific objectivity with political neutrality), I
think a better interpretation is that the founding members were more concerned with demarcating the boundaries between political science and
other disciplines and that it was only after these boundaries had become le-
gitimized by the successful creation of the APSA that practitioners felt secure enough to turn their attention to pedagogical issues.

14. The 1905 section report, published in 1906, was written by W. A. Schaper of the University of Minnesota. I assume that Schaper's lone authorship indicated the extent to which the section members were of like mind with his analysis.

15. See note 11.

16. The change in title of the group seems to have taken place at the 1906 APSA meeting, when the Committee of Five of the American Political Science Association in Instruction in American Government in Secondary Schools was created. Thereafter, all APSA reports on instruction would be delivered from a "committee."

17. I have been unable to find any evidence to suggest that the distinction we make today between the colleges and universities, on the one hand, and secondary and primary schools, on the other, was also made in the first decades of the twentieth century. This was to be expected, for many of the advocates of the movement for reform of higher education in America – including many of those who became influential in the discipline – strove mightily to distinguish the university from the old-time colleges. By running together the pedagogical missions of the schools and colleges, and distinguishing that mission from the mission of the universities, the authors of the 1907 report perhaps expressed the intentions of their predecessors.

    The fact that we tend to conceptualize the division differently today may be taken as evidence that these efforts were ultimately unsuccessful. On the other hand, the fact that we often distinguish between "major research institutions" and "teaching colleges and universities" may suggest that their distinctions still hold in a reconstituted form.

18. Somit and Tanenhaus (1967: 83–5) offer an interesting account of political scientists' engagement in public affairs, the content of major disciplinary journals, and the substance of research in the discipline, all of which may be read as a testament to the link between scholarship and administration in this period. It is also interesting to note that Somit and Tanenhaus's discussion of practitioners' political activities after the advent of behavioralism is remarkably thin in comparison with their accounts of these activities in the period before the 1920s and from the 1920s to the 1940s.

19. The characterization of this movement as Taylorism is meant to draw attention to themes of "scientific management" that appear to me to be central to the discipline's pedagogical identity in this period. For a discussion of Taylorism (and one that suggests very interesting parallels between what is going on in political science and in the field of industrial production), see Edwards (1979: 97–104). For a discussion that explicitly links the scientific management movement and the discipline's public administration emphasis, see Waldo (1948: 47–61). One should also note how Somit and Tanenhaus (1967: 54, 54n6) characterized the effects of

Taylorism as involving problems of "divided loyalties" and the dangers of disciplinary "bureaucratization."

20. For example, in his 1912 presidential address, A. B. Hart virtually claimed for the whole discipline an "administrative" emphasis, demanding that the discipline teach that "we need confidence in trained men, belief in experts, joyful affection for those who are to carry out the people's will" (Hart 1913: 26–7). Similarly, A. Lawrence Lowell (1913: 55) suggested that "a democracy, like every other community, needs the best tools it can find, and the expert of high grade is the best living tool of modern civilization." One need not dig too deep in the discipline's literature in this period to find many other claims of this sort.

21. This is Waldo's dating for the time when " 'public administration' reached self-consciousness – an event symbolized by the appearance of [Leonard D.] White's [1933] and [William Franklin] Willoughby's [1927] texts" (1948: 26n12). "Self-consciousness," perhaps, but this was only made possible by moving public administration out of the center of the discipline's intellectual identity.

22. As one should fully expect, the dominant pedagogical discourse was not the only one, for many still saw the discipline's tasks as the "moral education" of citizens. But even in these cases, their exception proves the rule. The best example of this is in an essay by Edgar Dawson, which appeared in the APSA *Proceedings* in the same issue as the preliminary report of the (third) Committee on Instruction in Government (1914). The title of Dawson's essay, "New Proportions in Political Instruction," itself suggests just how far the notion of moral education of citizens had been pushed to the discipline's margins, for Dawson's central thesis is that the purpose of political science "is to get the boy's heart right, to give him the right impulse, to establish a disposition to be a good citizen. Without this he may know all the political science in the books, and yet as a consequence be only a more expert demagogue" (1914: 234).

It is tempting to read Dawson's emphasis on moral education as evidence that citizenship was still taken seriously in the discipline's ranks. And rightly so. But one should also be aware that Dawson saw this moral education as part of the *colleges'* pedagogical task (as the vast body of the text indicates), that he thought this emphasis was "new" (as the title, again, indicates), that he confirmed the "empirical" and "descriptive" epistemic emphasis in the discipline (hence, his suggestion that the political science books were useless for the purposes of moral education), and finally, that he acknowledged the discipline's university orientation by distinguishing between the moral education of citizens and the objectives of "mak[ing] political scientists, or expert administrators, or able statesmen" (1914: 235). (Dawson's inclusion of "statesmen" may appear at odds with the division of labor I have described. However, it seems that he might have been ac-

knowledging the increasing tendency of those who would become statesmen to get their education in the universities; as he saw it, the colleges dealt
primarily with men who would be "going into business or the learned professions" [1914: 234], not those who would become politicians.)

23. It may be thought ironic that this recognition became more intense even
while one of the discipline's own – Woodrow Wilson – was president of
the United States. But one should also bear in mind that Wilson's "progressivism," while certainly conducive to the self-understandings of most
reform-minded political scientists, was hemmed in by the demands of
World War I, sandwiched between the antireform administrations of Taft
(1909–13) and Harding (1921–3), and marred by its complicity in the "Red
Scare" of the late teens and early 1920s.

24. An interesting example of the possible implications of this counterrevolu-
tionary movement can be found in John Burgess's *Reminiscences*. In 1917,
Burgess was encouraged to submit some of his early work to be published.
But after he had done so, he received "one of the rudest and most brutal
communications ever addressed by a publisher to an author." According to
Burgess, the publisher "informed me that the wonderful discovery of
'Prussianism' in my original work and the proposed reprint of its first chapters was not made by any member of his firm nor by any one of their read-
ers, but an ordinary typesetter; and he argued that if an ordinary typesetter
would take that view of it, the great American public would do so"
(Burgess 1934: 257).

25. See Elliott, *The Pragmatic Revolt in Politics* (1928), Corwin, "The Demo-
cratic Dogma and the Future of Political Science" (1929), and Beard,
"Time, Technology, and the Creative Spirit in Political Science" (1927).
For discussions of these thinkers, see Ross (1991: 458–67), and Somit and
Tanenhaus (1967: 117–22).

26. Somit and Tanenhaus (1967: 97–100) provide a useful summary of the activities of the Committee on Policy and the themes it articulated. I am indebted to their account for the arguments in this and the next few
paragraphs.

27. It may be that these sorts of outreach programs represented the beginnings
of activities that political scientists would later cite as "service activities"
on their vitaes. This is no minor matter, for it suggests that civic education
still remains central to the discipline's identity – but also that civic education had been reconceptualized as an auxiliary activity separate from
"teaching" and "research."

28. See, e.g., the passages from APSA Committee . . . in Civics (1922: 117),
Story (1926: 425), Ogg (1927: 403), and Spenser (1928: 962).

29. The remaining chapters dealt with teaching methods, curricular organization, integration with other social sciences, and substantive concerns in
teaching international relations.

30. This was a common claim in the period, as Somit and Tanenhaus (1967: 195–6) note.
31. The rise and fall of the CCH-NCEP is discussed in Somit and Tanenhaus (1967: 196–9).
32. For a sample of this literature, see the bibliography in Freeman (1991: 37–44).

4

"Public Opinion" in Modern Political Science

J. A. W. Gunn

It is commonly said that the crucial stage in the development of public opinion came when ordinary citizens found the means of communicating their views to their rulers on some regular and orderly basis. According to this criterion of significance, the rise of public opinion is held to come in the late eighteenth century and to encompass the half-century or so from the birth of the American republic through the French Revolution to the British Reform Bill of 1832. As I have argued elsewhere, both the expression and the phenomenon designated were well known and politically important a good deal earlier than has been supposed (Gunn 1989). That, however, does not significantly qualify the connection between public opinion and mass participation. For modern times, public opinion has become part of the practice of democracy and of the political theory associated with that form of rule. The life that belonged to something called "public opinion" in the aristocratic politics of the early eighteenth century remains of interest for purposes of assessing various modern assumptions. We can now, however, expect little change in the close connection that most political scientists have made between the concept and democratic politics. In the following account, emphasis will turn on the levels of analysis used in discussing public opinion. This allows us to identify different periods each dominated by a particular point of view. Thus, the traditional holistic vocabulary first gave way to an individualistic understanding, whereas of late, more holistic language has experienced a marked revival.

I. Definitions and Nondefinitions

At one time, one might have said that the significant watershed in the story of public opinion came with its ties to popular elections. But this is not, strictly speaking, true. Within modern thought on the subject, the great divide occurs in the twentieth century and marks the transition from speculative writings on public opinion and investigation that used the sampling techniques known to all of us as polls. As long as the voice of the people was held to speak chiefly through the ballot box, the conventions of political philosophy governed academic talk about public opinion. Only when supposedly typical citizens could be confronted individually, and their views related to their electoral behavior and other facts about them, was it in general feasible to contemplate public opinion as a collection of individual responses to particular questions. All of a sudden the prospect opened up of knowing exactly what people thought about public issues. Dubious talk of political mandates and ambiguous inferences about the meaning of elections might now yield to the precisely honed tools of science. The act of voting may have given to public opinion its modern significance, but it has been survey research that revolutionized how one talked about it. Public opinion came to be what the polls measured. If one still needed elections, as the pleasantry went, it was only to confirm the accuracy of the polls. The transition here described began in the 1930s and had been consolidated by a torrent of empirical studies in the twenty years that followed World War II.

Even though driven by improvements in technical expertise, the study of public opinion remains under the influence of the past if only because the political theory that attributes normative significance to the content of the public mind cannot be replaced by mere data. The issues that give significance to the phenomenon and the analysis that explored the meaning of the concept are with us still. Sometimes they have risen up to challenge the presuppositions of the more empirical students of opinion, but just as often they have been invoked by these same students. It is even true that scholars who have been critical of the treatment of public opinion by contemporary social science may appeal not just to the speculative works that antedated quantitative studies, but even to ways of viewing the issue that belonged to the time prior to the democratic revolution. More rarely, it may be the scientific researchers themselves who have reinvigorated their inquiries by dipping into the wisdom of prescientific formulations (Noelle-Neumann 1984).

No issue is better suited to illustrating the choices and echoes that inhabit the literature than the central question as to what public opinion is. In general, one may offer the hypothesis that investigations based on survey methods have assumed that public opinion is, in some sense, the aggregate of particular, individual, and perhaps even private opinions as revealed by sampling techniques. This is in line with the demands, familiar through the 1940s, to render the language of the study operational and thus to describe public opinion in terms of those procedures that would reveal its nature. The parallel with the earlier discovery that intelligence was what intelligence tests measured is too obvious to require emphasis. But operationalism had perhaps some firmer basis in the treating of opinion. Since the subjects of interviews were encountered individually, it did seem to make sense that one put the results of their interviews together to reconstruct the opinion of the entire community.

But the onset of scientific polling served only to give general currency to a way of referring to public opinion that already had roots deep in past usage. Democracy had preceded social science in encouraging the treatment of public opinion as some sort of aggregate. When George Gallup, a pioneer among American political pollsters, offered his understanding of what he was studying, he borrowed from Lord Bryce the formula that it was the "aggregate of the views that men hold . . . that affect or interest the community" (Gallup and Rae 1940, 16; Bryce 1921, I: 153). Such an understanding had already been relatively commonplace in the early twentieth century. It reflected, no doubt, the fact that people voted as individuals and that their views were brought to a sort of sum in the opinion of the public.

One can find similar conclusions at least as early as the Jacobin phase of the French Revolution (Salaville 1793). What is surprising is that this understanding was, on the whole, then comparatively rare and this despite the uncontested fact that public opinion must, in some sense, be composed of views held by particular persons. Yet not even convinced proponents of popular rule were necessarily agreed that the prestige of the public voice was best conveyed by calling it an aggregate. Robespierre himself seems rather to have favored the position that assumed a temporal priority for public opinion over opinions merely particular or private. It might then be argued, as he did, that the proper office for public opinion was to judge the views of individuals and to exercise control over them (Robespierre 1952, VII: 325–6). When we encounter this position on the part of the chief Montagnard of the revolution, we shall not be surprised to learn that more conservative souls shrank from depicting the public's verdict as a simple aggregate. Though aggregates were much in fashion in the vocabulary of early liberals, the enthusiasm stopped short of so describing opinion. Even among the French Physiocrats, a school of thought famous for its tendency to find public wealth in private wealth combined into a sum and public interest in a sum of particular interests, there was no strong disposition to pursue the same individualism in spelling out a program for enlightening public opinion. For them, the content of opinion began with the truth as conveyed by evidence, and individuals came to accept it according to their lights.

A traditional understanding of public opinion dealt in terms that were essentially holistic. For politicians in a predemocratic age there was a current of influence, especially manifest in capital cities, in the rumor of the day and in the gossip of the town. It was prudent to heed this opinion, and the victualling arrangements of Paris under the old regime, to cite but one example, are eloquent testimony of the power of the *vox populi*. When the cry was cheap bread, a people did not need to be enfranchised to be heard by its rulers. Practical politics has always entailed grasping by intuition (aided by police spies) what the buzz of the streets was saying. The philosophical essayist Joseph Glanvill gave the English language the metaphor of "climates of opinion," first coming in an essay of the 1660s (Glanvill [1661–76] 1970). This was essentially the entity or process about which rulers sought information, and the procedure for finding out had little to do with ascertaining individual views and somehow fitting them together.

Yet more holistic in nature was that traditional view of the public's judgment as a guide to truth and as a repository of wisdom. For centuries, the people of Western Europe had known of a tribunal that passed infallible judgments on what was good in morals, in the fine arts, and on occasion, in public policy. It was, in fact, least useful in the last-named capacity, since the verdicts were a long time in coming and settled reputations only after all of the evidence was in and sifted by time. This notion of a public that made up its mind slowly – and almost certainly with direction from the wisdom of a minority of the population – was what informed most treatments of public opinion prior to the present century. People had in mind a process that transcended the immanent wills of all of the members of the society, for public opinion, on this reading, was not something that revealed itself in an instant or responded equally to all members of the community.

This way of visualizing the phenomenon is still to be found in the classic study by Ferdinand Toennies. It appeared in 1922, after Bryce had given a definitive statement of the more modern formula. Toennies insisted that true public opinion was a sort of "unified social will," a condition that Toennies explicitly contrasted with the opinions of individuals that were expressed in public. In keeping with this commitment, Toennies strove to characterize public opinion as existing in various forms that corresponded to the physical states of solid, fluid, or gas (Palmer 1938; Toennies 1922, 137–41). The last significant statement of a view of public opinion that was organicist and holistic, and owed nothing to the practice of polling, was perhaps that by Wilhelm Bauer, author of two book-length studies on the subject, in the original *Encyclopedia of the Social Sciences* (1934). It is noticeable from research on public opinion that the central concept is less tied to national institutions than are many political ideas. Thus, scholars from one culture may readily address issues that arise, as well, in other cultures.

The United States was to replace Germany as the home of most of the work on public opinion, and the United States developed its characteristic response to the subject in the years immediately following World War I. Just as William James discovered the "multiverse" to replace the monolithic universe, so students of American government came to the conclusion that the public was marked by plurality rather than singularity. Professor Francis G. Wilson makes clear (Wilson 1962, 88–9) that this position was to be found in various sources before Walter Lippmann gave it a prominent place in his dissection of the populist myth of rule by a single informed and vigilant public. As Lippmann put it: "The public is not . . . a fixed body of individuals. It is merely those persons who are interested in an affair." Or again, "the membership of the public is not fixed. It changes with the issue" (Lippmann 1925, 77, 110). It is unfortunate that Lippmann's horror at the irresponsibility evident in public life came to confuse the issue of the plurality of publics; for in *The Phantom Public* (1925), the work in which he had most to say about the absence of any single, all-encompassing public, Lippmann also wrote of the "true public" as the disinterested residue, purged of the self-interested groups that passed themselves off as spokesmen for the whole. It is ironic that a very similar problem afflicted Dewey's *The Public and Its Problems* (1927), the work written to rescue American democracy from the strictures of Lippmann's pessimism. It has become normal for political scientists to attribute to Dewey a pluralistic account of the public (Westbrook 1991, 300, 305), when in fact he recognized the fact of diverse publics but regretted it and adhered still to the ideal of one concerned public (Dewey 1927, 137; Meyer 1975, 33).

It is evident that the legacy of Lippmann's enormously influential thoughts on the matter of public opinion was not all of a piece. Some scholars seized on his scorn for the naïveté of the populist faith in the competence of the citizen. This was a position that had never been without supporters, for it had firm foundations in various eminent Victorian

critics of democracy and more recent confirmation in the research of
Graham Wallas (1908) and of his fellow Englishman Norman Angell
(1927). In the 1920s, Lippmann and Angell were identified, along with
a number of lesser known figures, as having put to flight the vaporings
of political fundamentalism.

Edward M. Sait was one of the major political scientists of the interwar era who endorsed this verdict, though sometimes with an ironic air
that served to distance his views from those of the critics (Sait 1929).
Sait specifically took issue with another position that was equally at-
tributable to Lippmann. This was the notion of multiple publics and here
Sait's uneasiness in the presence of populist rhetoric made him equally
distrustful of an assumption that dissolved the single public of traditional language into a set of lesser bodies. It was not in fact true that, as
Lippmann sometimes suggested, only naïve democrats reified the public that held opinions. As his own writing made clear, a conservative vision of a community that took its lead from these who were morally and
intellectually superior might also find it important to think of the public
in global terms. This was presumably what Professor Sait had in mind
when he denied that "public" could ever be identified with a mere interest group (Sait 1938, 501–2). It speaks volumes for the divergence in
views among the scholars who have studied opinion that Kimball
Young, the social scientist whose usage of the word "public" (Young
1930, 510, 578) had provoked Sait's disapproval, was clearly confused
by the whole issue. He interpreted Sait to mean that the term "public,"
either as adjective or as noun, should be confined to the activity of politics (Young 1948, 388). This seems entirely to have missed the normative thrust in Sait's concern.

One reason why Walter Lippmann was such an important figure in
the emergence of our understanding of public opinion is that he recognized various unacceptable extremes in treating the subject. In his earliest thoughts about public opinion Lippmann was inclined to argue that
one ought to eschew references to social organisms, the spirit of the age,
and other kinds of "oversouls" as shortcuts to understanding (Lippmann
1922, 30; 1925, 97). Here, he seems to have had in mind the social psy-
chologies of McDougall, Trotter, Giddings, and others at a time when
the language of social psychology abounded in such constructs (Eulau
1956, 439). Often these terms seem to have been employed with no very
definite claim in view, as when Edward Bernays serenely combined the
methodological individualism of public opinion as an aggregate with the
holism of the "group mind" (Bernays 1923, 61). Some of the language

of President Lowell of Harvard suggests the same eclecticism (Lowell 1923, 71–126). Later in life, Lippmann was more given to commenting dismissively on the pollsters' image of an aggregate of individual opinions (Lippmann 1955, ch. 4). This seemed to embody the superficial philosophy of those opinion samplers – such as Gallup and Leo Crespi – who assumed that opinion, once collected, settled the issues of government or argued that the perfect association of democracy and polling meant that an attack on the latter was an affront to the former (cited in Rogers 1949, 16). Lippmann was ever less willing to allow the pollsters' claim that they could reconstruct an equivalent to that New England town meeting whose passing he had thought irreversible. A good number of Lippmann's references to the polls were hostile, since he thought that their presence rendered leaders more timid than otherwise, but he was ready enough to cite poll results when they served his purpose (Lippmann 1965, 99, 474).

Lippmann's articulate disenchantment came too close to a commitment to aristocracy to sit well with his countrymen. One might then have thought that his championing of the diversity of publics might have stood as his signal contribution, though shared with a good many others. However, this position too waned in popularity (Weissberg 1976, 11n), though the idea of "issue publics" remains a familiar one. The problem here seems to have been the triumph, in the 1950s, of probability sampling over the quota method. Should one assume the presence of a different public for every issue, that position would raise obstacles to any effort to pronounce on national opinion, but it would present particular problems for the ambition to determine the views of the American public from a sample, as now, of at most some fifteen hundred people. Probably Lippmann's true legacy will be seen as his contribution to a conservative rendering of the public voice that treats the relevant public in terms of an enduring corporate body not easily identified with the existing electorate (Nisbet 1975). It was not quite that oversoul that Lippmann had rejected in the early 1920s, but there were resemblances.

Another critic of the scientific treatment of public opinion was Herbert Blumer, the symbolic interactionist. Primarily, Blumer sought recognition of the unreality of treating opinions as equally weighted units that could be counted. As he put it, only in elections did people seem to obey this model; elsewhere, the unequal influence of various portions of the community was manifest (Blumer 1948, 547). Blumer's objections to the conceptual disarray of those who conducted survey research caused a storm, and perhaps for that reason, his position has not always been presented clearly or sympathetically.

It seems, for instance, to be incorrect to claim that Blumer stood for the notion of issue publics, with a separate audience or public for each issue (Weissberg 1976, 11). He appears consciously to have avoided expressing himself in these terms, and referred rather to a public that consisted of several groups and so of various opinions. But neither was Blumer's meaning adequately captured by references to a "complex organic whole" (Converse 1987, S13), which looks in fact to be the opposite extreme. What he argued for was an appreciation of public opinion as a "collective opinion," different from that of any one of the groups in the public. Alternatively, he made the suggestion that it could be seen as a "central tendency" among the separate opinions then current and reflective of their relative strength (Blumer 1950, 47–8). It might happen, however, he suggested, that a minority was disproportionately influential in defining the outcome. Though the public would never be unanimous, public opinion thus conceived did represent the entire public. In some respects, Blumer's efforts to chart a middle way between a mystical oversoul and methodological individualism has remained attractive, for it suggests scope for recognizing social interaction – the influence of one person on others – and interdependence (Glickman 1960). As we shall see, the history of electoral research strongly suggests that though one may err in creating mystical entities, one may equally go astray by offering too narrow a vision of the process.

One further contribution to a tradition of viewing public opinion from a conservative perspective was the work of Lindsey Rogers of Columbia. His book (1949) is much more difficult to dismiss than the literature's fleeting references to it seem to suggest. In several respects, it was, indeed, more sympathetic to the activity of polling than its reputation for sourness would imply. Rogers was respectful of the views of Tom Harrison of British Mass Observation and of the American Elmo Roper, two men who made their living from observing public reactions but who resisted the conclusion that the voice of a temporary majority should automatically rule. In contrast to Lippmann, who began with no explicit political theory of his own and rather criticized a theory of democracy that he deemed to suffer from an excess of enthusiasm, Rogers spoke for the traditional normative concern of political theory. By this reckoning, the failure of the new empiricism lay in its disinclination to articulate any political theory that made sense of the rule of public opinion and a corresponding reluctance to say what this opinion was.

The late 1940s were – despite the passing embarrassment of the election of 1948 – a time of confidence for public opinion researchers. Since these seem, for the most part, to have been psychologists, sociologists, and market researchers, it is not surprising that Rogers's call for political theory went unheeded. As one scans the pages of the *International Journal of Opinion and Attitude Research* one already encounters the claim that the very concept of public opinion was "a vague folk term" (Dodd 1948, 379) badly in need of operational definition. However, the best-known journal in the field continued to cling to the traditional expression. Later, the disrespect with which postwar behavioralists treated the concept of public opinion would be replicated by equally enthusiastic students of mass communications (e.g., Westley 1975, 187). Still, the concept survived and political theory would yet have its day.

II. Studying Voters

The techniques for measuring mass opinion had come first to be applied in commercial practice – marketing and public relations. In the 1930s, political opinions came under scrutiny. Paul Lazarsfeld and the staff of the Bureau of Applied Social Research studied the voters of Erie County, Ohio, in the presidential election of 1940, and the results, first published in 1944, introduced a new genre of social science (Lazarsfeld, Berelson, and Gaudet, 1948). From the first, it had become apparent that refinement in technique would dominate questions of wider political significance. The choice of electoral behavior as the setting of the study turned on the simple fact that election campaigns involved more people and focused their opinions on a single act in ways that had no parallel in commercial life. Here the noun "opinion" identified the important element, and the public or political character of the opinions in question was almost incidental. Thus, when Lazarsfeld and associates discovered that the campaign did not in fact focus judgments on public stewardship in nearly the way anticipated – voters were often acting out long-standing partisanship that was reinforced by the election campaign but not created by the issues – the original point of the study largely disappeared (Natchez 1985, 52). Nevertheless, the finding was of interest to social scientists and served to emphasize the antecedents of the electoral decision by individual voters rather than the meaning of the election for the political order as a whole. In such circumstances, it made ever more sense to view public opinion as an aggregate of individual opinions.

Epitomizing the relation between voting studies and public opinion was the fact that the final chapter in *Voting* (1954), the best-known study by Lazarsfeld's team, summed up the theoretical meaning of the book without reference to the concept of public opinion. The significance might, however, be given such an emphasis, for Bernard Berelson's article (1952), which had anticipated the conclusion of the book, made essentially the same points under the title "Democratic Theory and Public Opinion." Lazarsfeld's studies were succeeded by those of the Survey Research Center (SRC) at Ann Arbor, Michigan. Here the approach was different, with an emphasis on attitude psychology replacing Lazarsfeld's interest in socioeconomic variables. This had, if anything, the effect of rendering the relevance of the exercise to public opinion even less evident.

In *The American Voter* (1960) and *Elections in the Political Order* (1966) one finds little explicit mention of public opinion. Neither chapter headings nor index entries make references to the concept, though there were numerous references to "opinion" as in the expression "opinion leaders." Whereas Berelson had responded to the demonstrated limitations of the individual voter with an attempt to rework the theory of democracy and its relation to public opinion, the SRC studies offered first the "funnel of causality" by which to account for the formation of individual opinions and, later, the concept of a "normal vote." Neither construct made any direct connection either with public opinion or with the larger issues of democratic politics. It may of course be true that, in some sense, public opinion was what was being studied, but somehow explicit reference to it had become inessential to the task. This is suggested by a study, by yet a third team of social scientists, where public opinion received an initial bow as the point of the whole business (Nie 1976, 2–3), which business was then conducted in a language that dispensed with the expression "public opinion."

In the substance of their findings, the studies of the American voter, based on survey data, had given a scientific confirmation of what more impressionistic writings had long been saying. The individual members of mass publics knew remarkably little about political issues, cared little about them, and bestowed their trust on public figures for the flimsiest of reasons. Lippmann and a host of others had said the same in words more artfully chosen than those favored by students of voting. What the quantitative work had done was to put the message in forms much more precise than had hitherto been possible. This was no small accomplishment, but there had been a cost and not just in terms of a declining elegance in literary quality. V. O. Key Jr., a critic of Lazarsfeld and Berelson et al. for their apparent reduction of politics to sociological variables, can have found no greater cause for satisfaction in the Michigan studies, though he supported them and drew on their data for his own work.

In a private communication of 1960, Key had offered the judgment that the voting studies had been "primarily of sociological interest" (Natchez 1985, 185, 270n4). Earlier he had expressed the point, in print, by saying that a concentration on the demographic cohorts that made up the electorate "threatens to take the politics out of electoral behavior" (Key and Munger 1959, 281). This sort of language became quite popular in the early 1960s and had served, in a number of well-known studies, first to suggest the waning of ideology and political tensions and then to defend the practices of democratic politics against their supposed enemies. In regretting the apolitical air of voting studies, Key was joining forces with scholars whose general hostility to the normative insensitivity of behavioral science made their objections somewhat more far reaching than his own. One such critic joined to his condemnation of the focus on voters' social characteristics – it was study of the "subpolitical" – a reassertion of the importance of "opinion" as that factor that connected the voters' characteristics and the political consequences of their political choices (Berns 1962, 40–3). In his own way, Key was emphasizing the same deficiency, for his classic survey of the meaning of preceding empirical research would focus directly on public opinion as the center of the political process.

It is difficult to avoid the conclusion that this opinion had, indeed, been largely ignored in the studies of voting behavior. When Berelson and others discovered that voters in Elmira County had adopted their political loyalties and prejudices from people like themselves and not from debate with those with whom they disagreed, they were, to be sure, describing still a public or publics and not a mere mass (Park 1972). However, in Berelson's ingenious displacement of the role of guardians of the republic from the active citizen to the play of sociological regularities, much was lost. In place of the model citizen one was offered a celebration of diversity both of social affiliation and of political competence. American democracy flourished, it seems, by virtue of the shifting balance of political participants with different traits. The system, a bit mysteriously, seemed to draw in participants when they were needed and left them at other times to serve the common weal through their very passivity. Different distributions of individual characteristics translated into contrasting qualities of the polity as a whole. The result was a fortuitous equilibrium of cleavage, consensus, and the like. This has long been treated as a valuable, but seriously flawed piece of functionalist logic, destined for annual ritual sacrifice in undergraduate courses on democratic political theory. There seemed to be little by way of a useful public opinion at either the level of the citizen or of that of the system as a whole. Nevertheless, the work of the authors of *Voting* had accepted responsibility for trying to explain how the ship of state managed to stay afloat and provided suggestions that were embodied in some later studies.

If public opinion had apparently been mislaid in the process, it must be said that their successors from Ann Arbor did no better. Indeed, as Angus Campbell and associates sought to isolate the factors that moved the American voter, their psychological frame of reference made it yet more difficult to contemplate the larger meanings that might be attached to the formation of individual attitudes. In these studies it was the relative weakness of issues among the determinants of electoral choice that marked an electorate that, as always, emerged as less than rational. Such a finding seems to have had more relevance for the 1950s than for some later periods. However, the general proposition was subjected to methodological scrutiny of a refinement that was appropriate to the sophistication about method that was so apparent in the National Election Studies from Michigan.

Was it possible, critics wondered, that notwithstanding the apparent priority of party loyalty among voters to the emergence of electoral issues and notwithstanding the remarkable stability of party identification, issue saliency might still be salvaged? One line of argument sought to suggest that there might be more voting on issues than appeared in the data. It thus questioned the assumptions that had guided the interviewing of citizens. It makes a good deal of difference whether the issues on which voters are questioned are those deemed to be on the general agenda of the nation or whether one leaves the issue open to inclusion of issues that voters, for whatever reason, cite as relevant. Failure to construct questions that responded to the intensity with which relatively small numbers of voters related to each of a large number of different issues might then have serious consequences, for this assumption then doomed the recognition of voter rationality. Chisman, the most tenacious critic of the Michigan team, also appealed to the known propensity of voters to project their own preferences onto candidates or parties that did not share them (Chisman 1976, 132–3). Curiously enough, this irrational behavior might serve to shore up the crumbling case for the alert citizen who responded to issues.

Most remarkable in Chisman's sustained analysis was his claim that the authors of *The American Voter* were so much in the toils of traditional notions of public opinion as to hold that the public was a "monolithic majority" instead of a congeries of different-sized issue groups (Chisman 1976, 154–5). If nothing else, the observation captured the new tendency of survey research to deal with a uniform set of questions applicable to a nationwide sample. Little room here for recognition of the idiosyncratic concerns of small publics. The charge of excessive influence by traditional political theory does, however, give one pause, since there is little evidence that survey research has been much moved by an intellectual tradition much older than its own techniques. One's skepticism, moreover, grows in contemplating the narrowness of the inquiry into motivation and the readiness in which Campbell and his colleagues portrayed a voter whose behavior made little contact either with the general political process or with democratic theory.

The best answer to the alleged shortcoming of having underestimated the importance of issues had appeared in response to the study by Repass (1971). It was all very well, Philip Converse argued, to enhance the importance of issues by inviting respondents to say what political issues were important to them. However, in departing from a few issues that could reasonably be assumed to be of objective significance in a given election, one clouded the general concern about political meaning. The introduction of a great many different issues made it extremely difficult to interpret the meaning conveyed by electoral outcomes, whereas the limitation of questions to a few issues made possible the inference that voters were responding to these issues, though not to them alone (Converse 1975, 128). Finally, it might appear, politics had caught up to physics and had created its own indeterminacy theory. The belated recognition of issue saliency was accompanied by the suggestion that one could only do justice to the rationality of individual voters by introducing such a range of political issues as would render unintelligible the verdict of the whole electorate. This outcome would, of course, raise questions about the whole point of surveys as producers of information not available through elections. The two major concerns that had animated critics of the Michigan team had to do with the technical matter of their treatment of the importance of issues and the more normative question of how the data explained the working of the whole political system. Now, Converse suggested, one might have one or the other, but not both simultaneously.

The most influential reservation to be expressed about the major voting studies were those of V. O. Key Jr.; they continue still to reverberate through the literature. Key's major works of the 1960s, the second of which (1966) was published posthumously, together represented the major thrust to ground a study of opinion in the growing mass of facts about the voter, while simultaneously retaining a grip on the prescientific interest in judging the ultimate effect of public opinion on public policy and on government generally. Responding to the area of manifest weakness in the various studies of voters, Key (1961b) devoted the final section of his study of public opinion to the "linkages" that could be established between what the voters did and why they did it and the ramifications for the political system. These were translated through all of the familiar mechanisms of parties, elections, the behavior of representatives and pressure groups. Very soon, the term "linkages" began to figure in standard surveys of the literature on public opinion. Whereas many contemporaries had to respond to the charge of having sacrificed relevance on the altar of method, Key cheerfully offered a view of public opinion that he admitted to be difficult to apply in research. His definition was that it was "those opinions held by private persons which governments find it prudent to heed" (1961b, 24, 24n). Decades of increasingly sophisticated technique had culminated in research about opinions that omitted mention of public opinion at all. Here was something more robust.

For the remainder of his life, Key sought to define some priorities by way of making sense of public opinion in American politics. Part of the task entailed an exoneration of the much-maligned voter and much of the rest pointed the way toward a more conclusive attachment of responsibility. In some respects Key simply restated certain truths that tended to be overlooked in the chorus of dispraise for the performance of the individual citizen. More effectively than Lippmann, Key managed to make clear that public figures who claimed to be the passive tools of a capricious public will were seeking excuses for their own defects. Lippmann's condemnation of weak leadership was set against his insistence that, on crucial issues, the public had been at once ill informed and firm in its views. Key showed that the ignorance and inattentiveness of the American electorate left ample scope for leadership by those in office. Returning to the general theme of electoral incompetence, Key credited Lippmann with having destroyed the myth of the omnicompetent public. However, he added, the victory was over a straw man (Key 1961b, 5, 5n, 285, 559n).

Key's verdict is endorsed, in part, by scholarship on Lippmann (Wright 1973, 63). Nevertheless, one suspects, Key was being less than clear in his objection. The populists of early in the century had been quite real. So too were those pollsters – typified by statements of the elder Mr. Gallup – who thought that just as in the marketing of soap, one determined what the public wanted and then expected that the supplier (the government, in this case) would comply. It was then a worthwhile pursuit to discredit the very idea of such a sovereign popular will, in both empirical and in normative terms. So it seems that Key had not got Lippmann quite right. One reason was, no doubt, that Key had a different agenda. From his perspective, it was time to cease berating the incompetence of the public and to concentrate on political elites and their shortcomings. It was these influentials who occupied the still uncharted terrain on the political map. If the electorate failed in its task, responsibility lay with the political influentials; for according to Key, the voters had done their best with the political information that they had been given. This claim emerged as early as 1961 (Key 1961a), and *The Responsible Electorate* (1966) reaffirmed the change with the help of the notion of the "echo chamber."

Not surprisingly, Key's efforts to rehabilitate voter competence and the effectiveness of public opinion attracted not just wide attention, but also some trenchant criticism. Converse handled the "echo chamber" roughly with the retort that voters must always choose among competing accounts of varying credibility. They had no one to blame but themselves if they erred as to the nature of the world. He emphasized as well the potential for misreading Key's study of a responsible electorate that consisted entirely of those who had changed their party allegiance. A study of this small segment of the population did not offer conclusive evidence about the electorate as a whole, for naturally party loyalty could not be a factor in the behavior of those who had switched parties (Converse 1975, 122). The findings about the mass of voters thus remained unimpaired in their validity; consequently the attempt to immunize the public against criticism had failed. The matter of popular control and the issues where it is relevant, as well as those where electoral retribution was unlikely, has been considerably refined since it first emerged in the 1960s (Boyd 1972).

Another criticism of Key arose in Chisman's ambitious study of voting data and the inferences drawn from them. Chisman complained that

Key's interest had been limited to the impact of popular opinion on policy makers and that his insistence on an administration's autonomy from excess public pressure was not matched by any disposition to view linkage as allowing for a reverse flow of influence from the government to the people (Chisman 1976, 163, 168–9). True enough, Key's problematic had looked, in the main, at rule by public opinion and not (in Chisman's language) the rule *of* public opinion by elites. However, there is ample evidence that Key was in fact aware of both possibilities. He cannot, for instance, have been ignorant of Hadley Cantril's demonstration (Cantril 1944, 228, 244) of how the very fact of official adoption of policies increased popular support for them among those who had previously been opposed. Students of American foreign policy will have no problem in recognizing the pattern. Further, it seems imprudent to have ignored Key's clear affirmation (Key 1961b, 423) that Chisman's analysis reached a number of conclusions about Key's general position based mainly on the evidence of the final and unfinished book. The charge carries weight in relation to some of the works written about public opinion and especially those that did little to attach the opinion of voters to the entire political order. By contrast, it was Key, primarily, who sought to move the inquiry onto a broader stage and nothing in his premises suggested indulgence toward the behavior of the elites.

Though open to challenge in some of its claims and forbiddingly dense in argument, Chisman's work has been unduly neglected. The response in one review was not that the critique of voting literature could readily be refuted, but rather that it had all been said already, as by Berns (Luttbeg 1978, 280). Had that in fact been correct, and it was not, it was still an unconvincing rebuttal. Indeed, for students of opinion who are accustomed to counting the occurrence of points of view, one would think that each successive criticism might carry with it some significance. One factor that may account for the limited impact of Chisman's very methodical analysis is the simple fact that it had been a fairly late contribution to a wide-ranging effort to defuse the negative judgment of the voting studies about citizen competence. The fifteen-year flirtation with the notion of a new American voter, who had presumably emerged in the election of 1964, came to an end around 1979. It was rather conclusively established that a supposed upswing in the relevance of issues did not, in fact, herald the arrival of a dramatically different sort of citizen. Rather, it seems to have been, in good measure, a construct of the social scientists that owed its being to changes in the format of survey items and had coincided with a presidential election where ideological differences were more marked than usual (Neuman 1986, 44–5).

Recent and contemporary work on public opinion reveals a variety that cannot fail to bewilder those who seek direction from it. In that respect it reflects the process of decanonization that has visited the discipline of political science in general. Not only have there been a host of new possibilities put forward; there has been an apparent readiness to canvass possibilities once dismissed as outdated and to strive for what would be meaningful to those outside purely professional circles. Of course, a narrow empiricism had never been quite as bereft of vision as some critics would have it. Lazarsfeld (1957), for one, had been interested in prescientific views of the subject.

Certainly people working in the 1970s and after showed a disposition to welcome questions about the meaning of it all. Here, the fiftieth anniversary issue of *Public Opinion Quarterly* (Bogart 1987) is instructive, though such occasions do, of course, invite just that sort of graduation day reflection that is unlikely to govern the rest of mundane existence. One finds James A. Davis emphasizing the need for frameworks by which to make sense of all-too-numerous facts. J. Phillips Davison, another contributor to the symposium, even called for reopening the question as to what public opinion was. The black box in the middle of all the activity still has its fascination. Concern about tyranny of the majority came up, appropriately enough, by way of responding to vapid talk, in some quarters, about electronic democracy. Issues having to do with manipulation of the public by government raised matters more often discussed outside the ranks of opinion researchers. Few specialists seemed content with a purely technical agenda that confined itself to questions of reliability, validity, or the optimum timing of exit polls. Most wanted better theory and some wanted normative theory at that. Compared to the stock taking after twenty years, this occasion suggested a point of view less dominated by the technical demands of survey research.

III. Back to the Big Picture?

The political context of public opinion, as emphasized by V. O. Key, seems assured of continued recognition. He had urged his colleagues to carry the activity of probing voters' attitudes and opinions through to conclusions relevant to public life. There are, of course, various ways of doing this. An awareness of the ethical content of traditional democratic theory offers one way of securing relevance. An interesting version of this normative dimension is the demand, by a scholar engaged in survey research, that one distinguish good public opinion from bad. The former, Yankelovich argues, entails people who accept responsibility for the consequences of their views, and the sort of information that the public thus needs is information about probable consequences. Appropriate to the concentration on normative language is his insistence that the very content of public opinion is not so much factual propositions as value judgments (Yankelovich 1991, 24, 55).

Perhaps more familiar as the means to attach research to political relevance is the demand that public opinion must be a category that is construed within the polity. Inspiration here has come from various sources, including Key's impatience with social science that reduced voters to bundles of demographic information. Another more or less contemporaneous influence was the orthodox empiricism of Philip Converse and especially his emphasis on the puzzles created by comparing the data that traced the opinions of individuals over time with the portrait of the aggregate electorate. It is the major property of collectivities that they may change in certain respects without there being any change in the bulk of their continuing members. The introduction of a new generation of voters who had no past history of electoral behavior would be a case in point. It was characteristic of Converse's enormously influential work to seek connections between results at one level of analysis and another – typically, the citizen and the polity (Converse 1964, 238–9). In the 1970s, textbooks on public opinion began to divide the field into micro and macro sectors (Best 1973). This responded, no doubt, to the new awareness that data yielded generalizations at different levels and that there were arresting paradoxes involved in moving from one to the other. An interesting development of this approach has stressed the value of aggregate data even for purposes of portraying individual orientations to issues (Inglehart 1985).

Nor has it even been essential that one's vision extend to the entire polity. For some scholars, what has been important is that one somehow project one's analysis beyond the mere sifting of a collection of attitudes to find out, for instance, if influence on members of the public affects what they do even though not affecting the attitudes themselves. In this approach, there seems to be no holistic or macro level, but it is still possible to label as "reductionist" a disposition to confine one's attention to attitudes without inquiring about the wider ramifications (Lemert 1981, 2–10). From such premises, the habits of policy makers and their ways of processing information may become important, though the approach remains very much at the level of the individual actor. Of particular interest is the suggestion – reminiscent of V. O. Key – that one should view public opinion from the other end of the telescope. This entails asking what messages reach policy makers rather than focusing on the messages sent, after the manner of much earlier voting research. From the vantage point of the receiver of the message, public opinion becomes a "perception" about citizen attitudes on certain subjects. The fact that Lemert (1981, 12) accompanies his definition by the comment that public opinion is a "myth" reminds us that there is loss as well as gain in this perspective. To invoke public opinion as he does is to situate it within the political process. However to emphasize perception and myth is to deprive it of some of the substance associated with views that can, with some degree of firmness, be attributed to citizens. Another concession to changing priorities in research is the claim that opinions may be held to belong to organizations and not only to natural persons (Namenworth, Miller, and Weber 1981).

Though Lippmann's worry about an oversoul has not yet returned to haunt social science, there has undoubtedly developed a new readiness to treat public opinion as a quality of a particular polity at a particular time. Happily, this appears not to require our casting aside the accumulated knowledge about individual opinions, for some degree of eclecticism remains an attractive possibility. To express the point with other than the greatest care would threaten to revive the worst features of an outmoded organicism. Surely the elements generating a climate of opinion are individual beings in various combinations and reflecting group attitudes and other elements of socialization. One thus shrinks from the implications of a statement by an eminent student of public opinion that this opinion may come in the form of a "mood . . . maintaining a life of its own quite apart from what individuals think" (Bogart 1985, viii). One must insist that it is not *wholly* separated from what certain individuals think, for this rendering leaves the emergent property of public opinion more mysterious than seems useful or necessary. Still, it is of the greatest interest that such a possibility should come in the second edition of a work that, in its first version, only touched in the most tentative way on the possibility that the sum of opinions that seemed to emerge from polling need not be the best way of treating the phenomenon (Bogart 1972, 16).

Support for this new idiom for discussing public opinion comes from empirical work on the changing dispositions of large sectors of society, the realm once called that of mass opinion or "public mood" (Nimmo 1978, 243), now more often known as "policy moods." Here is scope for speaking once more the sort of political language that receded before the social science of the earlier twentieth century. Thus, James A. Stimson refers to "an informed and thoughtful public that knew its collective mind" (Stimson 1991, 125). Clearly, the presence of such a public has not usually been inferred from views of public opinion as the total of answers to survey questions. Of course, the raw material for the new perspective is nothing other than the recorded views of individuals, scientifically coded. However, a view of the public quite different from the accustomed one emerges when one compares aggregate survey "marginals" over time. These data record the percentage totals saying yes or no to certain questions with data on individuals washed out as "noise." By charting the movement of aggregates over time, Stimson departs from the model of public opinion that looked primarily to psychology.

Elites also enter the picture as the factor that renders those who share a policy mood orderly and rational in their conclusions. Gone, then, is the assumption that attitudes and opinions – like votes – were fungible, in other words, that one unit was a statistical surrogate for another. The methodological individualism of two generations of researchers seems in peril. The holistic quality thus lent to public opinion is unmistakable as the researcher is alerted to the presence of a mass of sentiment that waxes and wanes. The result may not be quite the spirit of the age, as understood by John Stuart Mill, but it does offer a way of talking about something that had previously seemed inimical to description in the dominant language. When police reports of the eighteenth century conveyed information about public spirit, they had addressed it in impressionistic ways. A comparable phenomenon is now, given Stimson's approach, amenable to more rigorous demonstration. Without building on half a century of empirical work, focused on the individual voter, the new precision would never have arrived.

Yet another challenging effort to link the individual and the social whole has gone under the intriguing name of the "spiral of silence" (Noelle-Neumann 1984). First emerging in articles of the early 1970s, Noelle-Neumann's construct is the most fruitful effort by a major student of survey research to link individual psychology and expressions of political opinion in ways that speak to the state of society as a whole. It draws on the understanding of the public's opinion that is far older than recommendations that government be leashed to the views of an electorate. The starting point is that climate of opinion that was first recognized as confining the ambitions and temptations of individual citizens as it formed their reputations and bound their conduct by the norms of the community. Through word of mouth or by resort to stronger sanctions, such as the charivari, the community usually had its way and gained at least that hypocritical tribute that vice pays to virtue. Applied to politics, the model accounts for the individual disposition, based on fear of social isolation, to refrain from vocalizing support for causes thought to be in decline.

Crucial to the analysis is the recognition that opinion, until it is voiced publicly, is private. The spiral of silence accounts for the process of keeping it private, thus underrepresenting the real strength of a party that accounts for a decline in manifest (and perhaps, real) support, and so on. Much here turns on perceptions that may become self-fulfilling. One aspect of the process has been labeled "pluralistic ignorance," or a situation where no one may believe in some position but all or most may think that everyone else believes. Misperception thus enforces conformity. The expression is commonly, but wrongly attributed to Robert Merton's use of it in 1965. It was in fact already current in the 1930s (Katz and Schanck 1938, 174). The phenomenon has been known, but not named, for centuries.

A very significant aspect of this fashion in analysis is that it strikes a further blow at any understanding of public opinion that treats it as a simple aggregate of individual opinions. No such view can be adequate when the spiral of silence suggests that prior to contributing to the public expression of opinion, individuals seem to be made aware of the presence of a climate of opinion that may encourage or inhibit their expressing views. Knowledge of this climate is alleged to come to people independently of the scientific sampling of opinion, though this point remains controversial. Acceptance of the model allows one to visualize the formation of a public as occupying a series of stages as information about the relative strength of positions draws in some people as it renders others mute. In the measure in which the spiral seems credible, one may put aside other aids to understanding such as that "looking-glass effect" whereby people merely assume that their own views predominate. The spiral has some future, it is claimed, in understanding the familiar paradoxes arising from the lack of transitivity in the decisions relating to public choice (Rusciano 1989). For present purposes, however, it is one more appeal to a more holistic interpretation of public opinion. It is consistent with the recognition that public opinion borders on collective behavior (Coleman 1990, 237) and the demand, still heard, that we still need yet more research on the psychology of public opinion (Kinder 1983; Kinder and Sears 1985). It is not easy, however, to reconcile a recent judgment that there was a "general shift from the collective to the individual side in conceptualizing public opinion" (Price 1992, 72) with the evidence presented here.

The other part of the agenda held over from the major voting studies is the matter of differential information and influence – the role, that is, of elites. In some formulations, this entails a recognition of that rather small proportion of the public whose sophistication leads to a vastly disproportionate contribution to political outcomes. In Neuman's version (Neuman 1986) there is an explicit reworking of Berelson's paradox of forty years ago, ending this time with the conclusion that mass incompetence fails to bring disaster because of the ministrations of the sophisticates. Of course, one has long suspected that something of the sort is what happens. Behind the "two-step flow" of Katz and Lazarsfeld (1955) lurks a vast literature that, in prescientific language, suggests the various routes – whether by differential influence on government or on one's fellow citizens – whereby the few may influence the many. Count Roederer (1857) described the process at length in several publications during the French Revolution. Similar to other developments of the past decade or so, Neumann's tribute to the knowledgeable minority stresses its significance for the body politic and understandably so. A rigorous methodological individualism is not easily brought to the task of normative inquiry into the state of the polity, but a moderate holism may easily move in that direction.

Most talk of elites is less inclined to follow Neuman in concentrating only on those that are in a private, unofficial capacity, and few studies treat the work of the leaders of opinion as entirely benign. There is a wide range of literature, much of which breathes a moral commitment to some form of that populism that attracted Lippmann's scorn. In certain versions, the possibility recognized by Key that government may direct the flow of influence toward the governed assumes the form of a transparent theory of conspiracy (Exoo 1987). Facile Gramscian assumptions about alliances among the corporate elite, the media, and political decision makers banish any recognition of the complexity of social causation. Real questions about the nature and extent of media influence – and indeed of whether the media may not, in some circumstances, follow rather than lead – evaporate in the high-tension talk about cultural hegemony and such matters. It may not be social science, but certain such efforts are most readable (Postman 1986) and come from people of great accomplishment (Chomsky 1989). In the decades after Watergate we may all have grown more suspicious of top leaders.

Studies written in more austere language cover the same ground in contemplating the possibility that convergence between the priorities of the people and the government may reflect movement by the one, by the other, or by both (Page and Shapiro 1989, 1992). It is, indeed, a quite remarkable indication of the great difficulty of confirming the most elementary assumptions of democratic theory that only recently have there been rather careful studies that suggest popular influence over the decision makers. The people, it is now said, may in a significant proportion of cases give the first signal and the government follows its lead. This comes with the cautionary note that celebrating the outcome as democracy may place too little credence in the possibility that public opinion might have been primed only to ask for what the governors were prepared to grant (Page and Shapiro 1983, 189).

The perspective finds an attractive statement (Ginsberg 1986) – though not one that is very convincingly supported – in the vision of a constant process of domesticating opinion in order to mold it into forms palatable to the powers that be. This is consistent with the familiar tale that casts the political history of the past century and a half in terms of palliatives that the world's more liberal regimes have used to ward off adversarial protest or revolution. It is capable of some nice touches, as in treating the polls as deflecting potential behavior into mere attitudes and in drowning extreme views in a mass of moderate opinions. It may seem, by contrast, tedious to insist that poll results do in fact reflect publics that are, on the whole, moderate. Certainly this is true of the American public. Is it somehow cheating to represent accurately the slender support for the highly committed minority?

Public opinion, we now hear, is not an independent variable. The implication is that this is an anomaly and that it should somehow be endogenous. But why, one wonders, need this be so? Governments have often been seen as having a duty to form citizens, to change them for the better, to educate their masters, as it were. Perhaps such views have flourished more in Britain than in the United States, but as Natchez (1985, 34) pointed out, the Founding Fathers and their work was hardly a simple bow to the *vox populi*. Governments need both to govern and to justify their policies to extragovernmental opinion. It is a matter of perception and of one's political values when they have become overzealous in creating a compliant public. Populistic slogans that suggest the people directing an otherwise passive government join with the one-time fear of propaganda as the weapon of regimes that lack effective constitutional controls (Qualter 1985). It is reinforced by fashionable talk of states that are autonomous from some interests to the ultimate benefit of others. If we are less fearful of propaganda than was true in the 1930s and 1940s, the fear may just have assumed new names.

Has there been progress, regress, or circular motion in the past half-century? It is not easy to pass judgment. What is most striking is that voices once apparently silenced have returned to some sort of favor. One thus finds a recent work that combines the enthusiastic pairing of polling and democracy with a recognition that Rogers may have been sounder in his views than the pollsters of his day (Crespi 1989, 89). Optimistic about growing understanding, the same author allows, in accord with the radical critique of hegemony, that most official use of polls has been, to date, manipulative in intent (Crespi 1989, 132–3). This displays sophistication and is an admirable effort at balance. One suspects, however, that there is no syncretism that can absorb all views and do justice to each.

Where public opinion is strong enough to make a difference, influential people will decline to leave it alone. To wish matters otherwise is to consign the voice of the public to nullity from the start. It is not surprising that whereas some deem public opinion to be intrusive and irresponsible, there will be others who complain that it is weak, derivative, inauthentic. Between these visions of imperfection one looks for some golden mean that pays sufficient respect both to popular sentiment and to the imperative of knowledgeable and firm leadership. And the search will continue. For the present, public opinion – monster or victim – remains at the very center of democratic politics and of political inquiry.

5

Disciplining Darwin: Biology in the History of Political Science

John S. Dryzek and David Schlosberg

Biological ideas permeate the history of political thought. Aristotle, as John Wahlke (1979, 27) reminds us, was not only the first political scientist, but also the first biopolitical scientist, in that he believed the state evolved organically from natural associations. The *body* politic is an age-old construct. Machiavelli used vivid natural metaphors to describe fortune as a woman and the prince as a lion or fox. The brutish world of Hobbes's state of nature justified Leviathan. Burke compared society to an organism. Malthus deployed the biology of food production and human reproduction to justify the suffering of classes and nations. And Hegel brought organic process and evolution into political theory.

Such applications of biology came mostly as metaphor. It is only in the wake of Darwin's voyages on the *Beagle* that we can speak of a distinctive biological approach to the study of politics that merits description as a true research program. So for the most part we will focus our examination of biology in political science on Darwinian ideas. However, it is impossible to write or grasp this more recent history without reference to the continuing uses of biological metaphors, to an advocacy of a science of politics modeled on the methods and aspirations of the life sciences, and to applications of non-Darwinian biological science to politics. Like it or not, the discourse of political scientists as they have noted, accepted, rejected, or developed biological ideas has not been confined to simple extension of Darwinian explanation, nor has the latter ever proceeded independent of these other uses of biology. We will do our best to sort out the various uses of biology, while stressing Darwinian analysis, which we believe constitutes the most long-lived, im-

For advice and criticism, we thank James C. Davies, James Farr, Stephen Leonard, and Albert Somit.

portant, and influential of these applications. Unless we indicate otherwise, it should be taken that all the adherents of a biological approach we discuss are practicing Darwinism. It will become clear that Darwinism has itself allowed a wide variety of interpretations.

We should also preface our account by noting that politically relevant Darwinian discourse often crosses disciplinary boundaries, especially in the late nineteenth and early twentieth centuries, when the social sciences as we now know them were only beginning to establish their separate professional identities. When threads cross discipline boundaries we shall follow them.

True research programs – sustained approaches with a distinct hard core or ontology, a methodology, and an interlinked set of theories (Lakatos 1970; Laudan 1977) – are rare in political science. But the Darwinian approach that predates the crystallization of the contemporary discipline and continues to the present can be reconstructed as such.

The Darwinian ontology consists of varied individuals who struggle for survival in a particular environment and try to maximize reproductive success. This ontology allows considerable latitude of interpretation. Struggle may emphasize individuals grouped into species or even races, though this is not what Darwin himself intended. What counts as a variation may differ, as can ideas about competition, environment, survival, and reproductive success. The basic ontology permits theories of group selection (selection of traits that benefit the group rather than the individual), Lamarckian inheritance of acquired characteristics (especially influential around the turn of the century), sociobiology's emphasis on inclusive fitness (i.e., maximization of shared genes in ensuing generations, which need not be transmitted through direct descent), and the interaction of nature and nurture.

The methodology of this Darwinian research program involves deduction from the maximization postulate (the maximand itself can vary), though observation of animal and human behavior, metaphor, and long chains of inference from natural conditions to human community also appear. Only in the past couple of decades has the program embraced more systematic empirical work, notably in its latest home, the subfield of biopolitics. This addition of empirical content may, however, say more about larger currents in the discipline than about this particular research tradition.

It is perhaps with regard to interlinked theories that the claim to be a true research program is weakest. There are substantial discontinuities across time and space, and political science practitioners have often turned straight to biology for inspiration rather than to the successes or failures of their disciplinary forebears. Some continuities can be established, though they are more often thematic than truly theoretical. So, for example, Ford (1915), Roberts (1938), and Masters (1989, 153–83) all use biology to explain the existence of the state, but in very different fashion. To Ford, the state is the culmination of a Darwinian "social hypothesis" in which groups are the consequence and then site of human evolution. To Roberts (who seems to have coined the term "biopolitics"), the correct model for the world society of states is the loose association of cell and protozoa colonies (see MacKenzie 1978, 82). To Masters, the state should be explained in terms of the association for convenience of individuals in pursuit of their personal genetic maximization projects.[1] Given theoretical discontinuity, progressive problem shifts in the research program (to use the Lakatosian terminology) can be hard to discern. Masters might improve on Ford in these terms inasmuch as his explanation of the state does not flirt with holism, and as such is more consistent with the individualist hard core of Darwinism. But Masters (1989, 159–60) himself admits that his explanation of the state is not entirely successful.

Aside from the state, persistent themes include competitive political relationships both within and between states, as well as cooperative relationships in small groups. Recurrent normative positions have related to the need to conquer nature for human purposes, acceptance of the perceived way of nature if *that* seems to assist human evolution, and the use of nature to justify human practices ranging from capitalism, socialism, war, imperialism, and hierarchy to democracy, community, and peaceful cooperation.

The past hundred or so years of Darwinian ideas in political science clearly provide much grist for the intellectual historian. Our inevitably selective history will focus on the program's persistent struggle with powerful ideological currents in American politics. This conflict is not one of science *versus* politics, for ideologies help to define empirical and conceptual problems that all social science research programs must solve if they are to flourish (Dryzek 1986). Moreover, practitioners of the Darwinian tradition have hardly been shy about engaging in political prescription themselves. Contra Degler (1991), whose more general topic is Darwinism in social theory, our story does not culminate in an eventual scientific escape from ideology.

Thus, our story is not told in terms of politically neutral (social) scientific problem solving. Some contemporary practitioners of biopolitics might object, on the grounds that whatever its past normative associations, the subfield has now reached a maturity in which it is guided by the canons of science rather than ideology. We are skeptical of such claims, and not just because of the frequency with which they have been made in the discipline's past by Whiggish historians on behalf of all manner of approaches and moments (see Dryzek and Leonard 1988, 1253–4). Nevertheless, it is up to us to justify our position through reference to not just the deeper history of Darwinian ideas in the discipline, but also the more recent history of biopolitics – and this we shall do. Those who would prefer an account that focuses on the explanatory accomplishments of biopolitics are referred to the excellent summaries of Somit (1972), Wiegele (1982), and Schubert (1989).

Our stance here does not betoken hostility to the Darwinian approach. Rather, we shall argue that recognition of the persistent and inescapable part played by ideology should sensitize us to the number of conclusions that can be reached when Darwinian ideas are incorporated in political and social science. Nature offers a wide variety of bases for such truth claims, and each may constitute the grounds for a contextually constrained but nonetheless objective analysis. In other words, there is no single truth about politics that nature can or should reveal. But at some level the biology in humanity – and so political science – is undeniable. And given current human abuse of the natural world, determining our collective place in relation to that world is surely crucial. With these considerations and caveats in mind, let us begin our history in earnest.

I. Early Days: Sumner and Ward

Biological metaphors pervade late-nineteenth-century social thought, and so social science. Some of these metaphors predate or are inconsistent with Darwin's own ideas, but it is often hard to disentangle their relative influence – especially given that these metaphors helped constitute the social and intellectual context in which Darwinism was received. Darwin's own simple yet far-ranging thesis was that given changes in an environment, species must adapt. Otherwise, the individuals involved find themselves at a competitive disadvantage and face possible extinction. The message for a nineteenth-century audience, in the midst of industrial and social revolutions, could not be confined to the quaint creatures Darwin described on the Galapagos Islands and elsewhere.

The early theories that deployed Darwin did not develop in an ideological vacuum. Stephen Jay Gould (1991) has recently commented that Darwin himself argued eloquently against popular biologically based racist views concerning the various peoples he came across in his travels but was quite comfortable with European cultural superiority and paternalism. Yet discourses now easily described as racist, sexist, or classist were ingrained at the time and, however much they were resisted by Darwin himself, became imprinted on the application of his ideas to human society.

Nowhere is this more apparent than in the American incarnation of social Darwinism, whose leading practitioner was William Graham Sumner. Social Darwinism is generally credited to the British sociologist Herbert Spencer, who was among the first to apply evolutionary biology to human society. However, Spencer was a complex thinker, held in high regard by Darwin himself (Gordon 1991, 412–38) and certainly no simple biological reductionist. While Spencer did subscribe to laissez-faire economics (see, e.g., Spencer 1895), it would be a mistake to dismiss him as a mere apologist for the barbaric side of capitalist competition. With Sumner there need be no such reservations. Sumner brings to social Darwinism a radical American individualism that runs wild with Spencer's "survival of the fittest" principle. To Sumner ([1883] 1952), social ills are simply natural and part of the struggle for existence in which some succeed and others fail. Thus, "everyman" has no responsibility for the "poor, weak, negligent, shiftless, inefficient, silly, and imprudent" ([1883] 1952, 17). Sumner rails against humanitarians and reformers who would toy with the "natural" development of society. "If the social doctors will mind their own business, we will have no troubles but what belong to nature" ([1883] 1952, 105).

Sumner justifies elitism as well as unregulated capitalism. Success and failure in the conflated natural and social realms are due solely to the performance and qualities of the individuals involved: "Probably the victim is to blame. He almost always is so" ([1883] 1952, 137). What results is due not to any kind of social conditions or exploitations, but to the qualities and conditions only nature has bestowed on both the individuals involved and the social world. Such ideas made obvious sense at a time when capitalism, red in tooth and claw, was flourishing as never before or since.

While Sumner is today best remembered for the political prescriptions of social Darwinism, it is worth recalling that he was also among the first – perhaps the first – to speak of the political effects of innate human drives such as love, vanity, and fear (see, e.g., Sumner and Keller 1927), a topic that would reappear in the 1960s (Davies 1986). Despite the fact that he was not a professional political scientist,[2] Sumner casts a long shadow over the fortunes of Darwinian ideas in the discipline that was crystallizing as he wrote.

Sumner's chief intellectual adversary in the 1880s was Lester Ward, the key figure in the early days of American sociology, who drew a very different lesson from Darwin. Like most good Victorians (and more clearly than Sumner), Ward equated evolution with progress; but he believed that environment and not biological endowment limited the attainment of individuals, such that all could participate and benefit (see Degler 1991, 21). Among humans, evolution produced an intelligence that resided in collectivities and not just individuals. In these collectivities, notably governments, individuals could cooperate and struggle against the forces of nature, rather than with one another. Social evolution could be brought under conscious central control, especially if informed by Ward's *Dynamic Sociology* (1883; for an echo, see Thorson 1970, 208, who speaks of "evolution become conscious of itself"). Ward recognized that much remained to be done in terms of the further evolution of collective human intelligence; hence, the need for a "sociocracy" in which social scientific expertise could be married to populist political impulses. This hope leads Seidelman and Harpham (1985, 27–40) to locate Ward squarely in their "third tradition" of American political science, which they define in terms of its commitment to reform science in the interests of a sick but not incurable democracy. In Britain, a strikingly similar and contemporaneous Darwinian analysis by David Ritchie (1890) could culminate in a more explicit call for a socialist program, but that kind of political option has always been unavailable in the United States.

Sumner and Ward give extreme expression and biological grounding to two very different strands in the American political tradition, one of unconstrained individualism, the other of hopes for effective state building. Neither was a professional political scientist, but they were writing prior to the confirmation of the disciplinary boundaries that we know today. And Ward was sufficiently influential in political science for Seidelman and Harpham (1985) to pair him with Woodrow Wilson as one of the two founders of the crucial third tradition of American political science. If Seidelman and Harpham are right on this score, then the kind of reform political science that would later engage figures such as

Charles Beard, Harold Lasswell, V. O. Key, and Theodore Lowi begins with a distinct Darwinian cast.

The political programs of both Sumner and Ward were ultimately frustrated, those of Sumner by growing recognition of the evils of naked capitalism and by the rise of progressivism, those of Ward by a recalcitrant political reality. Hence, the first significant appearances of Darwinian ideas in professional political science depart from them both.

II. To the Profession: Kelly, Ford, and Merriam

Professional political science first took note of Darwinian ideas mainly to criticize them. Thus W. W. Willoughby (1896) takes pains to deny that biological factors play any role in explaining the existence and development of the state – then the basic preoccupation of the discipline. He draws on Ritchie's (1890) justification for the intervention of enlightened thought into human evolution but, unlike Ritchie, sets human consciousness aside from evolutionary biology. Willoughby reasoned that the centrality of "conscious human action" in state creation and transformation excludes both the "instinctive" traits of humans and the idea that the state itself is like an organism subject to natural forces (Willoughby 1896, 32–8). More generally, Willoughby (1896, 334–5) asserts that "the entire distinction that is to be made between mankind and brute creation is contained in the fact that while the animal is transformed by its environment, man transforms the environment . . . thus to secure an improvement higher than the mere biological law could obtain."[3]

The political science of the Progressive era made much of this contrast between human agency and brute nature, and so rejected social Darwinism. Nowhere is this more apparent than in Edmond Kelly's (1900) tome on the proper ends and scope of government in relation to "natural" forces. Kelly establishes Progressive credentials in his preface, where he situates his study in the context of debates within the "Good Government Clubs" that helped break the grip of Tammany Hall over New York politics in 1894. Unlike Willoughby, Kelly allows some truth in social Darwinism. But his prescriptive conclusion resembles Ward and Willoughby rather than Spencer and Sumner: It is the task of enlightened human agency – and enlightened political science – to battle the dark natural forces revealed by social Darwinism. For civilization begins when "habit yields to deliberate, purposive conduct," and "the more civilized [society] is, the less it conforms to unconscious growth and the more it yields to human purpose" (Kelly 1900, 213, 272). Reviewing Kelly's book in *Political Science Quarterly*, Franklin Giddings (1900, 710) applauds Kelly's legitimation of government as "one of the chief agencies making for human betterment." However, Giddings, echoing Ward and Ritchie, would rather Kelly had grounded human reason in Darwinian nature than set the two apart. For though the Progressive movement could not accept the brutal and uncontrollable struggle celebrated by social Darwinism, it could, as Ross (1991, 155–6) notes, accept Darwinism so long as human consciousness, rationality, and creativity are allowed into evolution.

The first sustained application (as opposed to critique) of Darwinian ideas in professional political science has to wait until 1915 and the publication of Henry Jones Ford's *Natural History of the State*, which comes from the statist and conservative side of the discipline. Ford (1915, 6) is very conscious that he is writing against the disciplinary grain and that "the naturalistic concept has apparently been abandoned by political science."[4] Ford finds his precursors in Britain, in the tepid and hardly Darwinian evolutionism of Walter Bagehot ([1873] 1956),[5] the more emphatic Darwinism of Herbert Spencer, and the organic statism of Sir J. R. Seeley (1896). Very much the professional political scientist, Ford (1915, 6–8) bemoans the fact that biological ideas are more apparent in "political speculation," wherein he categorizes the work of Huxley, Marx, Kropotkin, Nietzsche, and (curiously) Spencer.

The bulk of Ford's book consists of a defense of what he calls the "social hypothesis" in human evolution. To Ford, our large brains in relation to our body size evolved for sociality (just as in social insects). Thus, human "natural selection shifted from the individual to the community," and man is "a product of social evolution" (Ford 1915, 77). Collectivization is "natural" in all kinds of human society, culminating in the state: "The undivided commune appears to be the primordial form of the state" (1915, 144). He applauds Aristotle for asserting the priority of the state over the individual, a principle Ford elevates to "the fundamental proposition of political science" (1915, 144). States become like organisms in that natural selection operates on them; some flourish, some wither and die. Ford does allow that there are limits to biological explanation once the state attains the "psychosphere" (1915, 167). But there is no doubting the place of the individual in relation to the state: "As in other organisms, the individual lives are subordinate to the general life" (1915, 174). Such organic statist political sentiments were hardly novel.

But there was a smaller American ideological constituency for them than for the very different analyses of Sumner and Ward.

Though sustained Darwinian reasoning of the sort engaged in by Ford was a rarity in early-twentieth-century political science, exhortation to imitate the natural sciences, including biology, was not. For example, A. Lawrence Lowell's 1910 American Political Science Association (APSA) presidential address likened the study of politics to that of physiology. In his 1916 address to the APSA, Jesse Macy (1917, 1) asserted that, with Darwin, scientists "had planted their feet firmly upon the solid earth." He assumed that all applied sciences would take on the Darwinian model, as that is the only model to link science and living systems. But neither Lowell nor Macy went so far as to actually apply Darwinian reasoning to the study of politics.

Shortly thereafter Charles Merriam would recommend democratization of the study of politics by bringing the life sciences (including but not limited to evolutionary biology) to bear. In 1921 he called for a study of the uses of geography, ethnology, and biology for political science. The life sciences would make political knowledge less dependent on authoritarian propaganda and closer to the domain of scientific technology. But Merriam argued, with LeConte, that any science – including the biological – must be brought into politics to counsel, not control: "Science must whisper suggestions rather than utter commands" (LeConte 1892, 353, quoted in Merriam 1921).

In the same piece, Merriam recognized that the differences between the cultural, humanitarian, and scholarly on the one hand and the scientific on the other might call for different methodologies. The larger point for Merriam was an argument for coordination and cooperation of the varied sciences and methods. As he asked in his 1925 presidential address to the APSA (Merriam 1926, 10), "At what point shall the geneticist, the environmentalist, and the student of social and political control come together, combine their results, and start anew?"

Merriam criticized the naiveté of those calling for the simple scientific "discovery" of preexisting human nature. Here he looked to the social psychologist E. L. Thorndike (1913). Thorndike was against any simplistic universalizing science that viewed behavior as nature as truth, and stressed instead the importance of local conditions, social surroundings, and the "interaction of the world of natural forces and the capacity to learn" (1913, 199). Thorndike's insistence on the variability of human "nature" led to his early arguments against ethnocentric bias in the sciences. He admitted, for example, the influence of his personal intuition (1913, 41), and while recognizing the abuse of anthropological studies, Thorndike believed "they have the great merits of being almost a sure cure for the acceptance of the customs of Europe from 500 B.C. to 1900 A.D. as laws of nature or of God" (Thorndike 1940, 727).

Merriam's acceptance of variability in human nature had its limits, revealed most tellingly in his embrace of the eugenics movement, which constituted his main use of (as opposed to exhortation on behalf of) Darwinian reasoning. Eugenics came to prominence in the early twentieth century with the decline of Lamarckian ideas about the inheritability of acquired characteristics (which, for different reasons, both Sumner and Ward had accepted); for if acquired characteristics are not inherited, and if the unfit and feebleminded are overbreeding, then social welfare policies will not produce lasting benefits, and the only remaining way to improve society is through controlled breeding (see Degler 1991, 24). Today eugenics connotes right-wing authoritarianism, but in that era it was embraced too by progressive social reformers (Degler 1991, 43). Merriam, for his part, believed:

Control is likely in the future to reach a point where it might be possible to breed whatever type of human being it is desired to have. Then we could breed morons and heavy-handed half-wits if we wanted them. We might even breed strange creatures as beasts of burden and toil . . . dominated by more spirited beings designed for higher walks of life. It is possible that we might . . . mix in a little too much spirit or sensitiveness by mistake or through too great sympathy, and thus cause restlessness and even breed revolution; but that is a part of the chance that the governing group would have to take in such a world. (Merriam 1931, 229–30)

Merriam admits the difficulties, but continues to assert the benefits:

It is unlikely that such methods will be adopted, but there is abundant opportunity, by forbidding certain unions on the one side and encouraging others, for the cultivation of a vastly improved breed of the human race, far transcending the present type of mankind. (1931, 230)

In the United States, eugenics found some reflection in laws for the sterilization of criminals and the mentally deficient. Delivering the Supreme Court's approval of Virginia's sterilization laws in *Buck v. Bell*, Oliver Wendell Holmes in 1927 declared that "three generations of imbeciles are enough." Eugenics may have influenced laws for the selective admission of immigrants, notably the Immigration Restriction Act of 1924. Whether this act was inspired by the biological "mismeasure of man" (Gould 1981, 232) rather than a simple desire for racial homogeneity (Degler 1991, 53) remains an open question.

III. Biology in Eclipse, 1925–1960

Just as professional political science in the form of Ford and Merriam began to take evolutionary biology seriously, Darwinian ideas were making an exit from the social sciences in general. We will not dwell on this story, as it has been chronicled by Degler (1991). By 1920 a cultural approach to human differences promoted by the anthropologist Franz Boas had largely displaced Darwinian explanation. At this time Darwinian analysis could not shake off an association with proponents of racial differences in intelligence, who in turn were successfully stigmatized as un-American for their denial of the principle of equality of opportunity. Eugenics for its part was undermined by biologists' realization that the presence of recessive genes means that selective breeding cannot really make much immediate difference to the distribution of population characteristics. As a political program, eugenics was finally killed by the efforts of Adolf Hitler, and Darwinian ideas in social theory more generally gained Nazi connotations.

The demise of Darwinism, begun in the 1910s and complete by the mid-1920s, was played out in psychology, anthropology, and sociology. Nothing done by political scientists made any contribution on either side of this struggle; political scientists had less at stake than members of these other disciplines and stood on the sidelines. From 1925 to 1960 there is nothing to report in the application of biological ideas in American political science, save mostly for an occasional appearance in the scientistic exhortation that is the staple of APSA presidential addresses (Roberts, whose 1938 book we mentioned earlier, was neither a political scientist nor an American). For example, in 1927 William Bennett Munro (1927, 10) wanted "to release political science from the old metaphysical and juristic concepts upon which it has been traditionally based. . . . It is to the natural sciences that we may most profitably turn, in this hour of transition, for suggestions as to the reconstruction of our postulates and methods" (Munro 1927, 10). Even here, however, Munro argues for a move from evolutionary biology to the new physics. Munro asserts what is to become a dominant theme in the discipline – using science to come up with a singular, pure, and simple *truth*.

Three decades later, Harold Lasswell's 1956 presidential address would reintroduce biological concepts and stress the need to keep politics up to the speed of new technologies. He argued for the need to increase our mastery of nature – making deserts and tropical forests habitable, making plateaus out of mountains – to advance the development and freedom of human beings (Lasswell 1956, 969–70). Later, Lasswell (1961) would discuss the possibilities of using new chemical and biological techniques to control individual human behavior. Emette Redford's 1961 presidential address asserts that political science is like biology in that just as a biologist seeks the origins of life, political science wants to know if there is a "universal plan in history and a destiny for man" (Redford 1961, 755). Echoing Munro, he admires biology only because it supposedly seeks a singular truth about nature, and that, likewise, is the ultimate goal for political science. But there is nothing in these presidential addresses that can be construed as a contribution to the Darwinian research program.

Aside from the exhortations of APSA presidents, the only work from the 1925–60 period worth mentioning consists of the occasional glance back to organic theories of the state (e.g., Wilson 1942), and biological associations in the stirrings of political psychology in the 1950s (e.g., Frenkel-Brunswick 1952). These works notwithstanding, the Darwinian research program was essentially dormant in these decades.

Just as political science played no part in the demise of Darwinian ideas in social science in the 1910s and 1920s, so it played no part in the comeback of such ideas in the 1950s. The behavioralism of the most self-consciously scientific wing of the 1950s discipline subscribed to, if anything, environmental determinism of behavior. Only in the 1960s does the second Darwinian wave hit political science. By then, developments in ethology (animal behavior) had already influenced psychology and anthropology. We hesitate to speculate on reasons for the lateness of political science's rediscovery. Perhaps memories of Nazi abuses of biology remained particularly strong in a discipline whose *political* emphasis made Naziism hard to forget, especially given the number of prominent political scientists in the postwar United States who were refugees from Nazi Europe. It is noteworthy that in American sociology, a discipline whose political center of gravity is further to the Left, Darwinian ideas are still banned – even though, as we have already seen, such ideas can be deployed by the Left as well as the Right.

IV. Biopolitics

One of the first political scientists to rediscover the biological sciences in the 1960s was James C. Davies. Davies (1963) argues that improvements in psychobiology, neurophysiology, and endocrinology can aid our understanding of human nature. These new sciences had some non-Darwinian dimensions. But they could, Davies believed, expose not just the biological but also the more specifically genetic (and so Darwinian) bases of politically relevant human desires such as autonomy and trust, and also ground Abraham Maslow's theory of human needs. Given that this hierarchy of needs culminates in self-actualization, Davies's practical interest lies in changing the political environment to allow for the fullest human biological potential to be realized – a far cry indeed from the interests of Merriam and Lasswell in social control.[6]

In 1964, Keith Caldwell argued that the simultaneous explosions of human population and biological knowledge raised issues that necessitated turning biological knowledge into political action. Biopolitics to him suggested "political efforts to reconcile biological facts and popular values . . . in the formation of public policies" (Caldwell 1964, 3).

But it was not until the late 1960s that biological ideas in general, and Darwinian analyses in particular, began to establish a stable niche in the discipline, and here the efforts of Albert Somit are central. By 1968 Somit had begun to examine the political implications of the link between behavior and genetic constitution established in ethology, as well as non-Darwinian topics such as psychopharmacology's success in manipulating behavior. He organized the first professional panel on biopolitical themes at the Southern Political Science Association meeting in 1967, cochaired the second with Davies at the Western Political Science Association meeting in 1969, and organized a number of biopolitics panels at the International Political Science Association (IPSA) meeting in Munich in 1970. Soon thereafter the IPSA recognized biopolitics as a distinct subfield. Somit (1972) also began to categorize the biopolitical literature, and his bibliographical efforts continue (Somit and Peterson 1990).

In the ensuing two decades the biopolitics subfield gradually added members, publications, and institutions. The Association for Politics and the Life Sciences was organized in 1980 and began to publish its own journal in 1982; in 1986 it became an official section of the APSA. Topics, too, have proliferated. Not everything within the subfield can be classified as Darwinian; it is also home to, for example, studies of the effects of nutrition and health on political participation, and the policy ramifications of biotechnology. We shall not dwell on these non-Darwinian applications. More explicitly Darwinian work explains power and hierarchy in terms of ethology, revolutionary action in terms of frustration of biological needs (Davies 1980), and war in terms of people's pursuit of inclusive fitness leading "genetically related individuals to band together in groups ready for conflict" (Shaw and Wong 1987, 8). Genetically programmed "tit for tat" selective cooperation has been shown to be evolutionarily stable (Axelrod and Hamilton 1981), and so social cooperation – culminating perhaps in the state – can be traced to biology (Masters 1989, 153–73). Put all these together and you have the makings of a general account of politics that would encompass political behavior, war, revolution, the state, and cooperation – the base perhaps for colonization of the whole discipline. Thus, political science may incorporate biopolitics "as Christianity [to use Somit's metaphor] was enveloped by and incorporated into the Roman Empire" (Wahlke 1986, 872).

Such hopes have yet to be fulfilled. Sam Hines, in the inaugural article of the journal, marks *Politics and the Life Sciences* "as a forum for communication among members of an 'invisible college' of scholars" (Hines 1982, 5). He had in mind a network of scholars with no shared physical location, but a lot of shared ideas and a lively interaction. However, the biopolitics "college" is also invisible in that other political scientists do not pay a great deal of attention to it (Wahlke 1986), and its members for their part concern themselves mostly with the work of fellow collegians. Some of them, such as Roger Masters and Glendon Schubert, have attempted to reach into surrounding literatures, as well as make their comprehensive works more accessible to the discipline – an example worth following by their more insular colleagues. Then again, all fault for this invisibility cannot be attributed internally, as insularity, fragmentation, and what Almond (1990) calls "separate tables" now pervade political science.

How can we account for the rise of Darwinism in biopolitics in the past quarter century? Part of the explanation resides no doubt in developments in biology with obvious political connotations, ranging from primate ethology in the 1950s and 1960s to E. O. Wilson's *Sociobiology* (1975), grounded in his study of social insects, in the 1970s. Politically, the ground may have been prepared by the fading memory of eugenics and Naziism. In addition, the hold that behavioralism gained in the 1950s created a discipline hospitable to both the methods and theories of natural science.

The biopolitics subfield and its Darwinian element in particular are very self-consciously postbehavioral, with all the ambiguity that term connotes. Wahlke's 1978 APSA presidential address gets to the heart of the matter. He accepts behavioralism's "epistemological premises" and methodologies but criticizes its "unsystematic, atheoretical character and limited range of research topics, and the erroneous conception of human nature on which research rests" (Wahlke 1979, 9). Presumably Darwinian analysis could rescue behavioralism from its nebulous, if not vacuous, theoretical condition by supplying the theory of behavior that has always been embarrassingly absent in that orientation to the discipline.

An intramural argument about the relationship with behavioralism begins in the first issue of *Politics and the Life Sciences* and remains unsettled. Hines (1982, 12) calls for a postpositivist biopolitics that "must always remain contingent and contextual." He concludes that "the real test is whether biopolitics can satisfy both the behavioral criterion of scientific rigor and the postbehavioral criterion of relevance" (1982, 16). White (1982, 23) replies that there is no need for any critical break with behavioralism, and sees instead the study of politics developing in stages from the "traditional" through the behavioral and "biobehavioral" to the "neuropolitical." William Kitchin (1986, 5) argues that "biopolitics represents only [a] minor change in the general behavioralistic framework of explaining political phenomena."

One way that some practitioners have attempted to transcend behavioralism is through proclamation of an "interactionist" paradigm. Moving beyond the opposition of nature versus nurture, interactionism takes into account the partial validity of the genetic determinism of the social Darwinists and biobehavioralists, as well as the environmentalism of those such as Boas. Behavioralism as such can accommodate both genetic and environmental influences, as in Davies's (1963) formulation that behavior is a function of the organism and its situation. But interaction need not stop there. So Masters (1990, 196) argues for the examination of culture as the place where the complex interplay of the two spheres occurs. Development is seen as a result of the interaction between human organism and environment, and of participation by the organism in continuance or change in that environment. Nature, in other words, does not simply *happen*. Rather, it is continuously created by the actions and interactions of organisms and their surroundings, and here the departure from behavioralism is apparent. Both human attributes and cultural institutions become part of the environment in which individuals and governments act. Yet while much is made of this advance, very few in the subfield work with it at any length. We should also note that interactionism (if not by that name) is not entirely novel, as our earlier dicussions of the nineteenth-century works of Ritchie and Ward should indicate.

A further disciplinary development conducive to the revival of Darwinian ideas comes with the inroads of rational choice microeconomics. Indeed, if one substitutes the maximization of inclusive fitness for the maximization of utility, then there is essentially no difference between microeconomic and Darwinian reasoning (see, e.g., Hirshleifer, 1977). Evolutionary strategies can themselves be explained in game theoretic terms (Axelrod and Hamilton, 1981). Finally, a discipline in the process of fragmenting into more specialized and arcane subfields is in no position to resist the inroads of *any* novel approach, no matter how controversial.

The establishment of biopolitics as a recognized subfield of the discipline does not mean that the ideological problems that once dogged the application of Darwinian ideas in social science are a thing of the past. The sociobiology controversy of the late 1970s is proof of the latent explosiveness of these ideas. Sociobiology explains society – and so politics – through reference to the idea that individuals engaged in an entirely selfish genetic maximization project may indeed behave cooperatively, as their genes tell them to maximize *inclusive* fitness. They will behave altruistically toward their kin in direct proportion to the number of shared genes, and reciprocally toward nonkin. The leftist critics of sociobiology charged it with racism, sexism, and even thinly disguised social Darwinism and eugenics. Many of these charges were ill considered; when it comes to race, for example, sociobiology stresses what is common in all races. More restrained critics such as Kitcher (1985) argued that the evidence mustered by sociobiologists is simply insufficient to warrant any intervention in human affairs. Perhaps the most telling criticism of sociobiology was that in asserting the genetic causes of behavior, it denies creative human potentiality (see, e.g., Gould 1981, 328–30). This criticism is a precise parallel to the charge leveled at social Darwinism by Willoughby and Kelly eight decades earlier. Sociobiology is profoundly conservative, for in casting around for genetic determinants of human behavior, be it kin altruism, aggression, war, hierarchy, or xenophobia, it denies that the world could ever be very different. Political scientists stood on the sidelines of the sociobiology debates; the real battleground was in anthropology, appropriate in that this was the disciplinary base from which Boas launched his ultimately successful crusade to expel Darwinism from social science earlier in the century. We should note that biopolitics practitioners are today divided on the merits of sociobiology.

So long as political prescriptions can be inferred from work inspired by Darwinian ideas, one can expect conceptual problems to remain. And it would seem that Darwinians in the field of biopolitics are in no mood to shrink from such evaluation and prescription; indeed, many such practitioners fear the nihilism that would result if they did. For example, Arnhart (1988, 173) believes that Darwinism gives no meaning to life beyond reproduction and survival; if we take it to heart, we are in danger of "declining into a state of self-indulgent hedonism" (1988, 174). His proposed solution, biological but hardly Darwinian (cf. MacIntyre 1984), is a return to an Aristotelian natural teleology of universal virtues.

Roger Masters (1989) shares this fear of nihilism in his portrayal of political regimes that, just like individuals, engage in "adaptive change" in response to their natural and social environment. Masters explains the modern state as an extension of cooperation for mutual benefit in small groups. As group size increases, free-rider problems necessitate coercive government. But Masters avoids a Hobbesian conclusion by emphasizing the benefits of governments that have both enforceable and changeable laws, flexible enough to adjust to changes in the environment. Here, he argues, liberal constitutionalism does quite nicely. For Masters, the biological basis of change banishes nihilism.

Masters (1989, 229) stresses that if there is variety in environments, then one can expect and should respect variety in cultures. No political system is natural in all conditions – only in its own. However, Masters does not pause to ask whether the extant variety of liberal, constitutional regimes truly exhausts the variety that nature warrants. Are these systems really open and variable enough to respond to variety and change in our environment? Masters stops at legitimization of the status quo, and so does not take his own argument to its logical, and less conservative, conclusion. Schubert (1989, xvii) is prepared to take matters further, on the grounds that modern biology "would revolutionize the study of politics by forcing its attention upon how change is the law of life, even if institutional stability is the law of the land." In his attempt to ground liberal constitutionalism, Masters tries to use the Darwinian approach to explain the particular form taken by complex social and political institutions, a task for which the approach is surely unsuited.

In a world where the idea of democracy is more popular than ever before, Masters's embrace of liberal democracy is of obvious utility to the Darwinian research program. But not all of his biopolitics colleagues share his political conclusion. For example, Somit and Peterson (1991) point to evidence from human evolution and primate (especially baboon and chimpanzee) ethology, underwritten by sociobiological reasoning, to suggest that hierarchy and dominance are ubiquitous and so humanity's natural condition. Thus, one should expect democracy to be rare, for "the course of human evolution may make it easier for us to create and live in autocratic or nondemocratic societies" (Somit and Peterson 1991, 16). Irrespective of the degree to which this conclusion is warranted by biological evidence, it raises once again the conceptual problem of inconsistency with dominant ideological beliefs that has dogged the Darwinian research program over the past century.

We believe that the history of Darwinian ideas in political science shows not only the persistence of ideological tangles, but also glimpses of how best to cope with them. The sensitivity to variety that appears in Merriam's appropriation of Thorndike and, later, in Masters is instructive. The key is to renounce the idea that nature has any single truth to tell us about human society.

V. The Truths That Nature Reveals

The past century or so reveals an extraordinary variety of political philosophies underwritten by interpretations of nature and evolutionary biology. The list includes Burkean classical conservatism (e.g., Ophuls 1977), capitalism run wild (Spencer and Sumner), libertarian microeconomics (Hirshleifer 1977), progressive liberalism verging on democratic socialism (Ward), dialectical materialism (Engels and Marx), anarchy (Kropotkin, Bookchin 1982), complex liberalism (Masters 1989), organic statism (Ford, Mussolini), social engineering (in the eugenics movement), authoritarianism (Garret Hardin 1968), and racism leading to exterminism (in Naziism). Recognition of this variety does not mean that "anything goes" in terms of truth claims, and we would not hesitate to dismiss some of the views we have just mentioned as manifestly false. Yet both this deeper history and the more recent intramural controversies within the biopolitics subfield (see, e.g., Johnson's 1990 critique of Masters) suggest that the politically relevant "truths" that Darwinian understandings of nature reveal are multiple and likely to stay that way. There are two reasons for this conclusion.

First, social constructivist accounts of nature argue that "nature is inaccessible to representation, because scientific knowledge is a thoroughly social construct" (Bird 1987, 256). Historians of both science and environmental attitudes, such as Evelyn Fox Keller (1985), Donald

Worster (1977), and Carolyn Merchant (1980, 1989), argue that scientific paradigms are sociohistorical constructs rather than progressively more accurate accounts of the "true" character of nature. Thus, nature is akin to a canonical text that is reinterpreted from time to time to meet current demands. This is not a denial of the idea of biological *science*, but only a reminder of the social influences involved.

Social construction may be easy to accept as we look back at Hobbes's horrific depiction of nature in the midst of the English civil war, or at Victorian capitalism's social Darwinism; it is more difficult to recognize within one's own era. But the variety of contemporary readings of the book of nature starting from Darwinian premises suggests that social construction is still with us.

Social constructivism remains controversial. But even if one rejects it, there is another reason why the application of Darwinian biology to human affairs should continue to produce a variety of interpretations, highlighted by the interactionist outlook we discussed earlier. If both nature and nurture can affect individual and social development, then many possible outcomes can result. Thorndike and Merriam accepted this point; and more recently, even sociobiologists such as Lumsden and Wilson agree:

No longer do the genes dictate one or a very few behaviors – instead the mind intervenes decisively. Ranging widely, it creates a much greater array of actions. It permits each combination of genes to have multiple expressions and offers alternative solutions to most problems within a single lifetime. (Lumsden and Wilson 1983, 154)

With this recognition that nature does not dictate a particular direction for humanity, these sociobiologists accept the "biological potentiality" position of Gould (1981, 328–30), one of Wilson's most severe critics. The interactionist paradigm to which many biopolitical scientists now subscribe – in principle, if not in the practice of their work – seems less prone to ideological controversy than narrower biological determinism of the sort associated with crude sociobiology.

This acceptance of interaction and variety is not universal. For example, it is still not hard to find quotes by sociobiologists claiming rigid genetic determinism. More surprisingly, the eco-anarchist Murray Bookchin (e.g., 1982) is quite ready to universalize his own reading of evolutionary biology. Stressing cooperation, he refuses to acknowledge the existence of competition in nature, and interprets all seemingly competitive acts as subtle forms of mutualism. Similarly, even Masters

(1989, 230) insists on the ultimate naturalness of large-scale constitutional states not unlike our own. And Somit and Peterson (1991) believe in the naturalness only of autocracy and hierarchy.

A connection can be made between the variety of which Darwinian nature is capable when it comes to humanity and the variety of interpretations we humans can generate. For if interaction allows a wide variety of "natural" practices, so can it generate a wide variety of stances from which to observe and interpret the natural and human worlds. Accepting the fact of multiple constructions may be one way to shed the ideological baggage the Darwinian field has carried, by recognizing the limits inherent in *any* naturalistic justification of a political program.

This acceptance might seem to come at the very heavy price of excommunication from the temple of science – but only on a monotheistic construction of that temple. If, on the other hand, variety is a key feature of the natural order, the temple doors may remain open. When it comes to the application of Darwinian ideas in political and social science, the "truth" that nature reveals is that nature reveals a variety of "truths" about itself. This understanding does not necessarily lead to the feared relativistic world of unsubstantiated warring claims to biological and moral truth, but rather to that fabled land "beyond objectivism and relativism" in Bernstein's (1983) terms. The variety of paths open for development of human culture and politics is not infinite, but dependent on existing natural and environmental conditions.

A kind of grounded or embodied relativity is argued for by both Masters and Donna Haraway, two otherwise very different figures. Masters is a political philosopher who turned to biopolitics, and to Darwinism in particular. Haraway is a biologist, less clearly Darwinist in her commitments, who now deals with the history and philosophy of science (as well as cyborg feminism). Masters (1989, 244) argues for what he calls "relative objectivity": No single political system or cultural view can claim to be natural in all social/ecological conditions – just in its own. But truths that depend on time and context are nonetheless truths, so one does not fall into "an excess of mere relativism" (1989, 242, 182). Masters's metatheory here is ahead of his political conclusions; if he took relative objectivity to heart, he could hardly treat complex liberalism as the culmination of political development.

Haraway both accepts and laments the social constructionists' deconstruction of science, which she believes "lays us out on the table with self-induced multiple personality disorder" (Haraway 1988, 578). She criticizes biologists in particular for their assertions of singular truth and concomitant inability to recognize the social and cultural influences on their science. On the other hand, she retains a belief in the value of biological science and a "no nonsense commitment to faithful accounts of a 'real' world" (1988, 579). She combines this commitment with a sense of historical contingency in advocating an embodied objectivity in which only a partial perspective can be considered objective (1988, 581). The alternative to relativism is not then a single, totalizing vision, but "partial, locatable, critical knowledges sustaining the possibility of webs of connections called solidarity in politics and shared conversations in epistemology" (1988, 584). "Situated knowledges" are about communities and shared visions, not about isolated individuals on the one hand or universalized conceptions of singular vision on the other. Haraway reaches her conclusions via scrutiny of the history of biology (and primatology in particular). It is not hard to reach similar conclusions via scrutiny of the history of biological ideas in political science.

Nature might, then, offer some ground between the chasm of relativism and a weakly supported set, singular nature. Darwinism might then also resist its own appropriation for the particular ends of limited interests. At the very least, universalistic claims could then be criticized without having to accept a relativism unattached to the natural world. The variety of pictures of natural *order* can be examined without reference to the limiting concept of natural *law*. And in that order, Lester Ward, W. W. Willoughby, Edmond Kelly, Charles Merriam, James C. Davies, Murray Bookchin, and Roger Masters might all be gratified by the room left for human agency and choice.

Notes

1. Non-Darwinian organic theories of the state may be found in the works of, among others, Aristotle, Burke, Hegel, and Mussolini.
2. Nor was he simply a Darwinian. Ross (1991, 106) points to the roots of his work in pre-Darwinian understandings, especially those of Malthus and Ricardo.
3. Willoughby's rejection of biological explanation in general and social Darwinism in particular does not prevent him from wanting to allow Darwinian competition to "operate as to eliminate those essentially unfit to survive" in the interests of "race improvement," provided only that this be done by the "organized effort of society" rather than natural selection (Willoughby 1896, 335–6).

4. This perception is corroborated by Dealey's (1915) condescending and dismissive review of Ford's book in the *American Political Science Review*.
5. Bagehot's *Physics and Politics* was written at a time when "physics" covered all of nature, including what became the province of biology.
6. We are aware that Lasswell in particular also had interests in extending meaningful democratic participation; see, e.g., Torgerson, Chapter 9, this volume.

6

Race and Political Science: The Dual Traditions of Race Relations Politics and African-American Politics

Hanes Walton Jr., Cheryl M. Miller, and Joseph P. McCormick II

I. Introduction

It was there at its birth. When academic political science was established in American colleges and universities in the late nineteenth century, the issue of race was already paramount and prominent in American society (Somit and Tanenhaus 1967: 86–98). Many in the first generation of academic political scientists had lived through the Civil War and the era of black Reconstruction, and the Compromise of 1877 (Logan 1965: 23–48) was fresh in the minds of the discipline's founders. Cognizance of these events helped to shape American political science.

At roughly the same time that academic political science emerged as a distinct discipline, there was the simultaneous emergence of the new social ideology of social Darwinism. In fact, this new form of social thought would become highly influential in the latter years of the nineteenth century. Richard Hofstadter, writing about the social Darwinist Herbert Spencer, noted the power that his ideas had for many Americans:

"The peculiar condition of American society," wrote Henry Ward Beecher to Herbert Spencer in 1866, "has made your writings far more fruitful and quickening here than in Europe." Why Americans were disposed to open their minds to Spencer, Beecher did not say . . . [but his] philosophy was admirably suited to the American scene. It was scientific in derivation and comprehensive in scope. It has a reassuring theory of progress based upon biology and physics. It was large enough to be all things to all men . . . It offered a comprehensive world-view, uniting under one generalization everything in nature from protozoa to politics. Satisfying the desire of "advanced thinkers" for a world-system to replace the shattered Mosaic cosmogony, it soon gave Spencer a public influence that transcended Darwin's. (Hofstadter 1969: 31)

Whether mere coincidence or not, the fact of the matter is that Spencer's theory of social selection, with its emphasis on the "survival of the fittest," also fit neatly with a dogma of racial inequality that informed racism in America and the imperialist expansionism of America abroad (Hofstadter 1969: 170).

By the time the fledgling discipline had established itself as a profession with the formation of the American Political Science Association in 1903 and its intellectual journal, the *American Political Science Review* in 1906 (Somit and Tanenhaus 1965: 22–41), a formal and legal rigidity on matters of racial differentiation was becoming an institutionalized feature of American society. This was a time when "segregation," given blessing by the Supreme Court's decision in *Plessy v. Ferguson* (1896) and supported by the prominent African-American leader Booker T. Washington (1856–1915), was being firmly entrenched (Logan 1965: 276–312). And in this, too, American political science seemed to be of like mind.

If the Civil War and Reconstruction made race a prominent feature of American politics, President Rutherford B. Hayes's Compromise of 1877 committed the federal government to a let-alone policy toward the South and made race a captive topic of states-rights arguments. And when combined with the federal government's hands-off policies toward the South, racial dogmas like social Darwinism and institutionalized practices of segregation meant nothing less than the political reality of disenfranchisement for African-Americans. Indeed, at the very moment that political science as an academic discipline was being institutionalized, the Fourteenth and Fifteenth Amendments were being circumscribed and nullified by an entire region of the country, if not the whole nation (see Woodward 1951, and Gillette 1979).

American political science responded to this concatenation of developments with its own hands-off policy; and when political scientists (like John W. Burgess) did take up the issue of race, they usually did so in terms that one can only describe as racist. Moreover, the solutions they sought for the race "problem" often turned out to be little more than justifications for segregation. In other words, political science was responding to realities and reflecting ideologies outside the walls of the academy.

A full three-quarters of a century after political science had become an academic discipline, Professors Mack Jones and Alex Willingham argued precisely this point, noting that the shape of the disciplinary treatments of race issues readily reflected a constellation of ideological forces "external" to the academy. These scholars developed a perspective flowing from an analysis of the problem of power in African-American politics. They argued that not only did "external" factors of race impact various intellectual disciplines, but that these factors forced many white scholars to see and write of the African-American experience from a consensual rather than a conflictual perspective – an attitude reflecting widely held social attitudes at the time (Jones and Willingham 1970: 31–5). This suggests to us that we may have good reason to believe that the attitudes toward race embodied in the work of the discipline's founders may well have reflected the dominant social attitudes of their day.

These historiographical assumptions are strengthened by the work of John Dryzek and Stephen Leonard, who, despite a different focus, arrived at essentially the same conclusions as Jones and Willingham, that is, that external forces helped shape the conceptual, theoretical, epistemological, and methodological outlooks of the field.[1] After reviewing several histories of the discipline, Dryzek and Leonard concluded that no social science discipline in general, or political science in particular, can fully escape or ignore external social, economic, and political upheavals taking place in the larger society (Dryzek and Leonard 1988: 1246). Sooner or later, these forces will influence the "meta theories, paradigms, research programs [and] research traditions" in the field. Political science is, then, in large part context dependent. They write:

Political Science is about theories of how we have lived, how we do live, and how we can and should live together. And theories are, as the postempiricists have shown, historical entities. They develop over time. But in Political Science theories are doubly historical in that they are also time-bound. (Dryzek and Leonard 1988: 1257)

Taking the arguments of Jones and Willingham, and Dryzek and Leonard as points of departure, we analyze how issues of race have been conceptualized in the history of American academic political science.

But external forces were not the only ones shaping the discipline's normative and political perspectives on race. There were forces internal to disciplinary development as well. In our view, however, these forces are complementary, not mutually exclusive.

Consider the racial composition of disciplinary membership. African-American political scientists in the early and formative years, as well as currently, were a very small part of the discipline's professional membership. In 1969 the profession created the Committee on the Status of Blacks in the discipline to improve and enhance the involvement and participation of blacks,[2] but the problem of numbers was not the only difficulty at hand. Those inside the discipline, both black and white, may have had a hard time producing and publishing scholarship on race because of the relative neglect of the issue in the mainstream of the discipline. The first African-American president of the American Political Science Association (to date there have been only two) "lamented that the publication prospects in political science for works on the political behavior of Negroes were somewhat limited," and he explained this problem as peculiar to political science:

In some field[s] this [publishing] is relatively easy. Anthropologists deal with the Negro as a respectable topic, and the journals of anthropology take such articles without hesitation. In respect to my own field, which concerns the status of the Negro, except insofar as papers having to do with colonial problems and the like are involved, there isn't a very cordial reception for papers dealing with the Negro. (Quoted in McLain and Garcia 1993: 247, see also Holden 1983)

In later years more work on race did begin to appear, and it should come as no surprise that increased coverage occurred at the same time that the number of African-American political scientists was growing. In this, then, we should recognize that the importance of internal considerations – like membership composition – are often linked in complex ways to external developments, and that together these can have a profound impact on the content of disciplinary scholarship.

The peculiar interplay of factors external and internal to the discipline have then shaped the ways that American political science has addressed the issue of race. As we shall argue, these factors have important implications for a broad set of concerns for scholarship on African-American politics as well as the political concerns of African-Americans themselves. In what we call the "dual traditions of race relations politics and African-American politics," one can locate both (disturbing) continuities and (some promising) discontinuities in changing approaches to race in political science, and one can also identify critical linkages between the substantive concerns of the discipline and racism in American society. In the next section we flesh out in more detail the methodological and analytical framework we use, after which we then turn to an analysis of the dual traditions of race relations politics and African-American politics.

II. Analytical Framework

As we suggested in our introduction, our research relies primarily on those resources that seem to be the most promising indicators of disciplinary self-understandings, namely, the published work of academic political scientists. These of course include books, journal articles, research notes, book reviews, and conference papers, as well as officially sanctioned statements about organizational policies, positions, and priorities. Given the constraints of the essay format, we focused almost exclusively on presidential speeches and journal articles, two particularly important forms of disciplinary expression. The presidential speeches permit us to see if and how the discipline's leadership fashioned the profession's normative values and political perspectives on race. Journal articles, on the other hand, permit us to see how individuals in the membership responded or did not respond to societal events dealing with race in their scholarship. Thus, our research program entails the hypothesis that if a linkage exists between social and disciplinary perspectives on race, it will be revealed by an interpretive analysis of presidential speeches and journal articles written by the discipline's leaders and membership.[3]

To support our hypothesis we have undertaken a longitudinal analysis of political science literature on the subject of race and political science. We focus primarily on the articles of two political science journals that started in the formative years of the discipline and have endured. The *Political Science Quarterly* began publication in 1885 and the *American Political Science Review* was started in 1906. Additionally, we use special sections and presidential addresses in these journals. These journals, unlike other political science journals, allow our analysis to cover almost a century of social events and upheavals. In fact, the time frame of our analysis, 1885 to 1990, encompasses the era of constitutionally sanctioned racial segregation to the modern era in which government sanctioned racial subordination has been declared unconstitutional.

In analyzing the content of these works, we utilized a twofold categorization scheme. The differences in our two categories turn on general attitudes toward the politics, roles, and position of African-Americans in American society (thus reflecting our interest in both the substantive content of scholarship and its implications for the lives of African-Americans).

Our first category, which we call the tradition of *race relations politics*, reflects some of the general attitudes toward race issues that we raised in our introduction. In particular, themes about the fundamental differences between whites and blacks, including in many instances a belief in the "superiority" of whites and the "inferiority" of blacks,[4] or

beliefs about the necessary dependence of blacks on the white majority's willingness to accommodate black concerns, are the earmarks of this
tradition. In short, the literature in the tradition of race relations politics
involves the subordination of African-Americans. As Mack Jones writes,
"Black–White politics . . . may be best understood as a power struggle
in which whites, as the superordinate group, act toward blacks in a manner designed to maintain whites' dominant position" (Jones 1991: 37).
This would be the essential nature of what we label the tradition of race
relations politics.

The second category, the *African-American politics* tradition, instead
of emphasizing black subordination and acquiescence to white interests,
supports parity and empowerment. Here, blacks would seek to eradicate
white dominance, to empower themselves. This category sees political
power not as an instrument of oppression but as a means of liberation.
The normative values and perspectives in this category are different.
The emphasis is on justice, equality, and liberty, ideals that do not rest
on the color of people's skin.

For the purpose of determining the appropriate category for any particular text, we have tried to be attentive to the effects of significant developments in the African-American political community, the changing
content and character of racial ideologies, and other relevant historical
changes in the broader sociopolitical system. In particular, we categorize our materials according to stances taken toward the identity and
functions of political leadership, normative accounts about the relations
between minority and majority leaders and citizens, attitudes toward the
cause of black empowerment, and views of white-led initiatives.

We place in the tradition of *race relations politics* articles that emphasize an implementation strategy to obtain peaceful and consensual
relations between the two races, even if the result is the domination of
one and the subordination of the other.[5] The category of race relations
politics includes those works that value and highlight stability over conflict, gradual and moderate change over strident or disruptive change; in
short, where calls for change are resisted or limited to demands for political adjustment in the context of existing institutions.

In the development of this tradition, one sees the unfolding of an approach to race problems that starts – as one would expect given its historical origins in the late nineteenth century – with the premise that there
are political inequalities existing between the two races, argues that
progress has been made, and maintains that progress will continue to be
made in the future, despite current difficulties. In this perspective, both

racial groups have duties and responsibilities to carry out in overcoming the crisis of race tensions. White leadership must work to improve the situation, and African-Americans must not only work with them (if in fact African-Americans can identify this group of leaders of goodwill); African-Americans must also accept the present limitations within which these "reformers" are working. Thus, the pace and broad goal of, if not the initiative for, change must remain with white leaders. African-Americans are assigned the role of followers.

The literature on race relations politics is thus not only prescriptive toward leaders in both races; it began with certain normative values about who is in charge, how fast leaders can stride toward the goal of racial harmony, and the supportive role that African-American leaders must play vis-à-vis white leadership and the control role they must play in their communities. This normative foundation inevitably leads to evaluation and assessment of any new African-American political initiative or innovation in terms of how these efforts will affect white political leaders and institutions. Evidence that African-American initiatives will impact existing political entities often support claims that such actions are premature, irresponsible, or potentially damaging. Typically, writers in this tradition respond to increased levels of racial tension by urging caution and calling for a continued search for "more responsible" black leaders.

By contrast, works in the African-American politics tradition typically advocate the empowerment of those of African descent. The prominent question here is whether or not a specific course of action increases the power of the African-Americans. Articles in the African-American politics tradition tend to focus on the analysis and evaluation of obstacles, limitations, and inadequate delivery of policy outputs/services. The political tone of these articles is informed by the belief that institutional barriers be removed in order to realize the demands of social justice and fair play.

The African-American politics perspective looks not only at the initiatives of white leadership or cooperative leadership to deal with political, social, and economic inequalities, but also at African-Americans' leadership initiatives, that is, African-American political parties, pressure groups, legislative caucuses, and the like as beneficial and on a par with the white ones. The perspective of race relations politics tends to see such initiatives as unnecessary, conflictual, nationalistic, and often ineffectual. The African-American politics perspective grows out of an experience that has taught blacks that white leadership cannot be entrusted to realize the needs of the black community, and that white-led initiatives – even when well intended – often stall, stop, and may be reversed. Moreover, white leadership, no matter how cooperative and well meaning, is in the final analysis paternalistic and emasculating for African-Americans.

Also inherent in this perspective is the willingness to strenuously analyze, and criticize where necessary, white-led initiatives. In the literature on race relations politics, such criticisms are (as we have seen) typically interpreted as ungrateful reactions, evidence that African-Americans do not understand the pluralist nature of the political system. But the African-American politics perspective sees criticism as essential to more and just democratic reforms. To simply wait until the political system responds leaves the African-American community in a reactive rather than a proactive mode, subject to others' goodwill. Works in African-American politics focus on the need to remove barriers to progress and the use of empowerment to solve community and national problems. Ultimately, while both traditions focus on the issue of race, they suggest different power configurations between the two races.

With these analytical points in hand, we now turn to an examination of the dual research traditions of race relations politics and African-American politics. As we continue, we will return to the preceding themes. We conclude by drawing out the lessons this inquiry has for how we should understand the past, present, and future of race in academic political science.

III. The Dual Research Traditions

Perhaps the most striking lessons of our review of presidential speeches and articles appearing in the *Political Science Quarterly* and *American Political Science Review* (as listed in Appendixes I and II) are fivefold. First, only three of the seventy-nine presidential addresses to the American Political Science Association even mention the words "Negro," "black," or "African-American." Second, only about 2 percent of the articles published through 1990 (on our count, 6,157) addressed the experiences of African-Americans. Third, nearly two-thirds of those articles that did tended to fall within the tradition of race relations politics. Fourth, works in the African-American politics tradition were quite infrequent in the opening decades of the century and began to appear in somewhat more significant numbers only in and after the 1940s. And fifth, it was not until the 1970s that the two traditions began to exhibit parity in frequency of publication.

Besides these general lessons, a number of related points emerge in this historical study. Both the *Political Science Quarterly* (hereafter, *Quarterly*), over its 105 years, and the *American Political Science Review* (hereafter, *Review*), over its 85 years, published an identical number (twenty-seven) of race-related articles. Most tellingly, these articles amounted to no more than 2 percent of the total number of articles. Moreover, the clear majority of the combined fifty-four articles reflect the tradition of race-relations politics. Little more than a third of the articles (in our count, twenty-one) were concerned with ways to enhance and improve the political power of African-Americans.

Some changes over time are noticeable and significant, however. Of the fifty-four articles published over the period in question, articles in the tradition of race relations politics were plainly dominant in the period from the 1890s through the 1970s. This dominance has not taken the form of a consistent linear pattern, but relative to works in the African-American politics tradition its influence is nonetheless marked. By contrast, articles in the African-American politics tradition were few and far between until the 1960s. During the 1960s and 1970s, one discovers some shift of influence as more articles in the African-American politics tradition are published alongside works concerning race relations politics. Indeed, articles in these two traditions begin to appear in more nearly equal numbers in the 1980s.

In making these claims about coverage over time, we are aware that the relatively low numbers of articles and speeches in question may make such claims statistically or empirically problematic for some readers. However, we still maintain that a pattern of change can be discerned, and if the meagerness of the data indicates anything at all, it is that the "negro problem" has been an issue that political scientists have largely ignored. This of course is no minor consideration, and we will return to it in our conclusion. For the moment, let us consider what can be learned from a more substantive analysis of the relatively few articles and presidential addresses that exist.

IV. Analysis of the Two Traditions

Beyond the matter of coverage over time are the substantive concerns of the articles. As one would expect, many of the articles in the tradition of race relations politics apologized for racially discriminatory institutions (including slavery, peonage, segregation, and political inequalities), addressed problems that these institutions faced in maintaining their existence, described how these social institutions worked and the benefits that occurred for those involved, or dealt with problems confronting the political and economic system as a result of these institutions.

A number of articles published in the *Quarterly* dealt more or less directly with the legacy of slavery. For the most part, these articles followed the analytical patterns we discussed in the previous paragraph (see the articles by Bugbee, Phillips, McClendon, Morris, and Curtin in Appendix I). Nor did these patterns change when racial segregation was the issue at hand. For example, the articles by Langdon, Brooks, and Weiss (see Appendix I) entail an analytical pattern not unlike those that dealt with slavery. In fact, the initial article on race in the *Quarterly* (by Langdon) justified southern segregation and urged northerners to not interfere. This article – written without footnotes or empirical support – concluded:

There are enough candid Northern men living at the South [*sic*] to assure Southerners that they may confidently put their trust in the sober second thought and honorable feelings of the North. And these Northern residents of the South will bear witness also that there is no race question there, save that which imaginative sociologists or unscrupulous politicians are themselves manufacturing and forcing upon it. But they will also plainly tell whom it may concern that no social crusade or political faction can even so much as attempt to impose negro equality on the South, or set up again the negro rule of the past, without the most disastrous results to the social, financial and political interests of the whole people. (Langdon 1891: 42)

A second segregation article, written in 1911 (by Brooks), concluded by stressing: "The blacks are naturally easy-going and improvident. They need the stress of competition and the presence of . . . industry. . . . The black man's powers of imitation are great; and where his energies are properly guided and he is encouraged to practice self-restraint and prudence . . . many a black man has become a prosperous and upright citizen" (Brooks 1911: 220). In short, these articles argued that segregation was beneficial to the African-American.

The third *Quarterly* article dealing with segregation, appearing in 1969 (by Weiss), argued that the success and the depths of President Woodrow Wilson's efforts to segregate the federal government and bureaucracy were due to the ineffectual nature of African-American protest organizations (Weiss 1969). Here we find an expression of the time-worn practice of blaming the victim: Since the presidency as an institution was firmly established by the time of Wilson's service, it was the ineffectiveness of black protests (the NAACP had just been organized in 1910) that explained Wilson's success.

In addition to these articles, there were works that addressed school desegregation (Rogers and Rossell in Appendix I), but in a manner that would not empower the African-American community. The other articles in this category (Fogelson, Leab, and Sonenshein in Appendix I) covered diverse issues but always with a dominant focus of improving racial relations and harmony within the context of existing institutional structures.

The articles on race relations politics in the *Review* embodied a similar pattern of argument. The initial article on race issues that appeared in the *Review* (by Rose; see Appendix II) tried to explain that the Negro's right to vote was based on the Constitution. Rose's defense of this claim is rather unremarkable, but what is most puzzling about his article is that his thesis and conclusions were inconsistent. On the one hand, he argues for what appears to be the usefulness of legislated equality:

The purpose of the Fourteenth and Fifteenth Amendments is to make the rights and privileges of every man born or naturalized in the United States dependent upon himself and not upon his race, color, or previous condition of servitude. . . . Those who so believe long for the day when the relations of the two races shall in truth and in deed be controlled by what they believe to be the real life principle of those amendments. That can never be until the white people of the South . . . believe that there should be legislation imposed. (Rose 1906: 42–3)

On the other hand, the article concludes by arguing that "God," not society and government, will one day ensure African-Americans their constitutional right to vote.

In the other three suffrage articles from the *Review* there is an obvious methodological shift from traditionalism to behavioralism, with the emphasis on the "individual" as the unit of analysis (see the article by Fenton and Vines, and the two articles by Matthews and Prothro in Appendix II). In these essays, as well as the six articles on various dimensions of political participation (by Orbell, Eisinger, Miller et al., Midlarsky, Leiske, and Shingles in Appendix II), there is both an emphasis on individual traits and practices as obstacles to black political activity, as well as a repeated tendency to call for compensatory programs as the means of redressing social and political inequalities. For the most part, systemic barriers to the political empowerment of African-Americans are not considered. Indeed, in most instances the American political system is judged to be adequate as it stands, requiring only tinkering reforms to "incorporate" African-Americans and thereby establish racial harmony.

The two *Review* articles on African-American political beliefs (both by Aberbach and Walker in Appendix II) address very similar problems and fall squarely in the tradition of race relations politics. The unique distinction of these articles is their special pleading for governmental action and intervention to give African-Americans their rights (Aberbach and Walker 1970: 1218–19). Once again, these articles, like the others, justify government intervention in guaranteeing African-Americans their rights on the grounds that it is "the best hope of obtaining and enduring race peace and building political trust" between blacks and whites (Aberbach and Walker 1970: 1218).

Not surprisingly, the articles in the *Review* addressing the issue of segregation (by Stephenson)[6] and desegregation (by Gatlin et al., and Meier and England) looked much like their counterparts in the *Quarterly*. Segregation was described as a necessary condition of good race relations, and compliance with segregation laws was advocated as the best means of improving those relations. Similarly, the successful desegregation of schools was often made contingent on the acceptance and willing compliance of "public opinion" (read: white opinion); enforced compliance, by implication, would do little more than exacerbate racial disharmony. At root, these articles made white opinion and attitudes toward race issues – and black acceptance of that fact – the primary focus of analysis and the primary source of progressive change. The fact that white attitudes and opinions often supported violations of the fundamental rights and needs of African-Americans was beside the point. Indeed, the logic of this position could be carried to an extreme, as was evident in an article written in 1934 by David Walter on the proposed federal antilynching bill (see Appendix II). Walter concluded that even if such a law were passed there would be noncompliance in the South. He concluded by saying:

It remains to be seen whether the present demand for such legislation can overcome the constitutional doubts and the sectional prejudices of Congress sufficiently to permit the enactment of a federal anti-lynching law. If so, we may expect an early attempt to have the Supreme Court decide upon the constitutional issues so sharply raised. (Walter 1934: 442)

Since southern whites would not comply there was little need for such a law; federal enforcement of the law would only inflame race relations and blacks would be the losers. Perhaps Walter believed it would be better to allow a few blacks to have their fundamental right to life violated if the consequence of making lynching a federal offense would be more lynchings. We will not push the point too far, but such arguments do intimate the problematic character of the logic of black submission and dependence on white "opinion" that is characteristic of the race relations tradition.

Substantively, both the *Review* and the *Quarterly* provide numerous articles in the race relations tradition that extol the virtue of achieving racial harmony and goodwill. The difficulties we have with this tradition, however, have less to do with the intent than the meaning of and means by which "harmony" and "goodwill" are to be realized. Whether one privileges individual behavior as the source of harmony and inclusion, or whether one privileges the harmonious effects of discriminatory institutions, the tradition of race relations politics tends toward a support of the status quo, or worse, the status quo ante – both of which, in historical context, denied African-Americans their constitutional and political rights. To illustrate the point, one need only consider the history of the "Lynch Law" section of the *Quarterly*'s "Record of Political Events" (see Dunning 1890, and Editors 1927). For the better part of three decades, the *Quarterly* reported – without comment – lynching incidents. One can only speculate on the reasons the *Quarterly*'s editors believed that lynchings were significant "political events" or the reasons they thought it no longer necessary to report them when lynchings were still a significant part of the African-American life experience. From what we have argued thus far, such speculation on our part would not be charitable to the *Quarterly*'s editorial leadership, but perhaps the point can be made another way. While lynchings were being recorded in the pages of the *Quarterly*, there was little else being published that addressed the issue of race and racism, and that which was published was hardly conducive to the interests of African-Americans. And the fact that this remained a feature of disciplinary discourse for many decades is hardly cause for celebrating the virtues of academic political science.

But the tradition of race relations politics is not the only tradition of inquiry into race issues in the discipline of political science. And if the race relations tradition may make us pause in our judgments about the virtues of academic political science, the African-American politics tradition may give us some reason to be hopeful.

Certainly the most notable difference between the two traditions is expressed in attitudes toward the empowerment struggles of African-Americans. This difference was expressed most clearly in articles on black suffrage and political participation (see the various essays by

Weeks, Fox, Stanley, Kousser, Hamilton, Smith, and Robinson in Appendix I and the essays by Gosnell, Strong, Salmon and Van Evera, Kernell, and Bobo and Gilliam in Appendix II). Where works in the tradition of race relations politics tended to view obstacles to suffrage and participation as the result of "individual" problems, "socialization" deficiencies, or "natural" resistance by whites, writers in the African-American politics tradition tended to view these obstacles as entailing a failure of political authorities at every level of government to fulfill their constitutional responsibilities. And where writers in the race relations tradition might argue that the expansion of black suffrage and participatory rights would work *against* black political advancement, those in the African-American politics tradition would argue that advancement, participation, and suffrage are mutually constitutive; without progress in participation and suffrage, there can be no advancement, and any advancement without progress in participation and suffrage is, at best, superficial.

We feel it significant to point out that six of the eleven articles (about 55 percent) in the African-American research tradition published in the *Quarterly* were written by African-American political scientists.[7] There are several likely explanations of this phenomenon. First, these scholars were most certainly influenced by the premodern (1932–54) and modern (1955–70) civil rights movements. Smith and Robinson began their college education during the latter, while Hamilton was intimately involved in the movement to empower African-American voters in Tuskegee, Alabama (Norrell 1985). Lewis, on the other hand, wrote during the height of the premovement. Hence, all of the African-American scholars were educated during, involved in, or worked through significant periods of the struggle for black empowerment – a fact that is reflected in the substantive content of their published work.

The African-American politics tradition in the *Review* was launched by one of great scholars of "Negro politics," Harold Gosnell, who wrote the now classic work on the subject.[8] Gosnell, who was a pioneering behavioralist, developed interesting insights into the character of African-American political practices in his study of black political meetings (Gosnell 1934).

Following Gosnell's *Review* article on African-American political participation, it was some time before more work appeared that addressed the issue of African-American political empowerment in a positive manner. In the 1940s three articles on suffrage issues were published by two white scholars at southern universities. These works were anomalous in their time given their criticisms of the poll tax, white primaries, and the negative white public opinion and attitudes that fostered these voting barriers. Yet there was no follow-up to this work. It would be two more decades before similar works were to again be seen in the *Review*. As with the *Quarterly*, some of these later works (dealing with the subject of empowerment) would be penned by African-American political scientists. In both the *Review* and the *Quarterly* there were a total of eight articles written by African-Americans and all of them dealt with the question of empowerment.

Our discussion of the substantive differences between the race relations and African-American politics traditions raises many questions about the relationship between disciplinary development and wider social and political trends and changes. To make sense of these matters, it may be useful to consider the implications of our discussion thus far for understanding the changing character of disciplinary discourse on race.

V. How Race Has Shaped Academic Political Science

While it is beyond the scope of this essay to consider at length the ways in which academic political science has responded to and reflected changing norms and values outside the discipline, there are a number of themes in literature we examine that provide a good barometer of these broader developments and trends. Among these themes, there are six we find particularly illuminating.

First, perhaps one of the best indicators of the discipline's understanding of the meaning and importance of race issues can be found in the concerns and focus of the discipline's *leadership*; here, the extent to which disciplinary leaders identified race as a critical social and political issue may tell us much about the discipline's relation to broader social trends. A second useful theme is the *epistemological* status of claims made about race issues – whether practitioners understood race issues as critical to scientific knowledge or merely secondary or derivative from other more central "truths." A third theme attends the ways that key issues in race-oriented inquiry are *conceptualized* with respect to both the interests of the African-American community and the maintenance of existing relations of power and authority. Fourth, a careful examination of *methodological* assumptions also provides provocative insights inasmuch as these assumptions reflect particular orientations toward causality, and thus identifications of the origins and explanations of race differences. Fifth, *policy* implications, that is, what kinds of policy proposals and suggestions followed from the arguments advanced, tell us a great deal about how political scientists understood the magnitude and character of race concerns. And, finally, one can glean interesting insights by considering the theme of *system support*, that is, whether the needs and concerns of the wider system, or those of the African-American community, are addressed.

Leadership

Our primary interest in the issue of leadership turns on the extent to which the discipline's leaders urged the profession to consider questions of race. Unfortunately, when we examined the presidential addresses of the American Political Science Association (APSA) for their perspectives on the importance of race, we found that none of them urged association members to see race as an important area of scholarly research or to consider racial conditions and upheavals in society as major social or disciplinary concerns.[9] Indeed, as we indicated earlier, of the seventy-nine APSA presidential speeches we analyzed, only four – Rowe (1922: 6), Brooks (1941: 7), Schattschneider (1957: 942), and Friedrich (1963: 845, 846, 847) – even mention the word "Negro."

This failure by APSA presidents to address the racial issue, particularly in the post–World War II era, is somewhat surprising given the heightened attention given to matters of race in the larger society during this time. Even in those four rare cases where the word "Negro" was used, considerations of race were always raised in the context of another (larger) issue.[10] Only the Friedrich address makes more than a passing reference to the Negro. At four different points in his 1963 address entitled "Rights, Liberties, Freedoms: A Reappraisal," Friedrich uses specific examples of the deprivation of rights to the Negro.[11] These exceptions noted, there was almost no reflection on race issues in the presidential addresses over the better part of a century. And even the exceptions proved meager; we were unable to determine how these works might fit into either of our analytical categories.

Simply put, for much of the leadership of the discipline, race was simply a nonissue when considerations bearing on "the state of the discipline" were being discussed. This is all the more surprising considering the fact that at least several APSA presidents might have been on solid intellectual grounds in raising race to the level of discipline-wide concern. Ralph Bunche, the first African-American to hold the position of

APSA president, did not use his presidential address to question the discipline's neglect of race, when he had done so in other venues. And V. O. Key, whose seminal work *Southern Politics* made the "Negro problem" a central feature for understanding politics in the South, also avoided raising the issue of race in his address to the association's members (Key 1958).

In light of this, it is not unreasonable to ask what, exactly, Samuel P. Huntington had in mind when, in his 1987 presidential address, he claimed that "Political Scientists want to do good . . . want to promote broader social goals or public purpose. Prominent among them are the promotion of justice, well-being, order, equity, liberty, democracy, responsible government, security for individuals and states, accommodation among groups, peace among nations" (Huntington 1988: 3).[12] Although Huntington does not list (racial) equality, this concern might be subsumed under the promotion of justice, responsible government, and accommodation among groups. Yet the reality is that the issue of race and politics was all but omitted from these two influential journals, if not from the "major issues" of concern to the discipline as a whole.

It appears, however, that these oversights may now be partially corrected. In his 1993 APSA presidential address, Lucius Barker – the second African-American to serve as association president – called for practitioners to make racial discrimination and inequalities central to their work, and he encouraged political scientists to seek those systemic factors that contribute to the continued marginalization of black Americans (Barker 1994). This clearly marks a moment of leadership informed by the perspective of the African-American politics tradition, but it comes many many years after it could – and should – have.

Epistemology

A second thematic indicator of how race issues at both the wider social and disciplinary levels might be related concerns the ways in which knowledge claims pertaining to race should be understood. Samuel Cook writes:

Unconsciously no doubt, American political science, despite its heavy emphasis on empiricism, behavioralism, and realism, has not done justice to the harsh treatment of the black political experience. It has been guided by categories, perceptions, interpretations, and applications which have not reflected the unsavory facts surrounding the status of blacks within the political system. These frames of meaning are not in themselves racist; they are, rather, tacit and unwitting vehicles of racism because of the manner of conceptualization and application.

... The categories and presuppositions, generally speaking, contain built-in filters that automatically block off significant sectors of experience, selecting certain phenomena to the exclusion of others. They are self-feeding and self-perpetuating – paralleling and reinforcing the racist character of political life. (Cook 1971: xxiv–xxv)

Ultimately, as Cook demonstrates, the question of race and politics forced many in the discipline to the sidelines. Not only did the issue become one of the least studied areas of the field, but when it was studied, the knowledge claims usually advanced by many scholars in their research tended to recapitulate the kind of exclusionary "knowledge" characteristic of broader social understandings of race.

What is more, one finds that it is during periods of significant social unrest or significant legal or political developments that these claims are articulated with greater frequency. In the period between 1890 and 1901, when blacks were being systematically disenfranchised, disciplinary writing on race increased; in the 1940s, when the Supreme Court handed down major decisions on the constitutionality of "white primaries" there was another increase in articles on race; and the civil rights movement in the 1960s was also accompanied by an increase in the number of articles about race.

In the face of these developments, the tradition of race relations politics responded by advancing legal, legislative, and attitudinal solutions that required black capitulation to white opinion and action. In most instances, there was little concern shown for the breakdown of law and order perpetrated by whites or for the failure of government authorities to enforce the laws and legislation already on the books. Even if the discipline did not see African-Americans as worthy of moral consideration, certainly the failure of governments to enforce the law or even realize their own responsibilities under the law might have been worth disciplinary attention. But it was not, and in this failure the discipline simply recapitulated in its own research practices the repressive social and political practices of American society.

These practices and their presuppositions have of course been challenged by those writing from the African-American politics perspective. Rather than seeking to explain race issues from the perspective of concerns about containing discontent and "harmonizing" race relations, the knowledge sought is about the political initiatives and empowerment efforts of African-Americans – and for the purpose of understanding these practices on their own terms instead of in terms of how acceptable or unacceptable they might be to the white majority.

It should come as no surprise that these works become more frequent later than those in the race relations tradition and that they also tend to appear with greater frequency during or following periods of heightened racial tensions. This is in large part a function of the dominant epistemological outlook of the discipline on matters of race, but it is also a function of the ways in which race itself was conceptualized.

Conceptualization

A third thematic indicator of the link between disciplinary and broader social changes is the ways in which race questions are conceptualized. Historians of the discipline have noted how "editors were less successful in living up to their . . . [scientific] promise. Not all items were characterized by the objectives of outlook normally associated with the term 'scientific.' In fact, the authors' [and editors'] political biases are often unmistakable" (DuBois 1962: 731). Journal editors such as John W. Burgess and William A. Dunning subscribed to widely held views about the differences between the races. One of their contemporaries, W. E. DuBois, says, "These authors believe the Negro to be sub-human and congenitally unfitted for citizenship and the suffrage" (1962: 731).

In the same vein, William R. Shepherd wrote, "It was Burgess . . . who founded the *Political Science Quarterly*" [and] argued in his second political science treatise, *The Reconciliation of Government with Liberty*, that suffrage should be "limited to men of intelligence, character, and means, and eligibility to a seat in the legislative body . . . upon the same qualities" (Shepherd 1965: 31, 43). Such ideas and dogmas clearly had consequences for the ways in which the discipline would treat the question of race and politics.

The *Quarterly*, under the tutelage of editors Burgess and Dunning, published a large number of articles portraying slavery, segregation, and disenfranchisement as positive institutions. Indeed, articles on suffrage limitations never spoke of the Negro (see, e.g., Hart 1892). When Dunning moved on to become president of the APSA, while discussing "liberty and equality" in his presidential address, he never alludes to African-Americans (Dunning 1923).

Evidence of racial bias is not always as clear as it was in the Burgess and Dunning cases, but it can be discerned, in part, from editorial practices. By editorial practices we simply mean whether editors permitted articles on race and politics to appear during their tenure, and whether such articles reflect a preference for the race relations or African-American politics perspective. For example, what the *Review* published for two and one-half decades was largely the consequence of the long term (1925–49) of managing editor Frederic Ogg. Ogg held the job longer than anyone else and was forced to resign under fire and much criticism (Somit and Tanenhaus 1967: 94–7). Yet during Ogg's tenure, a new conceptualization of race was taking shape, and it was reflected in Gosnell's pioneering insights in 1934 as well as in O. Douglass Weeks's and Donald Strong's unprecedented 1948 work. What Ogg made possible by enabling the articulation of an African-American politics approach to race issues, other editors made impossible by conceptualizing race in ways that precluded or constrained its treatment.[13]

It would seem, then, that until relatively recently, editors might have exercised great influence in constraining or encouraging particular conceptualizations of race. In this respect, the discipline's approach to race has both reflected and developed somewhat autonomously from broader social norms. The evidence from recent decades suggests that editors may actually wield less authority in determining the conceptualizations of race that will be represented in the journals – at least if the growing parity between the dual traditions is any indication. Nor does it seem that methodology might serve to preclude some conceptualizations of race as it may have in the past.

Methodology

It now appears that methodology in and of itself does not define either of the two traditions we discuss. "Traditional" and "behavioral" political science techniques have been employed in both the race relations politics and African-American politics research traditions. When the discipline shifted from traditional methodological approaches to more behavioral ones, the emphasis changed from philosophical, legal, historical, and institutional approaches to the behavior of individual agents as the grounding of political-scientific explanation (Wasby 1970, ch. 1).

Behavioralism, with its adherence to "scientific method," took the most basic unit of analysis, the individual, and developed a set of testable hypotheses that could be replicated and verified by others. This would not be a particularly problematic mode of explanation were it not for the fact that behavioralism also assumed that the behavior of the individual was conditioned by forces quite independent of systemic configurations. Not only did this allow behavioral inquiry to be passed off as "value free," but in doing so it systematically closed off examination of systemic forces in shaping the life experiences of African-Americans. Thus, where the traditional approach, which had focused on systemic factors, tended to support segregation and marginalization because it identified existing structures of power as desirable and defensible, behavioralism avoided any analysis of the systemic and thus cloaked its adherents' refusal to consider the effects of institutions and practices on the lives of African-Americans, all the while calling their method "neutral" (Walton 1985: ch. 1).

Behavioralism had the most impact on the *Review* especially after 1950, and this methodological approach forced many scholars to exclude systemic variables or discount them in their modeling efforts. Hence, many of the *Review* articles, starting in 1957, fall in the tradition of race relations politics because of this methodological focus. Most of these works use a sample of whites for comparative purposes and emphasize the important role of white public opinion in proposals for racial peace and harmony.[14] More recent work, much done by African-American scholars, has demonstrated that the same methodological approach can be used to treat the question of empowerment instead of racial goodwill.

Similarly, with regard to the use of traditional methodologies, the critical issue here seems to be *which* systemic factors one identifies as critical. And in this – as in the use of behavioral approaches – the real key may be how one conceptualizes key issues and also how one interprets the evidence at hand; hence, the occasional African-American politics tradition article that uses "traditional" methods.

Policy

Shaping policy recommendations, or implicitly supporting policy that serves the needs of the existing sociopolitical system, is a fifth area in which disciplinary and broader social trends might be linked. Articles leaning toward race relations politics ultimately supported the changing status quo – from slavery, to segregation, and finally desegregation. Not only did few of these articles call for systemic reform on a massive scale, but with the sole exception of Aberbach and Walker, few authors saw any other way for African-Americans to eliminate subjugation and oppression. The essence of these works – like the essence of widespread sentiment about race issues – is that blacks are best served by supporting the system as it stands.

Works that are in or lean toward the African-American politics research tradition speak of systemic reform, modification, and change, rather than tending to shape findings and proposals to the needs of the existing sociopolitical system. These articles address the need for more resources and structural arrangements that will weaken or eliminate institutional and legal impediments to black empowerment. Claims of policy limitations, bureaucratic inertia, and misguided leadership are harshly criticized. Occasionally, the latter occurs in the perspective of race relations politics, but the call for major institutional change and reform is seldom heard. In the African-American politics tradition, policy proposals link society's problem with systemic imperfections.

System Support

The sixth area of influence was in what we call system support – essentially, whether the needs and concerns of the African-American community are addressed. In some instances, institutions like slavery, segregation, and suffrage restrictions were justified by using traditional methods that emphasized the importance of historical continuity in systemic structures. In other instances, articles employing a behavioral methodology apologized for these practices by shifting the focus away from systemic flaws to an individual focus. Behavioralists often located economic, social, and political problems in the African-American community at the *individual level* and explained them as the consequence of apathy, poor socialization, limited education, unstable political beliefs and values, and lack of a work ethic. Thus, in the final analysis, it is not the failure of the American political and economic system, but the failure of African-American individuals.

At the group level, behavioral explanations sometimes rooted the cause of racial inequalities in cultural attributes and values that led to slums, crime, neglected housing, and the like. Once again it is not the failure of the system but the failure of African-Americans as a group.[15] Either way, neither the American system or white Americans are responsible. Few articles voiced a viewpoint different from the status quo. The majority of the articles that do so have appeared in the last two decades.

Finally, works in the African-American politics tradition offer no support for systemic outputs, like slavery, segregation, suffrage restrictions, token desegregation, and continued forms of discrimination. Political, social, economic, and legal arrangements that continue to restrict people on the basis of color are criticized as unconstitutional and anti-democratic. Support for proposals that promise a more just and equitable system tends to be in the works of this tradition.

In summary, our analysis of six areas of the discipline where the impact of race might be manifested suggests a link between society's attitudes on race and the discipline's journal publications. The dominant theme reflected in disciplinary discourse on race issues has been the maintenance of racial goodwill while preserving the political status quo. Not surprisingly, this has also been a dominant theme in American society and politics. Yet within the discipline – as within American society and politics – an alternative mode of understanding exists, one in which the realization of justice and empowerment for African-Americans takes precedence over racial "harmony" and system preservation. As we hope to have suggested, the strength of these perspectives, their substantive content, and their changing fortunes over time are intimately linked to broader developments in American society. What, then, might we conclude from this?

VI. Conclusion: Race and the Future of Political Science

Viewing academic political science purely in terms of its own internal dynamic and history would be narrow and partial. The internal history of political science, at least when it comes to the issue of race, is equally tied to the development of the external history of race and politics in America. Both internal and external developments are necessary to write an adequate history in this important area.

Looking back over the discipline, as reflected in its two premier journals, knowledge of the African-American political experience is limited, and its treatment was inadequate in at least three ways, the first being in terms of the discipline's avowed commitment to the principles of political democracy. Either the discipline and its instruments are committed to a better and more adequate functioning of democracy, or it is committed to a form of democracy that is built on limitations and restrictions where race plays a role. Moreover, inherent in the very nature of America's political democracy is the idea of equality. Articles in the race relations perspective suggest that an entire group, if it is of another race, can have its equality parceled out and infringed, as the racial majority deems necessary. Equality is either given or denied. Tolerance of piecemeal equality is in part support for a restrictive and a circumscribed political democracy. This is not consistent with the broader vision of American society as set forth by the Founding Fathers.

Second, from the perspective of African-Americans who have and must today continue to carry the burden and the legacy of racism – the relative paucity of disciplinary work that lends support to the struggle against racism, and the overwhelming influence of work that lends support to the maintainence of racism – there is cause for great concern. The history of race inquiry in political science has been inadequate because it has for the most part reassured the government and its organs that delayed responses and inadequate delivery of services are acceptable, and that injustice is preferable to change. In light of the long history of abuse African-Americans have suffered, there is little in political science that has promised relief from that suffering.

This brings us, finally, to the third way that political science has failed to address adequately the issue of race in the United States. From its birth academic political science has been, by common proclamation, committed to the cause of human progress and freedom. To be sure, the meaning of these ideals is open to disagreement, but whatever standards one might use, it would be difficult to claim that academic political science has contributed to progress and freedom for *all* Americans. Either freedom has to be made available to all citizens, or it may lead to what Bertrand Russell called the "moral superiority of the oppressed" – a response to the unequal application of moral and political standards of the governing and ruling majority. Such a development would be undesirable, but perhaps also understandable in light of the experiences of African-Americans. And American academic political science has done little to help remedy the lack of progress and experience of unfreedom that has brought African-Americans too often to the brink of revolt.

What then might be the future direction of the discipline on issues of race? Consistent with our findings, we believe that external events affecting the configuration of power between the races in this country will significantly shape the direction in which political science will move on this issue. To be sure, we will probably continue to see both traditions of inquiry on race that have dominated the discipline's history thus far. In light of the recent developments that have once again made questions of race visibly important in American social and political life – developments like the backlash against affirmative action, the increasingly dire economic conditions of a sizeable segment of African-Americans, the outbreak of racial hate crimes, the implicit racist appeals in many electoral campaigns, the rise of Afrocentrism, and the breakdown of "civil order" in Los Angeles in 1992 – it remains to be seen whether political science will fall back on its legacy of race relations politics, or whether it will embrace the ideals of empowerment, equality, and justice that have been reflected in the work of those writing in the African-American politics tradition.

Appendix I

Articles in the race relations politics and African-American politics categories: *Political Science Quarterly (PSQ),* 1886–1990. (Total number of articles published by the journal during this period was 2,474.)

Race Relations Politics

Brooks, R. P. 1911. "A Local Study of the Race Problem." *PSQ* 26 (June): 193–221.

Bugbee, L. G. 1898a. "Slavery in Early Texas: Part I." *PSQ* 13 (September): 389–412.

1898b. "Slavery in Early Texas: Part II." *PSQ* 13 (December): 648–68.

Curtin, Phillip D. 1968. "Epidemiology and the Slave Trade." *PSQ* 83 (June): 190–216.

Fogelson, Robert M. 1967a. "From Resentment to Confrontation: The Police, the Negro and the Outbreak of the Nineteen-Sixties Riots." *PSQ* 82 (June): 217–47.

1967b. "White on Black: A Critique of the McCone Commission Report on the Los Angeles Riots." *PSQ* 82 (September): 337–67.

Langdon, William C. 1891. "The Case of the Negro." *PSQ* 6 (March): 29–42.

Leab, Daniel J. 1973. "The Gamut from A to B: The Image of Black in Pre-1915 Movies." *PSQ* 83 (March): 53–70.

McClendon, R. Earl. 1933 "The Amistad Claims: Inconsistences of Policy." *PSQ* 48 (September): 386–412.

Morris, Richard B. 1960. "The Course of Peonage in a Slave State." *PSQ* 65 (June): 238–63.

Phillips, U. B. 1905. "The Economic Cost of Slave-Holding." *PSQ* 20 (June): 257–75.

1907. "The Slave Labor Problem in the Charleston District." *PSQ* 22 (September): 415–39.

Rodgers, Harrell R., Jr. 1974–5. "The Supreme Court and School Desegregation: Twenty Years Later." *PSQ* 89 (Winter): 751–76.

Rossell, Christine H. 1975–6. "School Desegregation and White Flight." *PSQ* 90 (Winter): 675–96.

Sonenshein, Ralphael J. 1990. "Can Black Candidates Win Statewide Elections?" *PSQ* 105 (Summer): 219–42.

Weiss, Nancy T. 1969. "The Negro and the New Freedom: Fighting Wilsonian Segregation." *PSQ* 84 (March): 61–79.

African-American Politics

Fox, Dixon R. 1917. "The Negro Vote in Old New York." *PSQ* 32 (June): 252–75.

Hamilton, Charles V. 1977. "Voter Registration Drives and Turnout: A Report on the Harlem Electorate." *PSQ* 99 (Spring): 43–6.

1979. "The Patron–Recipient Relationship and Minority Politics in New York City." *PSQ* 93 (Summer): 211–28.

1986. "Social Policy and the Welfare of Black Americans: From Rights to Resources," *PSQ* (Centennial Year, 1886–1986): 239–56.

Kousser, Morgan J. 1973. "Post-Reconstruction Suffrage Restrictions in Tennessee: A New Look at the V. O. Key Thesis." *PSQ* 88 (December): 655–83.

Lewis, Edward E. 1933. "The Southern Negro and the American Labor Supply." *PSQ* 48 (June 1933): 172–83.

Robinson, Pearl T. 1982. "Whither the Future of Blacks in the Republican Party?" *PSQ* 96 (Summer): 207–32.

Smith, Robert C. 1981. "Black Power and the Transformation from Protest to Politics." *PSQ* 96 (Fall): 421–43.

Stanley, John L. 1969. "Majority Tyranny in Tocqueville's America: The Factors of Negro Suffrage in 1846." *PSQ* 84 (September): 412–35.

Tannenbaum, Frank. 1946. "The Destiny of the Negro in the Western Hemisphere." *PSQ* 61 (March): 1–41.

Weeks, S. B. 1894. "History of Negro Suffrage." *PSQ* 9 (December): 671–703.

Appendix II

Articles in the race relations politics and African-American politics categories: *American Political Science Review (APSR)*, 1906–90. (Total number of articles published by the journal during this period was 3,683.)

Race Relations Politics

Aberbach, Joel D., and Jack L. Walker. 1970a. "The Meaning of Black Power: A Comparison of White and Black Interpretations of a Political Slogan." *APSR* 64 (June): 367–88.

1970b. "Political Trust and Racial Ideology." *APSR* 64 (December): 1199–1219.

Eisinger, Peter K. 1974. "Racial Differences in Protest Participation." *APSR* 68 (June): 592–606.

Fenton, John H., and Kenneth N. Vines. 1957. "Negro Registration in Louisiana." *APSR* 51 (September): 704–13.

Gatlin, Douglas S., Michael Giles, and Everett R. Cataldo. 1978. "Policy Support within a Target Group: The Case of School Desegregation." *APSR* 72 (September): 985–94.

Lieske, Joel A. 1978. "The Conditions of Racial Violence in American Cities: A Developmental Synthesis." *APSR* 72 (December): 1324–40.

Matthews, Donald R., and James W. Prothro. 1963a. "Social and Economic Factors and Negro Voter Registration in the South." *APSR* 57 (March): 24–44.

1963b. "Social and Economic Factors and Negro Voter Registration in the South." *APSR* 57 (June): 355–67.

Meier, Kenneth J., and Robert E. England. 1984. "Black Representation and Educational Policy: Are They Related?" *APSR* 78 (June): 392–403.

Midlarsky, Manus I. 1978. "Analyzing Diffusion and Contagion Effects: The Urban Disorder of the 1960s." *APSR* 72 (September): 996–1008.

Miller, Abraham H., Louis H. Bolce, and Mark Hallingan. 1977. "The J-Curve Theory and the Black Urban Riots: An Empirical Test of Progressive Relative Deprivation Theory." *APSR* 71 (September): 964–82.

Orbell, John M. 1967. "Protest Participation among Southern Negro College Students." *APSR* 61 (June): 436–46.

Rose, John R. 1906. "Negro Suffrage: The Constitutional Point of View." *APSR* 1 (November): 17–43.

Shingles, Richard D. 1981. "Black-Consciousness and Political Participation: The Missing Link." *APSR* 75 (March): 76–92.

Stephenson, Gilbert T. 1906. "Racial Distinctions in Southern Law." *APSR* 1 (November): 44–61.

1909. "The Separation of the Races in Public Conveyances." *APSR* 3 (May): 100–204.

Walter, David O. 1934. "Proposals for a Federal Anti-Lynching Law." *APSR* 28 (June): 436–42.

African-American Politics

Allen, Richard L., Michael C. Dawson, and Ronald E. Brown. 1989. "A Schema-based Approach to Modeling an African-American Racial Belief-System." *APSR* 83 (June): 420–42.

Bobo, Lawrence, and Franklin D. Gilliam Jr. 1990. "Race, Socio-Political Participation, and Black Empowerment." *APSR* 84 (June): 377–94.

172   *H. Walton Jr., C. M. Miller, J. P. McCormick II*

Eisinger, Peter K. 1982. "Black Employment in Municipal Jobs: The Impact of Black Political Power." *APSR* 76 (June): 380–92.

Gosnell, Harold F. 1934. "Political Meetings in the Chicago's Black Belt." *APSR* 28 (April): 254–58.

Kernell, Sam. 1973. "Comment: A Re-evaluation of Black Voting in Mississippi." *APSR* 67 (December): 1307–18.

Salamon, Lester M., and Stephen Van Evera. 1973a. "Fear, Apathy, and Discrimination: A Test of Three Explanations of Political Participation." *APSR* 67 (December): 1288–1306.

1973B. "Revisited: Rejoinder to 'Comments' by Sam Kernell." *APSR* 67 (December): 1319–26.

Strong, Donald. 1944. "The Poll Tax: The Case of Texas." *APSR* 38 (August): 693–709.

1948. "The Rise of Negro Voting in Texas." *APSR* 42 (June): 510–22.

Weeks, O. Douglass. 1948. "The White Primary: 1944–1948." *APSR* 42 (June): 500–9.

Notes

1. For an overview of recent discussions about the implications of disciplinary history, see Dryzek and Leonard (1988), Dryzek (1986), Farr (1988a,b), and Farr et al. (1990).

2. As late as August 1993, the Committee on the Status of Blacks in the profession filed a protest with the editor of the APSR requesting more African-Americans on the editorial board and more articles in the journal dealing with race and politics.

3. Although we cannot prove this to be the case in the context of this work, we believe that our analytical framework would readily accommodate the interpretation of additional materials besides those that we draw upon. By narrowing the range of materials we consider, our only intention is to keep this project manageable by focusing on those sources that seem most promising indicators of broader disciplinary attitudes.

4. A good example of this sort of thinking may be found in the social Darwinist thought of one of the most prominent founding fathers of the discipline, John W. Burgess. As Richard Hofstadter notes, "What [James K.] Hosmer did for Anglo-Saxon history, John W. Burgess did for political theory (political science). His *Political Science and Comparative Constitutional Law*, published in the same year as Hosmer's book," applied the concept of social Darwinism to political science and jurisprudence. It was Burgess's contention that political capacity is not a gift common to all nations, but limited to a few. The highest capacity for political organization, he believed had been shown, in unequal degrees, by the Aryan nations. Of all these, only "the

Teuton really dominates the world by his superior political genius" (Hofstadter 1969: 174–5).

5. For an overview of how race relations courses became institutionalized in the 1920s, first at white universities and later at black colleges, see Walton (1968).

6. Gilbert Stephenson wrote two articles and later put them into book form. See Stephenson (1969).

7. The black authors are Smith, Hamilton, Robinson, and Lewis. Hamilton authored three articles solely.

8. Gosnell's name appears in a ranking of the great men in the profession. See Somit and Tanenhaus (1967: 66).

9. Interestingly, Ralph Bunche, president of the APSA in 1953, the first African-American to hold this position, did not address the issue of race in his address. As will be seen, Bunche is not one of the four APSA presidents who even mentioned the word "Negro" in their presidential addresses.

10. The illustrative quotes where the word "Negro" was mentioned in the presidential addresses are (1) ". . . much in the same way and by the same slow and difficult process through which increasing numbers of negro tenants in our southern states are being transformed into land proprietors" (Rowe 1922: 6). (2) "Abolition of the privilege of slavery cost us a devastating civil war. But the Negro problem survived abolition, bringing forth the black disgrace of lynching which fortunately, now seems to be disappearing" (Brooks 1941: 7). (3) "We see its significance today in the migrations of the American Negro which have nationalized the question of race relations" (Schattschneider 1957: 942).

11. One of the four references (and the strongest in tone) is as follows: "The power resources of those Negroes who wished to insist upon their rights were not sufficiently developed to secure their enforcement. Recently, their organizations have been gaining sufficient strength to assert their right to vote as well as other rights with increasing determination" (Friedrich 1963: 847).

12. We should note that in the same 1987 address, Huntington mentions the term "black." However, Huntington's reference is to black South African political scientists. The quote is: "Political scientists – white political scientists have been in the vanguard of those working for the end of apartheid. . . . What has been most dramatically and tragically missing from the debate have been the voices of black political scientists. . . . Recognizing this need, . . . the council of our association advanced a proposal . . . to bring nonwhite South Africans to U.S. universities for graduate work in political science" (Huntington 1988: 6).

13. Our knowledge of the scholarship in the APSR during Ogg's twenty-four year tenure as editor has been greatly enhanced by a reading of Harold Zink (1950).

14. For a useful discussion on the problem of small subsamples of nonwhite respondents in national surveys, see Robert B. Hill (1984).
15. For an excellent statement of these theses, see Edward Banfield (1970) and Edward Banfield and James Q. Wilson (1963) particularly ch. 20, entitled "Negroes." For a critique of these untenable positions, see Hanes Walton Jr. et al. (1992).

7

Realism and the Academic Study of International Relations

Jack Donnelly

The tradition of political realism (*Realpolitik*, power politics) has a long history, going back at least to Machiavelli (Carr 1946: 63–4; Meinecke 1957) or Thucydides (Morgenthau 1946: 42; Gilpin 1986: 304; Ferguson and Mansbach 1988: 35, 82). This chapter explores realism as a style of analysis in the academic study of international relations in the United States (and, to a lesser extent, Great Britain).[1]

Self-identified realists such as E. H. Carr and Hans Morgenthau played central roles in establishing international relations as an academic discipline. Prominent scholar-practitioners, such as George Kennan and Henry Kissinger, have called themselves realists. And for most of the postwar era, realism has been the dominant paradigm in the Anglo-American study of international relations. In fact, tracing the fate of realism provides a partial yet still useful survey of the development of the field of international relations.

I. The Realist Tradition

Although there is considerable diversity to positions that are typically labeled realist,[2] three premises are widely shared. First, realists share a distinctive view of human nature. "Human nature has not changed since the days of classical antiquity" (Thompson 1985: 17). And that constant human nature is at its core egoistic, and thus inalterably inclined toward immorality. As Machiavelli put it, in politics "it must needs be taken for granted that all men are wicked and that they will always give vent to the malignity that is in their minds when opportunity offers" (*Discourses* I.3). Some realists, such as Reinhold Niebuhr (1944: 19) and

Morgenthau (1946: 202), see Machiavelli's claim as largely descriptive. Many, like Machiavelli himself, contend only that there are enough egoists to make any other assumption unduly risky. All, however, emphasize the egoistic passions and self-interest in (international) politics. "It is above all important not to make greater demands on human nature than its frailty can satisfy" (Treitschke 1916: 590).

Second, realism stresses the political necessities that flow from the anarchic structure of international relations.[3] Because of the absence of international government, "the law of the jungle still prevails" in international relations (Schuman 1941: 9). "The difference between civilization and barbarism is a revelation of what is essentially the same human nature when it works under different conditions" (Butterfield 1950: 31; cf. Schuman 1941: 9; Spykman 1942: 141). Within states, human nature usually is tamed by a hierarchical political structure of authority and rule. In international relations, anarchy allows the worst aspects of human nature to be expressed.

Third, the interaction of egoism and anarchy implies "the primacy in all political life of power and security" (Gilpin 1986: 305; cf. Schwarzenberger 1951: 17). Realism "is determined by an insight into the overpowering impact of the security factor" (Herz 1976: 74; cf. Schuman 1941: 7, 261; Spykman 1942: 41). "The struggle for power is universal in time and space" (Morgenthau 1948: 16). In the modern era, though, power politics is played out principally among sovereign states. International relations thus is largely a matter of the pursuit of the national interest, defined in terms of power (Morgenthau 1954: 5).

Realists differ in the relative emphasis they give to egoism and anarchy. Morgenthau, for example, stressed human nature: "Social forces are the product of human nature in action"; "The social world [is] but a projection of human nature onto the collective plane"; political problems are "projections of human nature into society" (1948: 4; 1962a: 7, 312). Others have emphasized the structure of anarchy. For example, John Herz argued that international anarchy assures the centrality of the struggle for power "even in the absence of aggressivity or similar factors" (Herz 1976: 10; cf. Waltz 1979: 62–3).

In addition, interpretations of all three core propositions vary:

International society is . . . a society without central authority to preserve law and order, and without an official agency to protect its members in the enjoyment of their rights. The result is that individual states must make the preservation and improvement of their power position a primary objective of their foreign policy. (Spykman 1942: 7)

In international society all forms of coercion are permissible, including wars of destruction. This means that the struggle for power is identical with the struggle for survival, and the improvement of their relative power position becomes the primary objective of the internal and the external policy of states. All else is secondary. (Spykman 1942: 18)

Although hardly ten pages apart in the same work, these passages reflect very different understandings of the priority of power and security. The first is modest and beyond dispute: The pursuit of power must be *a* primary objective of any state. The second advances the radical position that power and security must be *the* primary objective of *both* the internal and the external policy of *any* state.

One occasionally encounters a consistent "radical" realist, who adopts extreme versions of all three assumptions. The Athenian envoys at Melos in Thucydides' *History* advanced such a position. It is often attributed to Machiavelli. Most realists, however, adopt only relatively strong or relatively hedged versions of the theory. As Carr put it, "The impossibility of being a consistent and thorough-going realist is one of the most certain and most curious lessons of political science" (Carr 1946: 89).

"Strong" realists, such as Morgenthau and Kenneth Waltz, adopt the three core realist premises in a way that allows only modest space for politically salient "nonrealist" concerns. They also tend to present realism as a positive theory of (international) politics or statesmanship. "Hedged" realists adopt a realist definition of the "problem" of international politics – anarchy and egoism – but show varying degrees of discomfort with the realist "solution" of a politics of interest, power, and security alone. Robert Gilpin's recent defense of the realist tradition (1986) probably falls on the border between strong and hedged realism. Robert Keohane's *After Hegemony* (1984) begins with a heavily hedged realist argument that, by its conclusion, in my reading at least, is no longer realist.

Despite this variability, there is general agreement, among both realists and their critics, on the basic character and confines of the tradition. "Their intellectual style is unmistakable" and their analysis has "a quite distinct and recognizable flavor" (Garnett 1984: 29, 110; cf. Cusack and Stoll 1990: 19).

II. From Idealism to Realism: The Emergence and Transformation of International Relations

International relations has been studied by historians at least since Thucydides. By the mid-nineteenth century, diplomatic history was a well-established specialty. Lawyers have dealt professionally with international relations at least since Grotius. By the later nineteenth century, international law was a thriving discipline. The study of diplomacy was even part of the original mandate of the American Political Science Association (See Willoughby 1904). But international relations as a distinct discipline or subfield emerged only in the aftermath, and in reaction to the carnage, of World War I. Ekkehart Krippendorff exaggerated only slightly in arguing that "the discipline was born as a side product of the Versailles Peace Conference in 1919" (Krippenforff 1989: 34; cf. Olson and Onuf 1985: 11–13).

The first academic chair in international relations was the Woodrow Wilson Professorship established in 1919 at the University College of Wales at Aberystwyth. Its patron, Lord David Davies, a prominent industrialist, politician, and international reformer, hoped to turn Aberystwyth into "a Mecca of International Reformers." The mandate of the chair even included furthering the work of the newly created League of Nations (Porter 1972: app. 1). The Montague Burton Professors of International Relations, established in London in 1923 and Oxford in 1930, also were intended to promote the study of world government. In the United States, the explicitly pacifist Carnegie Endowment of International Peace (founded in 1910) played an important role in the emergence and development of the discipline, and liberal internationalist reformers, such as James T. Shotwell and Pitmann Potter, dominated the field. For example, eighteen of twenty-four American academic specialists in international relations with the rank of professor in 1930 concentrated on international law and organization (Thompson 1952: 438).

Realists often caricature the views of this first generation of professional students of international relations, beginning with the dismissive label "idealism." It is fair to say, though, that these (more neutrally labeled) liberal internationalists stressed the capacity of reason and international institutions to ameliorate, perhaps even eliminate, international conflict (Smith 1992). The interwar generation, galvanized by the failure of balance-of-power diplomacy to prevent war, was committed to using human reason and organizational ingenuity to replace the old order of national interests with a new order of common interests. As C. K. Webster put it in his inaugural lecture at Aberystwyth in 1922, the war "has so sapped the foundations of international order, and changed so remorselessly our conception of International Relations, that a recasting of our ideas [is] necessary" (quoted in Gelber 1982).

Even those who produced rigorous scholarly work of enduring value – for example, Alfred Zimmern, the first occupant of the Aberystwyth Chair and the holder of the Oxford Chair in the 1930s, whose *The League of Nations and the Rule of Law* (1936) is still worth reading – saw international relations as a distinctly practical field of study. "International Relations started life . . . prescriptive, normative and based on a conception of scholarly activity that stressed the immediate policy relevance of work" (Smith 1989: 7). As William T. R. Fox put it in a critical postwar essay, "The analytical model used for investigative purposes was a world commonwealth characterized by permanent peace. The real world was described in terms of deviation from this model" (Fox 1949: 77).

Consider, for example, Frank M. Russell's *Theories of International Relations* (1936), a mainstream text that reflected dominant modes of thought. There was no index entry for power, let alone realism (power politics), and only one passing seventeenth-century reference to raison d'état. Balance of power was discussed only historically. Not only was there no hint that it might have contemporary relevance; there was a very strong suggestion to the contrary. Meanwhile, full chapters were devoted to the League and to outlawing war.

The new field of international relations was so completely dominated by liberal internationalists that when the international crises of the 1930s discredited "idealism," there was no mainstream alternative to fill the void. Frederick Schuman's *International Politics*, arguably the first academic realist international relations text, had appeared in 1933. Schuman, however, was only a junior faculty member at Chicago, where the international relations program was dominated by the eclectic but decidedly nonrealist Quincy Wright. Nicholas Spykman was a full professor, but his major work did not appear until 1942. Niebuhr, although prominent, touched on international relations only in passing and had no discernible impact on the field before World War II.[4] Morgenthau spent the early and middle 1930s in Europe studying, practicing, and teaching international and administrative law. Carr remained in the British diplomatic service until 1936. And Georg Schwarzenberger in 1937 was, of all things, working as a research assistant for Lord Davies's New Commonwealth Institute, studying reform of the League.

Even obsolete theories, however, tend to persist until replaced by others. The final demise of interwar liberal internationalism thus had to await someone to deliver a fatal blow – or perhaps just an unceremonious push that would send the spent corpse tumbling into the grave. E. H.

Carr was the man who did the job. Upon taking up the Woodrow Wilson Chair in 1936,[5] Carr redesigned the curriculum, replacing the previous focus on the League with an emphasis on power and history. And in 1939 Carr published *The Twenty Years' Crisis*, perhaps the most enduring realist work of the century.

Liberal internationalist proposals for reform continued to appear, along with an occasional "idealist" work of scholarship of enduring importance (most notably David Mitrany's *A Working Peace System*, [1943] 1966). *The Twenty Years' Crisis*, however, marks the beginning of two decades of realist hegemony in the study of international relations. It was "the death knell for all those writers who had focused their attention on the world as it ought to be rather than as it was" (John, Wright, and Garnett 1972: 96).

The other major figure in the rise of realism was Hans Morgenthau, "the purest as well as the most self-conscious apostle of realism" (Parkinson 1977: 163). "Morgenthau's work was the single most important vehicle for establishing the dominance of the realist paradigm in the field" (Vasquez 1983: 17). His first major work, *Scientific Man versus Power Politics* (1946), was an all-out attack on progressive reformism in its scientific, moralistic, and totalitarian forms. In 1948, Morgenthau's *Politics among Nations: The Struggle for Power and Peace* provided the movement with a textbook.

A steady stream of major realist works followed. The year 1951 was particularly notable, witnessing the publication of the second edition of Schwarzenberger's *Power Politics*, George Kennan's *American Diplomacy*, Morgenthau's *In Defense of the National Interest*, and Herz's *Political Realism and Political Idealism*. As Grayson Kirk, an unreconstructed liberal internationalist, lamented, "Just now, the current fad . . . is to belabor what is called 'Wilsonianism' with all the sarcasm and dignified invective at the writer's disposal" (Kirk 1952: 110).

The new first chapter of the second (1954) edition of Morgenthau's *Politics among Nations*, which conveniently listed the "six principles" of realism, was particularly important in codifying the academic dominance of realism. These principles summarized a simple yet wideranging philosophical, theoretical, and political worldview, which Morgenthau presented in sharp, vigorous, accessible prose:

1. Political realism believes that politics, like society in general, is governed by objective laws that have their roots in human nature. (Morgenthau 1954: 4)

2. The main signpost that helps political realism to find its way through the landscape of international politics is the concept of interest defined in terms of power. (1954: 5)
3. Power and interest are variable in content over space and time. (1954: 8–9)
4. Realism maintains that universal moral principles cannot be applied to the actions of states. (1954: 9)
5. Political realism refuses to identify the moral aspirations of a particular nation with the moral laws that govern the universe. (1954: 10)
6. The difference, then, between political realism and other schools of thought is real and it is profound. . . . Intellectually, the political realist maintains the autonomy of the political sphere. (1954: 10)

By the mid-1950s, realism dominated the academic study of international relations as thoroughly as liberal internationalism had dominated the field in the early interwar years. In 1961, Fox and Fox could plausibly argue that "within the group of international relations and political science scholars, genuine anti-realists are hard to find" (Fox and Fox 1961: 343; cf. Ferguson and Mansbach 1988: 97). International relations had been in effect refounded. So thorough was the change that the section entitled "The Earlier Textbooks and International Theory" in James Dougherty and Robert Pfaltzgraff's *Contending Theories of International Relations* (1981: 10), the standard introductory survey in the field, is devoted entirely to the work of Morgenthau's generation.

III. Realism Triumphant

This first wave of realist writing initiated what is often called the "first great debate" in international relations – although in fact is was largely a one-sided realist attack on "idealism." Those who came to their intellectual maturity during, and in reaction to, "idealist" hegemony understandably saw sweeping away the old errors as their first order of business. For example, Carr wrote "with the deliberate aim of counteracting the glaring and dangerous defect of nearly all thinking, both academic and popular, about international politics in English-speaking countries from 1919 to 1939 – the almost total neglect of the factor of power" (Carr 1946: vii). Schwarzenberger likewise stressed that "it was necessary to be on guard against naive day-dreaming on international relations" (Schwarzenberger 1951: xv).

Liberal internationalism's emphasis on reason and managed reform helps to explain the realist (counter)emphasis, even overemphasis, on constraints, on what could *not* be done in international relations. Although I defined realism as a set of positive theoretical propositions, their negative corollaries – especially the inappropriateness of moralism, legalism, rationalism, and institutionalism – were at least as central to the early academic realists. "The realists made their reputation exposing false gods and . . . false prophets" (Rosenthal 1991: 32). In particular, they emphasized the (alleged) fact that "universal moral principles cannot be applied to the actions of states" (Morgenthau 1954: 9; cf. Schwarzenberger 1951: 231; Kennan 1954: 48).

Even Morgenthau, however, recognized that this leads to implausible, even monstrous, results. For example, he noted "the curious dialectic of ethics and politics, which prevents the latter, in spite of itself, from escaping the former's judgment and normative direction" (Morgenthau 1946: 177; cf. 1948: 177). "Morality is not just another branch of human activity, coordinate to the substantive branches, such as politics or economics. Quite the contrary, it is superimposed upon them, limiting the choice of ends and means and delineating the legitimate sphere of a particular action" (Morgenthau 1962a: 326). He even argued that "a man who was nothing but 'political man' would be a beast" (Morgenthau 1954: 12). Nonetheless, Morgenthau insisted that statesmen are obliged to act solely on the basis of such beastly political standards and to ignore the judgments and directions offered by morality. "The autonomy of the political sphere must be protected from the encroachments of other spheres of action" (1962a: 359).

The negative, reactive character of postwar realism also helps to explain its ambivalence on the role of reason in politics. For example, Morgenthau argued that "reality is dominated by forces which are indifferent, if not actively hostile, to the commands of reason" (Morgenthau 1946: 172). Reason itself, "far from following its own inherent impulses, is driven toward its goals by the irrational forces the ends of which it serves" (1946: 154). The target in such passages clearly is idealist rationalism. But Morgenthau also argued that "political realism considers a rational foreign policy to be a good foreign policy" (1954: 7). And a foreign policy of the national interest, which Morgenthau advocated with single-minded passion, rests on the exclusion of all but instrumental reason from international relations – which he admitted was impossible.

Like most triumphant new thinking, realism achieved its dominant position not simply because its message was better than the old one, but also because that message better fit the times. Much as liberal internationalists blamed power politics for World War I, realists blamed World

War II on insufficient attention to power. "The straits in which the Western democracies found themselves at the beginning of World War II were, in good measure, the result of the reliance upon the inner force of legal pronouncements . . . legal agreements . . . [and] international organizations" (Morgenthau 1964: 105). "Instead of setting ourselves up as judges over the morality of others, we would have done better to search for a stable balance of power" (Kennan 1984: 159). The interwar period reflected

the sort of peace you got when you . . . indulged yourself in the colossal conceit of thinking that you could suddenly make international life over into what you believed to be your own image; when you dismissed the past with contempt, rejected the relevance of the past to the future, and refused to occupy yourself with the real problems that the study of the past would suggest. (Kennan 1951: 61–2)

No less than their liberal internationalist predecessors, the postwar realists were obsessed with preventing the preceding world war. In particular, they stressed the importance of a realistic power politics to the mission of preserving "democracy" while avoiding a third world war. Robert Strausz-Hupé and Stefan T. Possony offered a particularly colorful expression of this perspective:

It should have been clear after the thirty years' war between democracy and dictatorship that the cause of freedom cannot be defended successfully by sandwiches and candles. Sandwiches – a higher standard of living and more rapid economic progress than that offered by dictatorship – are necessary. Candles – the ideals of humanism, freedom, and reason – are indispensable. But something else is required: strength, and the foresight, the resolution, and the skill to use that strength.

It is the contention of this book that Democracy will win out over Dictatorship, *provided* Democracy develops an imaginative strategy of freedom that employs skillfully three potent weapons: sandwiches, candles, and military power.

Democrats of all nations rally, unite, and advance! You have nothing to lose but your Freedom!

You have the happiness of your children and the future of mankind to win. (Strauss-Hupé and Possony 1950: viii)

The crude rhetoric should not obscure how effectively the message suited the times, especially in the United States.[6]

Prior to World War II, the only rival to idealism as a coherent American diplomatic tradition was isolationism. The combination of the war and the Cold War, however, discredited isolationism nearly as thoroughly as idealism. Former isolationists and idealists alike thus faced the problem of organizing and managing American hegemony without the guidance of a viable indigenous diplomatic tradition. Realism seemed to fill the void. "For an American audience in need of a crash course in statecraft, it seemed to offer a convenient crib of European diplomatic wisdom, the more convincing on campus because it was expounded, as often as not, in a thick German accent" (Bull 1972: 39). "Hans Morgenthau, a refugee from the Old World, brought its knowledge and experience to the New" (Rosecrance 1981: 749).

Both idealism and isolationism had been radically suspicious of power. Realists in effect assured lingering idealists that they had the rules and the wisdom to achieve (at least some of) the good, without becoming corrupted by the exercise of power. Morgenthau even spoke of "the moral dignity of the national interest" (Morgenthau 1951: 33–9). At the same time, Americans with lingering isolationist fears of "entangling alliances" were reassured that the balance of power, properly understood and operated, would allow the United States to play a central international role without corrupting its distinctive national character or interests.

We should be careful, however, of reductionism. Realism was nearly as dominant in Britain, whose power had been dramatically reduced by the war. Furthermore, American realists did not always preach what the American public and American politicians wanted to hear. In particular, Morgenthau and Kennan constantly stressed the danger of an ideological foreign policy. They were as critical of postwar anticommunism as they were of Wilsonian internationalism and McKinley's missionary imperialism. In fact, Morgenthau, Niebuhr, and Kennan, as often as not, were strong critics of actual American foreign policy, especially after the late 1950s.

Thus, I reject Steve Smith's argument that the American foreign policy agenda "closely mirrored the theoretical agenda of Realism" (Smith 1989: 11). Consider, for example, the purge of realists such as Kennan and their replacement by ideological cold warriors. In fact, the fourth and fifth of Morgenthau's six principles of realism were essentially critiques of the dominant ideological understanding of the Cold War. We must distinguish the appropriation of the language of power politics, which clearly did take place, from the adoption of a realist theory of power politics, which in my view simply did not penetrate very deeply into American foreign policy.

Robert Rothstein was somewhat closer to the mark when he argued that "the ease and pervasiveness of its [realism's] dominance in the post–World War II years owes a great deal to the fact that it always seemed 'natural' and 'right' to practitioners" (Rothstein 1972: 348). But there is huge gulf between being attracted to particular (realist) arguments (especially those that emphasized power, contingency, and the special wisdom and responsibilities of policy makers) and adopting realism as a theory or guiding perspective. Postwar American foreign policy, rather than being driven by – or even generally consistent with – realism, selectively appropriated realist arguments, largely out of context, on behalf of an ideological, anticommunist strategy.[7]

The relationship between academic realists and foreign policy decision makers (as well as the general public) in the United States was profoundly ambivalent. "At a time when the American discussion of international relations was heavily ideological, it [realism] appeared to provide a sharp instrument of criticism; when America looked for guidance as to how to conduct herself, it provided a sense of direction" (Bull 1972: 38). The postwar realists had an unusually easy and rapid academic success. They received access to the corridors of power. But they ultimately failed to get their message accepted. The strains and frustrations that must have resulted – especially if, like Morgenthau, one believed that one possessed perennial truths that could make a savage world much safer and more humane – are essential to understanding their work, especially its excesses.

Joel Rosenthal aptly titled his social history of this first generation of postwar American realists *Righteous Realists*. Although consistently opposed to the (self-)righteousness of rationalistic and moralistic reformers and critics, Morgenthau, Niebuhr, and virtually this entire generation of realists were as prescriptive as the interwar "idealists." "The realists, who warned against self-righteousness, obsessive moralizing, and false prophets, became prophets themselves. The message was delivered as a jeremiad . . . a political sermon filled with social criticism" (Rosenthal 1991: 34). For example, Morgenthau's essays bore titles like "The Subversion of Foreign Policy" (Morgenthau 1962a), "The Decline and Fall of American Foreign Policy," and "What is Wrong with Our Foreign Policy" (1962b). Again, Strausz-Hupé and Possony captured the spirit particularly well. "The main intellectual task before the American people is to develop a new sense of reality in order to walk upright upon its path through a world of decaying cultures and crumbling empires, which, in its entirety, is being rent asunder by revolution" (1950: 722; cf. Morgenthau 1951: 239–42).

This righteousness was largely lacking in Britain. Part of the explanation certainly was Britain's reduced circumstances. No less important, though, were the stronger roots of the idealist tradition in the United States, which increased both the need for (counter)polemics and the attractiveness of grand self-righteous schemes. The greater role of the public in American foreign policy also encouraged rhetorical excess and inflated expectations. In Britain, by contrast, the deeper roots of a balance of power perspective and the traditionally closer relationship between academics and policy makers eased the implementation of a realist perspective and reduced the need for impassioned appeals. Differences in national character and academic style also probably were important. Nevertheless, in Britain no less than in the United States, realism dominated the academic study of international relations in the decade following the end of World War II.

IV. Realism Reconsidered

In the 1950s and 1960s, however, increasingly critical scrutiny revealed that often there was much less to realism than first met the eye:

The laws of international politics to which some "realists" appealed in such a knowing way appeared on closer examination to rest on tautologies or shifting definitions of terms. The massive investigation of historical cases implied in the Delphic pronouncements about the experience of the past had not always, it seemed, actually been carried out. The extravagant claims made by some of them turned out to rest on assumed authority rather than on evidence or rigorous argument. Indeed, not even the best of the "realist" writings can be said to have achieved a high standard of theoretical refinement: they were powerful polemical essays. (Bull 1972: 39)

Attack centered on two key concepts, the national interest and the balance of power, which Morgenthau argued rested on "iron laws of international politics. . . . general laws of international politics applicable to all nations at all times" (Morgenthau 1951: 144, 147).

Morgenthau's argument that states "act as they must, in view of their interests as they see them" (1962a: 278), reflected not an uninteresting tautology but an extravagant theoretical claim. "We assume that statesmen think and act in terms of interest defined as power, and the evidence of history bears that assumption out" (1954: 5). It is one of the "eternal truths of foreign policy" that "there is no other standard of action and of judgment, moral and intellectual, to which a great nation can repair, than the national interest" (1952: 3, 7).

Even a sympathetic critic such as Robert W. Tucker (who in the 1960s emerged as a major realist voice) saw Morgenthau's work as riddled with "open contradictions, ambiguity, and vagueness" (Tucker 1952: 214). "If the national interest is analogous in nature to gravity [Morgenthau 1951: 33], then what is the reason for the repeated failure of statesmen to see what is self-evident?" (Tucker 1952: 216). If statesmen act according to the national interest defined in terms of power, then they should not need to be exhorted to do so, and there should be nothing for Morgenthau the policy analyst to criticize.

Tucker also aptly criticized Morgenthau's lingering liberal progressivist bias – which I would suggest was extremely important to his favorable reception in the United States. "There is, of course, some mystery as to how the national interest can have a 'moral dignity' if international politics is simply a struggle of power against power" (Tucker 1952: 221). As Tucker noted, Morgenthau's restriction of the substance of the national interest to self-preservation, rather than imperial expansion, was logically inconsistent (1952: 221n17). So was Morgenthau's underlying pluralist tolerance. "The logical consequence of asserting the moral supremacy of the national interest is to assert the moral inferiority of all other national interests. . . . Equality of moral status can be conceived only by asserting the existence of a moral order superior to the national interests of states" (Tucker 1952: 223).

The situation was similar with the balance of power, which Morgenthau described as a "necessary outgrowth" of international politics, a fact of international political life that "cannot be abolished" (Morgenthau 1948: 126; 1951: 155). "The aspiration for power on the part of several nations, each trying either to maintain or to overthrow the status quo, leads of necessity to a constellation which is called the balance of power and to policies which are aimed at preserving it. We are using the term 'of necessity' advisedly" (1948: 125). In the same work, however, he wrote that "the uncertainty of all power calculations not only makes the balance of power incapable of practical application, it leads also to its very negation in practice" (1948: 155).[8] On careful examination, even the meaning of "balance of power" proved obscure. For example, Ernst Haas (1953) uncovered eight major senses of the term in well-known realist works.

Efforts to clarify and strengthen realist theory, however, would have undermined much of its prescriptive power. A single consistent definition of balance of power would lead to a theory that was either so abstract that it provided little policy guidance or so precisely specified that it would no longer be universal. And if the national interest were treated descriptively, as something to be discovered by examining the actions of leaders and dominant groups in society, it could no longer serve as an allegedly objective point of reference for criticizing existing policies.

Later generations chose theoretical rigor and, thus, political marginalization. The present generation was unwilling to remain confined to the academy but could never reconcile its claims to practical political wisdom with the theory that allegedly supported them. "Correlating Morgenthau and Kennan on policy with Morgenthau and Kennan on 'Realism' requires a Talmudist's skill and patience, not to say a willing suspension of disbelief" (Rothstein 1972: 352). Stanley Hoffmann's judgment of Morgenthau holds more generally for this generation of realists: There was "a constant tension between his awareness of the diversity of politics – he was at his best as a subtle analyst of concrete situations – and his desire to reduce politics to a single type he deemed politically prudent and ethically wise" (Hoffmann 1981: 657).

The fact that, as Tucker put it, "Professor Morgenthau has not always taken the care to separate what he presents as a scientific analysis from his political judgements" (Tucker 1952: 214) was particularly damaging within the discipline. During the 1960s, realism in the United States was steadily pushed to the margins.[9] By the early 1970s, it usually was "simply ignored as an anachronistic remnant of the discipline's early years" (Rothstein 1972: 347). Like idealism a generation earlier, it was there to be kicked around when necessary or useful (or just for fun), but few leading figures in the discipline, and almost none of the best young scholars, still took it very seriously. Power, anarchy, and the nation-state remained a starting point for most work in the field. Realism in any significant sense of that term was marginalized in academic international relations.[10]

The fact that such fatal inconsistencies were evident in the early 1950s, however, suggests that broader social and political changes were also at work. Yale Ferguson and Richard Mansbach have argued that the early realists "were not especially innovative theoretically.... The key to their victory lay less in the power of their assumptions or logic than in the climate of the times." To the extent that this is correct – I see it as an insightful exaggeration – their decline also owed much to changes in "the frame of reference of scholars and the ethos of the society in which they were working" (Ferguson and Mansbach 1988: 99, 103). As Americans became more comfortable with the exercise of power, the wisdom of a Morgenthau seemed less necessary. Furthermore, the attractions of power theories declined as American power became less dominant in the world and as Vietnam led to fundamental questioning of its uses.

In addition, academic realism in the 1960s came under attack from a new generation of scholars seeking to apply the methods of behavioral and quantitative social science to international relations.[11] This "second great debate," which took its classic form in an exchange between Hedley Bull and Morton Kaplan in *World Politics* in 1966, was almost entirely methodological, revolving around the meaning and achievements of "science." So-called traditionalists or classicists either defiantly retained a continental notion of "science," meaning disciplined, scholarly study,[12] or argued that the new "science" of international relations, modeled on the natural sciences, could not deal with many of the most important international issues. Disputes over theoretical substance were almost completely lacking. "Behavioralism was not so much an attack on the assumptions of Realism as a dispute about the most appropriate methodology" (Smith 1989: 20). Only in the 1970s did a serious substantive and theoretical challenge arise within the mainstream of the discipline. Realism in the 1960s was displaced, even discredited, but not replaced.

V. Power and Interdependence

Interwar liberal internationalists had tried to develop an alternative to power politics based on reason, humane values, and international institutions. This style of liberal internationalism persisted on the fringes of the discipline even during the height of the realist hegemony (e.g., Grenville Clark and Louis Sohn's *World Peace Through World Law*, 1958). It even underwent a minor revival in the 1970s, most systematically in the work of Richard Falk (1975) and his colleagues in the World Order Models Project. The more serious challenge to realism, however, came from a fundamentally nonidealist brand of liberal internationalism that focused on newly developing processes of international interdependence and criticized realism largely on its own terms of interest and descriptive power.

Twentieth-century realism has been a radically state-centric perspective. States are seen as the only international actors able to provide defense and protect other basic values in an environment of anarchy. International order itself is seen to arise from the decisions and actions of states. Anarchy, however, severely restricts the opportunities for interstate cooperation. The absence of hierarchical authority to enforce contracts creates a high structural risk of others failing to cooperate. The egoism of human nature usually makes the risk insurmountable. Even if there are mutual benefits to cooperation, egoists in anarchy often face a "prisoners' dilemma": The risks of one's partner/opponent defecting are sufficiently high that the "rational" outcome is competition rather than cooperation, even where both parties would prefer and be better off by cooperating.

A key step in constructing a new liberal internationalist alternative was the Summer 1971 special issue of *International Organization*, edited by Robert Keohane and Joseph Nye, on transnational relations, that is, the cross-border activities of nonstate actors.[13] The transnationalists argued that other international actors were becoming sufficiently important that one could not adequately account for contemporary international relations by looking solely at states. Some even took to heart the title of Raymond Vernon's book on multinational corporations: *Sovereignty at Bay*. The more exuberant proponents of this view pronounced the nation-state, and thus a realist politics of the national interest, obsolete.[14]

This new generation of liberal internationalists also dramatically expanded the substantive focus of the discipline. Realists had traditionally emphasized the "high politics" of security relations, often to the virtual exclusion of everything else. Transnationalists stressed economic relations and opened a space for a variety of "new issues," such as human rights.

Instead of a realist world of largely autonomous sovereign states, alone and adrift in the sea of international anarchy, the new liberal internationalists of the 1970s presented a world of multiple actors, bound together in a complex web of conflictual and cooperative relations. In such a world, realism was not merely a misguided and vaguely embarrassing theoretical anachronism, but an impediment to progressive change:

The attitudes and predispositions which Realism fosters constitute a classically inappropriate response to these developments. With its overly narrow conception of politics, and with its antiquated notions of sovereignty, Great Power domination and the autonomy of foreign policy, the Realist response is bound to create conflict and destroy the possibility of working out new forms of cooperation. (Rothstein 1972: 361)

Keohane and Nye's *Power and Interdependence* (1977) pulled together these various strands under the label "complex interdependence."

They argued that a model of international relations characterized by multiple and varied international actors, a profusion of international issues that were not hierarchically ordered or centrally controlled, and the declining utility of force (accompanied by a severely reduced fungibility of power) was more accurate than the competing realist model.[15] Although this perspective never predominated – in fact, it was largely ignored in mainstream security studies and foreign policy analysis – it firmly established a substantive alternative to realism within the mainstream of the discipline. It also fostered the dramatic rise in the study of international political economy, which reshaped the definition of the field.

This change in intellectual perspective paralleled, and received additional impetus from, changes in international relations. The decline in the relative power and prestige of the United States suggested cooperation rather than dominance as the order of the day. And Vietnam delivered the finishing blows to hard-headed realism, especially in academic circles.[16]

Once more, though, we need to be wary of reductionism. Most of these authors saw their work as not merely an appropriate, but a demanded response to real and important changes in the world that were being given insufficient attention in the discipline. Furthermore, in the Nixon era, there was not much sympathy for liberal internationalist ideas in the corridors of power.

VI. The Neorealist Revival

Realism in its classic postwar form never completely died out. Even today it persists on the margins of the discipline, in the work of relatively isolated but respected figures such as Tucker and in academic enclaves such as the University of Virginia, where Kenneth W. Thompson, Morgenthau's former student, research assistant, and collaborator, has self-consciously sought to preserve and propagate the tradition. Realism's return to academic dominance in the 1980s, however, arose from the work of a new generation of scholars with a very different approach. If we follow Rosenthal in calling the postwar generation "righteous realists," emphasizing their prescriptive orientation, the new generation of neorealists, as they have come to be known, can be called "social scientific realists," to emphasize their overriding commitment to an explanatory social science.

The key figure in the neorealist revival was Kenneth N. Waltz. During the 1980s, Waltz's *Theory of International Politics* (1979) was the one indispensable text in the field and the point of reference, whether positive or negative, for much of the most important theoretical work in the discipline. Waltz presented a logically rigorous and elegantly spare theory of international politics that he claimed arose entirely out of the logic of anarchy. This has led to the common use of the label "structural realism" to distinguish it from the "classical realism" of Morgenthau, Niebuhr, Kennan, and company.[17]

The structuralism of neorealism is closely associated with its social scientific orientation. Neorealists, however, turned not to psychology and the behavioral sciences for a model of social science but to economics. Microeconomic rational choice analysis and a nomological deductive model of social scientific explanation have predominated, in contrast to the empirical, quantitative, and at times even inductive approaches of the behavioralists.

The result is grand theory, but with more modest and much more academic aspirations. For example, Waltz presents a very general and abstract balance of power analysis that provides an explanatory first cut, rather than detailed policy guidance. As he readily admits, such a theory does not aspire to determinate predictions of particular actions (Waltz 1979: 121). Its goal is firmly grounded theoretical understanding of the enduring constraints, patterns, and tendencies of international relations. Contemporary neorealism does not see social science as the source of a superior political wisdom capable of providing direct policy guidance. For example, where Morgenthau saw the national interest as objective and subject to discovery by realist analysis, neorealists usually see the national interest (beyond the objective of preserving sovereignty and territorial integrity) as not merely subjective but exogenous to the theory.

Not surprisingly, this change in intellectual fashion parallels changes in the real world of politics. The relationship, however, is complex. Reagan's emphasis on power and conflict certainly raised issues that realism was particularly suited to address. But Reagan's ideological, self-righteously nationalistic approach to politics was antithetical to classical realism, and at best irrelevant to neorealism. Thus, Tucker was a strong critic of the Reagan Doctrine (1985) and leading neorealists, such as Glenn Snyder, were critical of Reagan's security policies. Furthermore, the *structural* change in international relations in the late 1970s and early 1980s toward growing multipolarity and a deepening of complex interdependence, along with the continued increasing prominence of economics and other nonsecurity issues in international relations, should have strengthened neoliberalism, not neorealism.[18]

I would contend that the neorealist revival was rooted primarily in internal disciplinary developments. Many of the claims for interdependence were indeed extravagant, almost begging for rebuttal. The ruins of classical postwar realism, which for all its problems did contain some important fundamental insights, lay waiting for a more coherent social scientific reformulation. And the introduction of game theory and microeconomic models into political science offered a new and accessible methodology for such a reformulation.

In my view, it would be hard to overestimate the impact of the lure of a microeconomic social science in the neorealist revival. Waltz explicitly modeled his theory on microeconomics (Waltz 1979: 89–94), as did Snyder and Diesing (1977: ch. 2) and Gilpin (1981: ix–xii). Even Keohane (1984) was tempted down the road toward realism by microeconomic rational actor models. And many of Waltz's critics express a not always merely grudging admiration for his theoretical audacity, rigor, and power, which are largely rooted in his microeconomic orientation. Science, more than the politics, explains the rise of neorealism.

If microeconomics provided the method for resurrecting realism, the often extravagant claims for the transforming power of interdependence often provided an empirical focus. Waltz in particular developed his theory in opposition to the interdependence perspective, which he argued "both obscures the realities of international politics and asserts a false belief about the conditions that may promote peace" (Waltz 1970: 222). Likewise, an early work of Stephen Krasner, probably the leading young neorealist, criticized arguments that the Arab oil embargo was a harbinger of a radically new interdependent international system. In other words, neorealism owes much to its dialectical confrontation with interdependence,[19] which itself arose in significant measure in opposition to postwar realism – which in turn arose in opposition to an earlier style of liberal internationalism.

VII. Realism and International Relations in the 1990s

The hegemony of neorealism, however, proved short lived. After a few years, the indeterminate generalities of neorealist theory came to seem intellectually far less sustaining and practically much less helpful to the actual work of research than it initially appeared. The key blow, though, was the collapse of the Soviet empire.

Perhaps the most common critique of neorealism – certainly the thing that is most striking to first-year graduate students – is its inability to comprehend change. Waltz largely accepted such a characterization (1986: 338). And in defense of neorealism it must be noted that competing theories, including those that do try to explain fundamental structural change, did no better in predicting the end of the Cold War. Nonetheless, when the Cold War bipolar order collapsed seemingly almost overnight, this theoretical gap came to be seen as unacceptable even to many otherwise sympathetic observers – especially because that collapse was intimately tied to ideas of democracy and human rights and processes of technological and economic change, factors dear to liberal internationalism but beyond the analytical reach of neorealist structuralism.

Despite this disillusionment, I would expect neorealism not only to persist but to remain prominent throughout the 1990s. Because neorealists made much more modest claims than the postwar realists, the backlash is likely to be much less severe. In addition, their stress on theoretical rigor and consistency has left them much less open to wholesale ridicule and rejection. Although neorealism has been knocked from the commanding heights of the discipline, it is likely to remain one of the most robust campers at a lower elevation. And no other theory seems poised for an ascent to the top.

This, in my view, is unusually healthy for the discipline. Both idealism and realism have been dismal failures as grand theories of international relations (as have all other contenders, such as systems and dependency theories). Each, however, encapsulates important insights, as the best scholars in the field are increasingly willing to admit (e.g., Keohane 1986b: chs. 1, 7). Although some may bemoan the growing theoretical eclecticism, I think that it is immensely liberating and likely to contribute to richer, more diverse, and more insightful research.

In any case, the oscillation between realism and internationalism just charted suggests the true character of these "theories." As many commentators have noted, realism is less a "theory," in a strict social scientific sense of that term, than a general orientation: "a set of normative emphases which shape theory" (Ferguson and Mansbach 1988: 79); "a series of points that serve to structure debate" (Cusack and Stoll 1990: 53); "a loose framework" (Rosenthal 1991: 7).

The distinctive element of the realist perspective is its emphasis on power, constraint, and recurrence. Whenever the discipline undervalues these features of international life, we can expect a realist revival (especially when reality cooperates by providing a dramatic example). But when the discipline becomes obsessed with the limits and constraints of power and anarchy, realism is ready to be knocked from its pedestal. As no less a realist than Carr noted, "Consistent realism excludes four things which appear to be essential ingredients of all effective political thinking: a finite goal, an emotional appeal, a right of moral judgment and a ground for action" (Carr 1946: 89).

The discipline of international relations probably cannot, and should not, escape realism. But unless it goes beyond realism it will be sadly impoverished, both analytically and normatively.

Notes

1. This focus, in addition to reflecting my own knowledge and interests, corresponds to the fact that the academic study of international relations as a distinct discipline or interdisciplinary field was largely an Anglo-American phenomenon until the 1960s (the principal exception being the Geneva Program, established in the 1920s).
2. For a sampling of definitions, see Carr 1946: 63 and ch. 2; Morgenthau 1954: 4–13; John, Wright, and Garnett 1972: 96–7; Waltz 1979: 117; Maghroori 1982: 14–16; Vasquez 1983: 15–19, 26–30; Olson and Onuf 1985: 7; Cox 1986: 211–12; Gilpin 1986: 304–5; Keohane 1986a: 163; Smith 1986: 219–21; Ferguson and Mansbach 1988: 40–7, 102; Stein 1990: 4–7; Sullivan 1990: 9. The following paragraphs draw heavily on Donnelly 1992.
3. Throughout I use "anarchy" as it is ordinarily used in the international relations literature; that is, in the literal sense of absence of rule, lack of government. Anarchy does *not* imply chaos, absence of order; it is simply the absence of "hierarchical" political order based on formal subordination and authority. Thus, Hedley Bull (1977) could write usefully of international relations as taking place in an "anarchical society" of states.
4. He did, however, have a major impact after the war, both indirectly, through his impact on Carr and Morgenthau, and directly, through works such as *The Children of Light and the Children of Darkness* (1944) and a considerable body of occasional publications.
5. Lord Davies, whose candidate had been W. Arnold Forster (a professional painter who had been an active and zealous publicist for the League), broke his ties with Aberystwyth in protest (Porter 1972: app. 1).
6. We might note, however, that the Maginot line was hardly a candle and that the French, who when it came time to fight put up virtually no resistance to Germany, were nearly as dismissive of the League and liberal internationalism as Carr or Morgenthau. It is also at best disingenuous to blame idealists without mentioning the impact of the Depression, or otherwise accounting for the inadequate preparations and diplomacy of 1937, 1938, and 1939, when liberal internationalism was all but buried. And we should emphasize that the common association of appeasement with idealism simply cannot be

sustained. Carr supported the Munich agreement (these references, on pages 278 and 282, were removed from the 1946 reprinting), and most of its later realist critics were at the time silent. In fact, the most prominent contemporary criticisms of Munich actually came from idealists, who lamented the sacrifice of a guiltless country to "realistic" political expediency.

7. There were, of course, rabidly anticommunist realists, such as Strausz-Hupé and Possony. The leading intellectual figures of postwar realism, however, strongly opposed infusing ideological concerns into American foreign policy.

8. In a later work, Morgenthau even argued that "the rational deficiencies of the political world . . . present insuperable obstacles to rational understanding and management. The political world, domestic and international, in particular, is in good measure the realm of the unique, the contingent, the unforeseeable, the uncontrollable . . . not susceptible to theoretical understanding" (Morgenthau 1970: 67).

9. Realism in England, however, although no longer hegemonic, remained the most important perspective in the discipline. Several factors contributed to this more moderate decline. Carr and Schwarzenberger were radical value relativists, in sharp contrast to Morgenthau and Niebuhr, who believed in a single, universal morality (which simply had limited application to politics). They were also much less involved in public policy debates. As a result, they were less inclined toward either the righteousness or the political rhetoric characteristic of a Morgenthau. In addition, they had few aspirations to grand theory, resulting in a softer and more subtle theory that was less subject to devastating refutation. Much the same was true of Martin Wight, whose more restrained, historically grounded realism had a great impact in the 1970s and 1980s (both directly and indirectly through the work of Hedley Bull). See also note 11.

10. I am thus uncomfortable with Vasquez's distinction (1983: 15–19, 26–30) between "the realist paradigm," defined by a stress on the state, international anarchy, and the struggle for power, and what he calls realism or power politics, which involves additional assumptions and attitudes and is essentially what I have called realism here. Using "realist" in such an extended sense obscures important theoretical differences. My preference is to sharply focus the discussion by a narrower definition that downplays affinities across theories. Another way to make the point is to insist on a distinction between "realist theories," in a narrow sense of that term, and theories or bodies of work that may be compatible with, but are not driven or fundamentally informed by, realism.

11. In Britain, by contrast, virtually no quantitative work was undertaken in the 1960s, systems theory had a significantly smaller impact, and behavioral approaches in general won few adherents. This lack of an aspiration to "social science" probably further mitigated the decline in the fortunes of

British realism already noted. (Incidentally, it should be noted that the biggest gap in this essay, seen as a general survey of the development of the discipline, is its inattention to the large and diverse body of behavioral scholarship.)

12. This was the sense used by earlier realists, such as Carr (1946: 9–10). It was also the sense underlying Morgenthau's reference to universal laws.

13. This work had strong roots in Haas's neofunctional theory of international organization (1958, 1964), which itself was an explicit modification of Mitrany's more classical (although largely technology-driven) liberal internationalism. In fact, Nye's *Peace in Parts* (1971) is one of the classic restatements of neo-functional theory.

14. Morgenthau shared this view, as he emphasized as early as the preface to the second edition of *Politics among Nations* (1954: vii). For Morgenthau, though, nuclear weapons rather than interdependence explained this change.

15. A decade later, Keohane and Nye (1987: 728–30) claimed that they saw their work more as a complement to realism than a replacement. At the time, however, most scholars, on both sides of the issue, took *Power and Interdependence*, not unreasonably in my view, as an alternative to and critique of realism.

16. It is ironic, however, that a war that was a largely ideological struggle in the backwaters of the international system and was roundly criticized by leading academic realists – most prominently Morgenthau – contributed to realism's demise.

17. In fact, though, there were important structuralists among the postwar generation as well. For example, Herz was as self-consciously structural as Waltz. And even Morgenthau, for all his stress on human nature, argued no less emphatically than Waltz that anarchy necessarily leads to balance-of-power politics. The real generational contrast, in my view, has much more to do with differing attitudes toward or conceptions of social science than with differing interpretations of the role of anarchy or human nature.

18. In addition, the maintenance of a more or less realist mainstream in Britain, throughout all the ups and downs of realism in the United States over the past forty years, should caution us against simple reductionist accounts.

19. We should also note the importance of the conflict with dependency theory and other quasi- or neo-Marxist approaches. Chapter 2 of Waltz's *Theory of International Politics* is devoted to a critique of the Hobson–Lenin theory of imperialism and its descendants. In a similar vein, Krasner's *Defending the National Interest* (1978) – the title of which echoes Morgenthau's *In Defense of the National Interest* – is structured as a comparative test of liberal, neo-Marxist, and realist theories.

8

Remembering the Revolution: Behavioralism in American Political Science

James Farr

The discipline of political science may be identified in terms of its research programs, political traditions, institutional locations, or academic leaders. It may also be identified forensically, in terms of its arguments and debates, especially those reflexive ones about what it is to be a discipline avowing a "science of politics." Periodically, these arguments and debates prove to be particularly sharp and pointed about what politics is or science should be. Their consequences effect a fundamental transformation in the identity of the discipline as a whole. Such was the case in the arguments and debates about behavioralism in American political science in the third quarter of the twentieth century. What has come to be known as the "behavioral revolution" marked a dramatic moment in the forensic history of political science in the United States.

The behavioral revolution was marked by some distinctive features and phases that, with a little license, appear paradigmatically revolutionary. An initial protest against tradition soon became a movement of widespread change. Certain precursors of the movement were hailed by the revolutionaries as exemplars who envisioned how the new order might be. Heroic individuals emerged in the movement whose self-consciousness of the meaning of events around them came to be the

I would like to thank Heinz Eulau and my coeditors John Dryzek and Stephen Leonard for their very helpful comments on an earlier draft of this essay. They were, in their different ways, particularly instructive in helping me to clarify what sort of history of this disputed era that I was attempting to write. I would also like to thank them, as well as Terence Ball, Mary Dietz, Edwin Fogelman, John Gunnell, Robert Holt, Raymond Seidelman, and Frank Sorauf, for many discussions about behavioralism and the history of political science. As a result of these discussions, I am convinced that behavioralism still excites strongly held and extremely divergent views, and that trying to write a short, balanced historical account of it may well please no one.

self-consciousness of the revolution itself. An ancien regime was swept away as the revolutionary leadership became ensconced as a new establishment. Soon enough, the new establishment would itself become the object of popular criticism. Mounting crises would prompt some revolutionaries to call for yet a new revolution. But with its enthusiasm quenched, the revolution's more ambitious promises could be laid aside as the unattainable ends of an otherwise successful protest. A postrevolutionary consciousness would settle in for quite some time, including a certain sense of longing for the purposiveness that the revolution had inspired.

I have invoked revolutionary imagery in introducing this remembrance of behavioralism for the simple reason that scientific revolutions are not unlike political revolutions (Cohen 1985). But even more importantly, revolutionary imagery was used by many of the political scientists who effected the behavioral transformation of the discipline in the first place – even though there were plenty of continuities with the past.[1] It was the language of the moment. The tone was dramatic, and the terms evinced struggle, tumult, and change. Behavioralism polarized professional attitudes in the discipline, drawing down upon itself a heated and vociferous reaction. It thereby inaugurated a particularly argumentative and noisy period in the forensic history of the discipline. The arguments and debates about the proper identity of a science of politics raged around a number of striking and provocative proclamations that captured a sense of considerable transformation. These proclamations were first issued at the expense of a "traditional" political science and were later criticized in turn by antibehavioral opponents. The quieting or perhaps the exhaustion of these proclamations characterize the postbehavioral era in which we arguably still reside.

In focusing on the proclamations of behavioralism – and, more generally, on the forensic arguments and debates over them – this essay attempts to give voice to the articulated self-understandings of the principal figures of the behavioral revolution. It also hopes to do so without the partisan polemics that attended the rise of behavioralism in the first place. This historiographical stance is neither uncritical nor without its own commitments. Nor is it the only way to proceed in narrating this important stretch of disciplinary history. Attention to the proclamations of the behavioral revolution, it bears underscoring at the outset, tends to exaggerate certain differences with what came before and to displace a certain amount of attention away from the actual practices and products of behavioral research. But the proclamations themselves – about science, behavior, and liberal pluralism – were very prominent in the writings of the 1950s and 1960s. They figured in presidential addresses to professional associations, review articles, the prefaces and introductions to volumes on research, glosses of research grants, departmental constitutions, and much else besides. Countless political scientists weighed in, pro and con. The proclamations reveal how highly self-conscious political scientists were about their goals, hopes, and promises, as well as about the challenges to them. It is this that makes the period much more intriguing than what came before (arguably excepting the 1890s when political science was associating itself as an academic discipline and the Progressive era when the pitch of reform was high), as well as anything that has come since. The proclamations, in short, are every bit a part of the "real" history of the discipline, as much as any catalog of research, any recording of institutional developments, any honor role of important figures. Thus, a history whose narrative structure turns upon debates over those proclamations not only seems to be in order; but any account of behavioralism that avoided them would be remiss.

The historiographical stance of this essay, moreover, does not depend on any models of science drawn from the natural sciences, such as found in the work of Thomas Kuhn (1962) or Imre Lakatos (1978). This is fortunate if only because, should we actually follow Kuhn or Lakatos, there would be no genuine "science" of politics and so no history of it to narrate. It is certainly true that Kuhn's *Structure of Scientific Revolutions* made an enormous impact not only on philosophers and historians of science, but on political scientists as well. Indeed, the language of revolution made Kuhn's work all the more attractive to a number of behavioralists who were in the process of making over the discipline. Some even thought that behavioralism was itself a "paradigm" in Kuhn's technical sense (Almond 1966). Closer scrutiny, however, has shown that Kuhn's analysis of paradigms and their revolutionary overthrow had little to do with the structure or history of the social sciences – a point that Kuhn himself originally made (Kuhn 1962; cf. Gutting 1980). One might say that the reception of Kuhn was an important event *in* the history of political science, but that his historiography has not proved to be an adequate understanding *of* that history. Lakatos's model of scientific research programs, on the other hand, would appear to have replaced Kuhn's model of paradigms in the minds of many political scientists. Yet the "sophisticated falsificationism" that Lakatos developed when attempting to advance upon Karl Popper's account of science – with its armory of positive and negative heuristics, progressive and regressive problem shifts, hard cores and protective belts – seems better fitted to the advanced natural sciences than to the social sciences – a point that Lakatos also made clear at the outset (Lakatos 1978; cf. Ball 1976). Behavioralism – as a self-styled revolutionary program that issued proclamations about a science of politics and that encouraged research of considerable diversity and interdisciplinarity – simply does not fit the terms of Lakatos's model of science, any more than it did Kuhn's. It is the story of those proclamations – not Kuhnian paradigms or Lakatosian research programs, should they even exist in political science – that I wish to capture here.

In this essay, then, I will summarize what I take to be the principal proclamations of the behavioral revolution, trace their articulation by key behavioralists during the 1950s, recount the reaction to them during the 1960s, and briefly note the condition of a postbehavioral political science without them. I hope to evoke thereby the sense of revolution – a sense of energy, excitement, promise, and now loss – that emerged in the words and documents of key behavioralists (and some antibehavioralists) in the 1950s, 1960s, and at times today. There is not space here to develop all this in the detail that it deserves, especially to the very diverse (and some would say fragmented) audience that presently makes up the discipline of political science. Necessarily, then, there will be considerable abbreviation and simplification in my account, as well as only a glance at the considerable diversity of substantive research that presented itself as the results of the proclamations of behavioralism. Moreover, there is always a certain danger in historical remembrance following so hard upon the events themselves, particularly when some of the principal actors are still in the process of remembering and reflecting on their own roles and achievements (as in Baer, Malcolm, and Sigelman 1991). But whatever the difficulties and dangers, the topic is too important to neglect in a volume of historical essays on the discipline of political science in the United States.

I

Behavioralism in political science was part of a much broader intellectual movement that had been influencing the social sciences since the early twentieth century. The upshot of this movement can be captured by its most general proclamation: Study political behavior according to the canons of scientific methodology. What "behavioralism" (or sometimes "behaviorism")[2] meant beyond this is harder to state with much precision, and the behavioral revolutionaries of the 1950s and 1960s variously characterized it themselves not only as a revolution but as a movement, a protest, a persuasion, even a mood. We can discern, nonetheless, two general themes or lesser proclamations that were subsumed under the most general one, as well as a third that contributed to the broader tradition of American political thought. In brief, these dealt with (1) a research focus on political behavior, (2) a methodological plea for science, and (3) a political message about liberal pluralism.[3]

First, the behavioralists proclaimed that research in political science should focus on behavior and on the groups, processes, and systems within which behavior could be explained. This reoriented the subject matter to be studied by a science of politics and provided a new vocabulary and conceptual framework for the discipline. What the behavioralists called "traditional" political science, in their view, had long made much ado over the formalities of the state, constitutions, and law, as well as the normative ideals of the great political theorists like Plato, Locke, and Mill. What was desperately needed, they argued, was to turn to political behavior as such – to what people did and actually undertook, not to what they thought, taught, wrote, or paid lip service to. In short, "Human behavior is the root of politics" (Eulau 1963, 5). Behavioralism was, then, something of a wordplay on "behavior" that reflected a change in *what* was to be studied by political scientists and in *what terms*. For behavioralists, however, behavior could not be construed adequately in the reductionist mode popularized by twentieth-century psychological behaviorists, like John B. Watson or B. F. Skinner. Political behavior was still infused with attitudes, meanings, and beliefs about politics; and these could not be reduced to bodily movement or to " 'behavior as such' in a purely physical or mechanistic sense" (Eulau 1963, 114). Behavioralists were not physiological reductionists, especially in recognizing what was "political" about political behavior.

Moreover, the settings or consequences of political behavior were best captured by the idea of the processes of politics – not its fixed formalisms or ethical ideals – especially as revealed in groups or larger systems. In departments of political science across the country "processes and behavior" came to be the code words for the new behavioral studies. The language of "system" replaced or displaced the language of the "state" that had identified the discipline in the nineteenth century and much of it until the mid-twentieth century (see Farr 1993; and Gunnell, Chapter 1, this volume). With the concepts of behavior, groups, processes, and systems, the new behavioralists thereby revolutionized the very language within which the research objectives of political science could be discussed.[4] The study of the franchise became the study of electoral behavior; interests became embodied in interest groups; law metamorphosed into judicial process; and everything touching on the state became the inputs and outputs of the political system.

Second, a new methodology accompanied the research focus and vocabulary of behavioral political inquiry. A revolution in research techniques was underway, especially in the other social sciences. The behavioral revolutionaries, who were expressly interdisciplinary in their orientation, argued quite vociferously that political science could advance if and only if it adopted (or invented) new techniques of research, such as the use of polling data, survey questionnaires, psychological experimentation, scaling techniques, and statistical methods. Whatever particular techniques were adopted or invented, the general emphasis plainly fell on the need for quantification.

Besides quantifiable research techniques (i.e., "methodology" in the technical sense of the word), a more philosophical understanding of scientific methodology was proclaimed as well. Behavioral revolutionaries openly admitted their aspirations to genuine science and frequently drew on the account of the natural sciences then being provided by neopositivist philosophers of science (especially Morris Cohen, Carl Hempel, Ernest Nagel, and a certain reading of Karl Popper, all of whom had moved beyond the austere strictures of the logical positivism associated with the Vienna circle).[5] Political science, on this account, was to be a form of factual or empirical inquiry. It was rooted in the demonstrable facts of political behavior. Facts were, by definition, observable; or, rather, only what was observable was admissible as fact into behavioral research. Some behavioralists were particularly wont to underscore the centrality of fact-finding in science. Other behavioralists, however, criticized a conception of science that was purely factual or even "hyperfactual" (Easton 1953) because science aspired to general theories that were comprised of laws or lawlike generalizations that organized and explained the facts. Indeed, the very aim of science, it was argued, was to discover laws or lawlike generalizations and then to deploy them in theoretical explanations of political behavior, groups, processes, and systems.

If behavioral political science was to be "theoretical" in an explanatory sense, it most assuredly was not to be theoretical in a normative sense or in a sense allied to the history of political thought. Many departments indeed continued to use the term "theory" to characterize that subfield that did in fact undertake such normative and historical investigations. But according to the behavioral revolutionaries, this was an unfortunate usage of the term that lingered from an earlier period in the discipline's history (and, of course, would persist). In being empirical and explanatory, however, theory in behavioral research was to be value-free and objective. There was, it was argued, a logical gulf between fact and value, between "is" and "ought," which in no way could be spanned. Normative topics like freedom, justice, or authority – the staples of a prescientific study of politics – were best understood in terms of one's subjective emotions or expressive states. They were also laced with "a strong dose of metaphysical discourse" (Eulau 1963, 10), and no behavioralist operating with an eye to science – not to mention a neopositivist conception of science – could countenance metaphysics.

There was also in this new methodological orientation – what some critics called a new "methodism" (Wolin 1969) – a polemical intent that helped to transform the discipline. "Traditional" political scientists not only studied the wrong things, the behavioralists proclaimed; they did so in the wrong way, whether by prescribing what it was to be a good citizen or a just state, or by "textual exegesis of the classics as if they were sacred writings" (Eulau 1963, 8). Endlessly reinterpreting the great books of dead men and tirelessly disputing the meaning of the good life had nothing to do with science (even if these activities happened in departments of political science, so-called). In the name of a genuine science of politics, the behavioralists demanded the abandonment of the prescientific preoccupation with texts, glosses, and homilies.

Third, the behavioral revolution brought in train a new or renewed political message about liberal pluralism in the United States. In their research on the United States – and most behavioral research centered largely on American politics – behavioralists alleged to discover, explain, and confirm the basic outlines of a pluralist political system animated by liberal values. Such a system was composed principally of individuals acting in groups to realize their collective interests. These groups sorted themselves out into different arenas within which they vied for influence and across which they made a series of accommodations in order to have an impact on governance and the distribution of power in the kind of representative democracy found in the United States. The overall system, then, was stabilized by these sets of overlapping and competing interest groups that operated within the bounds of law, but without the dictates of the state (to use the traditional vo-

cabulary). A general consensus on the values of liberalism – especially
on individualism, rationality, openness, and toleration – animated this
pluralistic system of individuals and groups. Indeed, these were the societal values that operated underneath the political system, despite their
occasional violation. This message about American society and its political system was more-or-less accepted by most citizens, especially the
self-selecting elites among them, behavioralists argued. But it was also
generally accepted by more ordinary citizens who were otherwise apathetic or indifferent to the actual practices of self-government and likely
to express somewhat less liberal opinions when asked.

This picture of the American political system was, in the first instance, taken to be the consequence of behavioral political research.
That is, a liberal pluralist political system was simply the way it was in
the United States, quite independently of its intrinsic value or of the values of behavioral political scientists. No doubt this proved to be some
consolation to the large majority of behavioralists who were themselves
liberal in their own values, whether about education, speech, liberty,
equality, or participation. Nonetheless, this led to a sense of tension and
even contradiction, especially when pointed out by some critics of behavioralism whose own values fell somewhere to the left or to the right
of liberal pluralism. Alleging to be value-neutral, the categories of
behavioral political science proved to be quite value-laden, these critics
argued (and some behavioralists, too, later agreed). But many behavioralists, when in fact they addressed this issue, did not see themselves
smuggling into political science the kind of value-laden inquiry that they
stated should not ethically, and could not logically, be done. Rather, they
either came clean with their values at the outset of their empirical studies as a sort of prescientific confession of political faith or they found
these values implicated in the very categories and practice of empirical
science. Without toleration and openness, for example, no science was
possible. As long as behavioral research could continue to discover and
attempt to explain a liberal pluralist system in the United States, there
was a kind of preordained harmony between facts and values, as it were,
that obviated any need to perform the impossible, namely, to argue from
one to the other.

Looking back to the period roughly between the late 1940s and the
late 1960s, and most dramatically during the 1950s, these three proclamations – about behavior, science, and liberal pluralism – were sufficiently precise to galvanize many political scientists into a behavioral
movement conjured against a "traditional" political science. They were

also sufficiently vague to allow for countless differences and endless debate between behavioral political scientists about the precise character
of scientific research and American politics. At the level of discourse,
this should be taken as the mark of great and lasting success. Sufficiently
coherent to enable its advocates to share some sense of a common project, yet sufficiently open to allow for debate about how that project
should proceed, behavioralism proved to be a resilient and adaptable
mode of discourse.

The success of the behavioral revolution can also be seen in professional terms. Those political scientists who most clearly and persistently
made these proclamations about behavior, science, and liberal pluralism
were also those who were (or were to become) the most influential authors of scholarly texts and the highest office holders in the professional
associations, including especially the American Political Science Association (APSA). (A sociological analysis of behavioralism would make
this its central point.) A revolution had indeed made over the discipline
of American political science.

To give some more textual specificity to the proclamations of the behavioral revolution, as well as to trace their ancestry and assess their
fate, we may now turn to a brief historical sketch of behavioralism, especially as found in some of the more important documents and writings
of its principal spokesmen. We will look here mainly to David Truman,
David Easton, Robert Dahl, Heinz Eulau, and a few others – and even
then to their grander proclamations about the discipline, as opposed to
the details of their extensive substantive research in many different
fields. While many other behavioralists should and would figure in a
longer account, I hope that no reader will gainsay the choice to emphasize these particular political scientists. We may begin as they began, by
looking back further still to those moments in history that prefigured the
revolution.

II

In the *Eighteenth Brumaire of Louis Bonaparte*, Marx observed that revolutionaries bring in the new by dressing in the old. He had in mind
Luther and the Protestant Reformers solemnly playing the role of the
biblical saints, and the French revolutionaries parading about as Roman
republicans. Some revolutions in academia, it deserves observing, reverse the roles. They drag in the old by proclaiming it new. A bit of this
happened perhaps during the behavioral revolution. But the more sober,

influential, and historically minded of the behavioral revolutionaries presented their new scene with an eye to the various thinkers whose thoughts on science and politics were precursors of their own, however undeveloped in formulation or needy of transformation.

Some precursors were those titanic figures in the history of political thought, beginning with Aristotle. In the opening words of the single-most important manifesto lodged against traditional political science during the behavioral revolution – *The Political System: An Inquiry into the State of Political Science* – David Easton began by observing that "from the days of Aristotle, political science has been known as the master science" (Easton 1953, 3). Later, when John Wahlke delivered his 1979 presidential address to the APSA criticizing those segments of political science that were still "pre-behavioral," he too could glance back to Aristotle as "not only the first political scientist, but, indeed, as the first *bio*political scientist" (Wahlke 1979, 27n; discussed in Dryzek and Schlosberg, Chapter 5, this volume). Other behavioralists thought of Machiavelli or Hobbes in this connection, the former because of his realism, the latter because of his psychological premises and deductive rigor. Someone like David Hume could also be numbered "a major precursor of the behavioral sciences" (Miller 1971, 167) because of his conscious attempt "to reduce politics to a science." Honorary mention could go to the likes of Bentham, the Mills, "Helvetius, Condorcet, Diderot, [and] Montesquieu," as well as to "Comte, Marx, and Spencer" (Easton 1953, 11). In the United States, the new republic began its liberal career with repeated invocations of "the science of politics," as the *Federalist* made clear and as behavioralists remembered. In a general way, in short, it was acknowledged that "the behavioral persuasion represents an attempt, by modern modes of analysis, to fulfill the quest for political knowledge begun by the classical political theorists" (Eulau 1963, 7).

But for all their importance, the behavioralists found these distant echoes of their own science of politics too caught up in the normative, practical, and metaphysical struggles of their own times. Accordingly, the behavioralists were keener to acknowledge – though not uncritically – the relatively more recent thinkers from American (and sometimes European) political science that preceded them. Casual mention would be made to a host of nineteenth- and early-twentieth-century figures including Francis Lieber, John W. Burgess, Woodrow Wilson, Frank Goodnow, A. B. Hart, A. Lawrence Lowell, James Bryce, Jesse Macy, Henry Jones Ford, and the Willoughbys. But these thinkers had been too mired in the formalities of the state, the behavioralists thought, to anticipate a genuine explanatory science of behavior, even when, as in Goodnow's case, administration was meticulously studied, or when, as in Hart's case, "actual government" was deemed to be the realistic subject matter of political science. As Robert Dahl recounted, the term "political behavior" figured in the titles of books by the journalist Frank Kent in 1927 and by the Swedish political scientist Herbert Tingsten in 1937 (Dahl 1961b, 763). The bare terminology of "behavior" had appeared somewhat earlier[6] and with increasing regularity after World War I, thanks mainly to psychologists. By 1927, for example, John Dewey could contrast "political science" with political philosophy mainly by underscoring the former's attention to the "factual phenomena of political behavior" (Dewey 1927, 6). Yet mere mention of the term "behavior" did not of itself clarify the meaning of a science of behavior appropriate to a liberal pluralist political system.

Such a science, however, could be gleaned from a few significant works from the past. Indeed, it was the remembrance in the 1940s and early 1950s of two prominent figures – Arthur Bentley (whose principal works dated from the first two decades of this century) and Charles Merriam (from the second two decades) – that took center stage in the historical imagination of the behavioral revolutionaries as they set about their own programmatic efforts to transform the science of politics. These two figures were treated to more than a casual invocation; they were closely read and genuinely remembered (even if, as it turned out, the reading and remembrance were rather selective).

Bentley's *The Process of Government* (1908) was rescued from near obscurity by a few political scientists in the late 1940s, most notably David Truman. Despite the fact that it was a brilliant and scathing work, *The Process of Government* had fallen "stillborn from the press" (as David Hume remarked about his own brilliant and scathing *Treatise of Human Nature* a century and a half earlier). Barely (and even then dismissively) reviewed upon publication and only fitfully remembered in the 1920s and 1930s, Bentley's work was praised and relied upon in Truman's instantaneously successful book of nearly the same title, *The Governmental Process* (1951a). Albeit with much more sustained analysis and deeper factual grounding, Truman nonetheless recapitulated the conceptual framework of a science of the behavior of groups that he found in Bentley's work. Government was, for both of them, "the process of the adjustment of a set of interest groups in a particular distinguishable group or system" (Bentley 1908, 260). Similarly congenial to Truman was Bentley's criticism of a traditional – Bentley called it a

"dead" and Truman a "pretty damn dreary" – political science that conceptualized and studied politics in terms of "barren formalisms" (Bentley 1908; Truman in Baer et al. 1991, 143). This was especially true of
the concept of "the state."[7] While the term "pluralism" does not appear
in *The Process of Government*, it is used aptly enough by Truman in his
gloss of Bentley, with nods to the reception in the United States of the
English pluralists, especially Harold Laski, whose attack on the very
idea of a monistic and metaphysical state found favor in an American
society long accustomed to divided sovereignty and the give-and-take
of group dynamics.

All of this was still refreshing news in the late 1940s and early 1950s
when *The Process of Government* was republished (in 1949) and frequently cited. Along with Graham Wallas's *Human Nature in Politics*
(1908), Bentley's belated classic was seen to mark "the beginning of the
modern political behavior approach" (Eulau, Eldersveld, and Janowitz
1956, 7). Some of its other distinctive features, however, were notably
ignored or repressed. Bentley's view of science, for example, was much
more radical in design and effect than the later behavioralists found necessary for their study of groups, processes, and political behavior. It
owed quite a bit to his friend John Dewey's relentless pragmatism and
to the critique of mind language. Thus, where Truman could speak in a
psychological mode about the attitudes and interests behind behavior or
in group processes, Bentley had expressed deep suspicions that behavioral science could proceed coherently in such terms. In his more polemical moments he referred to such things as "mind stuff" or "soul stuff."[8]
Furthermore, Bentley was initially a reformer whose Progressive in-
stincts and muckraking journalism directed and sustained his scientific
impulses. The motto for *The Process of Government* – "This Book is an
Attempt to Fashion a Tool" – prefigured not only a science of political
process, but a science *for* practical politics as well. True to behavioralist historiography, Truman read the motto mainly in methodological
terms, as did other behavioralists in the heady days of the 1950s.

Charles Merriam was the other great and well-remembered figure in
the late prehistory of the behavioral movement. Largely ignoring his
role in local and national politics – as well as his writings on the history
of political thought (1900, 1903) and on citizen education (1934)[9] – the
behavioralists found in Merriam both an intellectual and an institutional
force that helped to pave the way for the behavioral revolution of the
1950s. Merriam stood out because of the profusion of his enthusiastic,
integrative, and futuristic essays on political research, the importance of

psychology, and the interdisciplinary unity of social science (in the singular). The behavioralists remembered it as a defining moment when these essays were bound together as *New Aspects of Politics* (Eulau et al. 1956, 7). The collection not only looked ahead – what with the many "new" and "recent" things whose "tendency" was "progress" – but it connected the present and the future to the past in a particularly influential and expressly methodological way. Merriam indicated what to him (and to many later behavioralists) were "the chief lines of development of the study of political processes":

1. The a priori and deductive method, down to 1850.
2. The historical and comparative method, 1850–1900.
3. The present tendency toward observation, survey measurement, 1900– .
4. The beginnings of the psychological treatment of politics. (Merriam 1925, 49)

Merriam also chose to distinguish old from new political science in terms that expressly contrasted the study of "political behavior" from what was merely "formal" when he delivered his inaugural address as president of the APSA in 1925. Later behavioralists repeatedly cited his deck-clearing proclamation that "some day we may take another angle of approach than the formal, as other sciences tend to do, and begin to look at political behavior as one of the essential objects of inquiry" (Merriam 1926, 7; significantly quoted in Truman 1951b, 37; Eldersveld et al. 1952, 1004; Eulau et al. 1956, 65; and Dahl 1961b, 763).

As striking as were his expressed sentiments, Merriam's other and arguably more important contribution to behavioralism was institutional. He proved to be "one of the greatest academic entrepreneurs in American history" (Westbrook 1991, 280). In particular, he assumed the leading role in founding the Social Science Research Council (SSRC) in 1924. The intellectual influence of the SSRC on the research agenda of the social sciences proved to be immediate and lasting. At the University of Chicago, he similarly sought to realize his vision of interdisciplinary research, to bring in the funds to accomplish this, and to build a department of innovative like-minded political scientists, whether as students or colleagues. Within the span of his years at Chicago, these included Harold Gosnell and Harold Lasswell (whose subsequent influence on the discipline has yet to be fully appreciated), as well as V. O. Key, Herbert Simon, Gabriel Almond, David Truman, and many others who collectively were remembered as "the Chicago school."

The younger members of the Chicago school were to be numbered among the more important of the behavioral revolutionaries in the 1950s. They carried over Bentley's and Merriam's belief that the traditional study of politics had exhausted itself for both theoretical and practical problems. The immensity of social and political change – especially in the light of fascism, communism, and a second world war – added to this belief. So, too, did the political and governmental experiences of many political scientists during World War II. As Robert Dahl later remembered it:

The confrontation of theory and reality provoked, in most of the men who performed their stint in Washington or elsewhere, a strong sense of the inadequacies of the conventional approaches of political science for describing reality, much less for predicting in any given situation what was likely to happen. (Dahl 1961b, 764)

The specter of politics took a Cold War form in the years immediately following World War II, and this also played a causal role on an expressly behavioral social science. In Senate hearings on science legislation in 1945, for example, an interdisciplinary colleague of Merriam's at Chicago – the sociologist William Ogburn – could say that behavioral social science could "aid in the national defense." But it should do so as all "true sciences" do, namely, in the form of value-free, ethically neutral, and otherwise "dispassionate inquiry," added John Gaus, then president of the APSA (quoted in Ball 1993). Besides expressing a shared view that had emerged from the critique of traditional inquiry, this vision of a politically useful but nonetheless value-free political science helped to blunt some criticisms of the social science disciplines that lingered through the McCarthy era (Easton 1990) with all the attendant "tensions and insecurities of the cold war" (Fellman 1952, 81). Indeed, the very term "behavioral" science had its advantages in a political climate in which, as reported in a 1952 House committee, "many of our citizens confuse the term 'social,' as applied to the discipline of the social sciences, with the term 'socialism' " (quoted in Ball 1993; cf. Easton 1962).

The very idea of a behavioral political science gained considerable momentum in this charged context through the offices of the Social Science Research Council's newly formed Committee on Political Behavior. After V. O. Key took over the chairmanship from E. Pendleton Herring in 1949, a series of important working papers – as well as conferences and summer seminars – issued from the committee and were reported in the SSRC's *Items*. For behavioralism, 1951 was something of a banner year when judged by the publication of a series of important and overlapping papers and reports connected with the committee's work. David Truman, author of that year's *Governmental Process* and a later chairman of the committee, drew some "implications of political behavior research" (Truman 1951b:39). "The ultimate goal of the student of political behavior," he proclaimed, "is the development of a science of the political process" based on systematic evidence, rigorous hypotheses, quantifiable techniques, cumulative knowledge, and interdisiplinary cooperation. Although "inquiry into how men ought to act is not a concern of research in political behavior," it was nonetheless true that "a major reason for any inquiry into political behavior is to discover uniformities [and their consequences] for the maintenance or development of a preferred system of political values" (Truman 1951b). The nature of those values was fairly clear to a behavioral audience and made even clearer in a committee working paper entitled "Research in the Political Process" by Oliver Garceau that was published in the 1951 *American Political Science Review*. Garceau began by noting the dilemma inherent in seeking causal generalizations of behavior while believing in "the liberal, democratic faith in man's individual capacity." But in a deft maneuver that not so much reconciled as held in suspension this dilemma, he went on to say:

Students of political behavior need not grasp either horn of such a dilemma in order to push on with their immediately pressing work. Their commitments to constitutional democracy can remain imbedded in philosophical and historical analysis, or conceivably in such empirical evidence as derives from modern studies of comparative cultures. Not only is the liberal faith no barrier to research in political behavior. More than this, our frame of reference concerning the good society is, as commonly observed, essential in threefold fashion: as a determinant of priorities in research, as datum of political behavior and as guide to the use of new insights and understanding. (Garceau 1951, 69)

The body of the paper set out a program of research for the study of voting, communications, public opinion, and leadership. The call for better hypotheses, fuller descriptions, and causal explanations inherent in such a program provided its own avenue to return to the question of the discipline's liberal identity. "It is evident," he concluded, "that more appropriate hypotheses and more complete description can contribute fundamentally to the operation of, and to confidence in, the modern democratic polity" (Garceau 1951, 84–5).

In the crucial decade from 1951 to 1961, the proclamations that were identified with behavioralism – on behavior, science, and liberal pluralism – were increasingly and prominently heard throughout the discipline. The year 1953 witnessed the publication of Easton's manifesto, *The Political System*. Here was a work – quite unlike Bentley's, for example – that immediately galvanized the sentiments of a new generation. Published soon after Easton took up residence at the University of Chicago (in Merriam's old office, no less), *The Political System* set out a thoroughgoing critique of what had passed for previous political science and political theory (from Aristotle to G. E. G. Catlin, as it were). Alternatively wrapped up in normative speculation and textual historicism, the story of the prebehavioral past could best be told in terms of "blighted hope," "malaise," and "decline" (Easton 1953, chs. 1–2, 10). The state came in for particular disapprobation: "Bearing in mind the actual history of the political use of the concept, it is difficult to understand how it could ever prove to be fruitful for empirical work; its importance lies largely in the field of practical politics" (1953, 112). Related criticisms were aimed at a view associated with James Bryce that political science simply needed "Facts, Facts, Facts" – a syndrome Easton labeled as "hyperfactualism." The practical or policy orientation of the discipline was premature because the theoretical work and value clarification had yet to be completed, or even properly begun. Political science should become much more theoretical in its use of situational and behavioral data, and it should generally model itself on the methodological assumptions of the natural sciences. More programmatically, Easton suggested centering research around the concept of "system," as well as defining "politics" in terms of the "authoritative allocation of values" (Easton 1953, chs. 4–5). This definition turned out to be incredibly persuasive throughout the discipline, and the program of "systems analysis" sustained Easton and other political scientists for several years (Easton 1965a,b).

Although the term "systems" was used quite extensively throughout the discipline, not every behavioral political scientist followed the precise program of "systems analysis." Quite the contrary. The categorical framework of behavioralism, as intimated earlier, was broad enough to countenance very diverse kinds of particular research and specialized theories. Proof of this had been made clear before *The Political System* appeared. It was evident not only in *The Governmental Process* by Truman (1951a), but in *The Analysis of Political Behaviour: An Empirical Approach* by Harold Lasswell (1947), in the research agenda on electoral behavior begun in 1948 and later published as *The American Voter* by Campbell, Converse, Miller, and Stokes (1960), in *Administrative Behavior* by Herbert Simon (1949), and in the collaborative project of the SSRC's Committee on Political Behavior by Samuel Eldersveld, Alexander Heard, Samuel Huntington, Morris Janowitz, Avery Leiserson, Dayton McKean, and (again) David Truman (as reported in Eldersveld et al. 1952). The breadth of behavioral research became even clearer in the later 1950s and throughout much of the 1960s. A good sampling – and a very influential collection – was evident in *Political Behavior* (1956), edited by Heinz Eulau and colleagues. Aptly titled and eminently timely, this volume reprinted selections from Bentley, Wallas, and Merriam, as well as Garceau's article on political research, the collaborative report of Eldersveld and company, and an expansive bibliography on methodology. The claims to forging ahead with a science of behavior – and with it the conceptual framework provided by groups, processes, and systems – stand out in the wide range of substantive articles it included between its covers. Amidst these highly visible works in the mid-1950s, it was an appropriate time to declare that a "revolution" was plainly underway in the behavioral sciences as evidenced by its impact on political science (Truman 1955).

The success of the revolution was soon quite consciously recognized and hailed. By 1961, Robert Dahl could look back on the behavioral approach in political science and pen an "Epitaph for a Monument to a Successful Protest" (1961b). The epitaph, not incidentally, preceded by only a couple of years Dahl's presidency of the APSA, and it followed upon his – and arguably the discipline's – most important contributions to liberal pluralism during the behavioral revolution, *A Preface to Democratic Theory* (1956) and *Who Governs?* (1961a).[10] The *Preface* put forward a model of "polyarchal democracy" that was argued to be more adequate as a description and an explanation of the American political system than were the Madisonian and especially the populist theories of democracy. (The latter, in particular, was "not an empirical system. It consists only of logical relations between ethical postulates. It tells us nothing about the real world. From it we can predict no behavior whatsoever" [1956, 51].) The *Preface* paid special attention to the electoral requirements of polyarchy, as well as to a fundamental consensus on liberal democratic norms. Its message that public policies were the product of the pluralistic struggle among competing groups led Dahl to conclude that in America there was rule not by a majority or a minority, but by minori*ties* (1956, 132). This vision of rule by minorities – and of "consensus as a process" of group struggle in a pluralistic system – was reinforced in the *Who Governs?* study in New Haven. Dahl's account of the political system having moved "from cumulative to dispersed inequalities" (1961a, 85, 228) seemed to vindicate the progress of democracy in the United States without overlooking the plain fact that "resources are [still] unequally distributed" (1961a, 228). (Other behavioralists – like Seymour Martin Lipset, who was hailed for his empirical work in Dahl's epitaph – were somewhat more sanguine. Despite admitted problems, the liberal democratic political system as found in the United States was nonetheless "the good society in action" [Lipset 1960, 403].)

Dahl's account of the development of the behavioral approach in his epitaph dealt with the scientific-methodological rather than the pluralistic-political aspects of behavioralism. It was intriguing in part because of its explanatory diversity. He gave equal billing to Merriam, World War II, the SSRC Committee on Political Behavior, survey methods, and philanthropic foundations. These historical sensibilities were complemented by textual ones, particularly in the case of Truman's "neglected" 1951 essay from which Dahl quoted generously and extensively. The behavioral approach would "gradually disappear," Dahl prophesied, not out of having failed but of having succeeded in being "incorporated into the main body of the discipline."[11] There was no complacency in this, in Dahl's mind, because there were many important tasks ahead – those that, as it turned out, the critics of behavioralism would emphasize, as well. These included addressing "what ought to be," avoiding "ahistorical theory," abandoning the "search for mere trivialities," and finding a place for "speculation" (Dahl 1961b, 770–2). But for the moment at least, Dahl wryly noted (1961b, 766), "The revolutionary sectarians have found themselves, perhaps more rapidly than they thought possible, becoming members of the Establishment."

III

The 1960s will be remembered for attacks on the establishment, as well as for the established success of the erstwhile revolutionaries themselves. During the decade, leading behavioralists were to serve as presidents of the APSA, including Truman, Dahl, and Easton. Others would follow during the next decade, including Eulau and Wahlke. Graduate departments in political science were to become much more markedly behavioral in their orientation, as were the leading journals.

New institutes for behavioral research burgeoned, for example, the Inter-University Consortium for Political and Social Research (see Eulau 1969). A new generation of students were to emerge with increasingly sophisticated methodological skills and a behavioral self-understanding (even if without much of an informed judgment or historical memory about the deficiencies of traditional political science or about what occasioned the revolution in the first place). But the institutional successes of the new behavioral establishment were complemented by some exceedingly uncomplimentary attacks on the proclamations of behavioralism.

The attacks on behavioralism began early in the 1960s, raged late into the decade, and spilled over into the 1970s. They came from those who had been stigmatized as "traditionalists," as well as from reformers and radicals who thought that behavioralism was part of the problem in coming to grips with power and privilege in pluralistic America. None of the major or lesser proclamations about behavioralism proved to be immune from these attacks. The very idea of "behavior" was criticized as devaluing "action," "meaning," and "the political." It was also evident how "behavior" had become so stretched as to cover intentional actions, deliberate decisions, procedural rules, negotiated bargains, role playing, verbal communication, personality traits, conscious attitudes, expressed opinions, as well as the inputs and outputs of whole systems. These jostled for primacy amidst the great diversity of behavioral research; and the attempt to contrast all of them with the "traditional" study of institutions, ideals, and legal formalities had become increasingly less coherent. Suspicions that the concept of equilibrium precluded systems analysis from accounting for changes of behavior within or across systems led one later commentator to observe that systems analysis was "a mad millenarian dream" (MacIntyre 1971, 269).

The adoption of an allegedly "positivist" conception of science by behavioralists was repeatedly lambasted, particularly the claim to be able to discover truly general or cross-cultural laws of political life (Gunnell 1969). The proclamation that political science should seek to explain politics in value-free terms or try to remain value-neutral about the political world proved to be especially vulnerable to attack. Many critics argued that the effort was a misguided or even an impossible quest (e.g., Sibley 1962; Taylor 1967), others that it was a contradiction of the discipline's oft-expressed desire to be policy-relevant (Bay 1965). Behavioralism was thereby criticized for advancing "an apolitical politics" through its methodological categories and its vain attempts at value-neutrality (McCoy and Playford 1967). The "scientific study of politics" as a whole – especially the studies of groups, psychology, and administration as found in Bentley, Lasswell, and Simon – came under fierce attack in a volume of essays edited by Herbert Storing. Leo Strauss, the essayists' mentor, concluded the volume with a fiery denunciation of behavioral political science. "One may say of it that it fiddles while Rome burns. It is excused by two facts: it does not know that it fiddles, and it does not know that Rome burns" (Storing 1962, 327).

Strauss also alleged that there was "a mysterious pre-established harmony between the new political science and a particular version of liberal democracy" (Storing 1962, 326). This had been noted a few years earlier by one of the discipline's few mid-twentieth-century historians (Crick 1959), as well as by contemporary critics of pluralism. But whereas Strauss sought to criticize the discipline for mirroring "the dangerous proclivities of democracy" (Storing 1962, 326), the other critics scored it for not being democratic enough. They came out squarely against "the bias of pluralism" (Connolly 1969; cf. Bachrach and Baratz 1962, 1963). Pluralist political scientists were criticized for being blind to the disparities of power among individuals and interest groups, as well as to the brute realities of a political system that excluded the great mass of citizens from effectively expressing their interests, much less from participating in the political community as a whole (Green and Levinson 1970). Some saw in this an essentially apologetic function of the discipline as regards American political life; others, more apocalyptically, saw in it the "end of liberalism" as a coherent description much less a normative account of modern politics as such (Lowi 1969).

Behavioralists responded in various ways to these attacks. One way was simply to return the favor either by renewing the assaults on traditional political inquiry or by taking up new positions against the radical and reformist critics (Polsby 1963). Another way was to proclaim that "the behavioral persuasion in politics" had become an established "way of life" in the discipline, and then go on without "polemics" to survey its successes and "dilemmas" (Eulau 1963, vi, viii, 132). Still another way was to refuse to respond altogether. Indeed, it was a sure sign of disciplinary success when it was left to political theorists (Schaar and Wolin 1963) – who were otherwise no friends to "methodism" (Wolin 1969) – to mount a counterattack on the stridently antibehavioral essays in the Storing volume (cf. Eulau in Baer et al. 1991, 193). Yet another way to respond to the attacks on the new behavioral establishment was to qualify or amend the program of behavioralism itself. In the case of the proclamations about behavior and science, this was already presaged in Dahl's epitaph and would be heard in presidential addresses like Truman's (1964). Liberal pluralism, too, was to undergo a series of important qualifications and amendments at the hands of Dahl and others.[12] Some of these bordered on the virtual abandonment of the grander proclamations of behavioralism.

The dynamics of internal change might be seen in these various attacks and responses. However, an arguably greater impetus for change – particularly in connection with the liberal pluralist view of American political life that had come to be so identified with behavioralism – came from outside the debates over behavioral ideas and scientific ideals. They came, in part, from the institutional structure of the discipline. They also came, in even greater part, from outside the academy altogether. The image of a liberal pluralist society based on a consensus over fundamental norms and values was effectively shattered for behavioralists (and everyone else) by the racially charged urban riots of the mid-1960s and the massive protests against the Viet Nam War in the late-1960s. Not only did the riots and protests suggest the fragility of a liberal pluralist system of values, but they undermined the proclamations by behavioral political scientists to be able to describe, explain, and predict actual political behavior.

Against the backdrop of these spectacular public events, a number of antibehavioral political scientists formed the Caucus for a New Political Science in 1967. Its bylaws took a debater's stance: "Whereas the APSA has consistently failed to study, in a radically critical spirit, either the great crises of the day or the inherent weakness of the American political system, be it resolved that this Caucus promote a new concern in the Association for our great social crisis" (quoted in Lowi 1973, 43). While the caucus ostensibly pledged a reform of the profession, some of its documents more ominously portended "an end to political science" (Surkin and Wolfe 1970).

It was a defining moment in the history of behavioralism and indeed of the discipline as a whole when, in this context, David Easton delivered his presidential address to the APSA. He began his address fully cognizant of the political and intellectual turmoil that was raging in and out of the discipline:

A new revolution is under way in American political science. The last revolution – behavioralism – has scarcely been completed before it has been overtaken by the increasing social and political crises of our time. The weight of these crises is being felt within our discipline in the form of a new conflict in the throes of which we now find ourselves. This new and latest challenge is directed against a developing behavioral orthodoxy. This challenge I shall call the post-behavioral revolution. (Easton 1969, 1051)

Easton spoke frankly – and in ways that cost him the support of many erstwhile allies – about behavioralism's failures. It had identified too strongly with a neopositivist conception of natural science, especially in its claims to be value-free. It had neglected its social responsibilities and thus its contribution to the intelligent formulation of public policy. It had failed "to anticipate the crises that are upon us" and in such a way as to display "the failure of the current pluralist interpretations of democracy." "We have appeared," Easton allowed, "more as apologists of succeeding governmental interpretations of American interests than as objective analysts of national policy" (1969, 1057). Postbehavioralism promised, more constructively, to establish a new "Credo of Relevance" for the discipline, to reintroduce the moral dimensions of political science research, and to embrace a postpositivist (mainly Kuhnian)[13] image of science. It also transformed the older interdisciplinary concerns of behavioralism into an appeal for a Federation of Social Scientists "to satisy our growing sense of political responsibility in an age of crisis" (1969, 1061).

"The New Revolution in Political Science" dramatized and itself contributed to much of what had transpired over the course of twenty years in terms of behavioralism's general proclamations about behavior, science, and liberal pluralism. Easton's own speculations about "postbehavioralism" suggested change, of course, but also continuity (as he made clear in an appendix to the second edition of *The Political System* in 1971). After all, "postbehavioralism" makes sense only inasmuch as its root "behavioralism" does (as do all things which are post-this or post-that, like postindustrial or postmodern). Even when espying postbehavioralism, then, behavioralism was remembered as giving to the discipline of political science in the United States its principal identity and enduring denomination.

As a credo or a positive doctrine, "postbehavioral*ism*," as it turned out, did *not* galvanize the discipline. If anything, it prompted reactions that political science was still too "prebehavioral" (Wahlke 1979; cf. Eulau 1992). Postbehavioralism neither inspired the allegiance nor provoked the challenges that its namesake had. The concern with the practical relevance of the discipline's empirical findings did persist, as can be seen in the APSA presidential addresses of Eulau (1973) and Leiser-

220   *James Farr*

son (1975), among other places (see Torgerson, Chapter 9, this volume). But this was something far far less than a revolution or even the bold proclamations of behavioralism. The status of postbehavioralism as a revolution was symbolically downgraded, as it were, to a "reformation" by Easton himself in order to avoid unnecessary arguments (1971, xvi; cf. Eulau 1992). Even this seemed to overstate the main point genuinely at issue, namely, that the discipline's mood had changed for the simple fact that the behavioral revolution was over. Eulau was soon to speak of the "drift of a discipline" (1977). Other erstwhile behavioralists would remark its evident "decline" (Ladd and Lipset 1978, quoted in Finifter 1983).

Temporally speaking, political science is still in a nominally *post*behavioral era, without the overarching organization or intellectual vigor of a postbehavioralism – or any other "ism" for that matter. Until something as dramatic as behavioralism in fact comes along, political science will doubtless continue to think of itself as simply marking time *after* behavioralism. Without postbehavioral*ism*, political science is simply *post*behavioral. Behavioralism thereby continues to identify the discipline long after its passing, particularly in recent reflections on the discipline that pursue the themes of drift and decline. Prompted by Gabriel Almond's reflections on a discipline "divided" and seated at "separate tables" (1990), a roundtable discussion on the nature of contemporary political science uniformly agrees that political science is fragmented, dispersed, and lacking a "core" (Monroe et al. 1990; cf. Moon 1991). In an important historical essay in *Divided Knowledge*, David Easton notes:

There are now so many approaches to political research that political science seems to have lost its purpose. During the 1950s and 1960s, in the behavioral phase, there was a messianic spirit and collective effort in the promotion and development of the methods of scientific inquiry even while there continued to be opposition to it. Today there is no longer a single, dominant point of view or one that unmistakably catches the imagination, especially of younger members of the profession. Nor is there even a single defensive adversary. The discipline is fragmented. (Easton 1990, 48)

This is not a mere fact about the present, as Easton has made clear even more recently. It was one of the consequences of the realization that the behavioral revolution simply "was not the millennium" (in Baer et al. 1991, 212). Millennium or not, Heinz Eulau looks back to suggest that "the expression 'revolution' was unfortunate" because there was no real overarching "paradigm." There is surely no paradigm now, and much "unfinished business" (in Baer et al. 1991, 193–4). Even the thirty years of American election studies, so central to behavioral research, amount to little more than detailed information for the historian, states Eulau. "So much for the behavioral revolution."

Two recent and none-too-flattering studies of the discipline – *The Tragedy of Political Science* (Ricci 1984) and *Disenchanted Realists* (Seidelman and Harpham 1985) – come to somewhat similar conclusions about the behavioral revolution and the postbehavioral condition. "The behavioral era marked a major watershed in the history of the third tradition," Seidelman avers, only to note that the reformist "third tradition" has come to its own end (Seidelman and Harpham 1985, 185). Ricci finds that behavioralism tragically reenacted that "old-time tension in political science – between scientific findings and scholarly support for democracy" (Ricci 1984, 175). There are good reasons, I believe, to resist interpretations of the history of the discipline couched historiographically in the terms of traditions or of tragedy (Farr 1988b). But the important point here is that Ricci and Seidelman show us – as do Easton and Eulau and many other remembrancers – that our interests in the behavioral revolution and its proclamations are not contingent or antiquarian ones. They make clear that the present postbehavioral era can be understood only with reference to behavioralism and that, even then, the behavioral revolution is open to different interpretations. Our interpretations of the behavioral revolution are necessarily bound up with our search for a present and future identity. In that sense, at least, we may all agree. So much for the revolution.

Notes

1. Heinz Eulau has argued recently that "the expression 'revolution' was unfortunate, which some people used, I probably did. The word, as far as I can determine, was first used in connection with the title of that book David Truman edited for the Brookings Institution. That was called *The Impact of the Revolution in the Behavioral Sciences on Political Science*" (in Baer et al. 1991, 192–3, about Truman 1955; cf. Eulau 1988 and 1992 for similar comments). It is certainly true that behavioralism was also characterized in other ways. But the language of "revolution" did and continues to capture a sense of the transformation that behavioralism promised; and the behavioral revolution is by now nearly standard reference to those years.

2. The term "behavioralism" has come to be the accepted term, and I will follow that usage throughout. "Behaviorism," however, was a frequent syno-
nym, though never in the sense of the reductionist program in psychology.
Somit and Tanenhaus (1967, 183n) note that " 'behaviorism' was common
until the early 1960s, and then gave way to the longer variant." In the influential collection edited by James C. Charlesworth, *The Limits of Behavioralism in Political Science* (1962), David Easton and Mulford Sibley
would consciously use the longer variant, whereas Heinz Eulau would speak
in "behavioristic" terms. By the 1970s, "behavioralism" was the nearly standard usage, but "behaviorism" could still be found, for example, in Jaros and
Grant (1974). Words as such do not matter, of course, as is true of "revolution." However, it is interesting that the choice of appropriate words and
phrases was then, and is still, a matter of some dispute.
3. More extensive lists are possible, of course. Some particularly clear and
helpful ones may be found in Easton, "The Current Meaning of 'Behavioralism' " (1962), in Somit and Tanenhaus (1967, esp. ch. 12, where "the
anti-behavioral brief" is also listed), and in Ricci (1984, ch. 5).
4. In 1967, Somit and Tanenhaus captured the linguistic transformation of the
discipline that had attended the success of behavioralism (1967, 190–1):
"Consider also the dramatic changes in vocabulary. An older generation
spoke knowingly of checks and balances, *jus soli*, divesting legislation,
brokerage function, quota system, bloc voting, resulting powers, propor-
tional representation, pressure group, sovereignty, dual federalism, lobby-
ing, recall and referendum, quasi-judicial agencies, concurrent majority,
legislative court, Taylorism, state of nature, item veto, unit rule, and natural law. From today's younger practitioners there flows trippingly from
the tongue such exotic phrases as boundary maintenance, bargaining, cognitive dissonance, community power structure, conflict resolution, conceptual framework, cross-pressures, decision making, dysfunctional, factor
analysis, feedback, Fortran, game theory, Guttman scaling, homeostasis,
input–output, interaction, model, multiple regression, multivariate analysis, non-parametric, payoff, transaction flow model, role, simulation, political systems analysis, T test, unit record equipment, variance, and, of
course, political socialization."
5. The reading and reception in behavioral political science of the doctrines of
these particular authors – as of the positivist movement more generally (to
which Popper has denied belonging, in any case) – is something that has yet
to be studied in any detail. To do so properly would also require investigating the influences (if any) of legal positivism, economic positivism, and
pragmatism in the mold of Dewey and Peirce. This would be a welcome development because the term "positivism" has come to be used to mean so
many different things – including, unfortunately, as an all-around term of
abuse. The behavioralists were surely interested in making political science

more "scientific." And some self-identified behavioralists did at times invoke the term "positivism" to characterize this interest. See, e.g., Dahl (1958, 91), Presthus (1965, 17–19), and Easton (1990). But the question of actual philosophical influence (if any) remains uninvestigated.

6. Indeed it went back further still, as can be seen in the pages of *Elementa Philosophica*, a long-forgotten American textbook on morals and politics published by Samuel Johnson in 1752, whose second part contains "Ethica, or Things Relating to Moral Behavior." The behavioral revolutionaries need not – and assuredly did not – remember this item from the deep vaults of moral and political science in America.

7. Bentley's critique of "the idea of the state" – its being at best "among the intellectual amusements of the past" and at worst a "propaganda" device – has been frequently noted, including most recently by Rodgers (1989). I here pass on this received and generally correct assessment. However, a more sustained study would look more closely at Bentley's admission that "if an effort were being made [in *The Process of Government*] to restate theoretical political science it might be a serious question how far the exclusion of the term 'state' would be justified" (Bentley 1908, 263, 263n). How far subsequent political scientists – including many behavioralists – refrained from using the language or thinking in terms of "the state" is something of an open question and worthy of further study.

8. Truman has more recently attributed this to the fact that Bentley was "afraid of psychology" (in Baer et al. 1991, 144). In this connection, compare the different assessments of Bentley's attitude toward psychology in Storing (1962, ch. 3), Kress (1973), and Ward (1984). The best account of Bentley's philosophy of social science is found in Ward (1984).

9. Reference to Merriam's work on civic education was made in the APSA committee report entitled *Goals for Political Science* (1951, 26), as also later in Somit and Tanenhaus (1967, ch. 7) and Karl (1974). But these works – on teaching, on the discipline's history, and on Merriam himself – emphasize aspects of Merriam's contributions to the discipline that were not well remembered by the behavioral revolutionaries when discussing behavioral research or behavioralism itself. For further discussion, see Seidelman and Harpham (1985, 119–26) and Leonard, Chapter 3, this volume.

10. Dahl used the language of "polyarchy" – as had Sir Ernest Barker in the 1910s – to describe the regime of groups and the access to power characteristic of the American political system in the first of these works. The terminology of "pluralism" was in greater evidence in the second, as well as in related works of Dahl's during this period and later.

11. This point is expressly challenged in Eulau (1962). Also see Wahlke (1979) on the persistence of "pre-behavioralism" in the discipline.

12. Dahl's work on democratic theory became increasingly more concerned with elite "guardianship." He also made quite plain that 1950s pluralism had underestimated the power of corporations and business interests to dominate other interests and groups. At the same time, his early life commitments to an egalitarian political order and even to democratic socialism returned to his theorizing – or, at least, they became much harder not to detect. Dahl has recently wondered aloud why his commitments were "missed by readers of *Who Governs?*" (in Baer et al. 1991, 169).

13. Thomas Kuhn's *Structure of Scientific Revolutions* (1962) had already made quite an impact on political science, as can be seen in Truman (1964) and Almond (1966). It is not clear if this represented a profound shift in methodological orientation or a sign that the allegiance to positivism or neopositivism had been rather superficial (see note 5). Positivist methodology was in any case being transformed or abandoned by the very philosophers who had originally advocated it. A breathtaking summary of that transformation, and one reason for it, can be found in a remark by the erstwhile positivist A. J. Ayer. When asked by Bryan Magee what, if any, were the defects of positivism, Ayer answered, "Well, I suppose that the most serious of the defects of positivism was that nearly all of it was false" (Magee 1978, 131).

9

Policy Analysis and Public Life: The Restoration of *Phronēsis*?

Douglas Torgerson

The study of politics has since antiquity shown an enduring concern with its relationship to public life. This relationship has often been viewed in the modern era, however, as but one aspect of a progressive acquisition and application of knowledge, in which political perplexities would eventually be overcome by enlightened administration.[1] In the contemporary period, the American behavioralist quest for a science of politics deliberately distanced itself from practical concerns, advancing instead ideals of basic research and detached observation. Nonetheless, there remained in the background a hope for the eventual application of political science, and this hope was dramatically revived in the face of controversy over the relevance of behavioralism. A focus on application developed with the inauguration of a postbehavioral era and a turn toward policy analysis. Yet public life retained a political character that suggested the continuing relevance of ancient ideas.

What was immediately evident to critics of the policy turn, as it came to prominence in the 1970s, was its positivist and technocratic orientation. The effort to establish an applied political science retained much of the tone of behavioralism while drawing the discipline into closer association with developments in policy-related fields such as management science and economics. Yet critics, following the emergence of postpositivism, maintained that the prevailing orientation was inadequate as a guide to practice. What was missing was Aristotelian *phronēsis*, prudence or practical wisdom, or some form of political understanding attuned to the complexities of particular contexts.[2] By the 1980s, this critique allowed for the conception of an alternative ap-

I thank John S. Dryzek and the reviewers for valuable criticisms and suggestions.

proach to policy analysis, a postpositivist policy analysis that would be hermeneutic or interpretive, even critical, and that would counter technocratic tendencies in public life by encouraging the democratic participation of the citizenry.[3]

Attempts to understand policy analysis have often vacillated between two complementary approaches – (1) wide-ranging literature reviews (e.g., Heclo 1972) that attempt to classify varieties or schools of policy analysis, and (2) accounts of policy analysis that focus on its emergence as part of specific political, institutional, and historical contexts (e.g., Wittrock, Wagner, and Wollman 1991). While indebted to both approaches, this essay takes a different tack. No attempt is made here to impress a set of sharply defined categories on the full expanse of the field or to portray in any detail how prevailing policy-analytic practice and conventional training relate to the administrative state or other institutions of advanced industrial societies.

The focus is instead generally narrowed to certain key figures and themes in the emergence of the policy orientation, chosen for their significance in highlighting major intellectual continuities, points of divergence, and crosscutting lines of influence. The approach particularly avoids skimming through fragments and impressions from a wide range of figures only to tie them together with a single thread; the aim is to develop a thicker, though perhaps more ragged, weave. Focusing on complexities of particular figures and themes, this essay proceeds through a series of interrelated interpretations that, taken together, are meant to convey a different kind of story about policy analysis.

The rationale for this approach is not only that it can draw attention to significant patterns in intellectual history, but also that it offers orientation to the problem of political understanding as it has newly been exposed by the postpositivist intervention. The 1970s policy turn, in this regard, was significant in the sense that it dramatically revived the old goal of fashioning a political science relevant to application. But it was a curiously awkward, even reluctant, revival; and its significance appears sharply diminished if viewed in the context of prior and subsequent developments. Thus viewed, the policy turn becomes a pivot, a turning point, particularly significant for its peculiar inattention to political understanding in relation to public life.

Taking the policy turn of the 1970s as such a pivot (section I), this essay proceeds to look both backward and forward from that event. The backward focus (sections II and III) examines earlier efforts to advance a policy orientation, particularly initiatives associated with progressivism and pragmatism. Looking backward in this way supports a consideration (sections IV and V) of the continuing influence of these earlier efforts and their relevance, following the policy turn, to present postpositivist initiatives.

With positivist and technocratic presuppositions, there is nothing peculiar about inattention to political understanding or public life. Given the preoccupations of the period, even the policy turn of a discipline devoted to the study of politics could hardly focus on these issues. Such inattention of course continues, across disciplines, to pervade the broad range of policy-analytic training and practice, especially where inquiry remains narrowly instrumental. The typically apolitical focus of policy discourse, clear enough in academic work yet strikingly evident in applied professional and administrative contexts, does not mean that the tenor of the policy turn in political science was, by itself, particulary significant. The focus testifies rather to the persistence of positivist and technocratic expectations in the wider context of discourses associated with contemporary administrative institutions. The postpositivist policy genre, posing a direct challenge to these discourses, becomes particularly significant to political science as a discipline by returning to its attention problems of public life and political understanding.

With the postwar rise of positivistic behavioralism and the ensuing policy turn, the discipline had largely relegated these concerns to the province of a moribund political theory. The unexpected advent of postpositivism throughout the literature of social inquiry has, however, helped bring renewed vitality to political theory and the perspectives on politics that it preserved (Torgerson 1992a). In a postpositivist context, then, elements of the discipline are positioned to make a distinctive contribution to the policy literature – to establish a connection between theory and practice that reinforces intellectual and institutional challenges to positivism and technocracy while refocusing attention on democratic possibilities (Fischer 1990). In this way, postpositivism promotes forms of policy discourse that go beyond service to established institutions and that thereby potentially involve the interests and insights of a broader citizenry, including democratic social movements seeking alternative policy directions and realignments of power.

The postpositivist policy genre, however, pays a price for its present identity inasmuch as it is defined in opposition to positivism (cf. Hawkesworth 1988). The positivist and technocratic expectations that pervade conventional policy analysis – and that particularly characterized the policy turn in political science – have obscured a story that now needs to be told. It is a story that goes back to the origins of the policy orientation in the pragmatism and progressivism of the early twentieth century, particularly to the figures of John Dewey and Charles E. Merriam; a story that continues with multiple threads involving three subsequent attempts – those of Harold D. Lasswell, Herbert A. Simon, and Charles E. Lindblom – to give shape to the policy orientation; and a story that culminates, but does not end, in current efforts to create a policy orientation that escapes and challenges the technocratic vision. This essay does not venture far into the methodological and political implications of the story, but suggests that it needs to be told if the postpositivist genre of the policy literature is to achieve a more coherent and potent identity.

Political understanding and its relationship to public life, as the story will show, have regularly appeared as a problem in attempts to promote a policy orientation. Postpositivism serves to make the problem obvious but does not provide a neat solution. Indeed, exhibiting divergent approaches to the problem, postpositivism both mirrors earlier efforts and, as we shall see in the conclusion, generates a perplexity of its own. A historical perspective cannot, of course, resolve such perplexity, but it can allow it to be recognized.

I. The Policy Turn

The Paradox of Applied Knowledge

The modern quest to develop knowledge and apply it for the improvement of the human condition featured a paradoxical duality. The relevant knowledge of general laws, of invariant regularities in nature and society, was typically to be gained through a science that, by rigorously abstracting from common understandings, found itself detached from the context of application. The positivism of the nineteenth century reinforced this duality and sought to institutionalize it with a knowledgeable, governing elite who would foster order and progress. A belief that problems could be solved by calculation removed from the context of application set the course for the technocratic project as it emerged in the twentieth century.[4]

The positivism of this century retained a tone consistent with technocracy but, by clearly separating fact and value, created a space for the development of a "pure" science detached from application. Here concern with the immediate use of knowledge would be suspended in the, at least implicit, hope of more effective future application. This was the program that behavioralism took up in the 1950s.

The behavioral movement of this period lacked a clearly articulated doctrine but brought a new scientific "mood" to the study of politics (Dahl 1961b, 770). Despite the lack of a coherent grounding, the positivist character of this mood was unmistakable (Gunnell 1975). Political science thus implicitly distanced itself from the influence of pragmatism, which, in an earlier period, had helped to shape a behavioralist program for a new science of politics focused on application (cf. Ascher 1986). Pragmatism had, indeed, sought to overcome the duality between knowledge and application by stressing knowledge acquisition and application as interrelated, at times perhaps even indistinguishable, dimensions of human activity.

Applying Political Science

When announcing the advent of the "post-behavioral revolution" in 1969, David Easton declared a decisive break with the position on applied research that he had advanced in the 1950s. No longer was it possible to maintain "the ideal scientific stance of behavioralism" – the position "that because of the limitations of our understanding, application is premature and must await further basic research" (Easton 1971a, 335). The trend toward a policy orientation had been emerging throughout the postwar period, and while Easton had quickly recognized and resisted this trend, he now moved to embrace and reinforce it. The policy turn had, by the mid-1970s, developed to a point where both proponents and critics saw policy as central to the discipline, leading it into an interdisciplinary domain, even eclipsing its distinctly political perspective (see, e.g., Heclo 1972; Dye 1975, 1976; Lowi 1975; Gunnell 1976; cf. Dolbeare 1970).

A systems framework has been Easton's key proposal for political science, and this was his main influence as well on the policy turn. The rhetorical significance of a systems vocabulary was that it projected an implicit mechanistic metaphor, reinforcing a sense of distance between political science and the common understandings of political life (Winner 1969). It was thus ironic that in an attempt to become relevant to political life, the most prominent initiative of political science employed an Eastonian systems framework in identifying the determinants and outcomes of public policy. Centering particularly on the statistical analysis of factors related to budgetary expenditures in American states, this mode of policy analysis typically conceptualized data in terms of an input–output model treating political life as a "black box." The approach quickly attained enough prestige that it could be described as "a near-paradigm for public policy research" in political science (Munns 1975, 665; cf. Sharkansky 1970).

Only by a reductive form of analysis, "chopping the world up into manageable units of inquiry," could political science, in Easton's view, contribute "reliable knowledge" to the complex demands of contemporary society (Easton 1971a, 330). In an explicit reference to antiquity, he argued that applied political science should be distinguished from the "prudential knowledge" of the statesman (1971b, 87n). Scientifically based, a technical knowledge of the necessary means to achieve desired ends would progress beyond common understandings (1971a, 363).

Nonetheless, Easton discerned a necessary relationship between applied political science and political understanding because of existing limitations of scientific knowledge. However, he did not indicate how to link scientific and "prudential" knowledge (1971b, 87n) or how to tell when one would be more relevant or reliable than the other (1971a, 353–7). Interpreting prudence as filling gaps in an immature technical knowledge, Easton's conception of applied political science paid inadequate attention to political understanding and neglected its relationship to public life.

The policy turn of the 1970s followed a tendency within behavioralist political science to insulate inquiry from the language and experience of politics. In criticizing this tendency, figures such as Sheldon Wolin had argued earlier that behavioral methods "presuppose a depth of political culture" that behaviorialism itself undermines by seeking to circumvent a "cultivation of political understanding" (Wolin 1969, 1069, 1077–8).

Yet concerns about political understanding and the character of public life were clearly present in earlier anticipations of a policy focus. In this respect, the positivist character of the policy turn in the 1970s provides a sharp contrast to earlier developments: to the prevailing pragmatism of the early twentieth century and to versions of the policy orientation that emerged from this context. With pragmatism, there is a type of "practical reason," which has been called "almost precisely the Aristotelian ideal of *phronēsis*" (Anderson 1991, 364). John Dewey's approach to the intelligent solving of public problems was, in particular, to provide a point of departure for the policy orientation and remains relevant in a postpositivist context where attention again focuses on public life and political understanding.

II. Precursors of the Policy Orientation:
Dewey and Merriam

John Dewey and Charles Merriam have been described as the founders of contemporary American political science (see Shklar 1991).⁵ The obvious implication is that the contemporary scene should largely be regarded as a product of progressivism. Indeed, the advent of the 1970s policy turn, signaling the inability of behavioralism to sustain its drive for a pure science of politics, clearly bore the marks of the progressive impulse.

In the reform movement of the early twentieth century, progressivism – with its adoration of science, expertise, and organization – was accompanied by a promotion of popular democracy (Hofstadter 1955; Haber 1964; and Nuechterlein 1980). Whatever the tensions between these dual elements of reform, the two were also drawn together and viewed as complementary parts of a single, progressive whole. Science and democracy, in short, went together. Both Dewey and Merriam sought not only the application of scientific knowledge to public problems, but also the education of citizens to participate actively in public life (Karl 1974; Damico 1978). The progressive hope to join science and democracy was badly shaken, however, in the aftermath of World War I as attention turned to deficiencies of public opinion and its manipulation through propaganda. The resulting ambivalence carried through from the waning of progressivism to the emergence of the policy orientation.

Dewey: Problem Solving and the Public

Dewey's pragmatic theory of inquiry proceeded from an analysis of thinking as a problem-solving activity, first clearly advanced in *How We Think* of 1910. A central concern for Dewey in the United States of the early twentieth century was how the method of problem solving discernible in human thought could be applied systematically to the solution of public problems. The difficulty was exacerbated by what Dewey viewed in *The Public and Its Problems* of 1927 as an "eclipse of the public" evident in the decline of the community basis of democratic life. Allying his pragmatism with progressivism, Dewey sought to join expert problem solving to an active, democratic society. In doing so, he recognized a problem with popular democracy but resisted the disillusionment voiced in progressive quarters after World War I.

For Dewey, the movement of thought is distinctly active, practical in the sense of being oriented to the solution of problems. Indeed, a problem-solving orientation guides both commonsense activities and those activities, such as science and art, that are informed by specialized and refined methods. What all forms of problem solving have in common, moreover, is a method that can be described in terms of "five logically distinct steps" ([1910] 1978, 236). The process initially proceeds from (1) a sense of perplexity to (2) the definition of a problem; then alternative solutions are (3) identified, (4) considered in terms of their implications, and (5) tested out ([1910] 1978, 236–41).

Stated in such a terse manner, this stepwise framework may suggest a rigid and mechanical procedure. However, this was not Dewey's intention. "No cast-iron rules can be laid down," he maintained, emphasizing the importance of context. He saw the method as a process that humans follow, whether implicitly or explicitly, in their problem-solving activities. An explicit statement of the method as part of a broader educative process, he believed, could enhance problem-solving capabilities and the cultivation of an intellect capable of judging "how far each of these steps needs to be carried in any particular situation" ([1910] 1978, 241). Time and again, Dewey indicates that in this complex, often ambiguous process, there is but one recurrent point of reference: judgment, "the good judgment, the good sense, of the one judging" ([1910] 1978, 261). Evident here are two sides to Dewey's approach to problem solving, dimensions that are apt, as we shall see, to be construed as divergent alternatives: one focusing on an explicit, replicable problem-solving method, and the second emphasizing a less precise, open-ended process.

The propagandistic manipulation of mass populations during the war, however, unsettled the progressive faith that had comfortably situated Dewey's problem-solving agenda in a democratic context. Portraying public opinion as biased and uninformed, Walter Lippmann in the 1920s was the most prominent figure in progressive quarters questioning faith in the public. What he proposed was an organization of experts to guide public affairs. Responding directly to this proposal, Dewey had no quarrel with an organization of experts and indicated that Lippmann had offered the clearest presentation yet of "the fundamental problem of democracy." Still, Dewey called for an active and enlightened public: "The enlightenment of public opinion still seems to me to have priority over the enlightenment of officials and directors" ([1922] 1983, 344).

In *The Public and Its Problems*, Dewey went on to warn of an oligarchy of experts and to emphasize the need for communication in a participatory democratic society: "The essential need . . . is the improvement of the methods and conditions of debate, discussion and persuasion. That is *the* problem of the public" ([1927] 1984a, 365). Yet Dewey's position is not altogether unambivalent. He wants an emerging, active public to assume a key role, but he also retains a place for specialized inquiry. Generally, he is imprecise about the relationship between experts and public in the "framing and executing of policies" because he feels that the capacity of the public "for judgment" cannot be gauged under present conditions of "secrecy, prejudice, bias, misrepresentation, and propaganda" ([1927] 1984a, 365–6). However, he would thus seem to restate the fundamental problem of democracy rather than provide a solution.

Focusing on cultivated judgment and reasoned discussion in the context of action, public problem solving in pragmatism does bear a resemblance to Aristotelian *phronēsis* (cf. Anderson 1991). Simple recourse to antiquity, however, would be out of the question for Dewey. Expressing a certain sympathy with the Aristotelian idea of politics, he accepted its pertinence in the context of the *polis* but viewed modern efforts to revive the idea as inappropriate to new forms of the state (Dewey [1927] 1984a, 239). Yet does Dewey entirely escape a similar difficulty?

For Dewey, the focus of social problem solving is on a process of trial and error applied to the specific, the concrete, the particular (see Damico 1978, 43, 55–6, 78). Yet his treatment of the public would seem to advise a thoroughgoing transformation of the character of public life. The logic of his position anticipates a cooperative interplay of judgment among experts and the public – institutionalized relationships modeled on the pragmatist idea of a community of inquirers. What Dewey indeed envisions is a remaking of politics on the model of a scientific community so that a common commitment to inquiry would displace conflicts inhibiting the intelligent conduct of public affairs ([1927] 1984b, 115–18; see also Damico 1978, 60–5; Kaufman-Osborn 1985). Yet reconstructing politics along these lines would be a project of sweeping scope, one difficult to envision in terms of piecemeal trial and error. Change would have to start in the context of a politics generally inhibiting, rather than promoting, the communication necessary for a new public life.

Merriam: Political Prudence and the New Science of Politics

If there is a resemblance between Aristotelian *phronēsis* and Dewey's intelligent problem solving, Merriam in the 1920s draws a clear connection between a "new politics" and the old Aristotelian idea.[6] While Merriam's new scientific politics is to employ methods more systematic, precise, and accurate than those previously used in political inquiry, he retains a place for "political prudence" – "the conclusions of experience and reflection regarding the problems of politics: wisdom that does not reach the state of science, yet has its own significance" (Merriam 1931, 163; cf. 16–17).

Just as Merriam provides an explicit role for "political prudence," he indicates its limits. In a manner later echoed by Easton, he argues that imperatives of decision often allow "no time to wait for political science" (Merriam 1931, 163). Yet wisdom still does not measure up to science: "Political science must rest upon a more fundamental basis than 'prudence' " (1931, 217).

Nonetheless, Merriam suggests a broader significance for political prudence in shaping the character of public life, in providing the very conditions for the application of political science to political practice. Against the backdrop of the disillusionment with public opinion led by Lippmann, Merriam suggests that "a representative group of wise men and women," practiced in reasoned discussion and supplied with facilities for inquiry, could avoid "many misunderstandings, misstatements, half truths"; yet he also emphasizes that political prudence is not restricted to "savants," but extends to "the generality of citizens" (Merriam 1931, 165, 178; cf. Karl 1974, 98).

Referring explicitly to Aristotle, Merriam proposes an institutionalization of political prudence that relies on "the insight and judgment of the citizens." Prudence develops with self-government by "the whole community," and without this there is no ensuring the "prudent political conduct of the commonwealth." Indeed, the very application of science to government conduct depends on the judgment and insight of the community (Merriam 1931, 178–80). Merriam thus suggests that only political prudence in a democratic context can provide adequate ground for the institutionalization of an applied political science.

Like Dewey, Merriam sought to maintain the progressive link between science and democracy. That link was to be dramatically weakened with the advent of technocratic propensities in the policy field. Nonetheless, the emergence of the policy orientation reveals a diversity of approaches, significant tensions, even points of resistance to the smooth coordination between a technocratic research agenda and the administrative state.

The current appearance of a postpositivist genre in the policy literature has amplified this resistance. Even though figures in the postpositivist genre do not seek to recapture the comfortable progressive association between science and democracy, they are in accord with Dewey and Merriam in advocating the cultivation of a rational public life that involves the active participation of the citizenry. This effort to connect reason with participatory democracy recalls a particular accent of Merriam.

If one can detect in Dewey a tendency to assimilate politics to science on the model of the pragmatist community of inquirers, Merriam retains the distinctiveness of the political. Here, again, there is a clearer Aristotelian tendency in Merriam than in Dewey. Indeed, when a motto was selected to adorn the new Social Science Research Center at the University of Chicago, Merriam was infuriated when Lord Kelvin's dictum, equating the knowable with the measurable, was chosen over the more popular central sentence of Aristotle's *Politics*, the statement that defines humans beings as political beings (Karl 1974, 154–5, 204, 217).

III. Varieties of the Policy Orientation

To interpret policy analysis as invariably technocratic does fit the main thrust of developments in the postwar period and captures the basic character of the 1970s policy turn in political science. What the interpretation neglects, however, are complexities that become particularly visible in light of the profound influence of pragmatism and such figures as Dewey and Merriam. This influence can be traced specifically with regard to the emergence of three leading varieties of the policy orientation: Harold D. Lasswell's promotion of the policy sciences, Herbert A. Simon's appeal to administrative science, and Charles E. Lindblom's reliance on a science of muddling through.

Each of these varieties of the policy orientation can largely be gauged in terms of its response to Dewey, in particular to his treatment of problem solving in *How We Think*. With the origins of the policy orientation, moreover, the issue of expert and public is tied to a questioning of the relationship between common understandings and scientific knowledge. The current ability of the antitechnocratic critique to strike a responsive chord in the policy field suggests the continued influence of this questioning.

Lasswell: Policy Sciences in Context

The accent of the 1970s policy turn suggested that making political science relevant through application was a fresh idea. However, when Easton in the early 1950s counseled an emphasis on pure research rather than application, he was already rejecting the project of the "policy sciences" that Lasswell had explicitly formulated in the 1940s and was to refine and promote for the remainder of his career. The immediate context in which Lasswell conceptualized this project was his work as a policy advisor in wartime Washington. Yet the basis of the idea was clearly present in his thought as far back as the mid-1920s, when he was a graduate student under Merriam at the University of Chicago. His vision of an intellectual leadership promoting an "intelligent social order" was formulated then amid diverse influences, of which pragmatism and progressivism were of central importance.[7]

In a late work, *A Pre-View of Policy Sciences*, Lasswell explicitly portrayed the policy sciences as "a contemporary adaptation of the general approach to public policy that was recommended by John Dewey and his colleagues in the development of American pragmatism" (Lasswell 1971, xiii–xiv). That book provided a summary framework of inquiry with three key principles to guide an emerging policy sciences profession: the policy sciences were to be "contextual, problem-oriented, multi-method" (1971, xiii).

In promoting his framework, Lasswell was given to a repetition of terse formulations, a reliance on abstract models, and a painstaking enumeration of elements: for example, five intellectual tasks; a range of eight values with corresponding institutions; a policy, or decision, process mapped as a seven-phase sequence. Following a pragmatist view of inquiry as problem oriented, Lasswell developed the framework over the course of his career. As early as 1924, his point of departure was Dewey's *How We Think*: "We are impelled to think when our habitual mode of adjustment to a situation fails to work smoothly" (Atkins and Lasswell 1924, 193).[8] Lasswell's enumeration of intellectual tasks and his portrayal of a sequential policy process both reflect the influence of Dewey's stepwise formulation of problem solving. Yet it is significant that Lasswell did not neglect judgment.

The principle of contextuality is central to Lasswell's framework of inquiry. Inquirers, both individually and collectively, are to escape errors of fragmentation by orienting themselves to the entire context of which they and their work form a part; there is to be a deliberate project of mapping "self-in-context" (Laswell 1971, 155). While the scope of this project is in principle comprehensive, there is no expectation that it is ever to be finished. Not only is the total context vast and complex, it is also changing. An orientation to the dynamic sequence of events is thus provisional and speculative. Yet agnosticism provides no alternative, for an at least implicit orientation to context is inescapable. And any orientation, as itself part of the pattern of events, has consequences for the wider context. In particular, a model of historical development, coupled to images of possible futures, is part of the shaping of the future. A continuous project of contextual orientation thus is necessary in the development of a policy sciences profession.

The future role of intellectuals was central to Lasswell's concerns, and from the 1920s on, he was attuned to ambivalent tendencies of modernity. The rationality of the age, the advance of technology, the promise of a secure civilization of intelligent communication and aesthetic cultivation – these were mirrored by chaos, scarcity, propaganda, and psychopathology (Torgerson 1985, 1990b). Eventually, Lasswell viewed this ambivalence in terms of two sharply divergent trends: one toward a democratic commonwealth of freedom and dignity, the other toward a "garrison state," even "a world concentration camp" (e.g., Lasswell 1965b). With either direction, Lasswell was convinced, intellectuals would have key roles; and in proposing the policy orientation, he was quite explicit about his own stance. Professional commitment to the "policy sciences of democracy," he hoped, would counter oligarchic and bureaucratic threats.

Lasswell's promotion of the policy sciences thus followed the lead of Dewey and Merriam in seeking to enhance the role of intelligence in public life. Like them, he stressed the importance of the education of citizens and of a participatory dimension in a democratic culture; but he also went much further than either in probing the domains of propaganda and psychopathology and thereby exposing shortcomings in ordinary democratic discussion. While Lasswell's proposals for a psychiatrically oriented "politics of prevention" ([1930] 1977, 197) strike the clearest technocratic notes in his work, one should not miss the critical import of his focus.

Attuned to the propaganda and psychopathology evident in World War I and its aftermath, Lasswell came to intellectual maturity just as progressivism, led by Lippmann, was experiencing a profound disillusionment with public opinion. Like Dewey, however, Lasswell resisted this disillusionment and was to assert the possibility of "democracy through public opinion": Democracy needed "a new way to talk," and this could be promoted through the education and enlightenment of the public if professionals adopted the role of "clarifier" (Lasswell 1941, ch. 7; cf. Lasswell 1926). The policy sciences of democracy, as Lasswell conceived them, would be committed to widespread, rather than narrow, participation in the "shaping and sharing" of power (see, e.g., Lasswell 1971, 44–8).

The policy sciences, Lasswell was aware, might succumb to "the threats and temptations of power" (Lasswell 1974, 177), but he believed that contextuality would weigh against this possibility. Even though adhering to ethical noncognitivism and acknowledging diversity and unpredictability in value commitments, he found it difficult to understand how anyone could genuinely seek enlightenment through the contextual principle and not also be committed to the goal of a democratic commonwealth (Lasswell 1968, 182). He believed the contextual principle necessary as a guide both to individual inquirers and to a profession.

When Lasswell speaks of mapping "self-in-context," he means the self both in its depth psychological dimensions and as located in the pattern of world history (see, e.g., Lasswell [1935] 1965a). Freud and Marx, the critique of psychopathology and of ideology, both loom large here, and the critical import of Lasswell's contextual principle becomes clear (Torgerson 1985). The point is to bring the liberating capacity of self-reflective rationality to bear in the policy process, with the effect expanding beyond the profession to enlighten the broader population and thus transform the character of public life. Indeed, the central goal of a policy sciences profession is not to assert control, but to promote conditions for freedom. Dewey wanted much the same thing, but by placing an emphasis on the whole and by explicitly viewing the policy sciences profession as part of a pattern of world historical development, Lasswell steps beyond the particularistic focus of Deweyan problem solving.

Despite his interdisciplinary approach, Lasswell's point of departure remains political science, a discipline that proceeds from the "working knowledge of politics" among political actors. Lasswell draws explicitly upon Merriam's treatment of "political prudence," yet implicitly introduces a contrast to his mentor's position by portraying such prudence as the basis of political science: The chief theoretical task is to reformulate political prudence (Lasswell and Kaplan 1950, xxii).

To reformulate the working knowledge of politics does not directly serve political practice but is a theoretical task necessary for the conduct of political inquiry (Lasswell and Kaplan 1950, xxii). This task is part of a "contemplative" moment of inquiry, which is distinguished from an "active" or "manipulative" one (Lasswell [1935] 1965a, 5–6, 16–17; Lasswell and Kaplan 1950, xi–xii). Yet there is an interplay between these moments of theory and practice in which the practical, problem-solving orientation remains central. Systematic inquiry is capable of refining political prudence, not of replacing it; political prudence remains the ground of theoretical development and the constant medium of political practice: "The practitioners of politics . . . need a 'positional sense'; the maxims of prudence require 'good judgment' for successful application" (Lasswell and Kaplan 1950, xxii). Neither action nor contemplation alone, moreover, but the two together provide for the "political orientation" of inquirers (Lasswell 1965a, 215).

Contextual orientation was to promote creativity and flexibility for action and inquiry in a fluid, unpredictable political domain (Lasswell 1964, 147). Lasswell indeed advanced a "preference for creativity" in marked contrast to a common "preference for automation," a "desire to abolish discretion on the part of the chooser and to substitute an automatic machine-like routine" (1955, 387). Linking his preference to a hope for "liberating" events, Lasswell did not hesitate to employ non-logical methods, even to remark on intriguing similarities between pragmatism and mysticism (1964, 155). Psychoanalytic free-fantasy, in particular, provides a way out of "self-deception" and the limitations of logical thought ([1930] 1977, 36–7). Insights into the self-in-context bring to the focus of attention forces that have surreptitiously guided conduct. The effect is to deny them their hidden, "privileged position" and thereby to enhance freedom. Indeed, the goal of inquiry becomes "*freedom* rather than prediction," not only in a profession, but in the development of a democratic commonwealth (1951a, 524).

Free-fantasy is hardly apparent in Lasswell's terse terminology and stepwise models. Once insights have been achieved, however, a prolonged psychoanalytic process culminates in the identification of key symbols to guide the interpretation of self-in-context. A coherent conceptual order finally emerges out of a chaos of associations ([1930] 1977, 218). It is similar with Lasswell's overall framework, which not only draws upon psychoanalysis, but which can itself be viewed as the culmination of a prolonged exercise – of a wide-ranging career effort to identify key symbols capable of adequately guiding the focus of attention in policy-oriented inquiry.

Lasswell long supposed that the conduct of inquiry could issue in consensus, in a shared professional orientation to be communicated to the citizenry. At the end of his career, faced with obvious differences among professionals, Lasswell suggested that alternative perspectives be made systematically available to the public (1979, 63). Yet he did not seem to

240   *Douglas Torgerson*

see a paradox remaining in his framework; for the institutionalization of
any set of key symbols, however refined, comprehensive and effective,
can constrain divergent perspectives and inhibit insight.9

Simon: Administrative Science and Public Policy

Following World War II, the policy orientation entered the shadow of
an administrative state armed with a new array of decisional technology.
In a policy domain populated by operations research, cost–benefit
analysis, program budgeting, and systems modeling, the clear preference was for the automation of decision procedures that Lasswell rejected in favor of creativity. Yet this technocratic accent was not
exclusive to fields like management science and microeconomics: It
was already audible within political science itself, especially in public
administration.

With *Administrative Behavior* in 1947, Herbert A. Simon offered a
conceptual framework designed to promote the development of administrative science. This work began as a doctoral dissertation in Merriam's political science department at the University of Chicago.
Studying there with Lasswell and other faculty in an intellectual climate
set by Merriam, Simon was significantly influenced by pragmatism but
later turned deliberately to positivism and the attractions of its greater
formalism (1991a; 1991b, ch. 3). Simon's framework for administrative
science stands in contrast both to Lasswell's proposal for the policy sciences and to Lindblom's concept of a science of muddling through.

Simon's point of departure in *Administrative Behavior* was his critique of "the proverbs of administration" as being a kind of folk wisdom,
not principles of an administrative science ([1947] 1976, ch. 2). He rigorously distanced administrative science from common understandings
(see, e.g., 1950). Words like "creativity," "intuition," "judgment" were
but vague labels covering cognitive processes for which research sought
precise, formal models. With the postwar advent of management science, he distinguished between "programmed" and "nonprogrammed"
decisions, not only arguing that the former tend to displace the latter, but
also suggesting that problem solving is a process in which "nonprogrammed decisions" are reached "by reducing them to a series of programmed decisions" ([1960] 1977, 70).

While he draws explicitly on *How We Think*, Simon does not
mention the crucial role that Dewey affords judgment. Dewey is invoked rather as the inventor of a stepwise model of problem solving

that can help to clear up a mystery: "The secret of problem solving is that there is no secret" (Simon [1947] 1976, 43, 69). With the secret revealed, management science is well embarked on a "technological revolution" and poised for a significant advance: "We are gradually acquiring the technological means . . . to automate all management decisions, nonprogrammed as well as programmed" (Simon [1960] 1977, 31; cf. 54–6).

Despite the distinctly technocratic tone of Simon's approach, his explicit purpose in promoting a reform of administrative processes is to assert more effective "democratic control" over public administration ([1947] 1976, 177). Simon invokes Dewey's "democratic philosophy of the relation of expert to public," even citing *The Public and Its Problems* as advancing "the essential thesis" of *Administrative Behavior* ([1947] 1976, 195). Despite Dewey's ambivalence, however, the whole thrust of his argument anticipates the emergence of an active and educated public in a form of participatory democracy. In contrast, Simon restricts his concern to the responsiveness of administration in the context of a representative democracy.

Seeking to enhance "democratic responsibility in modern government" by returning "the legislature . . . to a place of influence in the determination of public policy," Simon invokes "the ideal of a rational budget process" ([1947] 1976, 59, 195–6). Of particular importance is finding a way to state goals in measurable terms so that a comprehensive budget can specify adequate levels as well as forms of service, while taking into account the type and amount of resources needed to attain them. Simon views a task of immense and difficult research as necessary if "rationality" is to have "any significant role" in administrative decision making. The problem cannot be solved by experienced judgment or insight, for these are usually but "the sheerest guesswork" ([1947] 1976, 189, 194–5; cf. Simon 1987).

Although Simon clearly recognizes and stresses the "bounded" character of rationality, the whole thrust of his work is to find a way to coordinate the limited rationality of individuals into the organizational rationality of a more comprehensive decision-making system ([1947] 1976, xxvi–xxxiii, 38–41, 76–7, 102–8). Simon's promotion of an "ideal" rational budgetary process constitutes a notable step along the path in public administration that culminates in the postwar emergence of advanced decisional technologies (Schick 1966, 250). In this period, Simon stresses the potential to develop programmed decision procedures that can replace nonprogrammed decision making.

Nearly everything must be routinized if the political and administrative system is not be "choked" (Simon 1967, 100). Despite advances in decisional technology, Simon acknowledges that there is a "judgmental remainder" (1967, 110); and given the unpredictability of judgment, he suggests that political control of administration can be safeguarded by a profession rendered reliable by being made predictable (1967, 93–100). Since this reliance on a predictable professionalism cannot be considered foolproof, Simon proposes pressing ahead further with automation and, more significantly, formalization. Stating the basis of decisions "explicitly and definitely" allows for political monitoring and control (1967, 113).

While Simon recognizes in "the increasingly technical nature of public affairs" a problem of maintaining "lay control over the expert," his solution is thus to render public affairs even more technical and to increase reliance on experts (1967, 113). To the extent that the technical nature of public affairs involves the promotion of a technocratic idiom and a distancing of policy discussions from common understandings, however, the tendency would not be to assert political control over administration, but to reshape politics in the image of administration.

Lindblom: Muddling Through

The premise of Lindblom's incrementalism – that only "partial analysis" is possible – bears a distinct resemblance to Simon's thesis of "bounded rationality." Indeed, both men recognize this similarity (Lindblom 1979, 519–20; Simon 1991a). However, a key contrast between the two emerges through Lindblom's antitechnocratic posture, a stance that is reflected in his distinctive reading of Dewey.

If there is a science to policy, it is, for Lindblom, one of "muddling through" – both in individual problem solving and in patterns of "partisan mutual adjustment" that give rise to an "intelligence of democracy" (1959, 1965). Aware that his work emerges from a "climate" marked by Dewey, Lindblom draws explicitly on the treatment of problem solving in *How We Think* to argue that comprehensive strategy is inconceivable in policy analysis (Braybooke and Lindblom 1970, 18–19, 44).[10]

The process of problem solving is uneven and indirect, moving in various directions, taking unexpected turns, dramatically changing focus, relying on both "chance" and "system" (1970, 81). Yet what Lindblom implicitly rejects from *How We Think* is Dewey's conceptualization of problem solving as a stepwise procedure. Lindblom focuses attention on the other side of Dewey: on problem solving as "a sequence of approx- imations," an unfolding process "marked by the mutual adjustment of ends and means" (Braybrooke and Lindblom 1970, 73, 135, 252n5).

Lindblom indeed takes exception to Lasswell's stepwise model of the policy process. While Lindblom allows that viewing the process as "a sequence of steps" or as "a set of interlocked moves" can have its uses, he insists that such a view encourages the misleading notion that policy is "the product of one governing mind" (Lindblom 1968, 4). He seeks to undercut the pretensions of a professionalism claiming the authority of a special, abstract knowledge designed to inform "the decision maker" (Lindblom and Cohen 1979, 33). Such a conception overstates the role of "analysis" in contrast to "interaction" and ignores a possible complementarity based on a central role for "ordinary knowledge" (1979, 11–27).

In this connection, Lindblom criticizes Lasswell's view of the policy sciences as "guiding the focus of attention of all participants in deci- sion" (Lindblom and Cohen 1979, 37; see Lasswell 1971, 61). What Lindblom overlooks, however, is the critical import Lasswell assigns to the "focus of attention." Lindblom's own recourse to ordinary knowledge signals a return to common understandings that, as in hermeneutics, avoids problems of ideology and psychopathology. Lasswell's framework of inquiry is designed to render these problems inescapable.

IV. From Technocracy to Reflective Practice

The technocratic project, reinforcing the modern paradox of applied knowledge, envisions reason set apart in its own domain, controlling an objectified social mechanism. While Lasswell's proposal for a policy sciences profession is often portrayed as a technocratic venture, it is Simon's reliance on automation and professional predictability that – notwithstanding its stated democratic rationale – gives clear expression to that vision. Indeed, Simon's theoretical work on administration pro- vides an imposing intellectual centerpiece to the technocratic project of the twentieth century.[11] Lindblom, in contrast to both Lasswell and Si- mon, draws technocratic professionalism sharply into question. While implicitly critical in rejecting the technocratic project, his position em- braces common understandings and lacks an explicit critical principle.[12] Yet critique itself paradoxically puts inquiry at odds with common un- derstandings and risks again dividing expert and public.

Rationality in the Policy Process?

Praising Lindblom's "seminal" work on social problem solving and thereby echoing a particular strain of Deweyan pragmatism, Aaron Wildavsky has sought to turn policy analysis away from a technocratic preoccupation that is deceptive, self-deceptive, and inattentive to the "world of action" (Wildavsky 1979, 27–8, 35). Against a policy analysis concerned with clearly defined problems, Wildavsky proposes a "creativity" that, emphasizing process, risks the "form" of rationality for its "substance" (1979, 3–9).

Policy analysis as "art and craft" is necessary to a "self-conscious society," which, recognizing "permanent problems," can have "no choice except to think." Thinking, though, does not become oriented to technocratic problem solving, but develops within and centers on processes of interaction that render "our failures more instructive and our dilemmas more expressive of our moral selves" (1979, 22–3). Being interactive, analysis is consistent with the participation of citizens as well as professionals (1979, ch. 11). Indeed, the partial "truth" that analysts can express is not so much to be found "in them" as in "their give and take with others" (1979, 405, 12).

Wildavsky thus opposes the technocratic project by stressing the limits of a policy analysis fixated on "cogitation" and by pointing to the potential of "interaction" as a process of policy-relevant social learning (1979, 404). The clear democratic implications of Wildavsky's position recall Dewey's earlier vision of communication among an active and enlightened public. From an explicitly postpositivist – indeed critical – perspective, John Forester (1985) has, however, objected that Wildavsky's reliance on interaction fails to make a key distinction between two fundamentally different kinds: a form that is conducive to learning and one that is not. This point is especially relevant to a political world in which common understandings cannot be taken for granted.

Forester introduces a contrast between strategic interaction and communication – that is, between a context in which participants merely seek successful outcomes for themselves and one in which they share the goal of reaching mutual understanding. Given this contrast, Forester maintains, one cannot avoid the task of judging the different forms of interaction as being more or less appropriate for learning. Confusion, deception, manipulation, and misinformation all arise from interaction but, in themselves, do not constitute genuine learning. For an educative process to be secured, it is necessary that "citizens step outside their immediate contexts of interaction and seek recourse to domination-free discourses" (Forester 1985, 273). From a postpositivist perspective, Forrester thereby reasserts the concern with communicative distortion that, though once clearly troubling Dewey and Merriam, was not cogently addressed until Lasswell followed them with his critique of psychopathology and ideology (Torgerson 1985).

While exposing technocracy as an emperor without clothes, the pragmatism of figures like Lindblom and Wildavsky reaches a conceptual limit, lacking a standpoint from which to critically scrutinize prevailing community norms and perspectives. Indeed, their critique of technocracy shows pragmatism trying to reach beyond itself – to a point that Lasswell reached, on conceptual grounds, by drawing on Freud and Marx. With Lasswell, however, a focus on the threats of bureaucracy and oligarchy does not become an explicit critique of technocracy. Such a critique is blunted not because his proposal for a policy sciences profession conceptually accords with technocratic presuppositions, but because his chosen central symbol – "the policy sciences" – conveys connotations that inescapably recall scientistic notions of the progressive era. Only with the advent of a postpositivist policy genre in the 1980s does the critique of technocracy enter an entirely supportive intellectual terrain.

Like the efforts of other figures in the postpositivist genre, Forrester's move appeals to the critical theory of Jürgen Habermas, who proposes the standard of an "ideal speech situation" as a guide to inquiry and practice. Committed to a form of interaction beyond the strategic interplay characteristic of political life, critique turns against both the domain of common understandings and the restricted nature of technocratic reason, anticipating a mode of inquiry patterned on a model of "comprehensive rationality." Yet such a mode of inquiry is itself prone to demand "a methodological framework of established rules" to ensure that each element of comprehensive rationality receives its due; for inquiry promoting participation could become "a formula for trouble" without a "well-structured model" on which to proceed (Fischer 1990, 235, 377).[13] By following the call of reason and setting itself in judgment of common understandings, critique has an ironic potential to manifest itself as a mirror image of technocracy.[14]

Reflective Practice and Political Understanding

Pursuing the critique of technocracy and responding to disillusionment with professionalism, Donald A. Schön (1983) counterpoises to a positivist "technical rationality" a concept of "reflective practice" that, inspired by the advent of postpositivism, accentuates both hermeneutic and critical moments. Technical rationality has fostered the "dominant model" of policy analysis (1983, 339). Against this model, Schön describes the reflective practitioner in hermeneutic terms as engaging in a "conversation with the situation"; yet he also emphasizes the critical point that perspectives are "instruments of political power": Defining situations and problems means "struggle" as well as conversation (1983, 348).

In a formulation explicitly borrowing language from Dewey, Schön maintains that the presupposition of neatly formed problems is bound to mislead inquiry: "The situations of practice are not problems to be solved but problematic situations characterized by uncertainty, disorder, and indeterminacy" (Schön 1983, 16–17, 357n38). Schön here draws from Dewey the point that problems are defined amid situations found troublesome and challenging precisely because they are not neatly formed. Neither means nor ends are fixed from the outset but are defined "interactively" in a process of "naming and framing" that transfigures established categories (1983, 68, 40–8). The prospect is for "frame-reflective policy discourse" (Rein and Schön 1991).

While reflective practice promotes "a demystification of professional expertise" (Schön 1983, 345), Schön nonetheless distances himself from "counterprofessionals" who advance a "radical criticism of the professions" and propose "a utopian vision of reform" (1983, 343–5, 294, 340). Counterprofessionals overlook the extent to which they themselves are professionals: "Experts tend to behave like experts" (1983, 342). Radical counterprofessionalism, Schön thus suggests, is too self-assured, too lacking in critical self-reflection as a form of professionalism.

In the contemporary policy context, Schön sees "all sides" arming themselves with expertise immunized against reflection, and he worries that the consequence will be to inhibit the "reflective listening" needed to challenge perspectives (1983, 350), thereby undermining the prospect implicit in the idea of reflective practice: "a vision of professionals as agents of society's reflective conversation with its situation, agents who engage in cooperative inquiry within a framework of institutionalized contention" (1983, 342, 353).

Even though Schön rejects the "utopian vision" advanced by counterprofessionals, he here indicates that his concept of reflective practice fosters a vision that would require a transformation of political life. While this change is by no means conceived as a return to the ancient *polis*, the modern focus on politics as conflict is to be attenuated by a shared commitment to inquiry. Schön retains a clash of interests but also envisions a political community engaged in "reflective conversation" with itself – what Dewey would call a "public." Reflective practice indeed anticipates a particular form of political understanding – one oriented to community yet marked by the tensions of modernity.

V. Policy Analysis and Political Understanding

Demands of a Practical Focus

The problem of political understanding not only looms large in the new postpositivist genre of policy analysis, but has been present throughout the emergence of the policy orientation. Often with more or less direct reference to the Aristotelian formulation, the concept of political understanding has formed a recurrent point of reference in efforts to draw twentieth-century American political science into the realm of practice.

A practical focus in political inquiry indeed could not escape recourse to some form of political understanding capable of overcoming the modern duality of knowledge and application. In seeking relevance for political science, the policy turn of the 1970s initially replicated and reinforced this duality. Even though it proved unacceptable to wait for positivism to establish an applicable body of knowledge, positivism still provided the model for an applied political science. However, the applied focus could not avoid a nod to political understanding and the political prudence of antiquity.

The lingering positivism of the policy turn helped draw attention to a central flaw of the technocratic project. The price of the technocratic fixation was an inability to conceptualize and explore the complexities, nuances, and ambiguities characteristic of engagement in a context of common understandings. The perplexities arising from the policy turn constituted merely a rather awkward version of problems that, as we have seen, had been addressed earlier in the emergence of the policy orientation. This had been done, however, by figures whose pragmatist and progressive presuppositions still allowed them to consider forthrightly issues of public life and political understanding.

Political Understanding and the Context of Public Life

Political understanding suggests a way to overcome the modern duality of knowledge and application: Knowledge of politics remains continuous with the common understandings that guide the actual conduct of public life. Recourse to antiquity, in particular, discloses a form of political discourse in which the vocabulary, while refined to enhance "precision, consistency, and scope," nonetheless remained intimately related to "political experience": "A connecting thread," to quote Wolin, "persisted between the polished concept and the old usages" (Wolin 1960, 14–15).

Typically taking Aristotle's *phronēsis* as their point of departure, contemporary formulations of political understanding retain this connecting thread. *Phronēsis*, a way of knowing involved in practice, pertains to those domains, characterized by variability and contingency, in which the subject matter itself excludes the possibility of knowledge being fixed with precision, accuracy, and certainty. Deliberation, insight, and judgment are necessary, but *phronēsis* is manifest only in action, in the performance of deeds, and cannot be equated with a technique or craft. In Aristotle's conception, politics, like ethics, pertained to a domain of variability and contingency where action took account of a way of life, an *ethos*, shared in common. Political *phronēsis*, judging and acting politically in a manner appropriate to the circumstances, is inconceivable apart from the context of a political community. Politics presupposes the *polis*, embraced as a legitimate institution, with common understandings and norms that can be taken as a basis of judgment and action.[15]

The contemporary concept of political understanding typically contains the implicit aim of restoring meaning, of reaching and maintaining the common understandings necessary for the life of a political community. This hermeneutic move, however, can obtain direct access to Aristotelian political *phronēsis* only by ignoring the difference between present political conditions and those of the *polis* presupposed by Aristotle's concept. The modern idea of politics, as dramatically formulated by Machiavelli, cannot take such a political community for granted. Proceeding in a context where common understandings and norms are thrown into question and disrupted, politics assumes the character of technique capable, under fortuitous circumstances, of creating and securing political order.[16]

In promoting intelligent action and judgment appropriate to the public life of a modern democratic society, Dewey implicitly revealed a clear affinity with Aristotelian *phronēsis*, but explicitly rejected any restoration of ancient forms. By envisioning the democratic community on the model of a pragmatist community of inquirers, moreover, Dewey advanced a view of the modern democratic public that ultimately reflected a progressive propensity to deflect politics in favor of science.

While this propensity was also evident in the new science of politics proposed by Merriam, Dewey placed a distinct accent on politics, specifying a role for political prudence while explicitly stressing an Aristotelian reliance on a prudent community of citizens.

Even though both Dewey and Merriam were concerned about the problem of distorted communication in public life, neither faced the implications of the problem or the problematic character of modernity as fully as did Lasswell. Unlike Merriam, Lasswell portrays political prudence not as somehow separate from political science, but as the key focus of inquiry. The task of reformulating political prudence is a moment in a larger process of refining judgment through a connection between theory and practice. Indeed, Lasswell's approach perhaps suggests less affinity with Aristotle's virtue of *phronēsis* than with the prudence of Machiavelli's *virtú*, for the political community cannot be taken at face value; in a "rivalrous culture" marked by institutionalized deception on a large scale, there are clear reasons for distrust (Lasswell 1971, 79–80; cf. 1974, 181).

With his conceptual framework focused clearly on problems of psychopathology and ideology, Lasswell would subject elements of political prudence itself to suspicion and exposure through critical insight. Clearly, such a move has the potential – as Lasswell (1979, 533) knew – to foster a divide between a policy sciences profession and a broader population. Yet such a move also has the capacity to keep community norms and perspectives open to scrutiny, including those of the professionals themselves. This point is particularly pertinent to a world still beset by a technocratic politics of expertise (cf. Fischer 1990).

Political understanding today cannot avoid the awareness that besides relying on common understandings, public life is also characterized by conflict, distortion, and manipulation. A postpositivist policy analysis seeking to restore political understanding to the conduct of inquiry must not avoid the critical move needed to give this awareness its due (Torgerson 1986b).

Restoring Phronēsis? A Perplexity for Postpositivism

The policy focus now intersects with the hermeneutic emphasis in postpositivism. Like those delighted to learn that they have been speaking prose, policy analysts become aware that they are engaged in a hermeneutic activity; and it thus appears a short step to the restoration of *phronēsis* (Jennings 1983, 15; 1987, 129).[17] Political *phronēsis*, though, presupposes the shared norms and understandings of a political community. Restoring *phronēsis* would indeed mean restoring the *polis*. Political understanding is not simply a knowledge of means to attain ends: A form of political understanding is also part of a form of political life and at least anticipates a political community.

Emphasizing the hermeneutic dimension of inquiry accentuates the place of discussion in a domain of common understandings. Yet a hermeneutic posture also tends to presuppose the legitimacy of an existing context of community and tradition. The effect is to obscure the strategic character of political understanding attuned to the interplay of power. This is why the problem of distorted communication, if fully confronted, pushes pragmatism beyond itself in the direction of a critical frame.

A critical approach does not take the legitimacy of community or tradition for granted but focuses scrutiny on them: The construction of a legitimate political community remains a goal to be accomplished. Even though critique stays in touch with the world of common understandings, the critical spirit also keeps its distance – employing its own frame of reference to challenge the terms of that world.

By embracing both hermeneutic and critical moments, inquiry guided by reflective practice anticipates a context of common understandings and mutual regard tied to a frame-reflective mode of policy discourse. This is surely neither the *polis* of antiquity nor any form of political community fixed in its identity or framework of understandings: It is an open-ended form of public life, vaguely imaginable yet unachieved. The new postpositivist genre in policy analysis faces the perplexing problem of fostering a political understanding that can envision and anticipate this form of public life while remaining critically attuned to the present political context.

Notes

1. Wolin's survey of political thought significantly culminates in a focus on "the age of organization" (1960, ch. 10). The vision of enlightened administration displacing politics has emerged as the hallmark of twentieth-century technocratic discourse but also extends back through the Enlightenment and is anticipated in the early modern period (cf. Torgerson 1990a; 1986a), not to mention antiquity (cf. Arendt 1968).
2. This admittedly vague formulation is simply meant to convey a tendency in the literature. A point to be emphasized later is that Aristotelian political *phronēsis* constitutes a particular form of political understanding, presup-

posing the context of a particular form of public life. This point is relevant
to a tension between hermeneutics and critique in postpositivist approaches
to policy analysis. See notes 16 and 17 and the corresponding text.

3. Tribe (1972) provided a point of departure for many who proposed postpositivist alternatives. For a helpful overview, see Amy (1984); cf. Dryzek
   (1982) and Torgerson (1986a). Also see the elegant and insightful essay by
   Archibald (1980), which portrays the entry of analysis into a hermeneutic
   wonderland.

4. This duality emerges prominently at the focus of Habermas's discussion of
   the modern bifurcation of "lifeworld" and "system" (1984/1987). For a recent treatment of the "technocratic project," see Fischer (1990); cf. Torgerson (1992a) and Fischer (1992).

5. See Shklar (1991). Ricci discusses the influence of a broadly conceived
   "Deweyism" on mid-century American political science (Ricci 1984,
   101–14; cf. Braybrooke and Lindblom 1970, 18–19), while Seidelman
   and Harpham (1985, ch. 4) associate Merriam (and Lasswell) with a
   reform-oriented "third tradition" of the discipline.

6. Karl discusses the influence of Merriam's initiatives in the 1920s and places
   them in the context of Deweyan pragmatism (Karl 1974, 106, 251; cf. 259).

7. See Lasswell (1943a,b), Goldsen (1979), Almond (1990); cf. Lasswell
   (1951b). Seidelman and Harpham (1985, 133–45), in part following
   Easton (1950), stress a dramatic 1940s shift in Lasswell. However, their
   reading is an oversimplification that obscures continuities and complexities that become especially evident from unpublished material (Torgerson
   1990b, pp. 341, 345, 349).

8. This reference to Dewey comes in Chapter 8, a discussion of the "machine
   age" for which Lasswell was responsible. See his March 20 letter to his
   parents (Lasswell 1924). Lasswell also indicated the seminal importance
   of Dewey's *How We Think* to Myers S. McDougal, Lasswell's chief associate in developing the policy sciences framework (interviews with Mc-
   Dougal, Yale Law School, June 1986).

9. For a sophisticated account and defense of Lasswell's framework, see
   Brunner (1991).

10. Lindblom (1958) was apparently the first to use the term "policy analysis."
    See Melzner (1976, 1–2n1). All references to Dewey in Braybrooke and
    Lindblom (1970) come in chapters for which Lindblom had primary re-
    sponsibility, except for one reference in the shared first chapter (see p. viii
    on the division of responsibilities).

11. Chester I. Barnard, who wrote the foreword to Simon's *Administrative Be-
    havior*, detected a difference between himself and Simon in appreciating
    the value of democratic participation: "I probably give a somewhat higher
    value to political democracy than you . . . because I think the exercise of
    political democracy adds something to the dignity of the individual, or

should do so" (letter of Barnard to Simon, December 6, 1946, quoted in Wolf, 1974, 47). Compare, nonetheless, Simon's more recent discussion of the relationship between expert and public (1983, 87–107).

12. Compare, however, Lindblom's more recent assessment of critique (1982) and his discussion of "impairments" to inquiry (1990).

13. Also see the relevant exchange between Torgerson (1992a) and Fischer (1992).

14. Even though Habermas's focus on communication was meant to remedy this flaw in the Marxian tradition, his accent on rational discourse modeled on the formal principles of the ideal speech situation has often been portrayed – from both hermeneutic and postmodernist perspectives – as harboring such a potential (cf. Benhabib 1986; White 1991). The institutionalization of discourse in Habermas, however, should be viewed not only in terms of formal principles of communication, but also in light of his substantive, historical treatment of the public sphere (1989; cf. Calhoun 1992). Arendt stresses a substantive quality of public life she deems characteristic of the ancient *polis*, yet apparent only on the margins of modernity. While rejecting "truth" as alien to such public life, she also advances a treatment of judgment relevant to the idea of a rational form of public life (Arendt 1968, 241–2; Beiner 1983, 16). The Habermas–Arendt literature, to which Forester (1981) makes a notable contribution from the perspective of postpositivist policy analysis, provides a point of departure for considering further the relationship between form and content in public life (also see Dryzek 1989). With the tension between hermeneutics and critical theory a key issue (cf. Healy 1986; Torgerson 1986b), the literature of postpositivist policy analysis has only rather recently begun to give much serious attention to postmodernist interventions (see Throgmorton 1991; Dobuzinskis 1992; French 1992; Premfors 1992). White's (1991) effort to combine a "responsibility to act" (as in Habermas) with a "responsibility to otherness" (as in Derrida, Foucault, and Lyotard) may prove helpful. Especially relevant in regard to the problem of "otherness" are issues concerning public life and *phronēsis* identified from a feminist perspective (see, e.g., Bradshaw 1991).

15. The central text is Aristotle's *Nicomachean Ethics*, vi. Also see Beiner (1983), MacIntyre (1988, chs. 6–8), Gadamer (1979; 1989, esp. 312–24).

16. The prudence of Machiavellian *virtù* might be seen to differ from the Aristotelian virtue of *phronēsis* in the sense of being no more than the mere cleverness that Aristotle took to be necessary but not sufficient for *phronēsis* (*Nicomachean Ethics*, vi.12.1144a21–30). See, however, Kontos (1992); cf. Torgerson (1986b).

17. Cf. Hawkesworth (1988, 54–7, 190), Anderson (1987, 41), Healy (1986, 384, 393n7).

10

The Development of the Spatial Theory of Elections

John Ferejohn

I. Introduction

Formal theories of elections have a very long pedigree in political science, tracing back to Charles Dodgson's nineteenth-century explorations of the curiosities of voting procedures and E. J. Nanson's work on the design of electoral systems to the work of Condorcet and Borda in the late eighteenth century on methods of making collective choices (Arrow 1963). These works were, in an important sense, all motivated by a *normative* concern to find ways for a group to make choices rationally when there were more than two alternatives. The *positive* theory of elections has a much shorter history and can be traced to Harold Hotelling's (1929) publication of a theory of spatial competition in retail markets, in which he develops an application to competition among political parties. The positive theory of electoral competition remained largely unexplored after that until Anthony Downs published his Ph.D. thesis as *An Economic Theory of Democracy* (1957), which has since spawned a substantial literature.

In the thirty-five years since Anthony Downs exposited the spatial theory of electoral competition, the theory has evolved in a number of directions. This evolution has sometimes seemed puzzling to observers of real world elections. Empirical researchers regard it as striking that theorists seem to have paid little attention to how election contests actually look in choosing their research problems. Indeed, the "facts" that were to be explained – that plurality rule systems tended to have two

Parts of this essay were delivered at the Downs Conference, University of California, Irvine, October 28–9, 1989. While holding all harmless, I wish to thank Geoffrey Garrett, Judy Goldstein, Jim Morrow, and Barry Weingast for their comments on an earlier version of this essay.

parties (Duverger 1955) and that these parties tended to "converge" toward each other – were noted by Downs at the very beginning stages of theorizing and have not altered very much since then. Even though a number of empirical researchers have challenged whether these "facts" are facts at all, these disputes have had little influence on the development of the main body of the theory. Instead, for the most part, the history of spatial theory was largely driven by an internal logic.[1]

There are two kinds of dynamics that animate the development of a theory: an *external* one that relates the theory to the nature of the (empirical) phenomena to be explained, and an *internal* one that focuses primarily on questions of theoretical coherence.[2] Employing the external criterion, we say that one theory is *stronger* than another if it generates all the theorems of the second and some others besides, and if all the additional theorems are true according to whatever the prevailing standards of empirical evaluation are. The point of rational choice theorizing about a particular range of phenomena is to find the strongest possible theories of the phenomena in question according to the "stronger than" relation just defined.

This logic of theory comparison rests on the implicit notion that the nature of the "phenomena" to be explained is somehow fixed, so that we are always speaking of better or worse accounts of a given range of phenomena. But in important areas of social science theorizing, the nature of the phenomenon to be explained is itself in question. Thus, while economic science concerned itself initially with understanding the behavior of producing units, it came historically to concern itself with labor supply (the boundary between the household and production organizations) and, then, with consumption itself. This widening of the range of the phenomena under study pushed the development of economic theory, and the theory of rationality itself, to eliminate "inessential" substantive assumptions. Thus, the theory of the neoclassical, or profit-maximizing, firm became a special theory within economics and came to be understood as an "ideal" case or even an irrelevant one for general purposes.

The point is that from an external point of view, theory comparison has two aspects – strength and scope – and that they put opposing pressures on the elements of the theory. Pedantically, we might say that theories may be partially ordered both by their relative strength and by their relative scope, and that theory comparison proceeds by examining both dimensions. One theory is better than another, in this sense, if it has more strength and scope. Obviously, this standard does not generally lead to unique best theories: Rather, there will be a set of best theories according to the partial ordering, and best theories will be formally in-comparable. A theory with maximal scope will generally lack the power of a theory with smaller scope but maximal strength.

While external standards are doubtless important in accounting for the development of a theory, internal standards are often more impor-tant. The spatial model of elections is a special case of a *rational choice* theory, and as such, its development has been guided by the shared prin-ciple that we should try to understand human action as rational rather than by any special feature of electoral processes. The rationality hy-pothesis serves as an internal principle guiding the evolution of the the-ory and is not itself seen as an object of direct empirical investigation, remaining instead largely in the background.

For reasons of tractability, virtually every rational choice theory fails to employ fully the strength of the rationality hypothesis. Within neo-classical economics, for example, it is difficult to see why economic agents rationally must take prices as fixed; indeed, it is difficult to spec-ify a coherent (rational) account of how prices come to be determined from the general data about an economy. General equilibrium theory proceeds by making some more or less ad hoc assumptions (e.g., that people do act as price takers or that the prices faced by agents are those that clear markets) to get around these deficiencies. Thus, it is left to fu-ture researchers to construct foundational (i.e., rational) justifications for these assumptions. These assumptions permit "getting on with" the analysis but they do not thereby disappear from view. Instead, they be-come foundational issues that require more general settings within which they can be adequately addressed. As an example, issues of price formation have lately been reformulated outside of the neoclassical set-ting within game theoretic models.

A rational choice theory must, in this sense, always try to meet the challenge that the rationality hypothesis has not been fully employed. It is not fully employed when it is assumed that some actors in the model (voters, candidates, activists, contributors) are behaving in an appar-ently irrational or ad hoc fashion. In this sense, the rationality hypothe-sis provides force for an *internal dialectic* of theory development of the sort hypothesized in our historical framework. We can find instances of such a dialectic in the history of the theory of spatial competition. To take the most familiar example, it is assumed in some models of elec-tion that all citizens will vote, when it is evident from an examination of the voters' problem that it is difficult to provide a satisfactory rational justification of this assumption. Everyone knew that the assumption of universal turnout could not be defended either as true or as an approximation to the truth. Thus, it remained an internal or foundational problem for the theory.[3]

In this paper I shall explore one issue that is crucial to the coherence of the spatial model of elections as a rational choice theory and thus to the history of the research agenda in this area. That issue turns on the question of whether campaign platforms can have predictive or informational value for the voter within the spatial model. Obviously, unless platforms contain information as to what candidates would do in office, it would not be rational for voters to base their choices on them. In this sense, the spatial model rests on the assumption that campaign platforms are useful guides to the future behavior of politicians. It is by no means obvious that platforms can generally serve the function required of them by the spatial approach. There are, however, special settings within which platforms can have informational content, and in these settings, the spatial model can offer a coherent account of electoral phenomena. I begin by stating the analytical developments and then turn to the historical evolution of the spatial theory of elections as a rational choice theory.

II. The Spatial Theory of Elections

In the spatial theory of elections, candidates, who care only about enjoying the fruits of office, announce policies that they promise to implement as a means to win election. These policies correspond to points in an issue space.[4] Voters are assumed to be "policy oriented" in the sense of caring only about the policy that is implemented following the election rather than about the identity of the candidates or parties that win office, or about how they themselves cast their ballots.[5] Moreover, it is assumed that there are exactly two contestants for office and no possibility of "entry" by other candidates. In effect, then, the "pure" theory of spatial competition conceives of candidate competition as a two-person, zero-sum,[6] symmetric[7] game.[8]

For symmetric games, if x is an equilibrium strategy for one player it must also be an equilibrium strategy for the other player. Thus, if there are any equilibria in a spatial competition game, there must be "convergent" equilibria where both candidates play the same strategy. If there is a mixed strategy equilibrium – that is, an equilibrium in which the candidates randomize over a set of platforms rather than choosing specific ones – then there must be a convergent equilibrium at which both candidates randomize over the *same set* of platforms. If there is a pure strategy equilibrium, there must be a convergent equilibrium in which both candidates announce exactly the same platform. Moreover, again by symmetry, at any equilibrium, both candidates must have an expected payoff of zero.[9]

If the space of issues is one-dimensional with voters distributed according to a density function, Downs showed that there will always be a position – the position of the median voter – that cannot be defeated by any other in a majority vote and that both parties will, therefore, "converge" on it.[10] Thus, in this case there is a pure strategy equilibrium in the spatial competition game. This equilibrium has the property that each voter is indifferent between the two candidates and that the election is a tie. Most importantly, in this case, electoral competition produces an outcome – a median of the distribution of voters – that is functionally connected to the distribution of voter preferences. This is the by now familiar "Downsian analysis" of two-party competition.[11]

In the years following the appearance of Downs's book, analysts began wondering whether his theory of two-party competition could be extended to multidimensional issue spaces. If such an extension were impossible, the theory would need to provide reasons to believe that, somehow, important political decisions would come to be one-dimensional. Failing this, spatial competition theory would amount to little more than an amusing but irrelevant museum piece. In effect, this amounted to asking whether spatial competition games on multidimensional spaces could be expected to have pure strategy equilibria. Beginning with the work of Davis and Hinich, an impressive literature grew up that centered on this question (Davis and Hinich 1966). Over the ensuing two decades, a number of powerful and important results were found that indicated how this question could be answered. Without giving very many of the details, I will briefly sketch these developments.

First, the convergence result – that both parties adopt the same issue position in an equilibrium – obtains only if the distribution of voter preferences is symmetric in a specific sense. Results found in the 1960s by Charles Plott (1967) characterized these conditions mathematically and essentially showed that they were very difficult, indeed, virtually impossible, to satisfy. Whereas the convergence property always holds in one-dimensional spaces, it holds in two-dimensional spaces only for very unusual distributions of preference. Thus, in multidimensional spatial competition, if there are any equilibria at all, they will virtually always be in mixed rather than pure strategies.

Second, using a somewhat more restrictive set of assumptions on preferences, Richard McKelvey (1975) found, nearly a decade later, that when the convergence result fails – when there is no policy proposal that both candidates urge in equilibrium – every platform in the space is contained in the smallest "top cycle" of the space.[12] This implies that any platform *x* can be reached from any other platform in a finite number of steps. From this point of view, therefore, it might appear that virtually any platform might be announced in some mixed strategy equilibrium. But this turns out to be false.

Let $P(x,y)$ stand for the proportion of the electorate that prefers platform *x* to platform *y*. Then, we say that *x* (weakly) dominates *y* if $P(x,z)$ is at least as great as $P(y,z)$ for all *z*, with strict inequality holding for at least one *z*. McKelvey and Ordeshook (1976) showed that the set of platforms that could be played with positive probability in some mixed strategy equilibrium is confined to the set of weakly undominated platforms. This set is contained in the set of Pareto optimal outcomes and is usually significantly smaller than this set. Indeed, an argument of the sort reported more recently in Ferejohn, McKelvey, and Packel (1984) establishes that the set of strategies that can be played with positive probability can be shown to be small whenever the distribution of preferences "nearly" has a pure strategy equilibrium. Thus, in this sense, spatial competition can be expected to produce relatively restricted outcomes.

These results – which we may call the "neoclassical" theory of electoral competition – depend on two substantive hypotheses: that voters are *policy oriented* (i.e., they care only about which policy is implemented after the election) and candidates are *office oriented*, and that candidate platforms can *credibly* promise postelection policy. Both of these assumptions have come under sustained attack recently, not on the grounds that they are untrue in the world – everyone agrees that they are untrue empirically – but on the grounds that it is somehow inconsistent with the internal rationality project to assert them. The question posed is this: If voters and candidates really are rational, could it be true in an equilibrium that voting would be policy oriented or that candidate promises would turn out to be true?

III. The Paradox of Spatial Models of Electoral Competition

At the heart of Downs's spatial theory of elections is a paradox:[13] In general, if voters behave according to the assumptions of the spatial model and make their choice among candidates for office based on a comparison of their platforms, successful candidates would not rationally implement these platforms once they are in office. Instead, they would adopt policies that serve their interests from that time forward, and these will virtually never be those that were promised in the campaign. Thus, voters would have been irrational to have based their decisions on a comparison of platforms in the first place. In this sense, the assumptions of the model are self-refuting.

Downs presented this paradox in the context off his justly famous "coalition of minorities" argument (1957, ch. 4). He argued that, in a multidimensional setting, any platform – even one made up of the majority position on every issue – can be defeated in a majority vote by some other platform. Thus, incumbents, who must defend their policies, will always lose and, knowing that, would not have an incentive to keep their campaign promises.[14] Downs put the matter as follows: "If no government can possibly be reelected then party motivation for action cannot long remain the desire to be reelected. Experience will soon convince each party that this desire is futile" (Downs 1957, 62). Thus, incumbents might just as well do what they prefer to do (either shirk or follow their own policy preferences) rather than honor their campaign pledges.

The heart of the problem is this: Campaigning and governing take place in a multidimensional setting and in real time. Thus, the problem of "time inconsistency" – that best actions are different from those that were rationally promised ex ante – is inherent in the dynamic electoral relationship. Elected officeholders will not generally find it in their interest actually to carry out promises made during the campaign since, if they do, they cannot succeed in being reelected anyway. Voters will, in turn, anticipate that candidates would not rationally keep their promises, and so they have no reason to base their votes on campaign promises.

Ordinary citizens seem intuitively aware of this problem. When asked about whether they expect politicians to be truthful, they typically display a healthy (or, depending on your viewpoint, unhealthy) level of skepticism about the promises made by politicians. They know perfectly well that the political candidates are trying to win election to a valuable office and that they will promise many different things to achieve this end. They know too that when the time comes for delivering on campaign promises, the shadow of the past election will have faded and the prospect of a future one will be remote. Besides, there will be many ways to excuse or even to hide the failure to live up to a campaign promise by pointing to the occurrence of unforeseen circumstances or to the ambiguity of the promise itself. Perhaps then it is not too surprising that as appealing as the spatial metaphor may be, there is a good deal of evidence that it explains only a fraction of voting decisions and that voters ordinarily rely on other information about candidates in making their voting decisions.

For many years after the appearance of *An Economic Theory of Democracy*, researchers simply ignored this problem. They assumed that candidates somehow were able to commit themselves to implementing their campaign pledges whether or not they wished to carry out these promises when the time came to do so.[15] Instead, theorists concentrated their efforts on the classical, static, complete information formulation of the spatial theory in multidimensional choice spaces. It is fair to say that enormous advances were made in understanding the logical structure of (static) electoral politics as well as some aspects of real electoral politics. But it seems appropriate now to begin to ask about the nature of electoral competition when candidates cannot commit to carrying out their promises. What would a more fully rational spatial theory of elections look like in this case?

IV. Downs's Proposed Solutions to the Paradox

Downs himself was insensitive neither to this question nor to the problems for his approach that were raised by the paradox. Downs (1957, chs. 4, 7) suggests two forces that he argued would have the effect of inducing candidates to honor their platform promises and thereby providing a foundation for spatial theory. The first, which is by now quite familiar in game-theoretic literature, is essentially "reputational." It suggests that if incumbents fail to keep their promises in the current period, the voters may choose not to punish them,[16] or not to believe their promises when they next become challengers. The second argument is that uncertainty as to the preferences of the voters and the actions of the candidates will somehow alter the dimensionality of the space of electoral competition in an essential manner. Downs argued that, because of uncertainty, platforms will not be located in the high-dimensional space of issues but will be located, instead, in a one-dimensional space of *ideologies*.

We take up these arguments in reverse order and begin with a brief statement of Downs's ideology argument. He argued that because candidates are uncertain as to the preferences of voters and because voters themselves have little incentive to pay much attention to what the candidates are doing or saying, candidates are motivated to compete for office not in the (highly multidimensional) issue space but, instead, in a lower-dimensional space of ideologies. "In a world beclouded by uncertainty, ideologies will be useful to parties as well as voters" (Downs 1957, 100).

But in light of recent theoretical developments (McKelvey 1975), we know that the substitution of an ideological space of lower dimensionality than the original issue space is not sufficient to alleviate the effects of Downs's paradox unless the dimensionality of that space is less than two. On this issue Downs was, perhaps excusably, quite vague. His discussion (1957, ch. 7) made no explicit claims about the dimensionality of the ideology space. Rather, he began chapter 8 with a one-dimensional example, without comment on the choice of dimensionality. Whenever he discussed the relationship of the Left–Right continuum to the original issues, he spoke as though voters base their choice on some sort of weighted average. "Let us assume," he argued, "that each party takes stands on many issues, and that each stand can be assigned a position on our left–right scale. Then each party's net position on this scale is a weighted average of the positions of all the particular policies it upholds" (Downs 1957, 132). These and other remarks make it clear that Downs assumed implicitly that the ideological space in which parties and candidates position themselves is one dimensional.

Various justifications might be presented for this claim. Candidates may restrict themselves to a one-dimensional space of platforms either because (they know that) voters (1) are psychically unable to process multidimensional information (cognitive limitations of voters) or (2) do not find it worthwhile to process more complicated information (cognitive costs), or because (3) candidates want to economize on calculation or information transmission (advertising) costs. Whatever the actual mechanism he proposed, and he spoke most often about (2) and (3), Downs argued that the normal sources of uncertainty surrounding campaigns implicates one or more of these processes.

In this setting, if we assume (as Downs did) that the incumbent candidates' issue positions are identified with the policies they actually executed while in office, the time consistency problem dissolves. In this case, as long as office is sufficiently valuable and the candidates do not discount the future "too much," incumbents will be motivated to implement the median position since, if they fail to do so, challengers can announce that position and will prevail in the next election.

Downs's conclusion from this argument was that party ideologies will be *reliable* (or informative) predictors of their actions in office and they will be *stable* in the sense that they do not change much from one period to the next (Downs called this property "responsibility").

Obviously, everything in this argument turns on the claim that electoral competition will be reduced to a one-dimensional phenomenòn (analyzed in Downs 1957, ch. 8) a claim for which Downs provided little support. As long as party ideologies are confined to a single dimension, in equilibrium they will be good predictors of what the parties will do in office (since officials can do no better than to implement the platforms they promised during the election). Therefore, in equilibrium, voters would be well advised to rely on ideologies to make their voting decisions, and the paradox disappears. Incumbents and challengers would each take the same position in the ideological space, and whoever is elected would carry out their platform promises.

Thus, Downs's argument had two key components. The first is a reputational argument that relies on a repeated games story. It holds that candidates will keep their promises (even though they cannot commit themselves to do so) because they wish to continue to be elected in future elections. The second component appears to rest on some sort of cognitive limitation or information-economizing story. It claims that voters and parties will end up relying on one-dimensional predictors of party behavior in office rather than paying attention to the full space of issues. Most analysts nowadays find this second argument to be ad hoc in the sense that no theory is presented that would justify a one-dimensional ideological space. In any event, recent research has largely ignored this line of argument.

Instead, theorists have tended to extend more credulity to the reputational element of Downs's argument. They have attempted to develop a theory of electoral competition for cases in which candidates cannot commit themselves to keeping their campaign promises. In the next section we shall review a few such efforts. In the end I shall argue that the reputational argument is not sufficient to support the spatial theory. Some sort of reduction of the issue space to a single dimension seems necessary to provide appropriate incentives to candidates. Before turning to that argument, however, it is useful to look at the empirical view to see if there is any strong reason to believe that candidate campaign promises are in fact honored.

V. Empirical Research

Depending on how the question is asked, there is either very little research on the topic of whether candidates keep campaign promises or there is a great deal. On the one hand, there is relatively little literature that directly addresses the question of whether candidates honor campaign pledges. On the other, there is a great deal of writing that argues (and produces evidence) for the proposition that American political parties differ sharply and systematically from each other and that ordinary citizens can and do rely on these differences in behavior in making their voting choices. Thus, parties seem to be both stable and responsible (in Downs's sense). Among the most prominent of these studies is the work of Douglas Hibbs (1977, 1987). It suggests that the parties attempt to implement distinct monetary and fiscal policies. More evidence of this nature is also provided by the writings associated with the Manifesto Project (Budge, Robertson, and Hearl 1987). Evidence for the proposition that, in the aggregate, citizens perceive policy differences among the candidates is found in a well-known paper by Richard Brody and Benjamin Page (1972) and in many other places as well.

The literature that bears most directly on the former question of keeping promises measures candidate promises or platforms and then investigates the degree to which these platforms are implemented by the candidate who was elected. I found several such attempts, all of which suffer from characteristic methodological weaknesses that seem endemic to this genre of research. A good example of this sort of study is Jeff Fishel's book, *Platforms and Promises* (1985). Fishel develops codings of campaign platform promises, presidential efforts in office (from Kennedy to Reagan), and success in implementing platform promises. He finds, for example, that Presidents Carter and Reagan were both reasonably faithful in attempting to implement their campaign promises with legislative proposals. Carter, however, was not very successful in getting his promised policies through Congress (though he scored a bit better than Nixon in this respect). The percentages reported here seem reasonably high (as they are in other studies), but they are dependent on subjective codings and are therefore a fairly weak form of evidence. At best, studies of this sort might convince the skeptic that there is "some" information in platform promises.

Leaving aside issues of subjective coding, it's not clear what should be considered as a "large" percentage. As many recent presidencies illustrate, events can intrude and force presidents to alter their agendas and prevent them from pursuing promises in ways that are perfectly excusable by most voters.

Because of the inherent ambiguities of measurement and interpretation, in the end this kind of study seems not to be very useful in answering the most interesting questions in this area. Specifically, do elected officials systematically depart from keeping their campaign promises? We would expect that if candidates fail to keep promises, they would instead do what they want. That is, they would "shirk" by pursuing office perquisites, avoiding onerous tasks, or implementing their own ideological preferences.

There are a number of other studies that address promise keeping in a more indirect way, once some assumptions are made as to what kinds of objectives politicians might have. For example, a number of recent discussions of congressional roll call voting behavior focus on a phenomenon that Joseph Kalt and Mark Zupan (1984) have labeled "ideological shirking." (For an opposing view, see Peltzman 1984.) Kalt and Zupan demonstrate that roll call voting cannot be fully accounted for by constituency characteristics and that the residuals in voting regressions amount to the ideological tastes of congresspeople. They argue that congresspeople run for office in part because they have strongly held policy preferences that they want to implement and that this implies that congressional behavior cannot be wholly accounted for by constituency characteristics. In the context of a one-dimensional spatial model, one might expect ideological shirking to take on a characteristic form. Having promised to be centrist or moderate in their election campaigns, politicians return to their ideological preferences when in office (Reagan becomes Reagan), at least early in their terms.[17]

One might argue that insofar as unanticipated ideological shirking is observed, there is indirect evidence of a failure to keep campaign promises. Either incumbents have misled supporters into believing that partisan policies will be implemented, or they have misled centrists by implying that moderate policies will be adopted. On the other hand, such behavior, while perhaps not fully faithful to campaign promises taken literally, might still be predictable. In this case voters would be expected to anticipate that Democrats are more liberal than Republicans, irrespective of campaign statements (at least right after the election), and base their choices on those anticipations. It is not clear, of course, how precisely the voters will be able to place the candidates if they are known to be announcing platforms they do not intend to carry out. As shall be seen later, it may be that candidates with very different intentions will announce the same platform so that even though voters have rational expectations, they will be unable to tell the difference among candidates whose behavior in office will in fact diverge.

A related line of work concerns the existence of electoral cycle effects. The classical work in this genre has to do with macroeconomic effects on voting behavior. This work suggests that citizens are myopic in their voting decisions, paying more attention to recent events than more distant ones. In this case officials will respond by behaving differently as elections approach. Candidates would shirk early in their terms, returning to more attractive electoral positions as the election approaches. Evidence for such phenomena was presented initially by Nordhaus (1975) and Tufte (1978). Once again, candidate platforms would offer little guidance as to how elected officials will act early in their terms. Of course, electoral cycles may be anticipated: Voters may know that, early in their terms, Democrats will implement policies further to the left and Republicans policies further to the right than were promised. Thus, voters may employ other information besides campaign pledges in deciding how to vote.

While the original work in this area focused on macroeconomics and either presidential elections or aggregate congressional vote, more recent investigations show cyclical effects in a number of other domains. Kiewiet and McCubbins (1989) suggest that such effects exist in the budgetary process, and Robert Bernstein (1988) and Gerald Wright (1988), while disagreeing with each other to some degree, present evidence of such cycles in roll call voting in the Senate. Specifically, Bernstein and Wright both report election cycle effects: Senators who are more extreme than their constituencies tend to shift in a moderate direction during election years.

There is some related evidence on roll call voting over the course of a congressional career. One would expect that if congresspeople intend to retire after their current term, they would be free to pursue the sorts of policies they prefer. This "last-period" effect resembles the motivation for electoral cycles and ideological shirking and suggests that political actors will behave differently over the course of their careers. Somewhat surprisingly, John Lott (1987) shows that in their roll call behavior, congresspeople do not seem to shift their ideological positions in the "last period," although they do tend to vote less often. In other words, the ideological shirking that may be expected to occur seems not to be observed, but ordinary shirking is found instead. Lott and Reed (1987) suggest that there are mechanisms at work that sort out those politicians who are unrepresentative of their constituents. For example, the longer incumbents are in office the more likely it is that their preferences will resemble those of their constituents.

Indeed, other evidence suggests that Downs's ideas about ideology might deserve renewed attention. Recent empirical work by Keith Poole and Howard Rosenthal (1985) suggests that ideology may be a low-dimensional or even (in their bolder claims) a one-dimensional phenomenon. Politicians seem, whether for Downs's reasons or for others, to take positions in a low-dimensional ideological space and these positions seem to be remarkably stable over time. Although the interpretation of this work remains controversial, and we still lack a theory to explain the dimensionality of ideology, the data fit the Downsian hypothesis quite well.

While this survey is admittedly cursory, it is possible to draw some preliminary conclusions nonetheless. First, there is substantial evidence in the United States (and the evidence is much stronger in other nations) that the parties and their candidates differ systematically and consistently in a low-dimensional space of ideologies. Second, such evidence as we have on shirking suggests that such behavior is limited in its extent and can be anticipated by voters. In effect then, the empirical evidence we have, direct and indirect, suggests that politicians tend to be both predictable and reliable, in spite of powerful incentives to behave otherwise. I take it, therefore, that the external evidence is broadly congruent with Downs's hypotheses. Why is this so? What mechanisms are at work to induce candidates to behave stably and reliably, rather than doing as they please once in office? What induces them to keep the promises they make during the heat of a campaign in the absence of an enforcement mechanism that could induce them to?

VI. Campaigns without Precommitment

If candidates cannot precommit to keeping campaign promises, they will generally find it rational to behave differently once in office than they promised. In turn, voters will not rationally rely on platforms as predictors of the behavior of elected politicians. And if voters can better anticipate how candidates will behave in office by observing their characteristics and past behavior rather than by observing their promises, they would rationally base their votes on these data rather than on announced platforms. Thus, the following question arises: Under what conditions would campaign promises be informative as to subsequent policy-making activity?

Within this line of research, there are two sorts of models in which this question has been addressed. In the first – *moral hazard* models – citizens are assumed to know what the candidates' preferences are, but they cannot observe incumbent actions. They are restricted to observing policy outcomes that are produced jointly by incumbent actions, which are assumed to be costly to the incumbent[18] and externally generated "shocks."[19] Thus, citizens can only choose voting rules that depend on observable information about candidates (policy outcomes and campaign promises). In an equilibrium of such a model, citizens will cast ballots in such a way as to limit the amount of shirking that candidates will engage in while in office. Not surprisingly, in such models, the amount of shirking will depend on the ability of voters to monitor the actions of incumbent officials. If citizens could observe or infer policy choices perfectly, they would be able to induce officials always to act in their interest.[20]

Because candidate objectives are identical and commonly known, moral hazard models allow little scope for campaign promises to have an informational role. Because all candidates have the same underlying preferences (each wants to avoid taking costly actions), each would find the same actions to be optimal once in office, no matter what was promised during the campaign. For that reason, campaign promises cannot provide information about postelection actions. All the voters can do in such models is to provide postelection incentives for candidates to pursue their interests when in office. Specifically, they can adopt retrospective or performance-oriented voting strategies, which punish officials when policy performance is poor. If elections are sufficiently frequent and politicians (or parties) are infinitely lived, voters can choose restrospective strategies that limit official shirking in office. As we shall see later, this conclusion holds only in the case in which the set of alternative platforms is one-dimensional.[21]

With finitely lived politicians, the last-period problem causes unraveling: Voters would know that, in the last period, incumbents would surely shirk and so, in turn, they would certainly punish them by voting for the challengers. But if voters were to follow this policy, incumbents would then shirk in the penultimate period, and so on back to the first period. Thus, in equilibrium, the incumbent shirks every period. As a way to alleviate this unraveling and permit electoral control of officials, it is sometimes suggested that although politicians have finite lifetimes, parties are infinitely lived and can find organizational means to induce their candidates to honor platform promises.[22]

Alberto Alesina (1987, 1988) has recently published a series of papers in which he assumes that candidates have distinct policy preferences and that these are common knowledge within a finite-period model. Because of the finite horizon, campaign promises that are different from the candidates' true preferences are not credible. Candidates will rationally pursue their preferred policies when in office, and voters correctly anticipate this. In this model campaign promises play no role whatsoever, and officials also have no incentive to manipulate policy for electoral purposes. In an infinite-horizon model, however, supergame equilibria exist that allow the candidates to pursue "electoralist" policies that are distinct from the ones they actually prefer.

In an original departure that allows campaign promises to be credible, Banks and Austen-Smith (1989) have shown in a two-period moral hazard model that voters can credibly commit to punishing incumbents who deviate from their platform promises in the first period. The second-period incumbent would shirk in any case, so the voters incur no cost by punishing incumbents who fail to keep first-period promises. Thus, they are free to condition their vote on the relationship between first-period campaign promises and performance. This argument appears to extend to arbitrary numbers of periods. One problem with this approach is that it relies crucially on the existence of a known final period that does not depend on the career aspirations of the candidates. But this seems a rather artificial assumption. If, instead, each candidate is known to be willing to serve at most two periods, the usual unraveling argument will prevent the enforcement of campaign pledges.

In the second class of models – *adverse selection* or signaling models – candidate preferences are not known and cannot be directly observed by the electorate. Voters must infer these preferences from campaign statements in order to anticipate how these politicians would behave in office. Here most of the work that has been done is in a two-period model with a single election and in a single-dimensional ideological space. In this context, following the election, the candidates would simply do what they wished no matter what they promised during the campaign. Jeffrey Banks (1990) shows that if candidate preferences contain a penalty for executing policies much different than those promised, there are equilibria in which preelection promises are (sometimes) informative. Specifically, candidates whose preferences are far from the median will truthfully reveal their preferences, while those nearer to the median voter will "pool." Banks's assumption about candidate preferences may be justified as embodying "reputational" effects that would emerge in a multiperiod model.

Joseph Harrington (1988) shows that if voter preferences are unknown and if candidates are not penalized for carrying out policies divergent from their promises, informative equilibria may not exist. That is, in all equilibria, candidates with different preferences will essentially play the same campaign strategy, irrespective of their actual preferences, so that campaign promises will be uninformative. When Harrington assumes that candidates are less likely to be able to implement policies the more distant they are from the median voter, he finds that fully informative equilibria do exist. The idea here is that variable implementation costs can induce candidates to reveal their true policy preferences.

We should note the resemblance of the equilibrium strategies in these models to the "strategy of ambiguity" originally discussed by Downs. In equilibrium, candidates who announce that they are at the median position are, in equilibrium, actually telling the voter that their preferred position is distributed in an interval around that point. Thus, while it is often thought that as long as voters are risk averse, candidates would not announce ambiguous strategies, when candidates have private information as to their own preferences, they will generally choose to do so.

Alesina and Cukierman (1989) provide a model in which candidate preferences are not observed and demonstrate that candidates systematically "converge" toward the median voter in the first period and then they shirk in the second period. Thus, in a finite-horizon model, voters can induce incumbents to implement policies that voters prefer early in incumbents' careers by (credibly) threatening to replace them.

All of these published works suggest that in a multiperiod model with a one-dimensional issue space, independently of their characteristics, candidates will take moderate positions early in their careers and that these platforms will be good predictors of their actions in office. But as time goes on, candidates should shirk in the direction of their most preferred positions. If there are reputation-bearing mechanisms such as political parties, we might expect promises to be fully informative as to future actions (but not informative at all as to candidate preferences) at all times. In this case, the static spatial model would be a good heuristic for the analysis of real elections.

While this survey of recent theoretical work is too brief to have considered all of the relevant work in the area or to have presented in any detail the work of the various authors, I think that the general outlines are pretty clear. In one-dimensional moral hazard models, candidates can be induced to perform predictably *if* elections are repeated indefinitely and *if* voters are able to monitor the behavior of officials. If, alternatively, politicians have (known) finite horizons, things are more subtle. Either infinitely lived "reputation bearers" (like parties) might arise, or as in Austen-Smith and Banks, voters can credibly threaten to punish candidates who fail to deliver on promises until the last period. If the last period is not common knowledge but is instead private information held by one of the candidates, the situation is, once again, one of adverse selection.

In one-dimensional signaling models, voters seem to be able to induce politicians to make truthful promises (i.e., promises that will be kept) in early periods. Thus, either candidates will tell the truth about what they would do in office (if they have sufficiently extreme preferences) or candidates whose preferences are close to those of the median voter will pool at the median to get elected (and they would implement these preferences in early periods). In either case, in many of these models, behaving predictably (so that past actions are a good guide to future actions) or keeping campaign promises seems consistent with the hypothesis of equilibrium behavior.

I should emphasize that all of these "positive" results seem to rely essentially on the assumption that the issue space is one-dimensional. In a multidimensional setting – the setting of Downs's paradox – things are much less well understood. The mathematical techniques used in the one-dimensional models do not yield strong results in higher dimensions; indeed, it is hard to see how incumbents would have any incentive to convey information through campaign statements in multidimensional settings. For this reason, it is important to explore Downs's conjecture that spatial competition will take place at the level of ideology rather than at the level of issues and that the space of ideology will be one-dimensional.

Ideology

Downs's original statement of the paradox of truthful candidates relied essentially on the existence of majority rule cycles. But most of the theoretical discussions of campaigns without precommitment take place in one-dimensional settings in which such cycles cannot exist. The only exception I know of is my own multidimensional moral hazard model (Ferejohn 1986). That model showed that in a situation in which policies correspond to alternative distributions of wealth, candidates are entirely undisciplined by the electorate. Incumbents will shirk completely and the electorate will nevertheless have no reason to remove them from office. The voters could rationally expect no better of the challengers. Of course, the electors will anticipate this shirking and so they will not be surprised. Campaign promises would not be believed anyway. In a sense, then, this is a model in which candidates are truthful but depressingly so.

There is, however, another way to interpret this result, a way that provides a connection with Downs's story about ideology. My result suggests the possibility that there may be a strategic basis for a one-dimensional ideological space. Unless voters happen to locate their assessments of candidates on a one-dimensional space, incumbents would be completely uncontrollable. Thus, there is simply no purpose to using ideology at all unless it is essentially a single-dimensional concept. If ideology is multidimensional, it is useless as a method of disciplining politicians. In that case, one might conjecture that it would not play much of a role in politics. We would expect ideological argument, communication, and calculation to survive only if the ideological space is one-dimensional.

No theory has been developed that demonstrates just how a single-dimensional concept of ideology could arise or come to form the basis for electoral competition. Such a theory might well fall outside the class of game-theoretic models of the sort discussed in this essay. It may be that the best account of ideology is as a "focal" phenomenon of the sort discussed by Thomas Schelling (1960); related work along this line has been done by Kresps (1988). Here, however, what is "focal" is not the proposed equilibrium outcome, but the dimension along which competition will occur. All this is, of course, conjecture, but the pivotal idea is due to Downs: The structure of ideology may be traceable to competitive forces.[23]

If it turns out that a satisfactory theory of the structure of ideology can be generated, then a number of intriguing empirical results could be understood within a common framework. For one thing, campaign promises do seem more informative than one would expect if the space of competition is multidimensional. Candidates of different parties tend to take predictably distinct positions and attempt to implement distinct types of policy. Second, politicians do seem to locate themselves in more or less generally understood Left–Right terms, and their locations seem to be pretty stable over time and to predict their behavior accurately in higher-dimensional policy space (Poole and Rosenthal 1985). Third, such a theory might help us to understand the phenomenon that Joseph Kalt and Mark Zupan have termed "ideological shirking." They claim that politicians hold (unobserved) ideological positions that are not predictable from constituency characteristics and that explain their behavior in Congress. Perhaps instead, we should see politicians as choosing ideological positions (and perhaps even announcing them) as a way of developing what might be called a "brand name" that voters could use to calculate their anticipated behavior in office. For the reasons just discussed, brand names should be located in a one-dimensional space.

VII. Discussion

We return finally to the central issue of this paper: the historical development of the spatial theory of elections. Part of that development has been driven by external evidence. In the thirty-five years since the appearance of Downs's book, enormous advances have occurred in our capacity to describe and explain electoral phenomena. For example, we have a much better understanding now of the extent of voter ignorance, and this appreciation induces theorists to develop models of electoral competition that fit these facts and others. But I have argued that the internally generated agenda of rational choice theory is the more powerful force in shaping the research agenda. The fact that spatial theory is a rational choice theory commits its practitioners to pose certain kinds of questions and to keep asking them until more or less satisfactory answers emerge. I have suggested that this commitment has put pressure on the theory to develop in the direction of more fully incorporating the rationality assumption.

The central internal question for Downs's theory, within the framework of rational choice theory, is this: Why would voters rationally base their electoral choices on a comparison of the platforms of candidates? It would make sense to do so only if (rational) candidate behavior in office is reasonably consistent with these platforms; that is, only if platform statements are informative as to behavior in office. But if promises *are* informative, why is it that incumbents keep getting reelected?

The answer proposed long ago by Downs points to the emergence of a single-dimensional space of ideologies that permits the evaluation and control of politicians and parties. There is some external evidence that ideology can in fact be described as a low- or one-dimensional phenomenon. There is as yet, however, no genuinely persuasive rational choice theory that explains the emergence of a structure of ideology with the requisite characteristics. If ideology happens to be one-dimensional, there is quite a lot about electoral behavior we can explain, but we don't really understand why it must be so. The prominent nonrational choice alternatives seem not to do the work: There seems no strong reason to think that the costliness of information transmission or the structure of cognitive organization drives ideology to be one-dimensional rather than two-dimensional. Even if they did provide adequate explanations, rational choice theorists would only grudgingly accept the help.

Thus, from an internal viewpoint, there seems an overwhelming need for a theory that can account for the reduction of the dimensionality of the space of competition to a single dimension. Without such a reduction, it is not at all clear that we can have a coherent theory involving fully rational actors in which the assumptions of spatiality are satisfied. If such a reduction is not available, the commitment to rationality tempts theorists to jettison the assumption of spatiality in favor of more abstract game-theoretic models. The fact that there are powerful external reasons to think that spatiality fits empirical facts reasonably well will not long prevent this move.

Notes

1. More recently this situation may have begun to change as theorists have started to wonder whether either Duverger's law (1955) or convergence are genuine consequences of the spatial model. Partly this concern was driven by empirical observation: There are plurality rule systems that seem to have more than two dissimilar parties. (Britain's is the most prominent example, but the convergence hypothesis is under attack here in the United States as well.) But I think it more likely that, even here, attention to these problems was guided more by internal developments within rational choice theory – specifically, the rapid development of new techniques and perspectives in game theory (which is just the theory of rationality applied to multiperson interactions) – than by a resurgent interest in the "real world." Here too, inner logic seems a more potent force in theory development than a direct concern to explain events in the world.
2. My use of internal and external theoretical dynamics is substantially different from that offered by Lakatos (1978). The distinction drawn in this paper is between the exposure of the theory to evidence about the external world to which it refers and the internal aesthetic held by the community of scientists.
3. Ledyard (1984) and Palfrey and Rosenthal (1985) have addressed the internal theoretical problem, but in doing so they have sharpened the external criticism that could be levied at the theory. If voting is costly, then the theory cannot account for the nonnegligible turnout levels in large electorates.
4. If the issue space is sufficiently "large," the assumption that policies correspond to spatial locations has no real force. In this essay we shall be concerned with the case where the issue space is one-dimensional (i.e., "small"

in the sense just mentioned), and in this case the assumption of "spatiality" is quite restrictive.

5. The models also make additional technical assumptions: that voters have preferences that are representable by quasiconcave, differentiable utility functions.

6. Since the candidates care only about obtaining, without loss of generality, we may scale the payoffs so that the candidate that wins gets a payoff of 1, while the loser gets -1. We denote the payoff to candidate one of announcing platform x, while candidate two announces platform y, as $P(x,y)$.

7. $P(x,y) = -P(y,x)$.

8. Spatial competition games also have infinitely many strategies, and on the space of pure strategy pairs, the payoff function is discontinuous. In such games it is hard to guarantee the existence of equilibria. Kramer (1978) proved an existence theorem for games that are similar to these.

9. If there are multiple equilibria, there may be nonsymmetric equilibria as well.

10. This result is Black's (1948) famous "median voter" theorem. It is also essentially Hotelling's equilibrium (1929). The result for the case of mixed strategies might be regarded as a natural extension of Black's and Hotelling's theorems.

11. To assure uniqueness of equilibria wherever possible, we assume throughout that there is an odd number of voters or that the number of voters corresponds to a continuous density on an interval.

12. Let M stand for the strict majority rule relation. We write xMy in case x beats y by a majority vote. We write that xNy is in a set A if there is a sequence of alternatives, $z_1, z_2, \ldots, z_k$ contained in A such that $x = z_1$, $y = z_k$, and z_iMz_{i+1}, for each i. Then, a set A is a cycle if, for each pair of alternatives x,y contained in it, xNy is in A. A is a top cycle if there is no alternative x such that xMy for all y in A.

13. This is not, of course, the only paradox in Downs's theory of elections.

14. Downs assumes in that context that the incumbent will follow the "majority principle" on an issue-by-issue basis. Such an assumption is not relevant to the present argument and so I have dispensed with it.

15. One could construct a defense of this strategy in terms of the internal rationality program by pointing to mechanisms "outside" the model that might, in equilibrium, support the assumption that platforms are credible commitments. The most prominent candidate for such a mechanism is the political party. It is a long-lived vehicle that could develop and maintain a reputation for truthfulness and employ internal incentives to discipline its candidates to act in a way consistent with this reputation. This party-centered strategy has never seemed quite as plausible in the American context as in the British one.

16. It is not at all clear that voters can credibly threaten not to reelect an incumbent who has failed to honor a promise. For such a threat to be credible, the voters must expect to do better if a challenger is elected and, as long as challengers and incumbents have identical motivations, such expectations are difficult to justify. This use of reputation is essentially candidate-centered and is plagued with a variety of problems explored below.

17. For a direct argument of this sort, accounting for "honeymoons" and mandates, see Alt (1985).

18. The costliness of action is traceable to the fact that the incumbent will usually have policy preferences that differ from those of the electorate. Acting as the electorate wishes therefore entails forgoing preferred actions.

19. These external shocks are often thought of as arising from the economy but could as well come from the international sphere or the physical world. The important point is that they are not endogenously determined within the model. For developments of this model, see Barro (1973), Becker and Stigler (1972), and Ferejohn (1986).

20. Because we are speaking of a collective decision problem, the usual problems as to determining the interests of a collectivity remain. The models discussed in this section are one-dimensional and voters are assumed to have single-peaked preferences so that we may, conventionally, identify the preferred position of the median voter as the interests of the electorate.

21. Indeed, Ferejohn (1986) showed that in a multidimensional setting, candidate shirking is essentially uncontrollable.

22. Such means might include hiring retired politicians as consultants or promoting them for appointive positions.

23. I am not denying that other causal factors might have an influence on ideological structure. That ideologies help those who hold them to make sense of the world around them and identify useful ways of making choices and judgments surely limits the kinds of belief ensembles that could function as ideologies. Here the question is whether alternative sets of beliefs are scalable in a one-dimensional space.

11

Studying Institutions: Some Lessons from the Rational Choice Approach

Kenneth A. Shepsle

To my mind it is rather remarkable that a recent president of the Royal Economic Society could, in his inaugural address, report that the study of institutions "has become one of the liveliest areas in our discipline." He went on to assert that "it has . . . brought us more closely in touch with a number of other disciplines within the social sciences. A body of thinking has evolved based on two propositions: (i) institutions do matter, (ii) the determinants of institutions are susceptible to analysis by the tools of economic theory" (Matthews 1986: 903–4).

What is remarkable about this assertion is that for most of this century, economists, with some notable exceptions, had abandoned the study of institutions. The neoclassical paradigm took the institutional context as fixed, given, and exogenous. There were early warnings from John Commons and Thorstein Veblen about the inadequacy of the neoclassical approach, but their form of institutionalist scholarship was not clearly equilibrium oriented and soon faded. Ronald Coase (1937) took on the neoclassicists in terms more readily understood from an equilibrium perspective, but only in the past two decades have his contributions come to be recognized. Indeed, it is probably fair to say that institutions are, today, the objects of intense study by economists because of the inspiration Coase provided to the somewhat offbeat interests of organizational economists (Williamson 1975, 1985), economic historians (Davis and North 1971; North and Thomas 1973; North 1981), and business historians (Chandler 1962, 1977).

An earlier version of this essay was published in the *Journal of Theoretical Politics* (1989). For the present version I would like to thank John Dryzek and James Farr for some suggestions about the earlier history of institutionalism in political science.

There is a second sense in which the recent interests in institutions by economists is remarkable: Political studies have provided little of the inspiration or impetus. Until the behavioral revolution of the mid-twentieth century, it is not too much of an exaggeration to say that the study of institutions (together with the history of political thought) *was* political science. Nineteenth-century American political science was uncontestedly "the science of the state," and it is impossible to address the state without discussing institutions. Government for the most part was conceptualized as the institutional manifestation of the state, and the agenda so set for political science carried on into the early decades of the twentieth century. Whether dealing with the state in all its monistic and organic splendor or examining the minutiae of state functions, the discipline was thoroughly institutionalist.

This "old" institutionalism was not static, and over time changes in its form were apparent. So formalism faltered and empirical study gained ground beginning with the publication in 1885 of Woodrow Wilson's *Congressional Government*, which sought to investigate Congress as it actually worked, rather than as the Constitution declared that it should work. Wilson's was an early effort that examined the actual consequences of institutional arrangements, as opposed to explaining the origins of institutions (such as the state) or exhorting on behalf of particular institutions (such as the unitary national state) and their functions (such as developing national commerce). This kind of empirical study was facilitated, if not entirely consummated, by the efforts of Wilson, W. W. Willoughby, Frank Goodnow, and A. B. Hart to demystify the often elusive idea of the state by analyzing the tangible institutions of government.

These earlier political scientists notwithstanding, several features of turn-of-the-century political science's account of the state rendered it vulnerable to alternative understandings. Continued formalism, widespread aversion to empirical inquiry, pervasive partisan rhetoric on behalf of different functions for the state and government, and treatment of the state in organic, monistic, and sometimes reverential terms meant that the "old" institutionalism produced little in the way of cumulative theory. As such, it was open to attack from political scientists interested in more hard-headed empirical analysis. Leading the charge was Arthur F. Bentley. Bentley was a societal reductionist (at least as argued by Gabriel Almond 1990: 210). In *The Process of Government*, Bentley tried to reduce the study of politics, especially the politics of social groups, to the observation of process and activity. To Bentley, institutional forms were window dressing, and processes of social interaction could be understood quite well without them.

The old institutionalism was further undermined by the pluralist attacks on the statist focus of the discipline, which began in the 1920s and emerged victorious in the 1950s (see Gunnell and Farr, Chapters 1 and 8, respectively, this volume). The state was ejected from political science, both as empirical datum and normative desideratum. However, few pluralists followed Bentley in reducing politics to social processes and in completely ignoring institutions. So, for example, David Truman and other pluralists of the 1950s allowed government officials into pluralist interaction and allowed them to have interests irreducible to those of social groups. Yet pluralism treated institutions in highly limited fashion: as sources of interests for political actors or as a neutral arena for the interaction of interests. Thus, it was left to economists to go ahead and reinvent the rigorous study of institutions de novo.

In this brief essay I discuss some of these issues. In the first section, I describe in ever so circumscribed a fashion the behavioral and rational choice revolutions in political science. The second section is devoted to the rediscovery of institutional analysis and the important role played by rational choice modeling in this enterprise. In the third section, I address one side of the institutional coin explaining the consequences of institutional practices. The succeeding section examines the other side of the coin: endogenizing institutional practices. In the final section I conclude the discussion and resolve some loose ends.

I. The Behavioral and Rational Choice Revolutions in Political Science

It is something of an anomaly that in the nomenclature of political science, there is no distinction between political thought and political theory. In our discipline (and course catalogs) the two terms are taken as identical, encompassing a variety of intellectual activities but most of the time referring either to textual exegesis of classical works of political philosophy or to conceptual elaboration of ideas and values. Thus, for much of the discipline's history, there has been no theory in the sense that physics or biology or economics has theory (as distinct from the history of thought). There has been no political science counterpart to Isaac Newton or Albert Einstein, or even to Adam Smith, Alfred Marshall, John Hicks, or Paul Samuelson – that is, someone who is regarded as having offered up a unifying theoretical perspective.[1] There has been no body of theoretical doctrine that provides a coherent explanation of diverse phenomena. Indeed, until recently, there has been no professional consensus on the objective of explaining political phenomena.[2]

The behavioral revolution in political science represented a first attempt to break out of the more literary mold that characterized most political science through the mid-twentieth century (Gunnell 1988). Borrowing heavily from sociology and behavioral psychology, behavioral students of politics sought to understand empirical regularities by appealing to the properties and behavior of individuals. According to the behavioral persuasion, individuals constituted the fundamental building blocks, and political results were simply the aggregation of individual actions. The latter were to be understood as being founded on sociological and psychological principles.

Behavioralism was tremendously important to the scientific study of politics because it emphasized, in its many variations, precise observation, counting and measuring where possible, the clear statement of hypotheses, and unambiguous standards for accepting or rejecting them. In each of these respects there was a clear break with the past, a clear differentiation from literary essays and philosophical discourse.

There was a clear break in another sense as well. An earlier descriptive tradition, focusing principally on cataloging the minutiae of political institutions, was tossed overboard. In rejecting the legalistic, formalistic work that characterized this study of political institutions in the early part of the century, the behaviorialists (perhaps only implicitly) expressed a profound disinterest in institutions at all. To oversimplify, institutions were, in the thinking of many behaviorialists, empty shells to be filled by individual roles, statuses, and values. Once you had these individual-level properties and summed them up properly (as in Bentley's 1908 parallelogram of forces), there was no need to study institutions; they were epiphenomenal.

Now, institutions did not fade completely from sight during the behavioral era, and government did occasionally get treated as more than a dependent variable of social forces or as a neutral arena for interaction. Political scientists continued to study executives, bureaucracies, courts, and legislatures. But there is no doubt that institutions were deemed of decidedly secondary importance; for the behavioral revolution was a triumph of sociology and psychology. The rational choice revolution, which came in the 1960s and 1970s and continues today, is a triumph of economics. A superficial distinction between these approaches is given by Duesenberry's clever observation that "economics is all about how people make choices; sociology is all about how they don't have any choices to make" (Duesenberry 1960, 243). But it is the common presuppositions of these two paradigms that interest me here, for the renewal of interest in institutions is a response to blinders worn by *both* approaches.

There is a preprogrammed quality to the sociological man that populated the world of the behavioralist; responsiveness to environmental stimuli is foreordained by adherence to roles and by socialization. While behavioralists acknowledge learning and adaptive behavior, thereby distinguishing their model of man from that of a biological determinist, their emphasis on "the hand that rocks the cradle" occasionally brings them perilously close to the determinist camp.

What is interesting, and why I call Duesenberry's distinction superficial, is that there is a similar quality to *Homo economicus*. In place of responsive, passive, sociological man, the rational choice paradigm substitutes a purposive, proactive agent, a maximizer of privately held values. A rational agent is one who comes to a social situation with preferences over possible social states, beliefs about the world around oneself, and a capability of employing these data intelligently. Agent behavior takes the form of choices based on either intelligent calculation or internalized rules that reflect optimal adaptation to experience.

But rational man, like sociological man, is an atom unconnected to the social structure in which he or she is embedded. A behavioral theory aggregates individual behaviors based on role, status, and learned responses. A rational theory aggregates individual choices based on preferences or privately held values. Sociologically based theories emphasize (or seek to explain) the sources and causes of the learned responses, worrying less about the manner in which they are aggregated into social outcomes. Rationality-based theories worry hardly at all about the sources of preferences and beliefs, emphasizing instead how these data, however arrived at, get summed into social outcomes.[3] Despite these obvious differences, both theories involve, in Granovetter's (1985) terms, "undersocialized conceptions of human action." There is no glue holding the atoms together; there is no society.

In the past decade there have been responses to this difficulty from both the behavioral and rational choice camps. Since the focus of this essay in on the latter, I leave the reader interested in the sociological response to the problem with a recommendation to consult Granovetter's excellent essay. Let me only briefly indicate that his solution to the problem of an overly atomized conception of man is to focus on what he calls "embeddedness," the molasses-like connections among individuals that transform atomistic, impersonal, uncontingent behavior into social relations. While he and other sociologists have focused on *relationships* among individuals, rational choice theorists have turned to *institutions*. Like relationships, institutions may be thought of as part of what embeds people in social situations. They are the social glue missing from the behavioralist's more atomistic account.

II. The New Institutionalism

In the late 1970s a number of rational choice theorists, myself included (Shepsle 1979), became disenchanted with the overly atomistic conception of political life found in most social choice, game theory, and decision theory applications to politics.[4] Politics takes place in context, often formal and official (as in a legislative, judicial, or bureaucratic proceeding) but often informal as well (as in a club or faculty meeting).

Many of us were still prepared to believe that individuals brought privately held values and beliefs to such settings and that their behavior could be accommodated by an optimizing paradigm. But we felt that explanations based only on maximizing behavior were unnecessarily impoverished.[5]

In my own case, this conviction came from studying *real* social choices – namely, those that took place in the legislative process of the U.S. Congress. There I was struck by the importance substantive scholars placed on *structural features* (the division and specialization of labor in committees, leadership organization, staffing arrangements, party groupings) and *procedures* (rules of debate and amendment, as well as those regulating other features of daily official life).

In their quest for analytical generality, most formal theorists had suppressed institutional details such as these, thinking that to include them would be to specialize and render idiosyncratic otherwise general theories. Their view was that most empirical studies of institutions – of legislatures, courts, government bureaus, electoral systems – were so hopelessly time- and location-bound, so hopelessly tied to specific details, that they had no place in a general theory, one that sought to rise above idiosyncratic minutiae. However, in my view, by suppressing these details altogether, they robbed their own theories of any generality by modeling rational behavior in the most spartan of all institutional settings – that described only by a simple rule of preference aggregation (Shepsle and Weingast 1981, 1982).

"New institutionalism" is the general banner under which all of these concerns with institutional features have been elaborated. Like the rational choice theories that preceded them, and in contrast to the older institutional traditions both in economics and political science, these efforts are equilibrium theories. They seek to explain characteristics of social outcomes on the basis not only of agent preferences and optimizing behavior, but also of institutional features. The descriptive minutiae of an earlier tradition became, in a somewhat more general fashion, the specific details of a *game form*. They describe the strategic context in which optimizing behavior takes place by laying down the rules according to which (1) players are identified, (2) prospective outcomes are determined, (3) alternative modes of deliberations are permitted, and (4) the specific manner in which revealed preferences, over *allowable* alternatives, by *eligible* participants, occurs.[6] From this perspective, rational choice theories that begin "Assume a set $N = (1, 2, \ldots, n)$ of agents and a set $A = (a_1, a_2, \ldots, a_k)$ of alternatives . . ." are impoverished, since the sets N and A are precisely what institutional rules delineate. It is in this sense that structure and procedure combine with agent preferences to determine equilibria.

III. Structure-Induced Equilibrium: A Contribution of Rational Choice Theory

In my own work, and later in collaboration with Barry Weingast, I have sought to give the structural and procedural features that characterize most institutions of a general formulation. I do not review this work in any detail here,[7] but I do make several points. First, when I started thinking about formal models of institutions, I was alarmed at some of the inferences social choice and game theorists were making about political processes (especially their allegations of incoherence and instability) on the basis of an extremely spartan stylization of the political context. Second, I found it inconceivable that professional politicians would spend untold hours wrangling over matters of structure and procedure and that institutional handbooks of rules were extremely fine-grained and ran to hundreds of pages and multiple volumes if those rules were "merely" minutiae and not the stuff of general theory. Third, I believed there were ways to characterize some of these features so that while retaining some of the specialized flavor they exhibited in particular contexts, they nevertheless captured more general properties of these specific institutional features.

My contribution – a modest one – was to define an institutionally enriched equilibrium concept and give it a catchy name: *structure-induced equilibrium*. In earlier equilibrium theories, equilibrium was preference-driven. An outcome x was said to be an equilibrium if there existed no y preferred to it by a decisive coalition of agents (normally a simple majority of the set of agents). In the language of game theory, equilibrium was associated with the *core*. The unhappy conclusion of many of these theoretical stories, themselves generalizations and extensions of Arrow's impossibility theorem, was that in politics there typically were no equilibria; the core was empty. Hence, any outcome was provisional, a temporary resting place for a generally unstable process; all was flux. The story did not end there. In a remarkable theoretical development, McKelvey (1979) showed not only that no equilibrium existed in the sense just given; as well, it was entirely possible for *any* point to be a temporary resting place for the process.

As a student of congressional politics, I found these general conclusions inapposite. All was not flux; final outcomes were not arbitrary. For the past thirty years congressional scholars had been charting empirical regularities concerning legislative outcomes that displayed systematic features – for example, the disproportionate influence on outcomes of the preferences of members of a germane committee, of the majority party, or of senior members. In short, outcomes appeared to track the preferences of distinguished actors upon whom institutional structure and procedure conferred disproportionate agenda power. All the "action," so to speak, was not in the straightforward aggregation of preferences, but rather in the sometimes subtle influence provided by control over structure and procedure.

The concept of structure-induced equilibrium is based on the idea that an institutional process, described by its rules, can be graphed as an extensive form game. *Sequence*, the details of which are found in institutional rules of procedure and were suppressed in most earlier theories, matters because it determines which moves follow which other moves and who gets to move when; hence, sequence begets strategy. The *identity of individuals* matters because the rules confer the privilege of certain moves on certain specified subsets of N. In the extensive form game, named individuals (e.g., the committee chairperson, the majority leader) are assigned to specific nodes of the tree. Social choice models that assume "anonymity" (or in Riker's (1982) sense "undifferentiatedness") require revision because of this. In a parallel fashion, the assumption of an undifferentiated set A of alternatives (or, in the language of social choice theory, the assumption of *neutrality* among alternatives) seems inappropriate in many institutional settings; at specific nodes of the game tree (points in the process), the rules often delimit what (kinds of) alternatives are available for choice (e.g., germaneness rules for amendments).

With these notions as background, a structure-induced equilibrium may be defined as an alternative (a status quo ante) that is *invulnerable* in the sense that no other alternative, allowed by the rules of procedure, is preferred by all the individuals, structural units, and coalitions that possess distinctive veto or voting power. The idea can be made precise, but the more informal definition given here will suffice for present purposes. Perhaps the most important point to make is that the idea of equilibrium contained in this concept is founded on the structural and procedural features of the process being modeled. Process is made explicit and is given definition (as an extensive form game) by institutional context.

From the institution-free, atomistic specification of traditional social choice and game theory, the idea of structure-induced equilibrium is clearly a move in the direction of incorporating institutional features into rational choice approaches. Structure and procedure combine with preferences to produce outcomes. Equilibrium, if it exists, is affected not only by the distribution and revelation of agent preferences, but also by the way the collectivity goes about its business. Indeed, the strategic revelation of agent preferences will depend on this as well.

The research program spawned by this idea, however, leaves an important unfinished aspect. Institutional arrangements are taken as exogenous. With this approach we don't know *why* the collectivity goes about its business in some particular way. The structure-induced equilibrium approach elaborates the temporally subsequent effects of structure and procedure while ignoring temporally prior causes. It is my view that one cannot understand or explain institutions, however, without first explicating their effects. So it is quite proper to examine effects first. But the rational choice of institutions remains a challenge.

IV. Explaining Institutions: The Challenge to Rational Choice

If structure-induced equilibrium analysis has as its focus *institutional equilibrium* – the equilibrium in outcomes produced by a specific institutional configuration – then the challenge of explaining institutions is to formulate a theory of *equilibrium institutions*. There are really two questions here: How are institutions selected, and how are institutions sustained?[8]

Choosing Institutions

Imagine a group of children in a park considering a game like "hide-and-seek", "kick the can", or "capture the flag." In particular, because the park is filled with big rocks, dense bushes, and groves of trees, suppose they have settled on hide-and-seek. This game comes in a standard garden-variety (pun intended) form, with well-defined rules with which any child is familiar. But kids are known to alter the rules. Situation-specific features – time of day, number of children, age distribution of children, topography, length of the play period – often suggest specific variations that are agreed upon in advance (e.g., that an especially young child should not be "it" first). Other variations only occur to the children once play has commenced.[9] These instances are often associated with conflict because any resolution will have known distributional consequences. Ultimately, they are either resolved in the specific instance and serve as precedent for future occurrences, or lead to the disbanding of play.

I have earlier in this essay identified an institution with a game form. Thus, the story of children selecting rules for the play of a game in the park is an apt parable for institutional choice. According to this view (and it is certainly not the only view), choosing an institution is equivalent to choosing a game form. A theory explaining institutions, then, is one that explains why particular games are chosen.

In distinguishing among rational choice approaches to this problem, the role of information is crucial. One approach, associated with Rawls (1958, 1972) and Harsanyi (1977),[10] asks what institutions a collectivity would choose if information about individual biological, intellectual, and material endowments were unknown. That is, what game form would be chosen by individuals who were behind "the veil of ignorance"? Of course, as most readers will know, these theories of institutional choice are not usually offered as explanations for the choice of real institutions, but rather are suggested as metaphors for how institutions ought to be chosen and judged. As Rawls and Harsanyi suggest, if people, in constituting their political institutions, acted as if they were ignorant of personal endowments and therefore were capable of engaging in extended sympathy or of expressing "ethical preferences," then institutions that emerged would display qualities of justice.

The Rawlsian veil of ignorance is an artifice of extreme information incompleteness. In most institutional choice settings, the choosing agents, like the children in the park, are partially informed about a number of relevant parameters. And they are quite capable of fashioning institutions to accomplish a number of objectives. Some, like whether everyone should drive on the left or right side of the road, are pure coordination problems in which private knowledge about personal endowments has little relevance. The goal is coordination, and the distributional conflict involved in *which* outcome to coordinate on pales in comparison with the matter of arriving at *some* coordinated outcome.

In many situations, however, the objective is not coordination per se, but Pareto improvements in which the distributional conflicts are central (or at least more important than in pure coordination). In these instances individuals can imagine different institutional arrangements, which produce surpluses of different magnitudes, which entail different rules for sharing the surplus, and which offer different opportunities for ex ante commitment and ex post opportunism. In short, this view of institution selection regards an institution as an ex ante bargain the objective of which is to enhance various forms of "cooperation" and to facilitate the enforcement of agreements.

This approach, in contrast to the Harsanyi–Rawls formulation of the problem, assumes self-knowledge and is compatible with a wide range of common-knowledge assumptions. In the typical model of this sort, the agents may not know everything about one another, but they do know everything about themselves. Moreover, they typically have only imperfect information about the various contingencies in which the bargain will operate. This is not quite the same as a veil of ignorance in the Rawlsian sense, but it has something of the same effect. It should lead, in principle, to the ex ante selection of rules (read: game form), which, if obeyed, will not come to be regretted (as much as alternatives) by any of the parties ex post.[11] The theory of contracts (Hart and Holmstrom 1987), the theory of the firm (Coase 1937; Williamson 1975, 1985), the theory of principals and agents (Jensen and Meckling 1973; Fama and Jensen 1983; Pratt and Zeckhauser 1985), and transaction-cost economics (Williamson 1979) are now vast literatures that apply rationality to the problem of institution selection and deal with the twin obstacles of imperfect enforcement and imperfect foresight of future contingencies.

The conclusions in these literatures are too vast to summarize here, so let me simply indicate that perhaps the quintessential concrete example is the *employment relation*. It is an example of a contractual relation, many of whose clauses are explicit, but many of which are ambiguous or implicit and derive meaning only in concrete (but often unanticipated) contingencies. There are problems of enforcement (e.g., ambiguous clauses), of imperfect foresight (e.g., unanticipated contingencies), of opportunistic behavior (e.g., shirking on the job, pilferage), and of costly transacting (e.g., difficulty in measuring employee output in team production and monitoring effort) with which the *institution* of the employment relation seeks to cope. Indeed, many social relationships, ranging from that of the simple bilateral contract to complex organizational forms like the modern corporation and political party, are instances of imperfectly and incompletely informed individuals intelligently exercising what foresight they may command to select governance institutions.

From this brief survey I hope it is evident that there are rational theories of institution selection. Some seek to suppress contextual knowledge in order to derive the determinants of just institutions. Others allow for contextual information about oneself and one's colleagues, however incomplete, in order to determine the feasibility of cooperative "gains from trade" and the range of institutional forms that have "nice" properties – minimal transactions costs, satisfactory enforcement mechanisms and commitment capacities, and so on.

Although there are many unsolved problems and unsatisfactory features in the models found in this literature, let me draw the reader's attention to two. First, to the theorist as external observer an institution looks like a negotiated solution to some problem of cooperation. The institution may facilitate exchange, comity, or some other welfare-enhancing value. The theorist often yields to the temptation of concluding that what has been facilitated was the ex ante objective of the individuals involved. Yet what an institution facilitates may in fact be a byproduct of what its founders intended.

The institution of a committee system in the U.S. Congress, an instance with which I am familiar (Gamm and Shepsle 1988), illustrates this. To oversimplify the historical record, the committee system was an early-nineteenth-century creation that had a number of salutary effects for the legislature, especially in its struggle with the executive branch. Surely some of these effects were intended. Yet there is reason to suspect that Henry Clay, the activist Speaker of the House during this formative period (1811–25), had a hand in this institutional innovation, not so much to enhance the stature of the legislature in a separation-of-powers system, but rather to enhance his own stature. Specifically, it enabled him to remain leader of a once singleminded coalition that, after the War of 1812, had split into many factions. By decentralizing the operations of the House of Representatives, Clay was able to distribute pieces of turf to various factions as a substitute for a unified platform of political objectives around which the coalition had formerly unified (but which was now infeasible). The lasting effects of this institutional innovation could hardly have been anticipated, much less desired, by Clay. They were by-products (and proved to be the more enduring and important products) of self-interested leadership behavior.

The second issue I wish to underscore involves the ex ante veneer I have given the institution selection theories surveyed earlier. Returning to the children-in-the-park parable, recall that not all the rules of the game could be fixed in advance. Experience under the rules produced anomalies and unexpected events. In general, what *can* be anticipated in advance is that there will be unforeseen contingencies.

Many institutions with which we are familiar, anticipating this, possess short-circuiting procedures. Many contracts, for example, often specify the forum in which and the format according to which unanticipated contract disputes will be resolved or terms renegotiated. To give another example, most legislatures, clubs, and other organizations governed by rules of procedure possess methods by which those very rules may be suspended. Yet, for the most part, the theories discussed in preceding paragraphs (with some exceptions) conceive of institutions as ex ante bargains – as the one-time-only choice of a game form. In reality, institutions undergo transformation. In principle, these transformations may be modeled as "games within games." At any node in the game form, the option of changing the rules of the game is a possibility. This very possibility leads to the second aspect of "equilibrium institutions," namely institutional maintenance.

Maintaining Institutions

When an institution is transformed – endogenously, as when the rules of procedure are changed or a contract renegotiated in a prearranged fashion, or exogenously by some unanticipated shock to the system – it is not the same institution anymore. When the children in the park come to blows over some subtle interpretation of the rules of the game and "pick up their marbles and go home," the institution of play has been destroyed. When the Founding Fathers jettisoned the Articles of Confederation and, with the consent of enough of the governed, substituted for it the Constitution of the United States, a governance structure had been replaced. When the U.S. Senate changed its standing rules to make it easier to shut off a filibuster, an institution had been transformed. In each of these instances, in varying degrees, institutional arrangements were changed, transformed, evolved, adapted, or whatever. In the remainder of this section I want to address some alternative conceptions of institutional maintenance and change.

As noted earlier, the choice of an institution may be thought of as the selection of a game in which there are many uncertainties – unforeseen contingencies, unknown states of the world, incomplete information about the preferences of others. An institution is chosen by individuals, intelligently using what knowledge and information is available, but before the "values" of many parameters are known. It is, as I suggested, an ex ante selection. The question at issue is the degree to which it is robust ex post.

An institution may be said to be *renegotiation proof* if, even as experience unfolds and some previous uncertainties are resolved, no decisive coalition of agents wishes to alter the institution.[12] Renegotiation-proofness is a robustness requirement for institutions much as *perfectness* (Selten 1975) is a robustness requirement for strategies in extensive form games. Let me elaborate.

In an extensive form game, a strategy is a rule for an individual player mapping his or her nodes to actions. It says how the player would respond if a particular node in the game at which he or she had a move were reached. A set of strategies, one for each player, is said to constitute a *Nash equilibrium* if no player desires to alter his or her strategy given the strategic choices of all the others. A number of Nash equilibrium strategies, however, involve incredible threats. The subset of Nash equilibrium strategies that do not are said to be *subgame perfect*. When any node in the extensive form game is reached, the player whose turn it is is fully prepared to play as announced. That is, no matter how the game unfolds, no player wishes to alter his or her announced intentions.

An institution is robust in this same sense if, after no history of experience, any decisive coalition would wish to implement some alteration of the arrangements. To see what this entails, consider how Rawls's "just" institution fails this test. Behind the veil of ignorance, a just institution is selected by the collectivity. Then nature moves, removing the veil and allowing individuals to know their respective places in society. It is quite conceivable that some number of them, sufficient in quantity to disrupt the just institution, are unhappy with the arrangements in place. Because there is no way to bind oneself in the "original position" to maintain the institutional choices made there, Rawls's just institutions are vulnerable: The dissatisfied players may be in a position to force a renegotiation.[13]

Renegotiation-proofness of institutions, like perfection in strategies, is quite demanding. Were we to insist on this as the criterion of institutional robustness, it is my belief that virtually no institutional choice could satisfy it.[14] A somewhat less demanding notion, one I alluded to earlier, would regard an institution as "essentially" in equilibrium if changes transpired according to an ex ante plan (and hence part of the original institution) for institutional change. The regime of the United States is not thought to have changed whenever an amendment to the Constitution, passed according to procedures laid out in the Constitution, occurs; rather, the United States is said to have a "living" constitution.

Similarly, if children in the park agree, as part of their initial deliberations, to invent rules along the way by majority rule as unanticipated events occur, then it is fair to say that the original institution remains intact.

In making these points I want to make clear that rational choice theorists have only just begun to tackle the problem of institutional robustness. We have come a considerable distance from simply assuming institutions are robust, as Rawls and most of neoclassical economics did in taking institutions as exogenously fixed. We have even advanced beyond an initial recognition that institutions, as choices, seem not to have inherited the same sorts of instability that ordinary political choices reveal.[15] I conclude this essay by pointing to several matters deserving further attention.

V. Concluding Discussion

Characterizing an institution as a game makes transparent the concept of institutional equilibrium (the first side of the coin I discussed earlier) – it is an equilibrium of a game. Thus, the analytical problem of a rational theory of institutionally enriched political life is one of "equilibrium selection" (Harsanyi and Selten 1988). In thinking, on the other hand, about equilibrium institutions (or what I have been referring to as the problem of robustness), especially if we are going to regard an institution not only as a forum for future choices but as a choice, itself, then we must be more explicit about the process of institutional choice. What are the rules of *this* game? Who are the players? What subsets are sufficient to effect changes – that is, which are the decisive coalitions? In sum, the process of the choice of institutions must be modeled explicitly.

Whatever the process, it will be no free lunch. When children, mid-game, need to amend their rules to take some unforeseen event into account, one of the factors that reduces incentives for long negotiations is time. Time spent on transacting is time unavailable for play. If the American revolutionaries of 1776 did not hang together in their efforts to change their governance structure and minimize haggling among themselves, they feared they would "hang separately." These two examples illustrate the two principal "taxes" on the deliberation involved in renegotiating institutional arrangements (Binmore, Rubinstein, and Wolinsky 1986): (1) *impatience* – the deferral of gratification from the arrangements under consideration while haggling takes place; and (2) *risk of breakdown* – the likelihood (which increases with the duration and convolutedness of haggling) of failing to come to agreement and thereby being forced down to some "reversion" payoff. Changing institutions imposes transactions costs of this sort on the participants. The transactions costs include not only those devoted to decision making, but also those required to enforce the procedures of the new regime and for individuals to adapt to the new procedures.

In terms of institutional robustness, the transaction costs of change provide an institution with something of a cushion, giving it a stability it might not otherwise enjoy in a transactions-cost-free world. Thus, even when institutional arrangements are not optimally suited to a given environment, they may nevertheless endure because prospective gains from change are more than outweighed by the costs of effecting them. In a world full of uncertainty about future states, imperfect information and a modicum of risk aversion of participants may make that cushion substantial.[16] As a consequence, institutions may be robust, not because they are optimally suited to the tastes of participants and the present environment, but rather because transactions costs price alternative arrangements too high. This, then, again points to the necessity of formalizing the process by which institutions are selected and to be sure to incorporate the costs of engaging in deliberation in any valuation exercise.

As a final matter, let be briefly deal with a question that I have suppressed to this point. Is it reasonable to think of institutions as "objects" that are chosen? Some older institutionalists, like Sait (1938), would think much of this essay silly precisely because institutions are *not* chosen. He writes:

When we examine political institutions, one after the other, they seem to have been erected, almost like coral reefs, without conscious design. There has been no pre-arranged plan, no architect's drawings and blue-prints; man has carried out the purposes of nature, we might say, acting blindly in response to her obscure commands. We approached with veneration the splendid edifice of Roman law. . . . Remarking its symmetry, its satisfying proportions, and the harmony of its various parts, we ask for the name of the architect. There was no architect; nobody planned it. (Sait 1938:16)

Now Sait does not deny that institutions change; he is merely silent on the process by which this change transpires.[17] From this above passage it is clear he has some glacial, incremental, evolutionary process in mind, but surely not one that can be comprehended by the individuals governed by an institution, much less caused by their choices.

Most modern theorists would find this silence a major shortcoming. If one has an evolutionary theory in mind,[18] then one must specify the process or mechanism by which evolution takes place. In biological evolution, for example, it is the mechanism of environmental suitability, or natural selection, that permits genotypes to prosper or decline and phenotypes to increase or decrease their presence in the gene pool. And since one would be hard pressed to point to a process of natural selection for human institutions without the helping hands of man,[19] it seems to me that, Sait notwithstanding, some rational theory of institution selection is required. Still, I have some nagging doubts about how satisfactory a micro theory will be. Just as economic historians delicately straddle the boundary between the micro and the macro, so it probably must be for students of equilibrium institutions.

In elaborating some of the insights from rationality on the causes and consequences of institutional practices and features, I have endeavored to underscore how rational choice theorists have departed from both the philosophical and the behavioral traditions in political science. I believe that the rational choice revolution, rather than jettisoning contributions from these earlier approaches, has sought to build on them. From the philosophical it has rescued a concern with institutions as the "glue" that holds otherwise atomistic and self-interested individuals together in organized society. From the behavioral it has taken a concern with empirical regularities, both as constraints on theory and as matters to be explained. In the end, rational choice theory promises to drive a wedge between political thought and political theory, making the latter both a synthesis of its earlier roots and a genuinely scientific enterprise. More importantly, political science need no longer concede the study of institutions to the economists.

Notes

1. Some might claim that Arthur Bentley or Harold Lasswell in the modern era come close. Their influence on subsequent scholarship is indisputable, but their work did not result in a unified theoretical perspective embraced by later scholars. Others argue that Hobbes, Madison, and Tocqueville constitute major theorists. But in the history of political thought, their work is regarded less as attempts at coherent theory building than as products of the upheavals and historical events that occurred as they were being written. This strikes me as an odd perspective, and it has had the unfortunate consequence of diminishing the prospects for theoretical cumulativeness. I thank Elinor Ostrom for pointing this out to me.
2. In a brief account, oversimplification is inevitable. And so it is here. Before midcentury, there were nascent scientific efforts within political science. Perhaps the most important were those associated with the work of Merriam, Lasswell, and others of the Chicago school in the 1920s and 1930s. This is not the place to develop the historical record further.
3. More dynamic rational theories do seek to understand how beliefs change as a result of experience. When agents' information about the world around them is incomplete or imperfect, they may alter prior beliefs (usually according to Bayes's law) on the basis of experience. Interestingly, most rational choice theories do *not* allow room for preferences to change according to a similar dynamic.
4. At about the same time, and very much in the spirit of Granovetter, the same disenchantment was expressed by political sociologists. This is reflected especially well in the contextual modeling work of Raymond Boudon, Adam Przeworski, John Sprague, and their students.
5. Excellent general statements may be found in Riker (1980) and Ostrom (1986).
6. In a much more thoroughgoing fashion, Ostrom (1986) describes seven classes of rules by which an institution is configured. Like her, I wish here only to point out that an institution, like a game form, may be characterized by rules, that those rules may be formulated in a reasonably general fashion, and therefore, that they need not be so "hopelessly time- and location-bound" as to frustrate general theory.
7. See Shepsle (1979, 1986a,b) and Shepsle and Weingast (1981, 1987).
8. Indeed, it might even be asked *whether* institutions are selected and sustained. I have more to say about this later.

294   *Kenneth A. Shepsle*

9. When I was a child I played baseball in a partially cleared wood. It was not until my friends and I had some experience playing on that field that we came to devise location-specific rules, e.g., a ball hit into the creek is a "ground rule" double; a ball striking an overhanging branch is a "take over."

10. The interested reader should also consult Binmore (1988) and Sugden (1986).

11. This statement is not entirely right in that in some unforeseen contingency or realization of an ex ante uncertain state of nature, an individual may indeed regret the particular game form in place. He or she might have done better under a different set of rules and, if foreknowledge of the unknown state had been available, would have sought an alternative institutional arrangement. The ex ante rational institutional choice is the one that the collectivity believes, on average, will generate the last ex post regret.

12. When I say "decisive coalition," this term should be taken quite broadly. A single individual may constitute one. One child, unhappy with a ruling in a pick-up baseball game, may quit playing, leaving the remaining children to carry on in his absence. This, in turn, may require further institutional elaboration: For example, with the departing player's inclusion it might have been possible to divide the children into two equal-sized teams; in his absence, some new convention must be established (e.g., one child will become the permanent pitcher for both teams).

13. This argument is developed by Binmore (1988), citing Hare (1975) among others on the general problems of timing in Rawls. For more general treatments of renegotiation problems, see Farrell and Maskin (1986) and Pearce (1987). Rawls (1972) assumed that individuals *could* commit themselves to abide by choices made in the original position, but failed to specify the mechanism by which such commitments could be enforced.

14. A weaker version of this criterion parallels the criterion of Nash for strategies – an institution need not satisfy renegotiation-proofness at *every* node, only at those that are actually reached in the subsequent play of the game. While technically weaker, I suspect this is not substantively very helpful.

15. Riker (1980) referred to institutions as "congealed tastes" and "unstable constants." Elsewhere I suggested that, in conjoining opposites, Riker posed something of a paradox (Shepsle 1986a). I believe Riker is the first to have characterized institutions in this fashion within a rational framework and to have recognized that their robustness is, indeed, an unexplained phenomenon. As I note in the text, we are beginning to make progress on this puzzle.

16. In private discussions, Weingast has suggested thinking of an institution as a piece of capital equipment. An individual does not replace his or her personal computer the moment a new generation model is available. To do so entails not only the expenditure of monetary resources, but also the time

and energy to get going on the new system ("set-up costs"). Instead, one treats a piece of equipment as though it had a normal life the value of which depreciates over time. At some point the depreciated value of the old equipment is less than the value of the new model, *net of set-up costs*. This point is usually before the depreciated value of the old equipment reaches zero but after the date the new model is first available. For a general treatment of institutions from the perspective of industrial organization theory, see Weingast and Marshall (1988).

17. This is somewhat of an exaggeration, since Sait did propose two "hypotheses" on institutional change and discussed them in some detail. The *convergence hypothesis*, according to Sait (1938: 201–53), suggests that institutional forms evolve directly from their respective environments (though he does not say how). The *diffusion hypothesis* suggests conscious imitation by one community of the practices of another (Sait 1938: 467–99).

18. Economic theorists who have wedded rationality to evolution include Alchian (1950) and Nelson and Winter (1982).

19. The whole of Roman law may not have sprung fully formed from any one person's forehead, but its bits and pieces, much like the bits and pieces of a European cathedral built over many centuries, were surely the result of human agency.

12

Order and Time in Institutional Study: A Brief for the Historical Approach

Karen Orren and Stephen Skowronek

A leading student of interest group politics writes, "In the 1990s, we are all 'neo-institutionalists'" (McFarland, 1991: 262). Indeed, the claim that "institutions matter" can be heard today in every corner of political science. Unfortunately, as the cutting edge of a critical departure in the study of politics, this claim leaves much to be desired.

In the first place, the assertion that institutions matter fails to distinguish current disciplinary interests from more traditional ones. Political science blossomed in the late nineteenth century as a study of the institutions of government, as a "science of the state." The so-called revolt against formalism, which gathered steam in the 1920s, broadened the scope of inquiry considerably, but scholars never really lost sight of institutions. It is hardly any wonder that some of the leading lights of behavioral political science have found their "rediscovery" (Almond 1988b) amusing and the critical thrust of the "new institutionalism" wide of the mark (Easton 1981; Binder 1986). The attention showered on the informal processes of politics and the social bases of power by the behavioralists was not so much an alternative to a study of institutions as it was an exploration of their connections to the larger social and economic system. The renewed emphasis on institutions in political study may elaborate these larger relationships in important ways, but it cannot afford to disregard them.

The confusion goes deeper than that, however. The claim that institutions matter not only falls short of being an effective critique of past

Colleagues who were kind enough to offer comments on this essay were Joyce Appleby, Paul DiMaggio, Morris Fiorina, Jeff Frieden, David Mayhew, David Plotke, Ian Shapiro, Alex Wendt, Larry Dodd and James Farr.

This essay has been published previously under the title "Beyond the Iconography of Order: Notes for a 'New' Institutionalism," Larry Dodd and Calvin Jillson (eds.), *The Dynamics of American Politics: Theories and Approaches*. Boulder, Co: Westview, 1993.

concerns, it fails to distinguish among currently contending intellectual currents. "New institutionalism" is a label associated with many different scholarly agendas. Although its pursuit appears to be a concerted movement, one having gained momentum in the wake of the discipline's recent disenchantment with behavioralism, its adherents vie over what is at the heart of political study: Should we turn to economics and formal modeling for our new institutionalism? To sociology and organization theory? To history and comparative case studies?[1] All are pursued under the same rubric. The proposition that there is such a thing as *a* new institutionalism bespeaks a false consensus on the most basic disciplinary concerns.

It is not our intention to build a consensus. We recognize that a variety of approaches is appropriate, and we welcome the debates that variety engenders. In this essay we seek to clarify the case for historically oriented study and indicate the challenge it poses to diverse treatments of institutions found in both political science and history. Of all the various permutations of the new institutionalism, the historical may seem easiest to dismiss. If the general assertion that institutions matter falls flat as the pronouncement of a new scholarly agenda, the insistence that "history is important" does so even more. We believe, however, that the distinctive thrust of a historically oriented institutional study is more incisive than either of these statements would suggest. This work is not new because it is historical, rather it is historical because it is bringing new questions of timing and temporality in politics to the center of the analysis of how institutions matter. The historical institutionalists are challenging the basic conception of order in time that has been the centerpiece of the study of American institutions in all of its incarnations past and present.

We begin with a review of the various conceptions of order that have been fundamental to political analysis over the course of our discipline's history. The intent of this historical sketch is to trace these conceptions to the point where we can – as we should – supersede them. We then go on to suggest how the study of institutions can generate a better, more penetrating conception of the relationship between order and time, the overall effect of which is to provide the foundation for an institutionalism genuinely worthy of the appellation "new."

I. Political Science and Institutional Order

Political scientists have always agreed far more than they have disagreed about how institutions matter. Institutions have been approached variously as normative entelechies, as system balancers, and as game forms. But in each, institutions are seen as the pillars of order in politics, as the structures that lend the polity its integrity, facilitate its routine operation, and produce continuity in the face of potentially destabilizing forces. Institutional politics is "politics as usual," "normal politics," or a politics "in equilibrium."

In the field of American politics (with which we will be primarily concerned in this essay) the study of institutions has advanced through successive reformulations that consider how this ordering function operates. Each formulation has generated a different and more sophisticated explanation concerning how institutions hold together a far-flung, loosely knit polity. But because the fundamental premise about what institutions do has remained pretty much the same, what political scientists have produced is an increasingly elaborate iconography of order. Over the years, the study of institutions by political scientists has yielded a succession of guiding images or "models" – the Constitution, the political system, the rational actor – from which the principles of order are deduced. The rationale of each successive "institutionalism" is that it has penetrated more deeply into the fundamentals of political order than the one before.

The old institutionalism, which dominated the discipline's initial half-century (approximately between 1880 and 1930), found the pillars of order principally in the formal arrangements of the Constitution. As the U.S. Constitution provided the framework for political life, so it provided the framework for political study. In this view the formal constitutional arrangements were fundamental not only because they were, historically, foundational, but because they were seen as the concrete expression of the political culture's most basic value commitments. Once its norms were deduced, the Constitution became a standard for critical inquiry.

Many practitioners of the old formalism, for example, John W. Burgess, W. W. Willoughby, and Edward Corwin, were specialists in public law, and their work elucidated the immutable principles of American constitutionalism that had guided the polity's evolution. At the climax of Corwin's study of the presidency (1940), for instance, we find a stunning indictment of Franklin Roosevelt for trampling on the separation of powers and threatening all that the constitutional system had theretofore guaranteed.[2] But formalism was not inherently antithetical to reform. On the contrary, in the early days of the discipline, reform was an important impetus to the study of politics. In the field of public administration, for example, by taking European examples of "what to do" and figuring out the American "how to do it" (Wilson 1885), political scientists like Woodrow Wilson and Frank Goodnow sought to help the operatives of the constitutional order accommodate to changing conditions while preserving distinctive constitutional ideals. Alternatively, political science could be used to expose discrepancies between the constitutional formalities and real-life practice. In Wilson's scorching study of Congress, the formalities themselves became the driving wedge of a reform critique (Wilson 1885).

The behavioral revolution of the 1950s and 1960s radically reoriented the study of politics and, with it, the study of institutions. The "soul stuff" of the old formalism about which Arthur Bentley had complained as early as 1908 gave way to more rigorous empirical investigation of how American government actually worked, addressing such issues as why, in fact, the American system was one of the few that did work during the 1930s and 1940s. If the old presumptions about how it should work did not fit the facts, the naiveté of these presumptions would have to be exposed and replaced with a more realistic account of current operations. Under this scrutiny, boundaries between government and politics, and between state and society, quickly broke down. Government became a "process," its institutions part of the larger political "system," and public elites just another set of "interests" with behavior of their own. By the time David Easton published his definitive work, *A Systems Analysis of Political Life* (1965b), the new icons of order – system and equilibrium – had fully eclipsed the old images of state and constitution.

The pillars of order in the behavioralized political system were the conditions that stabilized the process. These were at once more abstract and more context-specific than the concrete and fixed institutions of government. They were arrangements within a set time frame: "rules of the game," observed and enforced by elites in and out of government; "conditions of polyarchy," including the overlapping memberships in voluntary organizations that served as balance wheels of otherwise freewheeling sociopolitical action (Truman 1951a; Dahl 1956). More fluid than the older constitutional forms, these institutions were also understood to be less dependable. The reforming impulse of the formalists was replaced by a recognition of the system's essential precariousness. It was an anxious David Truman, for example, who in a later edition observed the failure of elites to enforce the rules of the game by silencing Joseph McCarthy (Truman 1951a [1971]).

The behavioralists were by no means antagonistic to institutional or historical analysis. Truman's *Governmental Process* (1951a) located government institutions within the larger system of political action, and he analyzed the dynamics of system change through the organization and impact of social interests across American history. Richard Neustadt's (1960) study of the presidency queried how "midcentury" incumbents could operate effectively in a political or institutional system radically altered by the New Deal and World War II. Observe that the behavioralists' analysis of institutions – of both their order and change – was essentially homeostatic; that is, disruptions were exogenous to the system and were resolved into new and stable equilibria. Thus, in Truman's history, labor–management relations were disturbed periodically by changes in technology, and equilibrium was restored through new forms of association. Neustadt defined "politics as usual" in terms of a historically bounded, midcentury governing environment, in which presidents had to act; incumbents were endogenous, working within this system rather than upon it; transformative changes came from outside.

The third and current phase of the study of order is the new institutionalism of rational choice. Attention to institutions entered rational choice theory as a resolution of a theoretical dilemma. Order, conceived here as equilibrium, is the central premise of all rational choice theorizing. The enterprise turns on the explication of historically abstracted and analytically formal covering laws that predict stability in the resolution of issues collectively contested by individuals who act on their own preferences. The problem, as rational choice theorists have been showing for years, is that such equilibria are inherently elusive. "Politics is the dismal science," William Riker has declared in the phrase coined for economics, "because there are no stable equilibria to predict." This instability might have provided an alternative premise for the study of politics, adjusting the conception of science accordingly. But rational choice theorists have turned instead to institutions, hoping to sustain the initial program of explaining law-governed regularities, now retrospectively, working backward from decisions made to the underlying conditions of choice. "The outcome of the search for equilibria of tastes," Riker concludes, "is the discovery that, failing such equilibria, there must be some institutional element in the regularities observed" (Riker, 1982c: 19).

The "positive theory of institutions" (PTI) has built on economists' postulates about the difficulties individuals have making collective choices, adding to them an understanding of "how institutional structure and procedure combine with agent preferences to determine equilibria" (Shepsle 1989: 145). Institutions solve problems of collective action by altering the strategic context in which individuals calculate their self-interest. When everyone agrees to follow a set of rules and to act under institutionally prescribed conditions, equilibrium may be induced in a way that is impossible without this structure. Note that the introduction of concrete institutions historicizes the rules of political action and therefore also historicizes the covering laws of the theory that can be derived from them. At present, however, the rational choice program is less concerned with the question of institutional origins than with determining how (and how well) a given set of institutional arrangements will perform by applying relatively timeless covering laws to particular situations. In "robust" institutions like the U.S. Congress, internal structures and procedures are seen to become incorporated into the preferences and strategic behaviors of those who act within them.

The point to underscore in this brief history of the discipline's conceptions of order is the essential complementarity of rational choice or PTI with the older forms of institutional analysis it intends to supersede. Kenneth Shepsle describes PTI's contributions to political science in precisely these terms, as an effort to reclaim and deepen the essential insights of both the old formalism and behavioralism.

From the philosophical, it has rescued a concern with [formal] institutions as the "glue" that holds otherwise atomistic and self-interested individuals together in organized society. From the behavioral, it has taken a concern with empirical regularities, both as constraints on theory and as matters to be explained. (Shepsle 1989: 145)

The metaphor for institutions as the "glue" of politics, holding various political actors together and making them cohere, is an apt summary of the historical continuities of institutional study in all of its phases. What the formal theorists have done, Shepsle claims, is to take "idiosyncratic," "time-bound," "descriptive minutiae" derived from the empirical study of how institutions actually work and translate them into the "specific details of a game form" (Shepsle 1989: 135). As this formulation itself suggests, there is really very little at issue in the translation proposed. Received presumptions about what institutions do in politics are merely transposed to a higher level of theoretical abstraction. The object of studying institutions is still, as before, to figure out the regularities, to make sense of institutional politics as a more or less stable game in play. The behavioralists took the rules of the game out of formal institutional arrangements; the formal theorists put them back in, showing how institutional rules, devised by individuals to better satisfy their goals, reproduce order. The result is not only a new institutionalism that formalizes the strategic behavior of individuals, it is also a "new behavioralism" in which self-interested individuals are led by institutional arrangements toward "structure-induced equilibria."

II. Order and Change

The persistence with which institutional study in political science has devoted itself to unveiling the secrets of order has yet to be appreciated for its implications. Most important, this understanding of institutions lies at the heart of otherwise very different treatments of political change offered by political scientists and historians alike. In each disciplinary phase described above, institutional politics appears as "normal politics," as politics as usual, explicitly or implicitly opposed to an extraordinary politics, in which equilibria are upset, norms break down, and new institutions are generated. If the association of institutions with "order" has been all but instinctive in the study of American politics, so too is the understanding of political change as a transition between institutionalized orders, and of transition periods themselves as resolving disorder through new institutional settlements.

Consider in this regard a recent award-winning history by Martin Sklar (1989), *The Corporate Reconstruction of American Capitalism.* Sklar's description of the systemic disruptions produced by the rise of corporate capitalism at the turn of the twentieth century, and of the complex of social, economic, political, and cultural factors accommodated in the readjustment, is a quantum leap beyond prior understandings of the institutional changes negotiated in the Progressive era. For our purposes, however, Sklar's account is revealing for its familiar conception of institutions as evoked at the story's climax. Corporate consolidation prompts an intense, systemwide search for order; the search centers on the construction of new institutions and institutional relationships; and finally, a new institution (the Federal Trade Commission) is created that redefines the rules for all the players:

In restoring the common law construction of the Sherman Act, in its Rule of Reason decisions of 1911, the Supreme Court laid the juridical basis of what may be called the corporate liberal solution of the trust question, that is, of a non-

statist accommodation of the law to the corporate reorganization of capitalism.
... It was a solution capped by the legislation of 1914. Historians have long puz-
zled over the suddenness with which the trust question thereafter receded from
the center of national politics, if not disappearing altogether. Some have thought
that the American people grew tired of the issue or that the legislation of 1914
lulled them into complacency. With the Rule of Reason decisions of 1911 and
the legislation of 1914, however, the American people (or the major American
political forces) had not become tired with, or complacent about the issue; they
had settled it. It was a settlement, that is, sufficiently satisfactory to the major
concerns and interests among them, however unsatisfactory it may have been to
the concerns and interests of historians. (Sklar 1989: 173)

Setting aside the uncomfortable history just beyond Sklar's periodization of trust regulation – the shattering of the 1914 settlement during World War I and the persistent turmoil over antitrust legislation until
after World War II (Sanders 1986) – Sklar's story of the establishment
of the Federal Trade Commission (FTC) as the "solution" or "settlement" to a problem that produced decades of systemic dislocation, conforms to the successive versions of how institutions "matter" as told by
political scientists. The FTC established a new game – a new set of
rules – that could reconcile the interests of politically significant actors
and restore order.

Indeed, the grandest of all expositions of order are the overarching
broad syntheses of American political history, the mutual efforts of political scientists and historians to periodize institutional order and political change in America at the macro level. For each stage in political
science's study of institutions, there is a corresponding historiographic
synthesis. Corresponding to the old institutionalism in political science
was a "presidential synthesis" in American historiography that took the
constitutional frame itself as a periodizing scheme for politics and organized the study of American history around constitutionally mandated
presidential elections (Cochran 1948). Political history *was* presidential
history, and presidential history was the story of individual incumbents,
who tested themselves at the bar of the system of checks and balances.

Rejecting the excessive formality of the presidential scheme, a later
generation of behaviorally oriented political scientists and historians
joined in elaborating the "realignment synthesis," where periods of politics as usual are more clearly distinguished from moments of significant change. Here we find five or six distinct political regimes, or "party
systems," defined by their contending coalitions vying for power and by
the institutions that keep their policy agendas at the forefront of national

attention (McCormick 1982). Once established, the peculiarities of the American constitutional system make these orders difficult to dislodge; they persist until pent-up frustration is mobilized, and in a "critical election" (or a more extended "realigning period") the old regime is displaced and a new one takes shape.

Efforts to supersede the realignment synthesis, which are premised on finding too much variance among transitional episodes and argue for the irrelevance of electorally driven change in a bureaucratized polity, have centered on an "organizational synthesis." The organizational synthesis is less attuned to coalitional structures and policy agendas than to the characteristic institutional modalities that integrate state and society over extended periods of time (Galambos 1970, 1983; McCormick 1979; Balogh 1991). While the realignment theorists claim the Civil War era and the New Deal as major period breaks, the organizational theorists collapse the first into a long "party period" beginning in the 1820s and the second into a "bureaucratic period" beginning near the turn of the twentieth century. Whereas realignment historians, like behavioralists, emphasize the role of the voters in catalyzing political-institutional change, organizational historians, like formal theorists, see the motor force of politics in elite managers and institution builders, public and private.

We conclude this review with a final complementarity – found between political historians, who synthesize a seemingly seamless flow of events around one or another ordering principle, and formal theorists, who translate "time-bound" "descriptive minutiae" into "a game form." With history ordered by historians, formal theorists have a gold mine of material with which to elaborate the games people play. These explorations have centered in earnest on congressional politics, where, for example, Barry Weingast has applied rational choice analysis to the Congress of the 1850s to explain the disintegration of the second party system and the rise of the Republican coalition (Weingast 1991); Mark Hansen has done so with the Congress of the 1920s to explain the decline of partisan agricultural politics in favor of bureaucratic forms of influence (Hansen 1987); and Morris Fiorina has used rational choice to explain Congress's repeated design of regulatory forms (Fiorina 1982, 1986).

Another historical application of rational choice is offered by Terry Moe (1987). Moe's critique is in many ways similar to our own. He criticizes PTI for having been too quick to identify Congress as the "keystone" of the political system, too narrow in its designation of other institutions as "exogenous," and ultimately, too intent on a timeless display of the "comparative statics" of institutional politics. In his view, PTI's potential power lies in its capacity to make the entire constitutional system "endogenous" and to model rule formation, equilibrium adjustments, and institutional breakdown systemwide. To this end, he outlines the politics of the National Labor Relations Board (NLRB), placing the Congress, the president, business, labor, and bureaucracy on an equal theoretical footing. He then periodizes the history of the agency in three stages: (1) the 1930s and 1940s, an unstable, conflict-ridden phase of rule formation, (2) the 1950s and 1960s, a phase of normal politics in which each interest subordinates its particular pursuits to the enforcement of agreed-upon rules, and (3) the 1970s and 1980s, a phase of institutional breakdown when "the stars line up" in favor of one contending interest (business) with the rules abandoned at the expense of another (labor).

Moe's critique of PTI pushes the exercise of modeling beyond "comparative statics" toward whole-system dynamics, and his sequence of creation, stability, and disruption comes tantalizingly close to being an explicit exploration of the institutional construction of temporality in politics. But upon inspection, his depiction of the stable system established under the auspices of the NLRB turns out to be quite familiar. It rediscovers the post–New Deal order, or what others have called the "fifth party system." At his most ambitious, Moe challenges rational choice theorists to show us again how the pieces fit together into a coherent whole. At the farthest reaches of his search for underlying principles of change, he repairs to the fundamentals of formalism – the distinction between a constitutional system of separate powers and a parliamentary system (Moe 1990). When all is said and done, Moe's institutional analysis brings us back to the same old insights into system processes and the institutional forms of political stability.

Moe wants to challenge the boundary between formal theory and the system's view of order. We want to challenge the boundary between order and time. According to Moe, what stands in the way of formal theorists better explaining what the historians have richly described are the technical problems involved in modeling the entire institutional system. We hold that technical mastery will not substitute for a fundamental rethinking of the relationship between institutions and history posited by the notion of a system itself. Fascination with how the pieces fit into a coherent whole has reached a point of diminishing returns. New approaches to institutional study do not write history afresh but merely

translate received understandings of order and time into a new terminology. If the aim is to learn something more about what institutions do
in and to politics, the discussion must proceed beyond both the homeo-
statics of behavioralism and the comparative statics of positive theory.
A different view of the subject will get us beyond descriptions of the
ways the stars line up and turn inquiry to the movement of the stars
themselves.

III. A *New* Institutionalism

The assumption that institutions are systemically ordering mechanisms
underlies a powerful boast to disciplinary authority. Those who search
for master programs of order in time, or regularity over time, claim to
be doing science; others are said to be doing something less. The leading proponent of the realignment synthesis has suggested that political
science will either choose among various ordering constructs or be left
to "assert with full radicalness that everything flows, everything is
change, or in short that history is just one damn thing after another"
(Burnham 1986: 265). Spokesmen for rational choice theory urge us to
move beyond "time-bound descriptive minutiae" toward the explanation of transhistorical regularities, arguing that those who "continue to
assert that it all depends on some critical incident or personality" will
have to answer when others "continue to ask what political science has
to say" (Fiorina 1985: 197).

We reject these alternatives and argue that the search for master programs of order and regularity has obscured a good deal of what is characteristic about institutions in politics and what they have to teach us
about political change. The choice between analysis that will systematically exaggerate the significance of order in politics and no analysis at
all is, we believe, as unnecessary as it is unacceptable. Ours is a genuinely "new" institutionalism precisely because it cultivates analytic
ground between the seamless flow of events and period synthesis, and
between time-bound descriptive minutiae and purportedly timeless covering laws.

This reorientation proceeds on the observation that at any given time,
institutions, both individually and collectively, juxtapose different log-
ics of political order, each with their own temporal underpinnings. Separate institutions and institutional arrangements, operating according to
distinctive ordering principles, structure the passage of time – the sequences and cycles, the changes and lulls – at varying rates. In this

sense, the ordering propensities of institutions are about so many points of access to a politics that is essentially open-ended and inherently unsettled. As institutions congeal time, so to speak, within their spheres, they decrease the probability that politics will coalesce into neatly ordered periods, if only because the institutions that constitute the polity at that time will abrade against each other and, in the process, drive further change.

Institutional analysis harbors a simple but radical alternative to the overriding preoccupation with political order in periods: Discard it, and focus instead on the incongruities that political institutions routinely produce. Against the background of institutional frictions that drive and shape political change, pictures of ordered space in bounded time fade away, and with them the boundary that has separated order from change. What is revealed is neither chaos nor a seamless flow of events, but rather the institutional construction of temporality that occurs as one institutional ordering impinges on another (Elchardus 1982).

The single presumption abandoned is that institutions are synchronized in their operations or synthetic in their effects; the more basic idea, that institutions structure change in time, is retained. But this strategy reverses the direction of analysis, which now moves no longer from history to order, but from order*s* (plural) back to history. The historical study of institutions remains no less dedicated than its predecessors to finding empirical patterns and structures and to formulating concepts with which to explore them. It is quite open to building on the historical work of others in this respect, however, not at the expense of simplifying the temporality of institutional politics. A concern for the institutional construction of change in time makes our approach less random than the "garbage-can" models of James March and others, for it argues that the sequences and conjunctures can be understood in terms of how change along one time line affects order along the others (Cohen, March, and Olsen 1972; Kingdon 1984). It proposes that political scientists investigate, head on, the contingent temporal alignments and simultaneous movement of relatively independent institutional orderings that riddle political action.

Research of scholars engaged in the historical study of politics has already been moving in this direction, and it may be drawn on briefly for examples of what this perspective comprises. That political institutions, both singly and in their interactions, characteristically manifest ordering patterns that are conflicting and contradictory is amply borne out in the recent work, for example, on Jacksonian America. In the area of institutional procedures, state judiciaries have been shown to have regulated commerce through the application of rules out of phase with the practices of a burgeoning industrial capitalism (Miller 1971; Horowitz 1992). Looking at structures, scholars have described the conflict between the articulation of a decentralized federalism and the increasing nationalism of the economy (Scheiber 1975: 57; Dunlavy 1991: 1), and they have noted the hierarchical ordering of personal relations in the family in tandem with the flourishing of voluntary organization elsewhere in civil society (Baker 1984: 85). Insofar as institutions embody culture, the reigning perspective of "the liberal tradition" has been seen to incorporate several meanings, each with its own implications for political action, that explain the pattern of northern political coalitions on the subject of slavery (Greenstone 1986). In contrast, divergent patterns of government among southern states have been shown to have promoted competing ideologies of slave-holding (Norton 1986; Ellis 1991).

For other periods, research demonstrates similar themes of dissonance, asymmetry, incongruity. Study of the "New Deal order" has identified divergent capacities among administrative agencies within the same electoral regime – the success of the Agricultural Adjustment Act and the failure of the National Recovery Administration tied, respectively, to distinctive trajectories of reform in agriculture and industrial relations (Skocpol and Feingold 1982). Institutions have been shown to collide along opportunity structures, meaning the pattern by which the operations of one institution interfere with the achievement of the goals of another. Thus, nineteenth-century workers, organized primarily around industrial issues, were impeded in their political efficacy by a party system organized primarily around regional and ethnic issues (Oestreicher 1989). Furthermore, contrasting worker ideologies were differently obstructed by separate constitutional structures (Hattam 1990). Other asynchronic elements have been identified, for instance, between allegedly formative ideas and their tardy implementation (if they are implemented at all) within institutions. One study has found that the mutual outlook and career exchanges between government administrators and professionals in private life, often seen as fueling the growth of American bureaucracy throughout the twentieth century, did not occur on any significant scale outside the field of agriculture until World War II (Balogh 1991).

None of these incongruities is especially startling; our claim is that what is in plain view, analytically speaking, has not yet been appreciated for its theoretical significance. These incongruities are not based on a distinction between the normal and the extraordinary, or between the stable and the transformative; it is their routine status that recommends incongruities as the central concern of a new analysis of how institutions matter. Are we saying the stars never line up right, institutionally speaking, for truly extraordinary changes? We are not. But more often than not, we expect to find that continuities along one dimension of order and time will be folded into, and formative of, the extraordinary changes we are observing along another. The task is to sort out the elements, attend to their temporal alignments, and explain the institutional dynamics that push and pull the stars into their various configurations.

That such asymmetries, layerings, and intersections are characteristic of politics has been remarked upon by contemporary theorists who are concerned, as we are, with the reformulation of questions about time (or "time-space") in social analysis. In discussing the "only teleology involved in social systems," Anthony Giddens says:

Such teleology [comprised within the conduct of social actors] always operates within bounded conditions of the rationalization of action. All social reproduction occurs in the context of "mixes" of intended and unintended consequences of action; every feature of whatever continuity a society has over time derives from such "mixes," against the backdrop of bounded conditions of rationalization of conduct. (Giddens 1979: 112)

Elsewhere Giddens criticizes both Marxist and Weberian theories of class domination in an approach to institutional analysis "generically," institutions being constituted and reconstituted in the "tie between the durée of the passing moment and the longue durée of deeply sedimented time-space relations":

The totality/moment relation is compatible with a variety of different "layers" . . . of relations of autonomy and dependence between collectivities. The significance of such a stress is that it enables us to avoid difficulties that have always been associated with functionalist views of the whole, or more broadly, those views in which the whole is a "present" combination of parts. Such approaches have only been able to deal with the participation of the part in the whole by assuming that the one share[s] certain of the features of the other: that there is an homology between them. (Giddens 1979: 110)

IV. Elements of a *New* Institutionalism

Why should these contrasts and incongruities appear? The assertion that institutions are characterized by conflicts and intersections of rules and that these are frequently rooted in history is still a good way from explaining specifically how "mixes" occur and what their substance is in any particular institutional case. To elucidate those processes is the major task of a historically oriented reseach agenda for political science. Still, it is possible to tentatively identify certain intrinsic features of political institutions that account for their asymmetric, impinging, and interactive character.

Let us add to the standard definition of institutions as rules ("congealed tastes" and so forth persisting through time) the fact that *political institutions have been created or instituted at disparate points in the past*. It is ironic that the neglect of this nonsimultaneity of institutional origins is most evident in political studies that would seem to be directly concerned with historical events or dependent on historical propositions. The field of public law, the most systematically historical subfield in the discipline, devotes little attention to continuities with institutional forms imported from England. Reconstructions of American political order as diverse as Robert Dahl's *A Preface to Democratic Theory* (1956), Louis Hartz's *The Liberal Tradition in America* (1955), and Samuel Huntington's *American Politics: The Promise of Disharmony* (1981) rest on the premise, though not the demonstration, of the absence of a feudal past. The assumption of historical synchronicity is pervasive, evident in such notions as market society, industrialism, and the party period.

The nonsimultaneity of institutional origins may be illustrated in the case of research involving disparities so structured that they lasted a century and more. A first example comes out of the historiological debates over whether American institutions in the eighteenth and nineteenth centuries may be best understood in their spirit and organization as "republican" or "liberal." One recent analysis argues that the liberal and voluntary activities, mainly conducted by men, in economic and political institutions, was made possible by the hierarchical and republican strictures imposed in the family and the military, and on women and boys (Kann 1990). In a related vein, American women, legally cut off from the democratic political institutions of white men, have been shown to have strategically extended their "separate sphere" to welfare state protection for mothers and their children, at a time when identical protections were denied men precisely through the limitations of the electoral system (Skocpol and Ritter 1991). Or in another example of nonsimultaneity, a common perspective on the relations of government and the economy has been the concurrent development of democratic political institutions and the growth and intensification of capitalism. Study of the labor sector in the nineteenth century, however, reveals that it was governed by the judiciary according to the common law of a pre-democratic and precapitalist age, based on prescriptive rather than voluntary principles, defined as nonpolitical, and immune from legislative change (Orren 1991).

Republicanism, family organization, judicial regulation – each has origins older than liberalism, party organization, and legislative regulation; none of these distinctions would be captured within a "synthesis" view. Since these examples refer to the interfaces among institutions, let us round out this point by observing discontinuities in a single institution, the American presidency, which has, in fact, been the focal point of several such syntheses. We have already referred to the periodization of political history around successive presidents' progress through the avenues and potholes of the Constitution, and this synthesis has already been challenged by others. Another type of synthesis, also associated with the "search for order," emphasizes the organization of politics by parties in the nineteenth century and by bureaucracies in the twentieth; still another is based on electoral realignments, with different party systems structuring presidential action. Each of these perspectives is itself a reflection of different origins and purposes built into the office: The first derived from the historical experience of kingship; the second was a response to the unruliness of Congress (in its party manifestations) and the unruliness of markets (in its bureaucratic phase); the third focuses on the changing political fragments, participation, and "tastes" in a democratic electorate. In the approach proposed here, these "syntheses" are most useful neither as alternative schemes of analysis nor as descriptions of the president's disparate "roles," but rather in terms of how these contrasting roles intersect and thereby structure the leadership dilemma of any particular administration. As with the other examples mentioned, they signal that segmented lines of development must be superimposed to bring the political moment into view. Consider the following mixes: Abraham Lincoln fought a civil war and realized a "Second American Revolution" without changing the patronage-based, partisan organization of governmental operations; Theodore Roosevelt imposed new bureaucratic forms and displaced much of the old partisan mode of governmental operations, but he did so to preserve "politics as usual" vis-à-vis the basic governing commitments of the established Republican coalition; Franklin Roosevelt, like Lincoln, made extraordinary changes in the nation's basic commitments of ideology and interest, but he did so by invoking bureaucratic formulas for governing that had been made familiar by Theodore Roosevelt, Woodrow Wilson, and

Herbert Hoover. Once we disaggregate the different ordering principles and sort through the different time lines of change, we can analyze each leadership experience along its several dimensions and, by comparing them, show how the political impact of institutional action is reshaped at each unique conjuncture (Skowronek 1993).

A second feature we see as fundamental is that *political institutions control (or attempt to control) the behavior of persons or institutions other than themselves.* Within political institutions there are, clearly, rules designed to control behavior of operatives and participants; characteristically, however, political institutions reach outward. It is the fact that institutional rules are intended to control outsiders that distinguishes political from purely social institutions, whose rules are characteristically self-referential. This is not to say that social institutions may never have political aspects or impacts or be usefully thought of as political institutions. The point is, rather, that this quality of "otherness" in the activity of institutions is what lends them political signficance.

The other-directedness of political institutions is reflected in the concepts used in all eras to describe them – authority, sovereignty, representation, legitimacy, public opinion, delegation. It is also suggested in the distinctions we draw between institutions of rule and the subject population – democracy, monarchy, polyarchy. The institution of American federalism, the distribution of powers between national and state government, is of more than descriptive interest only as it organizes the governance of various social activities outside itself. Thus, for example, it raises the abiding historical question of federalism's effects on an increasingly centralized system of commerce. The common law is interesting politically because it governed social behavior outside the institution of the judiciary. The interface of institutions with outsiders is so characteristic that any set of examples risks trivialization. Its importance is pervasive, engaging the diverse objectives and methods of operation entailed in various mixes, and going far toward explaining persistence and change of political institutions as well as the behavior of those who act within them.

There may seem to be a paradox here, in that the concept of institutionalization is associated with the differentiation of roles within an organization, rather than those outside it, and with the development of internal specializations and procedures. In our perspective, it is the interaction with other institutions that will be seen to drive the institutionalization process. This proposition would find support, for example, in the history of the U.S. Congress, where, quite apart from housekeeping and career benefits for insiders, such changes have historically been connected to relations with other constitutional branches and with the efficacy of the policy-making function, including the perception of it by the electorate. Once we discover the independent persistence of roles and norms within the boundaries of a single institution, the work of analysis has just begun; the political significance of the "relative autonomy" of an institution is not in its description but in its interaction with other persistent patterns.

This brings us to a third feature of political institutions that undermines systems perspectives and confronts the analyst with contingent mixes. *Institutions are purposive or intentional.* They are purposive in that the rules that compose them are constructed and reconstructed with reference to specific goals, thereby distinguishing the rules of political institutions from the more spontaneous regularities associated with political culture. Purposes may change or be entirely subverted; but the fact that rules are aimed at the achievement of particular ends evokes cued responses from within the institution and from outside, as well as sets up the processes of monitoring and strategic readjustment of rules characteristic of institutional activity. Purposes are also the basis on which actors within institutions may be required to explain their actions and establish their legitimacy. Notice that the question of legitimacy again derives from the environment, the "otherness" within which any institution operates and by which it may be called to account.

Insofar as they are operated by individual actors, institutions are also intentional in the further sense that they partake of the actors' personal motives and ambitions. These may be more or less coincidental with the purposes structured into the institution's rules upon its design. Institutions vary in the discretion they allow those who take up positions within them and in how permeated decisions are by outside influences. It is here that the question of structure is important, for a crucial element of political-institutional analysis concerns the extent to which an institution is structured or "voluntary" with respect to actors' behavior. This question will be seen to be separate from whether the institution is "robust," in the sense of its being resilient. The U.S. Congress is more structured than the presidency, and both of these are less structured than the federal court system, whereas all have proven themselves equally robust. The regulatory system in the 1970s was highly structured, though not, as it turned out, robust.

The notion of purposes includes connections immediately engaged by goal-directed actions but that are outside of actors' perceptions – se-

314 K. Orren and S. Skowronek

creted, so to speak, within the rules and contingencies entailed in any set of institutional purposes (Ferejohn 1991). Consider in this regard two models of presidential leadership: "responsible party leadership" implicit in the notion of a party system, and independent statesmanship implicit in the oath to "faithfully execute the office of President of the United States." Andrew Jackson built a new party and transformed the powers of the presidency by directing his energies against the political regime he came to power to displace. James Polk fractured the party of Jackson, the party he came to office to represent, and he did so by exercising the powers bequeathed to him by Jackson. Polk did not see any contradiction between his election as an "orthodox, whole hog" Jackson Democrat and his determination to exercise the full powers of his office in his own right. He penned the line "I intend to be myself President of the U.S." in the course of committing his administration to do "equal and exact justice" to every faction of the Democratic Party. Nonetheless, the inherently disruptive effects entailed in that exercise transformed his political nickname from "Orthodox Polk" to "Polk the Mendacious" (Skowronek 1993). The successful pursuit of both goals – party leadership and constitutional independence – has historically depended on opportunities presented by secular conditions of electoral realignment over which presidents may have little awareness or control. Yet to analyze the "rules" of the presidency abstracted from this connection would provide a formal but, on the whole, empty description.

Another example of "secretions" in institutional rules can be found in 1890s industrial regulation. Congress scrupulously, that is, purposively, separated administrative setting of rates and policing fair competition from the "labor question," assigning the latter to other agencies based on distinctive principles and procedures. In industry, however, rates and competitive methods were tied not only to labor costs but also to the ease with which regulated industries could adjust costs downward. This connection was acknowledged occasionally by regulatory actors, but was usually eclipsed by assumptions (already outdated) about managerial authority built into the regulatory scheme. Indeed, it is possible to tell the story of the rise and fall of American regulatory agencies as a gradual coming to terms with labor organization, beginning with the agency's recognition of labor in new procedures and leading to agency disfavor and regulatory decline (Orren 1991).

All of these examples point to a fourth and final characteristic. *Political institutions are typically created by other political institutions.* As such, they carry forward incongruities and asymmetries already structured into the status quo. Even in so-called founding and revolutionary periods, where institutions are (arguably) not created by other institutions, they will be constructed against the background of their predecessors. This was true of the U.S. Constitution, for example, designed in conscious opposition to the "mixed" constitution of eighteenth-century Great Britain. Viewing institutions in terms of their relations to other institutions not only reveals active interfaces with the institutions they seek to control, but with those that, as a prior political event, have sought to control them. This sequencing dissolves not only the boundary of space, the "whole" into which "the pieces fit together," but also the boundary of time. That is to say, presuming there is no whole, the movements of the pieces through history will themselves define the intersections that comprise any specific moment of institutional action.

The connections and intersections discussed here are not "functional" or indicative of "order." Indeed, although we have consciously eschewed the notion of chaos, what is produced is nonetheless a kind of patterned incongruity. The continuous monitoring of results by institutional actors might bring about institutional learning and adaptive changes in the rules. At any given historical juncture, however, measures aimed at alleviating strain will as likely exacerbate it as not. Thus, the attempt by the early Interstate Commerce Commission (ICC) to ease competition through the establishment of regional rate setting by railroads encouraged regional railroad labor organization, resulting in increased pressures on costs (Orren 1991). President Lyndon Johnson intended the War on Poverty to shore up his party's relations with urban blacks; instead, it mobilized black communities against the old Democratic machines and further fragmented the governing coalition. In retrospect, that these pieces hung together – regional rates and labor costs, blacks and the old machines – is apparent. But the intricacies of control were hidden from actors who did not anticipate the systemically disruptive consequences of their ordering pursuits.

On the other hand, these same examples would seem to argue for "the uses of disorder," the degree to which successful functioning of institutions (their robustness) may in certain cases depend precisely on the mix and ferment rather than the consistency of their principles and procedures. Congress's regulatory goal of imposing fixed rates depended on the responsiveness of an all-but-automatic system for coercing the labor force; when labor organized and asserted its own intentions, costs were passed through to a nonresistant consumer base; when consumers joined the contest and organized effectively, the original regulatory scheme, or at least leading parts of it, was abandoned by Congress. The model of the responsible party leader implies either voluntaristic performance on the part of the president, accompanied by party cohorts willing to stem their own voluntaristic interests and follow, or a president willing to sacrifice his personal ambitions when these clash with the intentions of leaders of his party. As institutions aim to control the behavior of others, their success will depend on the resistance or malleability of those so targeted and, thus, on the layers of discipline that exist at any given time.

V. Conclusion

There is no escaping a description of "the times" in the study of institutions. The outstanding question is how time is to be described. Indeed, if the priority of time over order in institutional study is evident anywhere, it is in the unreflected premise of simultaneous origins on which overarching conceptions of order have been built. Once we discard this premise on the solid ground of empirical observation, we will have to regain our historical bearings without it. Gone is the distinction between extraordinary politics (rule making) and politics as usual (game playing); gone is the icon of equilibrium readjustments; gone is the "system" that congeals time between reconstructions. Instead the field consists of relatively independent layers of institutional actions and is conceptually, if not analytically, boundless. It makes no more sense to describe all factors as endogenous than it does to describe them all as exogenous. The important questions are questions of timing.

In light of political science's historic preoccupation with order in the study of institutions, there is much to be gained from a general rethinking of the essential historicity of the subject matter. So long as the claim that institutions matter rides piggyback on old presumptions about how things change, to wit, between periods of order, the range of potential new insights will be narrow. We have argued here that the upshot of a new institutionalism should be a substantially different understanding of historical processes – a departure from those already available. Terry Moe is right to caution us against PTI's ahistoricism and to call us back from a search for timeless covering laws. But there is no need to retreat from there to the illusion of systemic "fit." To advance we need to break with presumptions of system coherence and alter our basic conception of temporality in a way that accounts for the *patterned disorder* that institutions routinely create.

To fix on questions of timing in institutional politics requires using history in ways that historians themselves seldom do. In our view, time is not the medium through which the story of this or that institution will unfold; it is itself the central problem. The discovery of patterns – provisionally, even of order*s* – is an indispensable step. This may entail uncovering several layers of institutional politics that compose a single moment, or reaching across historical periods to identify a repeated sequence or configuration. The idea is not to detach the analysis from time-bound descriptive minutiae, but to explicate the timing of such details and to explain institutionally the shifts and developments that are constantly changing the political landscape. There are no "time lags" in this perspective, no institutional delays where older arrangements "catch up" with new; pieces held over from earlier patterns are part and parcel of the institutional composition and of the institutional construction of temporality itself.[3]

Institutions make history by the routine engagement of the tensions and contradictions among their various ordering principles and by their bending and reshaping of each other into patterns of change in time. Layers, not systems; dissonance, not fit; conjunctures, not regularities: These are the points of entry to a genuinely "new" institutionalism.

Notes

1. We deal with rational choice and historical alternatives in this essay but give no attention to the new institutionalism in sociology. For a review, see DiMaggio and Powell (1991). For a stimulating discussion of work in sociology, also see Elchardus (1982).
2. Edward Corwin notes, "The implication [of Roosevelt's assumptions of power in World War II] seemed to be that the President owed the transcendent powers he was claiming to some peculiar relationship between himself and the people – a doctrine with a strong family resemblance to the leadership principle against which the war was supposedly being fought" (1940: 167).
3. In the Progressive Era, it is not the decline of localistic, partisan forms of governance and the rise of nationalistic bureaucratic forms that calls for our attention; it is rather the stubborn persistence of the localistic forms – and of the pre-partisan Constitutional frame itself – as these refracted and recast the designs of those who would build the new bureaucratic forms. See Skowronek (1982).

Bibliography

Aberbach, Joel, and Jack L. Walker. 1970. "Political Trust and Racial Ideology." *American Political Science Review* 64: 367–88.

Adams, Charles Kendall. 1881. "The Relations of Political Science to National Prosperity." Inaugural address at the opening of the Department of Political Science, University of Michigan, Ann Arbor, MI (in C. K. Adams Papers, University of Wisconsin).

Adams, Henry. 1880. *Democracy: An American Novel*. New York: Henry Holt.

Alchian, Armen. 1950. "Uncertainty, Evolution, and Economic Theory." *Journal of Political Economy* 48: 211–21.

Alesina, Alberto. 1987. "Macroeconomic Policy in a Two-Party System as a Repeated Game." *Quarterly Journal of Economics* 102: 651–78.

   1988. "Credibility and Policy Convergence in a Two-Party System with Rational Voters." *American Economic Review* 78: 796–805.

Alesina, Alberto, and Alex Cuikerman. 1989. "The Politics of Ambiguity." Hoover Institution Working Paper in Political Science.

Almond, Gabriel A. 1966. "Political Theory and Political Science." *American Political Science Review* 60: 869–79.

   1988a. "Separate Tables," *PS* 21: 828–42.

   1988b. "The Return to the State." *American Political Science Review* 82: 850–74.

   1990. *A Discipline Divided: Schools and Sects in Political Science*. Newbury Park, CA: Sage.

Almond, Gabriel A., and Sidney Verba. 1963. *The Civic Culture: Political Attitudes and Democracy in Five Nations*. Princeton, NJ: Princeton University Press.

Alt, James. 1985. "Political Parties, World Demand, and Unemployment: Domestic and International Sources of Economic Activity." *American Political Science Review* 79: 1016–40.

American Political Science Association. 1951. *Goals for Political Science*. New York: William Sloane.

Committee for the Advancement of Teaching (APSA CAT). 1951. *Goals for Political Science*. New York: William Sloane.

Committee of Five on Instruction (APSA COF). 1908. "Report of the Committee of Five of the American Political Science Association in Instruction in American Government in Secondary Schools." In *1907 Proceedings of the American Political Science Association*. Baltimore: Waverly.

Committee on Instruction in Government (APSA COS). 1914. "Report on Instruction in Political Science in Colleges and Universities: Portion of Preliminary Report of the Committee of the American Political Science Association on Instruction in Government." In *1914 Proceedings of the American Political Science Association*. Baltimore: Waverly.

Committee on Policy (APSA COP). 1930. "Report of the Committee on Policy." *American Political Science Review* 24: Supplement.

Committee to Define the Scope and Purposes of a High School Course in Civics. 1922. "The Study of Civics." *American Political Science Review* 16: 116–25.

Section on Instruction in Political Science (APSA SOI). 1906. "What do Students Know about American Government, before Taking College Courses in Political Science?" In *1905 Proceedings of the American Political Science Association*. Baltimore: Waverly.

Amy, Douglas J. 1984. "Toward a Post-Positivist Policy Analysis," *Policy Studies Journal* 13: 207–11.

Anderson, Charles W. 1987. "Political Philosophy, Practical Reason, and Policy Analysis." In Frank Fischer and John Forester (eds.), *Confronting Values in Policy Analysis*. Newbury Park, CA: Sage.

1991. "Pragmatism and Liberalism, Rationalism and Irrationalism." *Polity* 23: 357–71.

Angell, Norman. 1927. *The Public Mind: Its Disorders, Its Exploitation*. New York: Dutton.

Archibald, Kathleen A. 1980. "The Pitfalls of Language, or Analysis through the Looking Glass." In Giandomenico Majone and Edward S. Quade (eds.), *Pitfalls of Analysis*. New York: Wiley.

Arendt, Hannah. 1958. *The Human Condition*. Chicago: University of Chicago Press.

1968. "Truth and Politics." In *Between Past and Future*. New York: Viking.

Arnhart, Larry. 1988. "Aristotle's Biopolitics: A Defense of Biological Teleology against Biological Nihilism." *Politics and the Life Sciences* 6: 173–91.

Arnold, R. Douglas. 1982. "Overtitled and Untitled Fields in American Politics." *Political Science Quarterly* 96: 91–104.

Arrow, Kenneth. 1963. *Social Choice and Individual Values*. New Haven, CT: Yale University Press.

Ascher, William. 1986. "The Evolution of the Policy Sciences." *Journal of Policy Analysis and Management* 5: 365–89.

Atkins, Willard E., and Harold D. Lasswell. 1924. *Labor Attitudes and Problems*. New York: Prentice-Hall.

Avineri, Shlomo. 1972. *Hegel's Theory of the Modern State*. Cambridge University Press.

Axelrod, Robert, and William D. Hamilton. 1981. "The Evolution of Cooperation." *Science* 211: 1390–6.

Bachrach, Peter, and Baratz, Morton S. 1962. "Two Faces of Power." *American Political Science Review* 56: 947–52.

1963. "Decisions and Nondecisions: An Analytical Framework." *American Political Science Review* 57: 632–42.

Baer, Michael A., Malcolm E. Jewell, and Lee Sigelman (eds.). 1991. *Political Science in America: Oral Histories of a Discipline*. Lexington: University of Kentucky Press.

Bagehot, Walter. [1873] 1956. *Physics and Politics*. Boston: Beacon.

[1867] 1963. *The English Constitution*. London: Fontana Library.

Baker, Paula. 1984. "The Domestication of Politics: Women in American Political Society, 1780–1920." *American Historical Review* 85: 620–47.

Ball, Terence. 1976. "From Paradigms to Research Programs: Toward a Post-Kuhnian Political Science." *American Journal of Political Science* 20: 151–77.

1979. "Marx and Darwin: A Reconsideration." *Political Theory* 7: 469–84.

1988. *Transforming Political Discourse*. Oxford: Basil Blackwell.

1993. "American Political Science in Its Postwar Context." In James Farr and Raymond Seidelman (1993).

Balogh, Brian. 1991. "Reorganizing the Organizational Synthesis: Federal–Professional Relations in Modern America." *Studies in American Political Development* 5: 119–72.

Banfield, Edward. 1970. *The Unheavenly City*. Boston: Little, Brown.

Banfield, Edward, and James Q. Wilson. 1963. *City Politics*. Cambridge, MA: Harvard University Press.

Banks, Jeffrey. 1990. "A Model of Electoral Competition with Incomplete Information." *Journal of Economic Theory* 50: 309–25.

Banks, Jeffrey, and David Austen-Smith. 1989. "Electoral Accountability and Incumbency." In Peter Ordeshook (ed.), *Models of Strategic Choice in Politics*. Ann Arbor: University of Michigan Press.

Barker, Ernest. 1914. *Nietzsche and Treitschke: The Worship of Power*. Oxford University Press.

1915. "The Discredited State." *Political Quarterly* 1 (7): 101–26.

1918. "The Superstition of the State." *Times Literary Supplement* (July): 329–30.

Barker, Lucius. 1994. "Limits of Political Strategy: A Systemic View of the African-American Experience." *American Political Science Review* 88: 1–13.

Barro, Robert. 1973. "The Control of Politicians: An Economic Model." *Public Choice* 14: 19–42.

Barry, Brian. 1970. *Sociologists, Economists, and Democracy*. London: Macmillan.

Bauer, Wilhelm. 1934. "Public Opinion." *Encyclopedia of the Social Sciences*, edited by E. S. Seligman. New York: Macmillan.

Bay, Christian. 1965. "Politics and Pseudopolitics: A Critical Evaluation of Some Behavioral Literature." *American Political Science Review* 59: 39–51.

   1967. "Politics and Pseudopolitics: A Critical Evaluation of Some Behavioral Literature." In McCoy and Playford (1967).

Beard, Charles A. 1913. *An Economic Interpretation of the Constitution*. New York: Macmillan.

   1927. "Time, Technology, and the Creative Spirit in Political Science." *American Political Science Review* 21: 1–11.

Becker, Gary, and George Stigler. 1972. "Law Enforcement, Malfeasance, and the Compensation of Enforcers." *Journal of Legal Studies* 1: 1–18.

Beiner, Ronald. 1983. *Political Judgment*. London: Methuen.

Bellamy, Edward. [1888] 1960. *Looking Backward*. Boston: Ticknor. Repr. New York: New American Library.

Benhabib, Seyla. 1986. *Critique, Norm, and Utopia*. New York: Columbia University Press.

Bentley, Arthur F. 1908. *The Process of Government*. Chicago: University of Chicago Press.

Berelson, Bernard. 1952. "Democratic Theory and Public Opinion." *Public Opinion Quarterly* 16: 313–30.

Berelson, Bernard, Paul F. Lazarsfeld, and William N. McPhee. 1954. *Voting: A Study of Opinion Formation in a Presidential Campaign*. Chicago: University of Chicago Press.

Bernays, Edward. 1923. *Crystallizing Public Opinion*. New York: Boni & Liveright.

Berns, Walter. 1962. "Voting Studies." In Storing (1962).

Bernstein, Richard J. 1983. *Beyond Objectivism and Relativism*. Philadelphia: University of Pennsylvania Press.

Bernstein, Robert. 1988. "Do Senators Moderate Strategically?" *American Political Science Review* 82: 237–41.

Best, James J. 1973. *Public Opinion: Micro and Macro*. Homewood, IL: Dorsey.

Binder, Leonard. 1986. "The Natural History of Development Theory." *Comparative Studies in Society and History* 28: 3–33.

Binmore, Ken. 1988. "Game Theory and the Social Contract." Mimeo, London School of Economics.

Binmore, Ken, Ariel Rubinstein, and Asher Wolinsky. 1986. "The Nash Bargaining Solution in Economic Modelling." *Rand Journal of Economics* 17: 176–88.

Bird, Elizabeth Ann R. 1987. "The Social Construction of Nature: Theoretical Approaches to the History of Environmental Problems." *Environmental Review* 11: 255–64.

Black, Duncan. 1948. *Theory of Committees and Elections*. Cambridge University Press.

Blumer, Herbert. 1948. "Public Opinion and Public Opinion Polling." *American Sociological Review* 13: 542–54.

Blumer, Herbert. 1950. "The Mass, the Public and Public Opinion" (1946). In Bernard Berelson and Morris Janowitz (eds.), *Reader on Public Opinion and Communication*. Glencoe, IL: Free Press.

Bogart, Leo. 1972. *Silent Politics: Polls and the Awareness of Public Opinion*. New York: Wiley.

   1985. *Polls and the Awareness of Public Opinion*. New Brunswick, NJ: Transaction Books.

   1987. "The Future Study of Public Opinion: A Symposium." *Public Opinion Quarterly* 51 (supplement): S173–91.

Bookchin, Murray. 1982. *The Ecology of Freedom*. Palo Alto, CA: Cheshire.

Boorstin, Daniel. 1953. *The Genius of American Politics*. Chicago: University of Chicago Press.

Boyd, Richard W. 1972. "Popular Control of Public Policy: A Normal Vote Analysis of the 1968 Election." *American Political Science Review* 66: 429–49.

Bradshaw, Leah. 1991. "Political Rule, Prudence and the 'Woman Question' in Aristotle." *Canadian Journal of Political Science* 24: 557–73.

Braybrooke, David, and Charles E. Lindblom. [1963] 1970. *A Strategy of Decision*. New York: Free Press.

Brody, Richard A., and Benjamin I. Page. 1972. "The Assessment of Policy Voting." *American Political Science Review* 66: 450–8.

Brooks, R. R. 1911. "A Local Study of the Race Problem." *Political Science Quarterly* 26: 193–221.

Brooks, Robert C. 1941. "Reflections on the 'World Revolution' of 1940." *American Political Science Review* 35: 1–9.

Brunner, Ronald D. 1991. "The Policy Movement as a Policy Problem." *Policy Sciences* 24: 65–98.

Bryce, James. 1921. *Modern Democracies*, 2 vols. New York: Macmillan.

Budge, Ian, David Robertson, and Derek Hearl (eds.). 1987. *Ideology, Strategy and Party Change: Spatial Analyses of Post-War Election Programmes in Nineteen Democracies*. Cambridge University Press.

Bull, Hedley. 1966. "International Theory: The Case for a Classical Approach." *World Politics* 18: 361–77.

1972. "The Theory of International Politics: 1919–1969." In Porter (1972).

1977. *The Anarchical Society: A Study of Order in World Politics*. New York: Columbia University Press.

Burgess, John. W. 1934. *Reminiscences of an American Scholar*. New York: Columbia University Press.

Burnham, Walter Dean. 1986. "Periodization Schemes and Party Systems: The 'System of 1986' as a Case in Point." *Social Science History* 10: 263–314.

Butterfield, Herbert. 1950. *Christianity and History*. New York: Scribner's.

Caldwell, Keith. 1964. "Biopolitics: Science, Ethics, and Public Policy." *Yale Review* 54: 1–16.

Calhoun, Craig (ed.). 1992. *Habermas and the Public Sphere*. Cambridge, MA: MIT Press.

Campbell, Angus, Philip E. Converse, Warren E. Miller, and Donald E. Stokes. 1960. *The American Voter*. New York: Wiley.

1966. *Elections and the Political Order*. New York: Wiley.

Cantril, Hadley. 1944. *Gauging Public Opinion*. Princeton, NJ: Princeton University Press.

Carlyle, Thomas. 1883. *Heroes and Hero Worship*. New York: J. B. Alden.

Carr, Edward Hallett. [1939] 1946. *The Twenty Years' Crisis, 1919–1939: An Introduction to the Study of International Relations*. New York: Harper & Row.

Catlin, C. E. G. 1927a. "The Delimitation and Measurability of Political Phenomena." *American Political Science Review* 21: 255–69

1927b. *The Science and Method of Politics*. New York: Knopf.

1929. Review of William Elliott, *The Pragmatic Revolt in Politics*. *Political Science Quarterly* 44: 259–65.

Chandler, Alfred D. 1962. *Strategy and Structure*. Cambridge, MA: Harvard University Press.

1977. *The Visible Hand*. Cambridge, MA: Harvard University Press.

Charlesworth, James C. 1962. *The Limits of Behavioralism in Political Science*. Philadelphia: American Academy of Political and Social Science.

Chisman, Forrest P. 1976. *Attitude Psychology and the Study of Public Opinion*. University Park, PA: Pennsylvania State University Press.

Chomsky, Noam. 1989. *Necessary Illusions: Thought Control in Democratic Societies*. Montreal: CBC Enterprises.

Clark, Grenville, and Louis B. Sohn. 1958. *World Peace through World Law*. Cambridge, MA: Harvard University Press.

Coase, Ronald H. 1937. "The Nature of the Firm." *Economica* 4: 386–405.

Cochran, Thomas C. 1948. "The 'Presidential Synthesis' in American History." *American Historical Review* 53: 748–59.

Cohen, J. Bernard. 1985. *Revolution in Science*. Cambridge, MA: Harvard University Press.

Cohen, Michael, James March, and Johan Olsen. 1972. "A Garbage-Can Model of Organizational Choice." *Administrative Science Quarterly* 17: 1–25.

Coker, F. W. 1921. "The Technique of the Pluralist State." *American Political Science Review* 15: 186–213.

1924. "Pluralistic Theories and the Attack on State Sovereignty." In Charles Merriam and H. E. Barnes (eds.), *A History of Political Theories: Recent Times*. New York: Macmillan.

1934. *Recent Political Thought*. New York: Appleton-Century.

Coleman, James S. 1990. *Foundations of Social Theory*. Cambridge, MA: Harvard University Press.

Connolly, William E. (ed.). 1969. *The Bias of Pluralism*. New York: Atherton.

Converse, Philip E. 1964. "The Nature of Belief Systems in Mass Publics." In David Apter (ed.), *Ideology and Discontent*. Glencoe: Free Press.

1975. "Public Opinion and Voting Behavior." In Fred I. Greenstein and Nelson W. Polsby (eds.), *Nongovernmental Politics*. Reading, MA: Addison-Wesley.

1987. "Changing Conceptions of Public Opinion in the Political Process." *Public Opinion Quarterly* 51 (supplement): S12–24.

Cook, Samuel Dubois. 1971. "Introduction: The American Liberal Democratic Tradition: The Black Revolution and Martin Luther King, Jr." In Hanes Walton Jr. (ed.), *The Political Philosophy of Martin Luther King, Jr.* Westport, CT: Greenwood.

Corwin, Edward S. 1929. "The Democratic Dogma and the Future of Political Science." *American Political Science Review* 23: 569–92.

1940. *The President: Office and Powers*. New York: New York University Press.

Cremin, Lawrence A. 1980. *American Education: The National Experience, 1783–1876*. New York: Harper & Row.

Crespi, Irving. 1989. *Public Opinion, Polls and Democracy*. Boulder, CO: Westview.

Crick, Bernard. 1959. *The American Science of Politics*. Berkeley & Los Angeles: University of California Press.

Crotty, William. 1991. "Introduction: Setting the Stage." In William Crotty (ed.), *The Theory and Practice of Political Science*. Evanston, IL: Northwestern University Press.

Cusack, Thomas R., and Richard J. Stoll. 1990. *Exploring Realpolitik: Probing International Relations Theory with Computer Simulation*. Boulder, CO: Lynne Rienner.

Dahl, Robert A. 1956. *A Preface to Democratic Theory*. Chicago: University of Chicago Press.

1958. "Political Theory: Truth and Consequences." *World Politics* 11: 89–102.

1961a. *Who Governs?* New Haven, CT: Yale University Press.

1961b. "The Behavioral Approach in Political Science: Epitaph for a Monument to a Successful Protest." *American Political Science Review* 55: 763–72. Reprinted in Farr and Seidelman (1993).

1966. "Further Reflections on the 'Elitist Theory of Democracy.'" *American Political Science Review* 60: 296–305.

Damico, Alfonso J. 1978. *Individuality and Community: The Social and Political Thought of John Dewey.* Gainesville: University Presses of Florida.

Davies, James C. 1963. *Human Nature in Politics: The Dynamics of Political Behavior.* New York: Wiley.

1980. "Perspectives on Human Conflict." In Ted Robert Gurr (ed.), *Handbook of Human Conflict.* New York: Free Press.

1986. "Biology, Darwinism, and Political Science: Some New and Old Frontiers." *Journal of Social and Biological Structures* 9: 227–39.

Davis, Lance E., and Douglass C. North. 1971. *Institutional Change and American Economic Growth.* Cambridge University Press.

Davis, Lane. 1964. "The Cost of Realism: Contemporary Restatements of Democracy." *Western Political Quarterly* 17: 34–46. Reprinted in McCoy and Playford (1967).

Davis, Otto, and Melvin Hinich. 1966. "A Mathematical Model of Policy Formation in a Democratic Society." In Joseph Bernd (ed.), *Mathematical Explorations in Political Science*, Vol. 2. Dallas: Southern Methodist University Press.

Dawson, Edgar. 1914. "New Proportions in Political Instruction." In *1913 Proceedings of the American Political Science Association.* Baltimore: Waverly.

Dealey, J. Q. 1915. Review of Henry Jones Ford, *The Natural History of the State. American Political Science Review* 9: 798–9.

Deane, Herbert A. 1955. *The Political Ideas of Harold J. Laski.* New York: Columbia University Press.

Degler, Carl N. 1991. *In Search of Human Nature: The Decline and Revival of Darwinism in American Social Thought.* New York: Oxford University Press.

Dewey, John. 1916. *Democracy and Education.* New York: Macmillan.

[1910] 1978. *How We Think.* In Jo Ann Boydston (ed.), *John Dewey: The Middle Works*, Vol. 6. Carbondale: Southern Illinois University Press.

[1922] 1983. Review of Walter Lippmann, *Public Opinion.* In Jo Ann Boydston (ed.), *John Dewey: The Middle Works*, Vol. 13. Carbondale: Southern Illinois University Press. Originally published in *New Republic* 30: 286–80.

[1927] 1984a. *The Public and Its Problems*. In Jo Ann Boydston (ed.), *John Dewey: The Later Works*, Vol. 2. Carbondale: Southern Illinois University Press.

[1930] 1984b. *Individualism, Old and New*. In Jo Ann Boydston (ed.), *John Dewey: The Later Works*, vol. 5. Cardondale: Southern Illinois University Press.

Dickinson, John. 1929. "Social Order and Political Authority." *American Political Science Review* 23: 293–328.

DiMaggio, Paul, and Walter Powell. 1991. *The New Institutionalism and Organization Theory*. Chicago: University of Chicago Press.

Dobuzinskis, Laurent. 1992. "Modernist and Postmodernist Metaphors of the Policy Process: Control and Stability vs. Chaos and Reflexive Understanding." *Policy Sciences* 25: 355–80.

Dodd, Stuart C. 1948. "Concepts of 'Public' and 'Public Opinion.'" *International Journal of Opinion and Attitude Research* 2: 379–84.

Dogan, Mattei, and Pahre, Robert. 1990. *Creative Marginality: Innovation at the Intersections of Social Sciences*. Boulder, CO: Westview.

Dolbeare, Kenneth M. 1970. "Public Policy Analysis and the Coming Struggle for the Soul of the Postbehavioral Revolution." In Philip Green and Sanford Levinson (eds.), *Power and Community: Dissenting Essays in Political Science*. New York: Random House.

Donnelly, Jack. 1992. "Twentieth Century Realism." In Nardin and Mapel (1992).

Dougherty, James E., and Robert L. Pfaltzgraff Jr. 1981. *Contending Theories of International Relations: A Comprehensive Survey*, 2nd edition. New York: Harper & Row.

Downs, Anthony. 1957. *An Economic Theory of Democracy*. New York: Harper & Row.

1991. "Social Values and Democracy." In Kristen R. Monroe (ed.), *The Economic Approach to Politics: A Critical Reassessment of the Theory of Rational Action*. New York: HarperCollins.

Drukman, Mason. 1971. *Community and Purpose in America*. New York: McGraw-Hill.

Dryzek, John S. 1982. "Policy Analysis as a Hermeneutic Activity." *Policy Sciences* 14: 309–29.

1986. "The Progress of Political Science." *Journal of Politics* 48: 301–20.

1989. "Policy Sciences of Democracy." *Polity* 22: 97–118.

Dryzek, John S., and Stephen T. Leonard. 1988. "History and Discipline in Political Science." *American Political Science Review* 82: 1245–60.

DuBois, W. E. 1962. *Black Reconstruction in America*. New York: Russell & Russell.

Duesenberry, James. 1960. "Comment on 'An Economic Analysis of Fertility.'" In Universities National Bureau Committee for Economic Research (ed.), *Demographic and Economic Change in Developed Countries.* Princeton, NJ: Princeton University Press.

Duguit, Leon. 1919. *Law in the Modern State*, translated by Frida Laski and Harold Laski. New York: R. W. Huebsch.

Duncan, Graeme, and Steven Lukes. 1963. "The New Democracy." *Political Studies* 11: 156–77. Reprinted in McCoy and Playford (1967).

Dunlavy, Coleen A. 1991. Mirror Images: Political Structure and Early Railroad Policy in the United States and Prussia. *Studies in American Political Development* 5: 1–35.

Dunning, William A. 1890. "Record of Political Events." *Political Science Quarterly* 5: 357–88.

1917. Review of Laski, *Studies in the Problem of Sovereignty. Political Science Quarterly* 32: 503–4.

1923. "Liberty and Equality in International Relations." *American Political Science Review* 17: 1–16.

Duverger, Maurice. 1955. *Political Parties.* London: Methuen.

Dye, Thomas R. 1975. "Political Science and Public Policy: Challenge to a Discipline." In Robert N. Spadaro et al. (eds.), *The Policy Vacuum.* Lexington, MA: Lexington Books.

1976. *Policy Analysis.* Tuscaloosa: University of Alabama Press.

Dyer, Hugh C., and Leon Mangasarian (eds.). 1989. *The Study of International Relations: The State of the Art.* New York: St. Martin's.

Easton, David. 1950. "Harold Lasswell: Policy Scientist for a Democratic Society." *Journal of Politics* 12: 450–77.

1953. *The Political System: An Inquiry into the State of Political Science.* New York: Knopf.

1962. "The Current Meaning of 'Behavioralism.'" In James C. Charlesworth (ed.), *The Limitations of Behavioralism in Political Science.* Philadelphia: American Academy of Political and Social Science.

1965a. *Framework for Political Analysis.* Englewood Cliffs, NJ: Prentice-Hall.

1965b. *A Systems Analysis of Political Life.* New York: Wiley.

1969. "The New Revolution in Political Science." *American Political Science Review* 63: 1051–61.

1971a. "The New Revolution in Political Science." (Originally published 1969.) Appendix to 1971b.

1971b. *The Political System: An Inquiry into the State of Political Science,* 2nd edition. Chicago: University of Chicago Press.

1981. "The Political System Besieged by the State." *Political Theory* 9: 303–26.

1990. "Political Science in the United States: Past and Present." In David Easton and Corinne Schelling (eds.), *Divided Knowledge.* Beverly Hills, CA: Sage. Reprinted in Farr and Seidelman (1993).

Easton, David, John G. Gunnell, and Luigi Graziano (eds.). 1991. *The Development of Political Science*. London: Routledge.

Eaton, Dorman B. 1880. *The Civil Service in Great Britain*. New York: Harper.

Editors. 1927. "Notice to Members and Subscribing Members of the Academy of Political Science." *Political Science Quarterly* 42: i.

Edwards, Richard. 1979. *Contested Terrain: The Transformation of the Workplace in the Twentieth Century*. New York: Basic.

Elchardus, Mark. 1982. "The Rediscovery of Chronos: The New Role of Time in Sociological Theory." *International Sociology* 3: 35–59.

Eldersveld, Samuel J., et al. 1952. "Research in Political Behavior." *American Political Science Review* 46: 1003–45.

Elliott, William Y. 1924. "The Pragmatic Politics of Mr. H. J. Laski." *American Political Science Review* 18: 251–75.

   1925. "Sovereign State or Sovereign Group?" *American Political Science Review* 19: 475–99.

   1927. Review of Robert MacIver, *The Modern State. American Political Science Review* 21: 432–4.

   1928. *The Pragmatic Revolt in Politics: Syndicalism, Fascism, and the Constitutional State*. New York: Macmillan.

   1931. "The Possibility of a Science of Politics: With Special Attention to Methods Suggested by William B. Munroe and George E. G. Catlin." In Stuart A. Rice (ed.), *Methods in Social Science*. Chicago: University of Chicago Press.

Ellis, Ellen Deborah. 1920. "The Pluralistic State." *American Political Science Review* 14: 393–407.

   1923. "Guild Socialism and Pluralism." *American Political Science Review* 17: 584–96.

   1927. "Political Science at the Crossroads." *American Political Science Review* 21: 773–91.

Ellis, Richard J. 1991. "Legitimating Slavery in the Old South: The Effect of Political Institutions on Ideology." *Studies in American Political Development* 5: 340–51.

Erie, Steven P. 1989. *Rainbow's End: Irish-Americans and the Dilemmas of Urban Machine Politics, 1840–1985*. Berkeley & Los Angeles: University of California Press.

Eulau, Heinz. 1956. "From Public Opinion to Public Philosophy: Walter Lippmann's Classic Reexamined." *American Journal of Economics and Sociology* 15: 439–51.

   1962. "Segments of Political Science Most Susceptible to Behavioristic Treatment." In James C. Charlesworth (ed.), *The Limits of Behavioralism in Political Science*. Philadelphia: American Academy of Political and Social Science.

   1963. *The Behavioral Persuasion in Politics*. New York: Random House.

1969. *Behavioralism in Political Science*. New York: Atherton.

1973. "Skill Revolution and the Consultative Commonwealth." *American Political Science Review* 67: 169–91.

1977. "Drift of a Discipline." *American Behavioral Scientist* 21: 3–10.

1988. "Editor's Note." *Political Behavior* 5: 157–60.

1992. "David Easton and the Behavioralists: A Memoir on Revolutions, So-Called, in Political Science." Paper presented at the annual meeting of the American Political Science Association, Chicago.

Eulau, Heinz (ed.). 1989. *Crossroads of Social Science: The ICPSR 25th Anniversary Volume*. New York: Agathon.

Eulau, Heinz, Samuel J. Eldersveld, and Morris Janowitz (eds.). 1956. *Political Behavior: A Reader in Theory and Research*. Glencoe, IL: Free Press.

Evans, Peter B., Dietrich Rueschemeyer, and Theda Skocpol (eds.). 1985. *Bringing the State Back In*. Cambridge University Press.

Exoo, Calvin F. (ed.). 1987. *Democracy Upside Down: Public Opinion and Cultural Hegemony in the United States*. New York: Praeger.

Falk, Richard. 1975. *A Study of Future Worlds*. New York: Free Press.

Fama, Eugene F., and Michael C. Jensen. 1983. "Separation of Ownership and Control." *Journal of Law and Economics* 26: 301–25.

Farr, James., 1982. "Historical Concepts in Political Science: The Case of 'Revolution.' " *American Journal of Political Science* 26: 688–708.

1988a. "Political Science and the Enlightenment of Enthusiasm." *American Political Science Review* 82: 51–69.

1988b. "The History of Political Science." *American Journal of Political Science* 32: 1175–95.

1990. "Francis Lieber and the Interpretation of American Political Science." *Journal of Politics* 52: 1027–49.

1991. "The Estate of Political Knowledge." In JoAnne Brown and David van Keuren (eds.), *The Estate of Social Knowledge*. Baltimore: Johns Hopkins University Press.

1993. "Political Science and the State." In Farr and Seidelman (1993).

Farr, James, John G. Gunnell, Raymond Seidelman, John S. Dryzek, and Stephen T. Leonard. 1990. "Can Political Science History be Neutral?" *American Political Science Review* 84: 587–607.

Farr, James, and Raymond Seidelman (eds.). 1993. *Discipline and History: Political Science in the United States*. Ann Arbor: University of Michigan Press.

Farrell, Joseph, and Eric Maskin. 1986. "Renegotiation in Repeated Games." Mimeo, Harvard University.

Fellman, David. 1952. "Introduction to 'Recent American Political Theory.' " *American Political Science Review* 46: 81.

Ferejohn, John. 1986. "Incumbent Performance and Electoral Control." *Public Choice* 50: 2–25.

1991. "Rationality and Interpretation: Parliamentary Elections in Early Stuart England." In Kristen Monroe (ed.), *The Economic Approach to Politics: A Critical Reassessment of the Theory of Rational Action*. New York:
Harper.

Ferejohn, John A., Richard D. McKelvey, and Edward W. Packel. 1984. "Limiting Distributions for Continuous State Markov Models." *Social Choice
and Welfare* 1: 45–67.

Ferguson, Yale H., and Richard W. Mansbach. 1988. *The Elusive Quest: Theory and International Relations*. Columbia: University of South Carolina
Press.

Finifter, Ada W. (ed.). 1983. *Political Science: The State of the Discipline*.
Washington, DC: American Political Science Association.

Fiorina, Morris P. 1982. "Legislative Choice of Regulatory Forms: Legal
Process or Administrative Process." *Public Choice* 39: 33–66.

1985. "Group Concentration and the Delegation of Legislative Authority."
In Roger G. Noll (ed.), *Regulatory Policy and the Social Sciences*. Berkeley & Los Angeles: University of California Press.

1986. "Legislative Uncertainty, Legislative Control, and the Delegation of
Legislative Power." *Journal of Law, Economics, and Organization* 2:
33–52.

Fischel, Jeff. 1985. *Platforms and Promises*. Washington, DC: Congressional
Quarterly Press.

Fischer, Frank. 1990. *Technocracy and the Politics of Expertise*. Newbury
Park, CA: Sage.

1992. "Reconstructing Policy Analysis: A Postpositivist Perspective." *Policy Sciences* 25: 333–9.

Follett, Mary Parker. 1918. *The New State: Group Organizations – The Solution of Popular Government*. New York: Longmans, Green.

Ford, Henry Jones. 1903. "The Results of Reform." In *1902 Proceedings of the
American Political Science Association*. Baltimore: Waverly.

1906. "The Scope of Political Science." In *1905 Proceedings of the American Political Science Association*. Baltimore: Waverly.

1915. *The Natural History of the State*. Princeton, NJ: Princeton University
Press.

Forester, John. 1981. "Hannah Arendt and Critical Theory: A Critical Response." *Journal of Politics* 43: 196–202.

1985. "The Policy Analysis–Critical Theory Affair: Wildavsky and Habermas as Bedfellows?" In John Forester (ed.), *Critical Theory and Public
Life*. Cambridge, MA: MIT Press.

Fox, William T. R. 1949. "Interwar International Relations Research: The
American Experience." *World Politics* 2: 67–79.

Fox, William T. R., and Annette Baker Fox. 1961. "The Teaching of International Relations in the United States." *World Politics* 13: 339–59.

Freeman, Donald M. 1991. "The Making of a Discipline." In William Crotty (ed.), *The Theory and Practice of Political Science*. Evanston, IL: Northwestern University Press.

French, Richard D. 1992. "Postmodern Government." *Optimum* 23: 42–51.

Frenkel-Brunswik, Else. 1952. "Interaction of Psychological and Sociological Factors in Political Behavior." *American Political Science Review* 46: 44–65.

Friedrich, Carl J. 1963. "Rights, Liberties, and Freedoms: A Reappraisal." *American Political Science Review* 57: 841–54.

Fukuyama, Francis. 1989. "The End of History?" *National Interest* (Summer): 3–18.

Furner, Mary O. 1975. *Advocacy and Objectivity: A Crisis in the Professionalization of American Social Science, 1865–1905*. Lexington: University of Kentucky Press.

Gadamer, Hans-Georg. 1979. "Practical Philosophy as a Model of the Human Sciences." *Research in Phenomenology* 9: 74–85.

  1989. *Truth and Method*. 2nd revised edition. Translated by Joel Weinsheimer and Donald G. Marshall. New York: Crossroad.

Galambos, Louis. 1970. "The Emerging Organizational Synthesis in Modern American History." *Business History Review* 44: 279–90.

  1983. "Technology, Political Economy, and Professionalism: Central Themes of the Organizational Synthesis." *Business History Review* 57: 471–93.

Gallup, George, and Saul Forbes Rae. 1940. *The Pulse of Democracy*. New York: Simon & Schuster.

Gamm, Gerald, and Kenneth A. Shepsle. 1988. "The Evolution of Legislative Institutions: Standing Committees in the House and the Senate." Paper delivered at the annual meeting of the American Political Science Association. Washington, DC.

Garceau, Oliver. 1951. "Research in the Political Process." *American Political Science Review* 45: 69–85.

Garnett, John C. 1984. *Common Sense and the Theory of International Politics*. London: Macmillan.

Garson, G. David. 1978. *Group Theories of Politics*. Beverly Hills, CA: Sage.

Gelber, H. G. 1982. "International Relations Curricula: Some Comments." In Coral Bell (ed.), *Academic Studies and International Politics*. Canberra: Department of International Relations, Australian National University.

Gettell, Raymond G. 1924. "Pluralistic Theories of Sovereignty." In *History of Political Thought*. New York: Century.

Giddens, Anthony. 1979. *Central Problems in Social Theory: Action, Structure, and Contradiction in Social Analysis*. Berkeley & Los Angeles: University of California Press.

Giddings, Franklin H. 1900. Review of Edmond Kelly, *Government or Human Evolution. Political Science Quarterly* 15: 710–13.

Gillette, William. 1979. *Retreat from Reconstruction, 1869–1879.* Baton Rouge: Louisiana State University Press.

Gilpin, Robert. 1981. *War and Change in World Politics.* Cambridge University Press.

 1986. "The Richness of the Tradition of Political Realism." In Keohane (1986b).

Ginsberg, Benjamin. 1986. *The Captive Public: How Mass Opinion Promotes State Power.* New York: Basic.

Glanvill, Joseph. [1661–76] (1970). *The Vanity of Dogmatizing: The Three Versions,* edited by Stephen Metcalf. Brighton: Harvester.

Glickman, Harvey. 1960. "Viewing Public Opinion in Politics: A Common Sense Approach." *Public Opinion Quarterly* 23: 495–504.

Goldsen, Joseph M. 1979. "Harold Lasswell as Policy Adviser and Consultant." In Myres S. McDougal et al., *Harold Dwight Lasswell, 1902–1978.* New Haven, CT: Yale Law School.

Goodnow, Frank J. 1905. "The Work of the American Political Science Association." In *1904 Proceedings of the American Political Science Association.* Baltimore: Waverly.

Gordon, Scott. 1991. *The History and Philosophy of Social Science.* London: Routledge.

Gosnell, Harold, F. 1934. "Political Meetings in Chicago's Black Belt." *American Political Science Review* 28: 254–8.

Gould, Stephen Jay. 1981. *The Mismeasure of Man.* New York: Norton.

 1991. "The Moral State of Tahiti – and of Darwin." *Natural History* (October): 12–19.

Graham, George, and George E. Cary (eds.). 1972. *The Postbehavioral Era.* New York: McKay.

Granovetter, Mark. 1985. "Economic Action and Social Structure: The Problem of Embeddedness." *American Journal of Sociology* 91: 481–510.

Green, Philip, and Sanford Levinson (eds.). 1970. *Power and Community: Dissenting Essays in Political Science.* New York: Random House.

Greenstone, David. 1986. "Political Culture and Political Development: Liberty, Union, and the Liberal Bi-Polarity." *Studies in American Political Development* 1: 1–49.

Gross, Bertram. 1955. *The Legislative Struggle: A Study in Social Combat.* New York: McGraw-Hill.

Gunn, J. A. W., 1989. "Public Opinion." In Terence Ball, James Farr, and Russell L. Hanson (eds.), *Political Innovation and Conceptual Change.* Cambridge University Press.

Gunnell, John G. 1969. "Deduction, Explanation, and Social Scientific Inquiry." *American Political Science Review* 63: 1233–58.

1975. *Philosophy, Science and Political Inquiry.* Morristown, NJ: General Learning Press.

1976. "Social Scientific Knowledge and Policy Decisions: A Critique of the Intellectualist Model." In Phillip M. Gregg (ed.), *Problems of Theory in Policy Analysis.* Lexington, MA: Lexington Books.

1983. "Political Theory: The Evolution of a Sub-Field." In Finifter (1983).

1988. "American Political Science, Liberalism, and the Invention of Political Theory." *American Political Science Review* 82: 71–88. Reprinted in Farr and Seidelman (1993).

1990. "In Search of the State: Political Science as an Emerging Discipline in the U.S." In Peter Wagner, B. Whittrock, and R. Whitley (eds.), *Discourses on Society*, Vol. 15. Boston: Kluwer Academic.

1991. "The Historiography of American Political Science." In Easton, Gunnell, and Graziano (1991).

1992. "Continuity and Innovation in the History of Political Science: The Case of Charles Merriam." *Journal of the History of the Behavioral Sciences* (April): 133–42.

1993. *The Descent of Political Theory: The Genealogy of an American Vocation.* Chicago: University of Chicago Press.

Gutting, Gary (ed.). 1980. *Paradigms and Revolutions: Applications and Appraisals of Thomas Kuhn's Philosophy of Science.* Notre Dame, IN: University of Notre Dame Press.

Haas, Ernst B. 1953. "The Balance of Power: Prescription, Concept, or Propaganda?" *World Politics* 5: 442–7.

1958. *The Uniting of Europe.* Stanford, CA: Stanford University Press.

1964. *Beyond the Nation-State.* Stanford, CA: Stanford University Press.

Haber, Samuel. 1964. *Efficiency and Uplift: Scientific Management in the Progressive Era, 1890–1920.* Chicago: University of Chicago Press.

Habermas, Jürgen. 1984/1987. *The Theory of Communicative Action*, 2 vols. Boston: Beacon.

1989. *The Structural Transformation of the Public Sphere.* Cambridge, MA: MIT Press.

Haddow, Anna. 1939. *Political Science in American Colleges and Universities, 1636–1900.* New York: Appleton-Century-Crofts.

Hall, Arnold Bennett. 1926. Review of Walter Lippmann, *The Phantom Public* (1925). In *American Political Science Review* 20: 199–201.

Hansen, John Mark. 1987. "Choosing Sides: The Creation of an Agricultural Policy Network in Congress, 1919–1932." *Studies in American Political Development* 2: 183–229.

Haraway, Donna. 1988. "Situated Knowledges: The Science Question in Feminism and the Privilege of Partial Perspective." *Feminist Studies* 14: 575–99.

Hardin, Garret. 1968. "The Tragedy of the Commons." *Science* 162: 1242–8.

Hare, R. 1975. "Rawls' Theory of Justice." In Norman Daniels (ed.), *Reading Rawls*. Oxford: Basil Blackwell.

Harrington, Joseph. 1988. "The Revelation of Information through the Electoral Process." Working paper, Johns Hopkins University.

Harsanyi, John C. 1977. *Rational Behavior and Bargaining Equilibrium in Games and Social Situations*. Cambridge University Press.

Harsanyi, John C., and Reinhart Selten. 1988. *Equilibrium Selection*. Cambridge, MA: MIT Press.

Hart, Albert B. 1892. "The Exercise of the Suffrage." *Political Science Quarterly* 7: 207–327.

   1913. "APSA Presidential Address: A Government of Men." *American Political Science Review* 7: 1–27.

Hart, Oliver, and Bengt Holmstron. 1987. "The Theory of Contracts." In Truman F. Bewley (ed.), *Advances in Economic Theory – Fifth World Congress*. Cambridge University Press.

Hartz, Louis. 1955. *The Liberal Tradition in America: An Interpretation of American Political Thought since the Revolution*. New York: Harcourt Brace.

   1964. *The Founding of New Societies*. New York: Harcourt, Brace, & World.

Hattam, Victoria. 1990. "Economic Visions and Political Strategies: American Labor and the State, 1865–96." *Studies in American Political Development* 4: 82–129.

Hawkesworth, M. E. 1988. *Theoretical Issues in Policy Analysis*. Albany: State University of New York Press.

Healy, Paul. 1986. "Interpretive Policy Inquiry: A Response to the Limitations of the Received View." *Policy Sciences* 19: 381–96.

Heclo, Hugh. 1972. "Policy Analysis." *British Journal of Political Science* 2: 83–108.

Herring, E. Pendelton. 1929. *Group Representation before Congress*. Baltimore: Johns Hopkins University Press.

Herz, John H. 1951. *Political Realism and Political Idealism: A Study in Theories and Realities*. Chicago: University of Chicago Press.

   1976. *The Nation-State and the Crisis of World Politics*. New York: McKay.

   1986. "From Geneva 1935 to Geneva 1985: Roots of My Views on World Affairs." *International Studies Notes* 12: 28–31.

Hibbs, Douglas. 1977. "Political Parties and Macroeconomic Policies." *American Political Science Review* 71: 1467–87.

   1987. *The American Political Economy*. Cambridge, MA: Harvard University Press.

Hill, Robert B. 1984. "The Polls and Ethnic Minorities." *Annals of the American Academy of Political and Social Science* 472: 155–66.

Hines, Sam. 1982. "Politics and the Evolution of Inquiry in Political Science." *Politics and the Life Sciences* 1: 5–16.

Hirschmann, Albert O. 1977. *The Passions and the Interests: Political Arguments for Capitalism before Its Triumph*. Princeton, NJ: Princeton University Press.

Hirshleifer, J. 1977. "Economics from a Biological Viewpoint." *Journal of Law and Economics* 20: 1–52.

Hoffmann, Stanley. 1981. "Notes on the Limits of Realism." *Social Research* 48: 653–9.

Hofstadter, Richard. 1955. *The Age of Reform*. New York: Anchor.

    1969. *Social Darwinism in American Thought*. Revised edition. New York: Braziller.

Holcombe, Arthur N. 1922. Review of Walter Lippmann, *Public Opinion* (1922). *American Political Science Review* 16: 500–1.

Holden, Matthew. 1983. *Moral Engagement and Combat Scholarship*. Charlottesville, VA: Court Square Institute.

Horowitz, Morton. 1992. *The Transformation of American Law*. Cambridge, MA: Harvard University Press.

Hotelling, Harold. 1929. "Stability in Competition," *Economic Journal* 39: 41–57.

Hsiao, Kung Chuan. 1927. *Political Pluralism: A Study in Contemporary Political Theory*. New York: Harcourt, Brace.

Hume, David. 1888. *Treatise of Human Nature*. Oxford: Clarendon.

Huntington, Samuel P. 1981. *American Politics: The Promise of Disharmony*. Cambridge, MA: Belknap.

    1988. "One Soul at a Time: Political Science and Political Reform." *American Political Science Review* 82: 3–10.

Inglehart, Ronald. 1985. "Aggregate Stability and Individual-Level Flux in Mass Belief Systems: The Level of Analysis Paradox." *American Political Science Review* 79: 97–116.

James, William. 1890. *Principles of Psychology*. New York: Henry Holt.

    1902. *The Varieties of Religious Experience*. New York: Modern Library.

Jaros, Dean, and Lawrence V. Grant. 1974. *Political Behavior: Choices and Perspectives*. New York: St. Martin's.

Jennings, Bruce. 1983. "Interpretive Social Science and Policy Analysis." In Daniel Callahan and Bruce Jennings (eds.), *Ethics, the Social Sciences and Policy Analysis*. New York: Plenum.

    1987. "Interpretation and the Practice of Policy Analysis." In Frank Fischer and John Forester (eds.), *Confronting Values in Policy Analysis*. Newbury Park, CA: Sage.

Jensen, Michael C., and William H. Meckling. 1973. "Theory of the Firm: Managerial Behavior, Agency Costs and Ownership Structure." *Journal of Financial Economics* 3: 305–60.

John, Ieuan, Moorehead Wright, and John Garnett. 1972. "International Politics at Aberystwyth 1919–1969." In Porter (1972).

Johnson, Gary R. 1990. "Evolutionary Biology and Natural Justice: A New Version of an Old Fallacy." Paper presented at the annual meeting of the American Political Science Association, San Francisco.

Jones, Mack. 1991. "Political Science and the Black Political Experience: Issues in Epistemology and Relevance." *National Political Science Review* 3: 29–46.

Jones, Mack, and Alex Willingham. 1970. "The White Custodians of the Black Experience." *Social Science Quarterly* (June): 31–5.

Kalt, Joseph, and Mark Zupan. 1984. "Capture and Ideology in the Economic Theory of Politics." *American Economic Review* 74: 279–300.

Kammen, Michael. 1987. *A Machine That Would Go of Itself: The Constitution in American Culture*. New York: Knopf.

Kann, Mark E. 1990. "Individualism, Civic Virtue, and Gender in America." *Studies in American Political Development* 4: 46–81.

Kaplan, Morton. (1967). "The New Great Debate: Traditionalism versus Science in International Relations." *World Politics* 19: 1–20.

Kariel, Henry S. 1961. *The Decline of American Liberalism*. Stanford, CA: Stanford University Press.

Karl, Barry D. 1974. *Charles E. Merriam and the Study of Politics*. Chicago: University of Chicago Press.

Katz, Daniel, and Richard L. Schanck. 1938. *Social Psychology*. New York: Wiley.

Katz, Elihu, and Paul Lazarsfeld. 1955. *Personal Influence*. Glencoe, IL: Free Press.

Kaufman-Osborn, Timothy V. 1985. "Pragmatism, Policy Science, and the State." *American Journal of Political Science* 29: 827–49.

Keller, Evelyn Fox. 1985. *Reflections on Gender and Science*. New Haven, CT: Yale University Press.

Kelly, Edmond. 1900. *Government or Human Evolution*. London: Longmans, Green.

Kennan, George F. 1951. *American Diplomacy, 1900–1950*. Chicago: University of Chicago Press.

　1954. *Realities of American Foreign Policy*. Princeton, NJ: Princeton University Press.

　1984. *American Diplomacy*. Expanded edition. Chicago: University of Chicago Press.

Kent, Frank. 1924. *The Great Game of Politics*. New York: Doubleday, Page.

Keohane, Robert O. 1984. *After Hegemony: Cooperation and Discord in the World Political Economy*. Princeton, NJ: Princeton University Press.

　1986a. "Theory of World Politics: Structural Realism and Beyond." In Keohane (1986b).

　(ed.) 1986b. *Neo-Realism and Its Critics*. New York: Columbia University Press.

1989. *International Institutions and State Power: Essays in International Relations Theory.* Boulder, CO: Westview.

1991. "International Relations Theory: Contributions of a Feminist Standpoint." In Rebecca Grant and Kathleen Newland (eds.), *Gender and International Relations.* Bloomington: Indiana University Press.

Keohane, Robert O., and Joseph S. Nye Jr. 1977. *Power and Interdependence: World Politics in Transition.* Boston: Little, Brown.

1987. *"Power and Interdependence* Revisited." *International Organization* 41: 725–53.

Key, V. O. 1958. "The State of the Discipline." *American Political Science Review* 52: 961–71.

1961a. "Public Opinion and the Decay of Democracy." *Virginia Quarterly Review* 37: 481–94.

1961b. *Public Opinion and American Democracy.* New York: Knopf.

1966. *The Responsible Electorate: Rationality in Presidential Voting, 1936–1960.* Cambridge, MA: Harvard University Press.

Key, V. O., and Frank Munger. 1959. "Social Determinism and Electoral Choice: The Case of Indiana." In E. Burdick and A. J. Brodbeck (eds.), *American Voting Behavior.* Glencoe, IL: Free Press.

Kiewiet, D. Roderick, and Mathew D. McCubbins. 1989. *The Spending Power: Congress, the President and Appropriations.* Unpublished manuscript.

Kilson, Martin. 1993. "Political Science and Afro-Americans: Normative Problems of American Politics." In Vernon Van Dyke (ed.), *Teaching Political Science: The Professor and the Polity.* Highlands, NJ: Humanities Press.

Kinder, Donald E. 1983. "Diversity and Complexity in American Public Opinion." In Ada W. Finifter (ed.), *Political Science: The State of the Discipline.* Washington, DC: American Political Science Association.

Kinder, Donald, and David O. Sears. 1985. "Public Opinion and Political Action." In Gardner Lindzey and E. Aronson (eds.), *Handbook of Social Psychology,* 3rd edition (Vol. 2). New York: Random House.

Kingdon, John. 1984. *Agendas, Alternatives, and Public Policies.* Boston: Little, Brown.

Kirk, Grayson L. 1952. "In Search of the National Interest." *World Politics* 5: 110–15.

Kitcher, Philip. 1985. *Vaulting Ambition: Sociobiology and the Quest for Human Nature.* Cambridge, MA: MIT Press.

Kitchin, William. 1986. "The Place of Biopolitics in the Political Science Curriculum." *Politics and the Life Sciences* 5: 5–13.

Kontos, Alkis. 1972. "Success and Knowledge in Machiavelli." In Anthony Parel (ed.), *The Political Calculus: Essays on Machiavelli's Philosophy.* Toronto: University of Toronto Press.

Kramer, Gerald. 1978. "Existence of Electoral Equilibrium." In Peter Ordeshook (ed.), *Game Theory and Political Science*. New York: New York University Press.

Krasner, Stephen D. 1978. *Defending the National Interest: Raw Materials Investments and U.S. Foreign Policy*. Princeton, NJ: Princeton University Press.

  1988. Review of Robert Gilpin, *The Political Economy of International Relations*. *American Political Science Review* 82: 681–2.

Kresps, David. 1988. "Corporate Cultures and Economic Theory." Working paper, Graduate School of Business, Stanford University.

Kress, Paul F. 1973. *Social Science and the Idea of Process: The Ambiguous Legacy of Arthur F. Bentley*. Urbana: University of Illinois Press.

Krippendorff, Ekkehart. 1989. "The Dominance of American Approaches in International Relations." In Dyer and Mangasarian (1989).

Kuhn, Thomas. 1962. *The Structure of Scientific Revolutions*. Chicago: University of Chicago Press.

Ladd, Everett Carl, and Seymour Martin Lipset. 1978. *1977 Survey of the American Professoriate: Technical Report*. Storrs: Social Data Center, University of Connecticut.

Lakatos, Imre. 1970. "Falsification and the Methodology of Scientific Research Programmes." In Imre Lakatos and Alan Musgrave (eds.), *Criticism and the Growth of Knowledge*. Cambridge University Press.

  1978. *The Methodology of Scientific Research Programmes*. Cambridge University Press.

Langdon, William. 1891. "The Case of the Negro." *Political Science Quarterly* 6: 29–42.

Lanham, Richard A. 1992. "The Extraordinary Convergence: Democracy, Technology, Theory, and the University Curriculum." In Darryl J. Gless and Barbara Herrnstein Smith (eds.), *The Politics of Liberal Education*. Durham, NC: Duke University Press.

Laski, Harold J. 1917. *Studies in the Problem of Sovereignty*. New Haven, CT: Yale University Press.

  1919. *Authority in the Modern State*. New Haven, CT: Yale University Press.

  1921. *Foundations of Sovereignty and Other Essays*. New York: Harcourt, Brace.

  1925. *The Grammar of Politics*. London: Allen & Unwin.

  1935. *The State in Theory and Practice*. New York: Viking.

Lasswell, Harold D. 1924. Letter to Anna P. Lasswell and Linden Lasswell, March 20. Harold D. Lasswell Papers (Box 56), Manuscripts and Archives, Yale University Library.

  1926. Review of Walter Lippmann, *The Phantom Public*. *American Journal of Sociology* 31: 533–5.

1927. *Propaganda Technique in the World War*. New York: Knopf.

1929–30. Review of Elliott, *Pragmatic Revolt in Politics*. *American Journal of Sociology* 35: 134–5.

1941. *Democracy through Public Opinion*. Menasha, WI: George Banta.

1943. "Proposal: The Institute of Policy Sciences" and "Personal Policy Objectives." Memorandum, October 1. Harold D. Lasswell Papers (Box 145), Manuscripts and Archives, Yale University Library.

1947. *The Analysis of Political Behavior: An Empirical Approach*. New York: Oxford University Press.

1951a. "Democratic Character." In *The Political Writings of Harold D. Lasswell*. Glencoe, IL: Free Press.

1951b. "The Policy Orientation." In Daniel Lerner and Harold D. Lasswell (eds.), *The Policy Sciences*. Stanford, CA: Stanford University Press.

1955. "Current Studies of the Decision Process: Automation versus Creativity." *Western Political Quarterly* 8: 381–99.

1956. "The Political Science of Science: An Inquiry into the Possible Reconciliation of Mastery and Freedom." *American Political Science Review* 50: 961–79.

1961. "Communication and the Mind." In Seymour M. Farber and Roger H. L. Wilson (eds.), *Man and Civilization: Control of the Mind*. New York: McGraw-Hill.

1964. *The Future of Political Science*. New York: Atherton.

[1935] 1965a. *World Politics and Personal Insecurity*. New York: Free Press.

1965b. "The World Revolution of Our Time: A Framework for Basic Policy Research." In Harold D. Lasswell and Daniel Lerner (eds.), *World Revolutionary Elites*. Cambridge, MA: MIT Press.

1968. "Policy Sciences." *International Encyclopedia of the Social Sciences* 12: 181–9.

1971. *A Pre-View of Policy Sciences*. New York: American Elsevier.

1974. "Some Perplexities of Policy Theory." *Social Research* 41: 176–89.

[1948] 1976. *Power and Personality*. New York: Norton.

[1930] 1977. *Psychopathology and Politics*. Chicago: University of Chicago Press.

1979. *The Signature of Power*. New Brunswick, NJ: Transaction Books.

Lasswell, Harold D., and Abraham Kaplan. 1950. *Power and Society*. New Haven, CT: Yale University Press.

Latham, Earl. 1952. *The Group Basis of Politics*. Ithaca, NY: Cornell University Press.

Laudan, Larry. 1977. *Progress and Its Problems*. Berkeley & Los Angeles: University of California Press.

Lazarsfeld, Paul. 1957. "Public Opinion and the Classical Tradition." *Public Opinion Quarterly* 21: 39–57.

Lazarsfeld, Paul, Bernard Berelson, and Hazel Gaudet. 1948. *The People's Choice*. 2nd edition. New York: Columbia University Press.

LeConte, Joseph. 1892. "The Race Problem and the South." In *Man and the State: Studies in Applied Sociology*. New York: D. Appleton.

Ledyard, John. 1984. "The Pure Theory of Large Two-Candidate Elections." *Public Choice* 44: 7–41.

Leigh, Robert D. 1944. "The Educational Function of Social Scientists." *American Political Science Review* 38: 531–9.

Leiserson, Avery. 1975. "Charles Merriam, Max Weber, and the Search for Synthesis in Political Science." *American Political Science Review* 69: 175–85.

Lemert, James B. 1981. *Does Mass Communication Change Public Opinion After All?: A New Approach to Effects Analysis*. Chicago: Nelson Hall.

Lieber, Francis. 1880. *Reminiscences, Addresses, and Essays*. Philadelphia: Lippincott.

Lindblom, Charles E. 1958. "Policy Analysis." *American Economic Review* 48: 298–312.

    1959. "The Science of 'Muddling Through.' " *Public Administration Review* 19: 79–88.

    1965. *The Intelligence of Democracy*. New York: Free Press.

    1968. *The Policy-Making Process*. Englewood Cliffs, NJ: Prentice-Hall.

    1979. "Still Muddling, Not Yet Through." *Public Administration Review* 39: 517–26.

    1982. "Another State of Mind." *American Political Science Review* 76: 9–21.

    1990. *Inquiry and Change*. New Haven, CT: Yale University Press.

Lindblom, Charles E., and David Cohen. 1979. *Usable Knowledge*. New Haven, CT: Yale University Press.

Lindsay, A. D. 1914. "The State in Modern Political Theory." *Political Quarterly* 1 (1): 128–45.

Lippmann, Walter. 1914. *A Preface to Politics*. New York: Mitchell Kennerley.

    1922. *Public Opinion*. New York: Harcourt, Brace.

    1925. *The Phantom Public*. New York: Harcourt, Brace.

    1955. *Essays in the Public Philosophy*. Boston: Little, Brown.

    1965. *The Essential Lippmann*. Edited by C. Rossiter and J. Lare. New York: Vintage.

Lipset, Seymour Martin. 1959. "Some Social Requisites of Democracy: Economic Development and Political Legitimacy." *American Political Science Review* 53: 69–105.

    1960. *Political Man: The Social Bases of Politics*. New York: Doubleday.

Logan, Rayford. 1965. *The Betrayal of the Negro*. Revised edition. New York: Collier.

Lott, John. 1987. "Political Cheating." *Public Choice* 52: 169–87.

Lott, John, and Robert W. Reed. 1987. "Shirking and Sorting in a Political Market with Finite Lived Politicians." Working paper in political science, Hoover Institution.

Lowell, A. Lawrence. 1910. "The Physiology of Politics." *American Political Science Review* 4: 1–15.

1913a. *Public Opinion and Popular Government.* New York: Longmans, Green.

1913b. "Expert Administrators in Popular Government." *American Political Science Review* 7: 45–62.

1923. *Public Opinion in War and Peace.* Cambridge, MA: Harvard University Press.

Lowery, David. 1993. "A Bureaucratic-Centered Image of Governance: The Founders' Thought in Modern Perspective." *Journal of Public Administration Research and Theory* 3: 182–208.

Lowi, Theodore J. 1969. *The End of Liberalism: The Second Republic of the United States.* New York: Norton.

1973. "The Politicization of Political Science." *American Politics Quarterly* 1: 43–71.

1975. "What Political Scientists Don't Need to Ask about Policy Analysis." In Stuart S. Nagel (ed.), *Policy Studies and the Social Sciences.* Lexington, MA: Lexington.

1992. "The State in Political Science: How We Become What We Study." *American Political Science Review* 86: 1–7. Reprinted in Farr and Seidelman (1993).

Lumsden, Charles J., and Edward O. Wilson. 1983. *Promethean Fire: Reflections on the Origin of Mind.* Cambridge, MA: Harvard University Press.

Luttbeg, Norman. 1978. Review of Forrest Chisman, *Attitude Psychology and the Study of Public Opinion. Public Opinion Quarterly* 42: 280.

MacIntyre, Alasdair. 1971. "Is a Science of Comparative Politics Possible?" In *Against the Self-Images of the Age.* New York: Schocken.

1984. *After Virtue.* 2nd edition. Notre Dame, IN: University of Notre Dame Press.

1988. *Whose Justice? Which Rationality?* Notre Dame, IN: University of Notre Dame Press.

MacIver, Robert M. 1926. *The Modern State.* Oxford University Press.

MacKenzie, W. J. M. 1978. *Biological Ideas in Politics.* Harmondsworth: Penguin.

Macy, Jesse. 1917. "The Scientific Spirit in Politics." *American Political Science Review* 11: 1–11.

Magee, Bryan. 1978. *Men of Ideas.* New York: Vintage.

Maghroori, Ray. 1982. "Introduction: Major Debates in International Relations." In Ray Maghroori and Bennett Ramberg (eds.), *Globalism versus Realism: International Relations' Third Debate.* Boulder, CO: Westview.

Marx, Karl. 1963. *Eighteenth Brumaire of Louis Bonaparte.* New York: International.

Masters, Roger D. 1989. *The Nature of Politics.* New Haven, CT: Yale University Press.

——— 1990. "Evolutionary Biology and Political Theory." *American Political Science Review* 84: 195–210.

Matthews, R C. O. 1986. "The Economics of Institutions and the Sources of Growth." *Economic Journal* 96: 903–18.

McClain, Paula D., and John A. Garcia. 1993. "Expanding Disciplinary Boundaries: Black, Latino and Racial Minority Group Politics in Political Science." In Ada W. Finifter (ed.), *Political Science: The State of the Discipline*, 2nd edition. Washington, DC: American Political Science Association.

McClain, Paula D., and Albert Karnig. 1990. "Blacks and Hispanic Socioeconomic and Political Competition." *American Political Science Review* 84: 535–44.

McConnell, Grant. 1966. *Private Power and American Democracy.* New York: Knopf.

McCormick, Richard L. 1979. "The Party Period and Public Policy: An Exploratory Hypothesis." *Journal of American History* 66: 279–89.

——— 1982. "The Realignment Synthesis in American History." *Journal of Interdisciplinary History* 13: 85–105.

McCoy, Charles A., and John Playford (eds.). 1967. *Apolitical Politics: A Critique of Behavioralism.* New York: Crowell.

McFarland, Andrew. 1991. "Interest Groups and Political Time: Cycles in America." *British Journal of Political Science* 23: 257–84.

McKelvey, Richard D. 1975. "Intransitivities in Multidimensional Voting Models and Some Implications for Agenda Control." *Journal of Economic Theory* 12: 472–82.

——— 1979. "General Conditions for Global Intransitivities in Formal Voting Models." *Econometrica* 47: 1085–111.

McKelvey, Richard D., and Peter C. Ordeshook. 1976. "Symmetric Spatial Games without Majority Rule Equilibrium." *American Political Science Review* 70: 1171–84.

Meinecke, Friedrich. 1957. *Machiavellism: The Doctrine of Raison d'état and Its Place in Modern History.* New Haven, CT: Yale University Press.

Melzner, Arnold J. 1976. *Policy Analysts in the Bureaucracy.* Berkeley & Los Angeles: University of California Press.

Merchant, Carolyn. 1980. *The Death of Nature: Women, Ecology, and the Scientific Revolution*. San Francisco: Harper & Row.

1989. *Ecological Revolutions: Nature, Gender, and Science in New England*. Chapel Hill: University of North Carolina Press.

Merriam, Charles E. 1900. *History of the Theory of Sovereignty since Rousseau*. New York: Columbia University Press.

1903. *A History of American Political Theories*. New York: Macmillan.

1921. "The Present State of the Study of Politics." *American Political Science Review* 15: 173–85.

1922. *The American Party System*. New York: Macmillan.

1923. "Progress Report of the Committee on Political Research." *American Political Science Review* 17: 274–312.

1925. *New Aspects of Politics*. Chicago: University of Chicago Press.

1926. "Progress in Political Research." *American Political Science Review* 20: 1–13.

[1925] 1931. *New Aspects of Politics*. 3rd edition. Chicago: University of Chicago Press.

1934. *Civic Education in the United States*. New York: Scribner's.

Merriam, Charles E., and Harold F. Gosnell. 1924. *Non-voting: Causes and Methods of Control*. Chicago: University of Chicago Press.

Meyer, William J. 1975. *Public Good and Political Authority: A Pragmatic Proposal*. Port Washington, NY: Kennikat.

Miller, Eugene F. 1971. "Hume's Contribution to the Behavioral Sciences." *Journal of the History of the Behavioral Sciences* 7: 154–68.

Miller, George H. 1971. *Railroads and the Granger Laws*. Madison: University of Wisconsin Press.

Mitrany, David. [1943] 1966. *A Working Peace System*. Chicago: Quadrangle.

Moe, Terry. 1987. "Institutions, Interests and Positive Theory: The Politics of the NLRB." *Studies in American Political Development* 2: 236–99.

1990. "Political Institutions: The Neglected Side of the Story." *Journal of Law, Economics, and Organization* 6: 213–54.

Monkkonen, Eric. 1991. "Introduction: History and Other Social Sciences." *Social Science History* 15: 199–200.

Monroe, Kristen, et al. 1990. "The Nature of Contemporary Political Science." *PS* 23: 34–43.

Moon, J. Donald. 1975. "The Logic of Political Inquiry: A Synthesis of Opposed Perspectives." In Fred I. Greenstein and Nelson W. Polsby (eds.), *The Handbook of Political Science*, Vol. 1. Reading, MA: Addison-Wesley.

1991. "Pluralism and Progress in the Study of Politics." In William Crotty (ed.), *Political Science: Looking to the Future*, Vol. 1. Evanston, IL: Northwestern University Press.

Morawski, Jill G. (ed.). 1988. *The Rise of Experimentation in American Psychology*. New Haven, CT: Yale University Press.

Morgenthau, Hans J. 1946. *Scientific Man versus Power Politics*. Chicago: University of Chicago Press.

　　1951. *In Defense of the National Interest: A Critical Examination of American Foreign Policy*. New York: Knopf.

　　1952. "What Is the National Interest of the United States?" *Annals* 282 (July): 1–7.

　　[1948] 1954. *Politics among Nations: The Struggle for Power and Peace*. 2nd edition. New York: Knopf.

　　1962a. *Politics in the Twentieth Century*. Vol. 1, *The Decline of Democratic Politics*. Chicago: University of Chicago Press.

　　1962b. *Politics in the Twentieth Century*. Vol. 2, *The Impasse of American Foreign Policy*. Chicago: University of Chicago Press.

　　1964. "The Intellectual and Political Functions of a Theory of International Relations." In Horace V. Harrison (ed.), *The Role of Theory in International Relations*. Princeton, NJ: Van Nostrand.

　　1970. "International Relations: Quantitative and Qualitative Approaches." In Norman D. Palmer (ed.), *A Design for International Relations Research: Scope, Theory, Methods, and Relevance*. Philadelphia: American Academy of Political and Social Science.

Morison, Samuel Eliot. 1972. *The Oxford History of the American People*. Vol. 2, *1869 to the Death of John F. Kennedy 1963*. New York: New American Library.

Moynihan, Daniel P. 1979. "Pattern of Ethnic Succession: Blacks and Hispanics in New York." *Political Science Quarterly* 93: 1–13.

Munns, Joyce Matthews. 1975. "The Environment, Politics and Policy Literature: A Critique and Reformulation." *Western Political Quarterly* 28: 646–65.

Munro, William B. 1928. "APSA Presidential Address: Physics and Politics – An Old Analogy Revisited." *American Political Science Review* 22: 1–11.

Namenworth, J. Zvi, Randi Lynn Miller, and Robert Philip Weber. 1981. "Organizations Have Opinions: A Redefinition of Publics." *Public Opinion Quarterly* 45: 463–76.

Nardin, Terry, and David R. Mapel (eds.). 1992. *Traditions of International Ethics*. Cambridge University Press.

Natchez, Peter B. 1985. *Images of Voting/Visions of Democracy*. New York: Basic.

Nelson, Richard R., and Sidney G. Winter. 1982. *An Evolutionary Theory of Economic Change*. Cambridge, MA: Harvard University Press.

Neuman, W. Russell. 1986. *The Paradox of Mass Politics: Knowledge and Opinion in the American Electorate*. Cambridge, MA: Harvard University Press.

Neustadt, Richard. 1960. *Presidential Power: The Politics of Leadership*. New York: Wiley.

Nie, Norman H., Sidney Verba, and John R. Petrocik. 1975. *The Changing American Voter*. Cambridge, MA: Harvard University Press.

Niebuhr, Reinhold. 1932. *Moral Man and Immoral Society: A Study in Ethics and Politics*. New York: Scribner's.

1944. *The Children of Light and the Children of Darkness*. New York: Scribner's.

Nimmo, Dan. 1978. *Political Communication and Public Opinion in America*. Santa Monica, CA: Goodyear.

Nisbet, Robert. 1975. "Public Opinion versus Popular Opinion." *Public Interest* 41: 166–92.

Noelle-Neumann, Elisabeth. 1984. *The Spiral of Silence: Public Opinion – Our Social Skin*. Chicago: University of Chicago Press.

Nordhaus, William. 1975. "The Political Business Cycle." *Review of Economic Studies* 42: 169–90.

Norrell, Robert. 1985. *Reaping the Whirlwind: The Civil Rights Movement in Tuskegee*. New York: Random House.

North, Douglass C. 1981. *Structure and Change in Economic History*. New York: Norton.

North, Douglass C., and Robert Thomas. 1973. *The Rise of the Western World: A New Economic History*. Cambridge University Press.

Norton, Ann. 1986. *Alternative Americas*. Chicago: University of Chicago Press.

Novick, Peter. 1988. *That Noble Dream: The 'Objectivity Question' and the American Historical Profession*. Cambridge University Press.

Nuechterlein, James A. 1980. "The Dream of Scientific Liberalism: The *New Republic* and American Progressive Thought, 1914–1920." *Review of Politics* 42: 167–89.

Nye, Joseph S. 1971. *Peace in Parts: Integration and Conflict in Regional Organization*. Boston: Little, Brown.

Oakley, Francis. 1992. "Against Nostalgia: Reflections on Our Present Discontents in American Higher Education." In Darryl J. Gless and Barbara Herrnstein Smith (eds.), *The Politics of Liberal Education*. Durham, NC: Duke University Press.

Odegard, Peter H. 1925. *Pressure Politics*. New York: Columbia University Press.

1940. "The Political Scientist in the Democratic Service State." *Journal of Politics* 2: 140–64.

Oestreicher, Richard. 1989. "Urban Working-Class Political Behavior and Theories of American Electoral Politics." *Journal of American History* 74: 1257–86.

Ogg, Frederic A. 1927. "Reports of Round Table Conferences." *American Political Science Review* 21: 389–409.

Olson, William, and Nicholas Onuf. 1985. "The Growth of a Discipline: Reviewed." In Steve Smith (ed.), *International Relations: British and American Perspectives.* Oxford: Basil Blackwell.

Ophuls, William. 1977. *Ecology and the Politics of Scarcity.* San Francisco: Freeman.

Orren, Karen. 1991. *Belated Feudalism: Labor, the Law, and Liberal Development in the United States.* Cambridge University Press.

Ostrom, Elinor. 1986. "An Agenda for the Study of Institutions." *Public Choice* 48: 3–25.

Page, Benjamin I., and Robert Y. Shapiro. 1983. "The Effects of Public Opinion on Policy." *American Political Science Review* 77: 175–90.

   1989. "Educating and Manipulating the Public." In Michael Margolis and Gary A. Mauser (eds.), *Manipulating Public Opinion: Essays on Public Opinion as an Independent Variable.* Pacific Grove, CA: Brooks/Cole.

   1992. *The Rational Public: Fifty Years of Trends in America's Policy Preferences.* Chicago: University of Chicago Press.

Palfrey, Tom, and Howard Rosenthal. 1985. "Voter Participation and Strategic Uncertainty." *American Political Science Review* 79: 62–78.

Palmer, Paul A. 1938. "Ferdinand Toennies's Theory of Public Opinion." *Public Opinion Quarterly* 2: 584–95.

Park, Robert E. 1972. *The Crowd and the Public and Other Essays* (1904). Edited by H. Elsner Jr. Chicago: University of Chicago Press.

Parkinson, F. 1977. *The Philosophy of International Relations: A Study in the History of Thought.* Beverly Hills, CA: Sage.

Pearce, David G. 1987. "Renegotiation-Proof Equilibria: Collective Rationality and Intertemporal Cooperation." Mimeo, Yale University.

Peltzman, Samuel. 1984. "Constituent Interest and Congressional Voting." *Journal of Law and Economics* 27: 181–210.

Plott, Charles. 1967. "A Notion of Equilibrium and Its Possibility under Majority Rule." *American Economic Review* 57: 787–806.

Polsby, Nelson W. 1963. *Community Power and Political Theory.* New Haven, CT: Yale University Press.

Poole, Keith, and Howard Rosenthal. 1985. "A Spatial Model for Legislative Roll Call Analysis." *American Journal of Political Science* 29: 357–84.

Porter, Brian (ed.). 1972. *The Aberystwyth Papers – International Politics: 1919–1969.* Oxford University Press.

Postman, Neil. 1986. *Amusing Ourselves to Death: Public Discourse in the Age of Show Business.* New York: Penguin.

Pratt, John W., and Richard J. Zeckhauser (eds.). 1985. *Principals and Agents: The Structure of Business.* Cambridge, MA: Harvard Business School Press.

Premfors, Rune. 1992. "Knowledge, Power, and Democracy: Lindblom, Critical Theory, and Postmodernism." *Knowledge and Policy* 5: 77–93.

Prestage, Jewel. 1969. "Report of the Conference on Political Science Curriculum at Predominantly Black Institutions." *PS* (Summer): 322–36.

Presthus, Robert. 1965. *Behavioral Approaches to Public Administration.* Tuscaloosa: University of Alabama Press.

Price, Vincent. 1992. *Communication Concepts.* Vol. 4, *Public Opinion.* Newbury Park, CA: Sage.

Qualter, Terence H. 1985. *Opinion Control in the Democracies.* London: Macmillan.

Rawls, John. 1958. "Justice as Fairness." *Philosophical Review* 67: 164–94.

  1972. *A Theory of Justice.* Cambridge, MA: Harvard University Press.

Redford, Emmette S. 1961. "Reflections on a Discipline." *American Political Science Review* 55: 755–62.

Rein, Martin, and Donald A. Schön. 1991. "Frame-Reflective Policy Discourse." In Peter Wagner, et al. (eds.), *Social Sciences and Modern States.* Cambridge University Press.

Repass, David E. 1971. "Issue Salience and Party Choice." *American Political Science Review* 65: 389–400.

Ricci, David. 1984. *The Tragedy of Political Science: Politics, Scholarship, and Democracy.* New Haven, CT: Yale University Press.

Riker, William H. 1980. "Implications from the Disequilibrium of Majority Rule for the Study of Institutions." *American Political Science Review* 74: 432–47.

  1982a. "The Two-Party System and Duverger's Law: An Essay on the History of Political Science." *American Political Science Review* 76: 753–66. Reprinted in Farr and Seidelman (1993).

  1982b. *Liberalism against Populism.* San Francisco: Freeman.

  1982c. "Implications from the Disequilibrium of Majority Rule for the Study of Institutions." In Peter Ordeshook and Kenneth Shepsle (eds.), *Political Equilibrium.* Boston: Kluwer-Nijhoff.

Ritchie, David. 1890. *Darwinism and Politics.* New York: Humboldt.

Roberts, Morley. 1938. *Biopolitics: An Essay in the Physiology and Pathology and Politics of the Social and Somatic Organism.* London: Dent.

Robespierre, Maximilien. 1952. *Oeuvres.* Edited by Marc Bouloiseau, et al. Paris: Presses Universitaires de France, VII.

Rodgers, Daniel T. 1987. *Contested Truths: Keywords in American Politics since Independence.* New York: Basic.

Roederer, Pierre-Louis. 1857. *Oeuvres.* Edited by A. M. Roederer. Paris: F. Didot.

Rogers, Lindsay. 1949. *The Pollsters: Public Opinion, Politics, and Democratic Leadership.* New York: Knopf.

Rose, John C. 1906. "Negro Suffrage: The Constitutional Point of View." *American Political Science Review* I: 17–43.

Rosecrance, Richard. 1981. "The One World of Hans Morgenthau." *Social Research* 48: 749–65.

Rosenthal, Joel H. 1991. *Righteous Realists: Political Realism, Responsible Power, and American Culture in the Nuclear Age.* Baton Rouge: Louisiana State University Press.

Ross, Dorothy. 1991. *The Origins of American Social Science.* Cambridge University Press.

Rothstein, Robert L. 1972. "On the Costs of Realism." *Political Science Quarterly* 87: 347–62.

Rowe, L. S. 1922. "The Development of Democracy on the American Continent." *American Political Science Review* 16: 1–8.

Rudolph, Frederick. 1990. *The American College and University: A History.* Athens: University of Georgia Press.

Rusciano, Frank Louis. 1989. *Isolation and Paradox: Defining "The Public" in Modern Political Analysis.* Westport, CT: Greenwood.

Russell, Frank M. 1936. *Theories of International Relations.* New York: Appleton-Century.

Sabine, George H. 1923. "Pluralism: A Point of View." *American Political Science Review* 17: 34–50.

    1928. "Political Science and the Juristic Point of View." *American Political Science Review* 22: 553–75.

Sait, Edward M. 1929. *Democracy.* New York: Century.

    1938. *Political Institutions – A Preface.* Boston: Appleton-Century-Crofts.

Salaville, Jean-Baptiste. 1793. Unsigned article in *Annales patriotiques* 204 (24 July).

Sanders, Elizabeth. 1986. "Industrial Concentration, Sectional Competition and Anti-Trust Politics in America, 1880–1980." *Studies in American Political Development* 1: 215–45.

Schaar, John H., and Wolin, Sheldon. 1963. "Essays on the Scientific Study of Politics: A Critique." *American Political Science Review* 57: 125–50.

Schattschneider, E. E. 1957. "Intensity, Direction and Scope." *American Political Science Review* 51: 933–42.

Scheiber, Harry. 1975. "Federalism and the American Economic Order, 1789–1910." *Law and Society Review* 10: 57–118.

Schelling, Thomas. 1960. *The Strategy of Conflict.* Cambridge, MA: Harvard University Press.

Schick, Allen. 1966. "The Road to PPB: The Stages of Budget Reform." *Public Administration Review* 26: 243–58.

Schön, Donald A. 1983. *The Reflective Practitioner: How Professionals Think in Action.* New York: Basic.

Schubert, Glendon. 1989. *Evolutionary Politics.* Carbondale: Southern Illinois University Press.

Schuman, Frederick L. 1941. *International Politics: The Western System in Transition.* 3rd edition. New York: McGraw-Hill.

Schwarzenberger, Georg. 1951. *Power Politics: A Study of International Society*. 2nd edition. New York: Praeger.

Seeley, J. R. 1896. *Introduction to Political Science*. London: Macmillan.

Seidelman, Raymond, and Edward J. Harpham. 1985. *Disenchanted Realists: Political Science and the American Crisis, 1884–1984*. Albany: State University of New York Press.

Selten, Reinhard. 1975. "A Reexamination of the Perfectness Concept for Equilibrium Points in Extensive Games." *International Journal of Game Theory* 4: 25–55.

Sharkansky, Ira (ed.). 1970. *Policy Analysis in Political Science*. Chicago: Markham.

Shaw, Albert. 1907. "Presidential Address." *American Political Science Review* 1: 177–86.

Shaw, R. Paul, and Yuwa Wong. 1987. "Ethnic Mobilization and the Seeds of Warfare: An Evolutionary Perspective." *International Studies Quarterly* 31: 5–31.

Shepard, Walter. 1919. Review of Laski, *Authority in the Modern State*. *American Political Science Review* 13: 491–4.

Shepherd, William R. 1965. "John William Burgess." In Howard W. Odum (ed.), *American Masters of Social Science*. New York: Kennikat.

Shepsle, Kenneth A. 1979. "Institutional Arrangements and Equilibrium in Multidimensional Voting Models." *American Journal of Political Science* 23: 27–60.

　1986a. "Institutional Equilibrium and Equilibrium Institutions." In Herbert Weisberg (ed.), *Political Science: The Science of Politics*. New York: Agathon.

　1986b. "The Positive Theory of Legislative Institutions: An Enrichment of Social Choice and Spatial Models." *Public Choice* 50: 135–79.

　1989. "Studying Institutions: Some Lessons From the Rational Choice Approach." *Journal of Theoretical Politics* 1: 131–48. Revised version as Chapter 11 in this volume.

Shepsle, Kenneth A., and Barry R. Weingast. 1981. "Structure-Induced Equilibria and Legislative Choice." *Public Choice* 37: 503–19.

　1982. "Institutionalizing Majority Rule: A Social Choice Theory with Policy Implications." *American Economic Review* 78: 367–72.

　1987. "The Institutional Foundations of Committee Power." *American Political Science Review* 81: 85–104.

Shklar, Judith N. 1991. "Redeeming American Political Theory," *American Political Science Review* 85: 2–15.

Sibley, Mulford, Q. 1962. "The Limitations of Behavioralism." In James C. Charlesworth (ed.), *The Limits of Behavioralism in Political Science*. Philadelphia: American Academy of Political and Social Science.

Simon, Herbert A. [1947] 1949. *Administrative Behavior*. 2nd edition. New York: Macmillan.

1950. "The Semantics of Political Science: Discussion." *American Political Science Review* 44: 407–11.

1967. "The Changing Theory and the Changing Practice of Public Administration." In Ithiel de Sola Pool (ed.), *Contemporary Political Science*. New York: McGraw-Hill.

[1947] 1976. *Administrative Behavior*. 3rd edition. New York: Free Press.

[1960] 1977. *The New Science of Management Decision*. Revised edition. Englewood Cliffs, NJ: Prentice-Hall.

1983. *Reason in Human Affairs*. Stanford, CA: Stanford University Press.

1987. "Making Management Decisions: The Role of Intuition and Emotion." *Academy of Management Executive* 1: 57–64.

1991a. Letter to the author. May 30.

1991b. *Models of My Life*. New York: Basic.

Skinner, Quentin. 1984. "The Idea of Negative Liberty: Philosophical and Historical Perspectives." In Richard Rorty, J. B. Schneewind, and Quentin Skinner (eds.), *Philosophy in History*. Cambridge University Press.

Sklar, Martin. 1989. *The Corporate Reconstruction of American Capitalism*. Cambridge University Press.

Skocpol, Theda, and Kenneth Feingold. 1982. "State Capacity and Economic Intervention in the Early New Deal." *Political Science Quarterly* 97: 255–78.

Skocpol, Theda, and Gretchen Ritter. 1991. "Gender and the Origins of Modern Social Policies in Britain and the United States." *Studies in American Political Development* 5: 36–93.

Skowronek, Stephen. 1982. *Building a New American State: The Expansion of National Administrative Capacities, 1877–1920*. Cambridge University Press.

1993. *The Politics Presidents Make: Leadership from John Adams to George Bush*. Cambridge, MA: Harvard University Press.

Smith, Michael Joseph. 1986. *Realist Thought from Weber to Kissinger*. Baton Rouge: Louisiana State University Press.

1992. "Liberalism and International Reform." In Nardin and Mapel (1992).

Smith, Steve. 1989. "Paradigm Dominance in International Relations: The Development of International Relations as a Social Science." In Dyer and Mangasarian (1989).

Snyder, Glenn H., and Paul Diesing. 1977. *Conflict among Nations: Bargaining, Decision Making, and System Structure in International Crises*. Princeton, NJ: Princeton University Press.

Somit, Albert. 1972. "Biopolitics: A Review Article." *British Journal of Political Science* 2: 209–38.

(ed.). 1976. *Biology and Politics: Recent Explorations*. Paris: Mouton.

Somit, Albert, and Steven A. Peterson. 1990. "Biopolitics and Mainstream Political Science: A Master Bibliography." DeKalb, IL: Program for Biosocial Research.

1991. "Democracy as an Endangered Species: Toward an Evolutionary Perspective." Paper presented at the annual meeting of the American Political Science Association, Washington, DC.

Somit, Albert, and Joseph Tanenhaus. 1967. *The Development of American Political Science: From Burgess to Behavioralism* Boston: Allyn & Bacon.

Spencer, Herbert. 1895. *The Principles of Sociology.* 3rd edition. New York: Appleton.

Spenser, Richard C. 1928. "Notes on Instruction and Research: Significance of a Functional Approach in the Introductory Course." *American Political Science Review* 22: 954–66.

Spykman, Nicholas John. 1942. *America's Strategy in World Politics: The United States and the Balance of Power.* New York: Harcourt, Brace.

Steffens, Lincoln. 1904. *The Shame of the Cities.* New York: McClure, Phillips.

Stein, Arthur A. 1990. *Why Nations Cooperate: Circumstance and Choice in International Relations.* Ithaca, NY: Cornell University Press.

Stephenson, Gilbert. 1969. *Racial Distinction in American Law.* New York: Negro Universities Press.

Stimson, James A. 1991. *Public Opinion in America: Moods, Cycles and Swings.* Boulder, CO: Westview.

Storing, Herbert J. (ed.). 1962. *Essays on the Scientific Study of Politics.* New York: Holt, Rinehart, & Winston.

Story, Russell M. 1926, "The Content of the Introductory Course in Political Science." *American Political Science Review* 20: 419–28.

Strauss, Leo. 1962. "Epilogue" to Storing (1962).

Strausz-Hupe, Robert and Stefan T. Possony. [1950] 1954. *International Relations in the Age of Conflict between Democracy and Dictatorship.* 2nd edition. New York: McGraw-Hill.

Sugden, Robert. 1986. *The Economics of Rights, Cooperation, and Welfare.* Oxford: Basil Blackwell.

Sullivan, Michael P. 1990. *Power in Contemporary International Politics.* Columbia: University of South Carolina Press.

Sumner, William Graham. [1883] 1952. *What the Social Classes Owe to Each Other.* Caldwell, ID: Caxton.

Sumner, William Graham, and Albert G. Keller. 1927. *The Science of Society* New Haven, CT: Yale University Press.

Surkin, Marvin, and Alan Wolfe (eds.). 1970. *An End to Political Science: The Caucus Papers.* New York: Basic.

Taylor, Charles. 1967. "Neutrality in Political Science." In Peter Laslett and W. G. Runciman (eds.), *Philosophy, Politics and Society.* (3rd series). New York: Barnes & Noble.

Thompson, Kenneth W. 1952. "The Study of International Politics: A Survey of Trends and Developments." *Review of Politics* 14: 437–67.

1971. "Education for What: The Debate Over Goals." In Stephen D. Kertesz (ed.), *The Task of Universities in a Changing World.* Notre Dame, IN: University of Notre Dame Press.

1985. *Moralism and Morality in Politics and Diplomacy.* Lanham, MD: University Press of America.

Thorndike, E. L. 1913. *Educational Psychology.* Vol. 1, *The Original Nature of Man.* New York: Teachers College, Columbia University.

1940. *Human Nature and the Social Order.* New York: Macmillan.

Thorson, Thomas L. 1970. *Biopolitics.* New York: Holt, Rinehart, & Winston.

Throgmorton, J. A. 1991. "Rhetorics of Policy Analysis." *Policy Sciences* 24: 153–79.

Toennies, Ferdinand. 1922. *Kritik der öffentlichen Meinung.* Berlin: Julius Springer.

Torgerson, Douglas. 1985. "Contextual Orientation in Policy Analysis: The Contribution of Harold D. Lasswell." *Policy Sciences* 18: 241–61.

1986a. "Between Knowledge and Politics: Three Faces of Policy Analysis." *Policy Sciences* 19: 33–59.

1986b. "Interpretive Policy Inquiry: A Response to Its Limitations." *Policy Sciences* 19: 397–405.

1990a. "Limits of the Administrative Mind." In Robert Paehlke and Douglas Torgerson (eds.), *Managing Leviathan.* Peterborough: Broadview.

1990b. "Obsolescent Leviathan: Problems of Order in Administrative Thought." In Robert Paehlke and Douglas Torgerson (eds.), *Managing Leviathan.* Peterborough: Broadview.

1990c. "Origins of the Policy Orientation: The Aesthetic Dimension in Lasswell's Political Vision." *History of Political Thought* 11: 339–51.

1992a. "Reuniting Theory and Practice." *Policy Sciences* 25: 211–24.

1992b. "Priest and Jester in the Policy Sciences: Developing the Focus of Inquiry." *Policy Sciences* 25: 225–35.

Treitschke, Heinrich von. 1916. *Politics.* New York: Macmillan.

Tribe, Laurence H. 1972. "Policy Science: Analysis or Ideology?" *Philosophy and Public Affairs* 2: 66–110.

Truman, David B. 1951a [1971]. *The Governmental Process: Political Interests and Public Opinion.* New York: Knopf.

1951b. "The Implications of Political Behavior Research." *Items* (Social Science Research Council) 5: 37–9.

1955. "The Impact on Political Science of the Revolution in the Behavioral Sciences." In S. K. Bailey et al. (eds.), *Research Frontiers in Politics and Government.* Washington DC: Brookings Institute.

1964. "Disillusion and Regeneration: The Quest for a Discipline." *American Political Science Review* 59: 865–73.

Tucker, Robert W. 1952. "Professor Morgenthau's Theory of Political 'Realism.'" *American Political Science Review* 46: 214–24.

1985. *Intervention and the Reagan Doctrine*. New York: Council on Religion and International Affairs.

Tufte, Edward. 1978. *Political Control of the Economy*. Princeton, NJ: Princeton University Press.

Turner, Stephen Park, and Turner, Johnathan H. 1990. *The Impossible Science: An Institutional Analysis of American Sociology*. Newbury Park, CA: Sage.

Vasquez, John A. 1983. *The Power of Power Politics: A Critique*. New Brunswick, NJ: Rutgers University Press.

Voegelin, Eric. 1952. *The New Science of Politics*. Chicago: University of Chicago Press.

Wahlke, John. 1979. "Pre-Behavioralism in Political Science." *American Political Science Review* 73: 9–31.

1986. "What Does the Biological Approach Offer Political Science?" *PS* 19: 871–2.

Waldo, Dwight. 1948. *The Administrative State: A Study of the Political Theory of American Public Administration*. New York: Ronald.

Wallas, Graham. 1908. *Human Nature in Politics*. London: Archibald Constable.

Walter, David O. 1934. "Proposals for a Federal Anti-Lynching Law." *American Political Science Review* 28: 436–42.

Walton, Hanes, Jr. 1968. "Race Relations Courses in Negro Colleges." *Negro Educational Review* 19: 123–32.

1985. *Invisible Politics: Black Political Behavior*. Albany: State University of New York Press.

Walton, Hanes, Jr., et al. 1992. "The Problem of Preconceived Perceptions in Black Urban Politics: The Harold F. Gosnell–James Q. Wilson Legacy." *National Political Science Review* 3: 217–29.

Waltz, Kenneth N. 1959. *Man, the State and War*. New York: Columbia University Press.

1970. "The Myth of National Interdependence." In Charles P. Kindleberger (ed.), *The International Corporation*. Cambridge: MIT Press.

1979. *Theory of International Politics*. Reading, MA: Addison-Wesley.

1986. "Reflections on *Theory of International Politics*: A Response to My Critics." In Keohane (1986b).

Ward, James F. 1984. *Language, Form, and Inquiry: Arthur F. Bentley's Philosophy of Social Science*. Amherst: University of Massachusetts Press.

Ward, Lester. 1883. *Dynamic Sociology or Applied Social Science*. New York: Appleton.

Wasby, Stephen. 1970. *Political Science: The Discipline and Its Dimension*. New York: Scribner's.

Weaver, Gary R., and James H. Weaver (eds.). 1969. *The University and Revolution*. Englewood Cliffs, NJ: Prentice-Hall.

Weingast, Barry. 1991. "The Political Economy of Slavery: Credible Commitments and the Preservation of the Union, 1800–1860." Paper presented at the annual meeting of the American Political Science Association, Washington DC.

Weingast, Barry R., and William Marshall. 1988. "The Industrial Organization of Congress; or, Why Legislatures, Like Firms, Are Not Organized as Markets." *Journal of Political Economy* 96: 132–64.

Weiss, Nancy J. 1969. "The Negro and the New Freedom: Fighting Wilsonian Segregation." *Political Science Quarterly* 84: 61–79.

Weissberg, Robert. 1976. *Public Opinion and Popular Government*. Englewood Cliffs. NJ: Prentice-Hall.

Westbrook, Robert B. 1991. *John Dewey and American Democracy*. Ithaca, NY: Cornell University Press.

Westley, Bruce H. 1975. Review of Ithiel de Sola Pool et al. *Handbook of Communication*. *Human Communications Research* 1: 187.

White, Elliott. 1982. "Brain Science and the Emergence of Neuropolitics." *Politics and the Life Sciences* 1: 23–5.

White, Leonard D. 1933. "Administration, Public." In *Encyclopedia of the Social Sciences*, Vol. 1.

    1958. *The Republican Era: A Study in Administrative History, 1869–1901*. New York: Free Press.

White, Stephen K. 1991. *Political Theory and Postmodernism*. Cambridge University Press.

Wiegele, Thomas C. 1982. *Biology and the Social Sciences: An Emerging Revolution*. Boulder, CO: Westview.

Wildavsky, Aaron 1979. *Speaking Truth to Power: The Art and Craft of Policy Analysis*. Boston: Little, Brown.

Wilde, Norman 1924. *The Ethical Basis of the State*. Princeton NJ.: Princeton University Press.

Williamson, Oliver E. 1975. *Markets and Hierarchies: Analysis and Antitrust Implications*. New York: Free Press.

    1979. "Transaction-Cost Economics: The Governance of Contractual Relations." *Journal of Law and Economics* 22: 233–61.

    1985. *The Economic Institutions of Capitalism*. New York: Free Press.

Willoughby, W. F. 1927. *Principles of Public Administration*. Washington, DC: Brookings Institution.

Willoughby, W. W. 1896. *An Examination of the Nature of the State*. New York: Macmillan.

    1904. "The American Political Science Association." *Political Science Quarterly* 19: 107–11. Reprinted in Farr and Seidelman (1993).

    1907. "Report of the Secretary." In *1906 Proceedings of the American Political Science Association*. Baltimore: Waverly.

    1926. "The Juristic Theories of Krabbe." *American Political Science Review* 20: 509–23.

Wills, Garry. 1992. "The Presbyterian Nietzsche." *New York Review of Books* 34 (January): 3–7.

Wilson, Edward O. 1975. *Sociobiology: The New Synthesis*. Cambridge, MA: Harvard University Press.

Wilson, F. 1942. "The Revival of Organic Theory." *American Political Science Review* 36: 454–9.

Wilson, Francis Graham. 1962. *A Theory of Public Opinion*. Chicago: Henry Regnery.

Wilson, Woodrow. 1885. *Congressional Government: A Study in American Politics*. New York: Houghton Mifflin. Revised edition, 1895.

1887a. "The Study of Administration." *Political Science Quarterly*, 2: 197–222. Reprinted in Farr and Seidelman (1993).

1887b. "Of the Study of Politics." *New Princeton Review* 3: 188–9.

1889. *The State: Elements of Historical and Practical Politics*. Boston: Heath. Revised edition, 1898.

1901. "Democracy and Efficiency." *Atlantic Monthly* 87: 289–99.

Winner, Langdon. 1969. "Cybernetics and Political Language." *Berkeley Journal of Sociology* 14: 3–17.

Wittrock, Bjorn, Peter Wagner, and Hellmut Wollman. 1991. "Social Science and the Modern State: Policy Knowledge and Political Institutions in Western Europe and the United States." In Peter Wagner et al. (eds.), *Social Sciences and Modern States*. Cambridge University Press.

Woellner, Fredric P. 1923. *Education for Citizenship in a Democracy: A Text-Book for Teachers in the Elementary Schools*. New York: Scribner's.

Wolf, William B. 1974. *The Basic Barnard: An Introduction to Chester I. Barnard and His Theories of Organization and Management*. Ithaca, NY: Cornell University Press.

Wolin, Sheldon S. 1960. *Politics and Vision*. Boston: Little, Brown.

1969. "Political Theory as a Vocation." *American Political Science Review* 63: 1062–82.

Woodward, C. Vann. 1951. *The Origins of the New South: 1877–1913*. Baton Rouge: Louisiana State University Press.

Woolsey, Theodore Dwight. 1877. *Political Science, or the State Theoretically and Practically Considered*. New York: Scribner, Armstrong.

Worster, Donald. 1977. *Nature's Economy: A History of Ecological Ideas*. Cambridge University Press.

Wright, Benjamin F. 1973. *The Five Public Philosophies of Walter Lippmann*. Austin: University of Texas Press.

Wright, Gerald C. 1988. "Policy Positions in the U.S. Senate: Who Is Represented?" Paper presented at the Hendricks Symposium on the United States Senate. Lincoln, NE.

Yankelovich, Daniel. 1991. *Coming to Public Judgment: Making Democracy Work in a Complex World*. Syracuse, NY: Syracuse University Press.

Young, Iris Marion. 1987. "Impartiality and the Civic Public." In Seyla Benhabib and Drucilla Cornell (eds.), *Feminism as Critique*. Minneapolis: University of Minnesota Press.

Young, Kimball. 1930. *Social Psychology: An Analysis of Social Behavior*. New York: Knopf.

　1948. "Comments on the Nature of 'Public' and 'Public Opinion.'" *International Journal of Opinion and Attitude Research* 2: 385–92.

Zimmern, Sir Alfred. 1936. *The League of Nations and the Rule of Law*. London: Macmillan.

Zink, Harold. 1950. "The Growth of the American Political Science Review, 1926–1949." *American Political Science Review* 44: 257–65.

Index